INTERNATIONAL POLITICAL ECONOMY SERIES

General Editor: Timothy M. Shaw, Professor of Political Science and International Development Studies, and Director of the Centre for Foreign Policy Studies, Dalhousie University, Nova Scotia, Canada

Recent titles include:

Pradeep Agrawal, Subir V. Gokarn, Veena Mishra, Kirit S. Parikh and Kunal Sen
ECONOMIC RESTRUCTURING IN EAST ASIA AND INDIA: Perspectives on Policy Reform

Solon L. Barraclough and Krishna B. Ghimire
FORESTS AND LIVELIHOODS: The Social Dynamics of Deforestation in Developing Countries

Kathleen Barry (*editor*)
VIETNAM'S WOMEN IN TRANSITION

Ruud Buitelaar and Pitou van Dijck (*editors*)
LATIN AMERICA'S NEW INSERTION IN THE WORLD ECONOMY: Towards Systemic Competitiveness in Small Economies

William D. Coleman
FINANCIAL SERVICES, GLOBALIZATION AND DOMESTIC POLICY CHANGE: A Comparison of North America and the European Union

Robert W. Cox (*editor*)
THE NEW REALISM: Perspectives on Multilateralism and World Order

Mark E. Denham and Mark Owen Lombardi (*editors*)
PERSPECTIVES ON THIRD-WORLD SOVEREIGNTY: The Postmodern Paradox

John Healey and William Tordoff (*editors*)
VOTES AND BUDGETS: Comparative Studies in Accountable Governance in the South

Noeleen Heyzer, James V. Riker and Antonio B. Quizon (*editors*)
GOVERNMENT–NGO RELATIONS IN ASIA: Prospects and Challenges for People-Centred Development

David Hulme and Michael Edwards (*editors*)
NGOs, STATES AND DONORS: Too Close for Comfort?

George Kent
CHILDREN IN THE INTERNATIONAL POLITICAL ECONOMY

David Kowalewski
GLOBAL ESTABLISHMENT: The Political Economy of North/Asian Networks

Laura Macdonald
SUPPORTING CIVIL SOCIETY: The Political Role of Non-Governmental
Organizations in Central America

Gary McMahon (*editor*)
LESSONS IN ECONOMIC POLICY FOR EASTERN EUROPE FROM
LATIN AMERICA

David B. Moore and Gerald J. Schmitz (*editors*)
DEBATING DEVELOPMENT DISCOURSE: Institutional and Popular
Perspectives

Juan Antonio Morales and Gary McMahon (*editors*)
ECONOMIC POLICY AND THE TRANSITION TO DEMOCRACY: The Latin
American Experience

Paul J. Nelson
THE WORLD BANK AND NON-GOVERNMENTAL ORGANIZATIONS:
The Limits of Apolitical Development

Archibald R. M. Ritter and John M. Kirk (*editors*)
CUBA IN THE INTERNATIONAL SYSTEM: Normalization and Integration

Howard Stein (*editor*)
ASIAN INDUSTRIALIZATION AND AFRICA: Studies in Policy Alternatives
to Structural Adjustment

Geoffrey D. Underhill (*editor*)
THE NEW WORLD ORDER IN INTERNATIONAL FINANCE

Sandra Whitworth
FEMINISM AND INTERNATIONAL RELATIONS

David Wurfel and Bruce Burton (*editors*)
SOUTHEAST ASIA IN THE NEW WORLD ORDER: The Political Economy
of a Dynamic Region

Out from Underdevelopment Revisited

Changing Global Structures and the Remaking of the Third World

James H. Mittelman
Professor of International Relations
School of International Service
American University
Washington, DC

and

Mustapha Kamal Pasha
Assistant Professor of Comparative Regional Studies
School of International Service
American University
Washington, DC

First edition (*Out From Underdevelopment*) by James H. Mittelman 1988,
reprinted 1989
Second edition (*Out From Underdevelopment Revisited*) by James H.
Mittelman and Mustapha Kamal Pasha 1997

 Published by
MACMILLAN PRESS LTD
Houndmills, Basingstoke, Hampshire RG21 6XS
and London
Companies and representatives
throughout the world

ISBN 0-333-63644-9 hardcover
ISBN 0-333-63645-7 paperback

A catalogue record for this book is available
from the British Library.

This book is printed on paper suitable for recycling and
made from fully managed and sustained forest sources.

10   9   8   7   6   5   4   3   2
06 05 04 03 02 01 00 99 98 97

Printed in Great Britain by
The Ipswich Book Company Ltd, Ipswich, Suffolk

 Published in the United States of America by
ST. MARTIN'S PRESS, INC.,
Scholarly and Reference Division
175 Fifth Avenue, New York, N.Y. 10010

ISBN 0-312-16466-1 (cloth)
ISBN 0-312-16467-X (paperback)

For Linda, Alexandra, Jordan and Alicia (JHM)

For my parents (MKP)

Contents

List of Figures and Tables	x
Preface to the First Edition	xi
Preface to the Second Edition	xviii
Acknowledgements	xx
List of Abbreviations	xxiii
A Note on Style	xxv

PART I   INTRODUCTION

1 Public Platitudes and Unfounded Attitudes	**3**
American Rites	3
Misguided Attitudes	7
Political Economy	16
How Many Worlds?	19
Learning from our Children	23

PART II   IDEOLOGIES AND STRUCTURES OF ACCUMULATION

2 Sources of Received Ideas about the Third World	**31**
Liberal Reformism	34
Where have All the Modernization Thinkers Gone?	41
Third World Radicalism	43
Beyond Orthodoxy	46
3 Received Ideas and International Institutions	**49**
International Organization	49
Foreign Aid	52
Technology	60
Transnational Corporations	63
Transnational Banking	71
4 Back to the Nineteenth Century for New Ideas	**80**
Capital Accumulation	82
The Enigmas in Marx's View of History	87
Beyond Classical and Neo-classical Thought	91

PART III STRATEGIES OF ACCUMULATION

5 **The Conventional Route, Joining Global Capitalism:**
   Track 1 – Brazil   **105**
   Brazil in the Limelight   105
   The Backdrop   107
   The Stage Is Set   110
   Same Cast, New Characters   111
   Act One: The Drama Unfolds   115
   Act Two: A Failed Miracle   119
   Act Three: In Search of a New Miracle   123
   Curtain Call: The Debt Noose Tightens   125
   The Continuing Saga   127

6 **The Conventional Route, Joining Global Capitalism:**
   Track 2 – the Asian NICs   **130**
   'Miracle' Economies   130
   The Legacy   135
   Land Reform and Industrialization   136
   Command Capitalism   140
   City-State to Global City   144
   Laissez-Faire to Market-Leninism   147
   The Underside of Growth   149
   Conclusion   152

7 **The Exit Option, Withdrawing from and Re-entering**
   Global Capitalism: China under and after Mao   **154**
   'The East is Red'   155
   Out of the Ashes   156
   The First State Plan   160
   'Mass Production of Useless Products'   164
   Readjustment   168
   Capitalist Road or Socialist Road?   170
   Mao's Legacy   173
   China under Deng   173

8 **The Alternative Path, Weaving through Global**
   Capitalism: Mozambique   **181**
   The Colonial Legacy   181
   Mozambique's Strategy of Accumulation   183
   Achievements and Difficulties   194
   The Global Context   200

About-face 208
Problems and Promises 213

PART IV   THE BIG QUESTION

9   **What Works in the Third World?** 217
What Is the Problem? 219
What Has Been Tried? 228
Whether to Join, Leave or Weave? 233
What Has Been Learnt? 237
What Should Be Done? 242

Postscript 251

Notes and References 260

Index 275

List of Figures and Tables

Figure

4.1   The dynamics of development and underdevelopment   92

Tables

1.1   Human development index, 1992   13
1.2   Structures of production, 1993   14
3.1   Top 200 companies by country, 1960–80   65
3.2   Top 200 companies by country, 1994   66

Preface to the First Edition

As a petulant 20-year-old embarking on graduate school, I quickly lost patience wading through the standard fare of university education in the USA. My courses suffered from a kind of single-mindedness that seemed to stifle creativity. The faculty were so orthodox in their own work and with their students that there was little feeling of pleasure in learning. Scholarly activity was presented as a 'discipline'.

Frustrated by staid, unimaginative courses, I confronted the dean, a strait-laced drill-sergeant who politely listened to my reasons as to why I should be allowed to use my fellowship for travel abroad. The sergeant caught me by surprise when he uttered, 'All right, sir. Where do you aim to study overseas?' Improvising, I said, 'Africa,' a continent I knew nothing about. Cocking an eyebrow, he inquired, 'Where in Africa?' At a loss for an answer, I glanced fretfully at my watch, dutifully noting that I was late for my class. 'Could we meet again to discuss the details of my proposal?' I queried.

I immediately telephoned a friend far more experienced in world affairs than I and explained my dilemma. 'The sergeant asked me where I want to study in Africa. What should I say? Do they have universities there?' My friend, an Oxford-educated diplomat with an advanced degree in African studies, replied, 'Of course, there are excellent universities in Africa. I recommend Makerere in Uganda and Ibadan in Nigeria. Since Nigeria may soon erupt in civil war, I would choose Makerere.' This advice prompted me to thumb through my world atlas. Aha, I learnt that Uganda is a landlocked country in East Africa, the source of the Nile.

When the dean and I resumed our conversation, I stated my choice, Makerere. He reacted in a word: 'What?' I explained, 'Makerere is in Uganda. It's an outstanding university, you know.' Three days later his secretary called to say that he had approved my request.

Months slipped by without so much as an acknowledgement, let alone an acceptance or rejection from Makerere. One of my professors, an esteemed philosopher, consoled me and urged me not to go. 'Good God, man,' he exclaimed, 'do you intend to study #&*@ barbarism?' Finally, I placed my first overseas telephone call. The operator asked for the name of the city, not the country. I told her to try the capital city. Unrelentingly, she demanded the name of the capital. Back to my reliable atlas: 'Either Kampala or Entebbe,' I shouted. 'I can't tell from the map. The binding in the middle of the page runs right through Uganda.' Nonetheless, the call went through in a minute. 'Oh yes, my dear chap. We have received your application. Of course you are accepted. Can you come right out?'

PROVINCIALISM

When I stepped off the plane in Uganda, I gazed at Lake Victoria, royal blue under the tropical sun, encircled by a verdant quilt of banana trees and a patchwork of ruddy clay roads. To an unseasoned traveller, the 26-mile journey from Entebbe, the old colonial headquarters, to Kampala, the capital since the accession to independence in 1962, seemed otherworldly. My eyes were riveted on the lush plant life: brilliant purple bougainvillaea shrubs, fiery red flame trees, and sturdy witch-like baobab trees. The perfume of flowers was everywhere. Dotting the expanse were men clad in *kanzu*, long white gowns, topped by Western-style sports jackets. Trailing behind some of the men were their wives frocked in *basuti*, high shouldered, multicoloured dresses inspired by fashion during the Edwardian period of colonial rule, with babies resting on their backs.

At the university, I was shown to my room in Mitchell Hall, a dormitory named after a colonial governor. When the bell rang, I joined the crowd assembling in the dining hall. No one said a word to me. My first impression was that I was the only white student present. Although the medium of instruction at Makerere is English, the African students conversed in their own languages. I could not ask for the food because such staples as *matoke*, boiled green bananas, were unknown to me. After lunch I made my way to the town centre. I came upon the Clock Tower where, I was told, nearly every day the country's leading politicians and intellectuals would hold a public debate over burning social issues.

In the university community, I met an American professor from my home town. We became close friends and at the end of the academic year, he asked if I would give an exam to his first-year class while he was up-country lecturing at a high school. Gladly, I said. Now in those days Uganda had quite a reputation for its rollicking night club life. Not a person of great willpower, I accepted an invitation to accompany friends to 'the Susana' on the eve of the exam. And what a time we had! Consuming our fair share of beer and *waragi* (a potent gin-like drink brewed locally), we mingled with the other patrons – a convivial crowd ranging from local notables, including government ministers, to the common man and woman – and danced until the first flickers of morning summoned us away from the festivities. Mindful of my responsibilities at the university, I dashed back to campus at 7.00 a.m., one full hour before I was to appear in the classroom.

In the British educational system, I found out, exams are taken very seriously. There is no periodic evaluation, as is the North American custom. Rather, since undergraduates are often tested only twice – at the end of their first and third years in a three-year degree programme – the results of a single exam can determine one's future life chances. The gravity of the occasion was impressed upon me by the appearance of solemn students bedecked in red gowns, a remnant of the Oxford-Cambridge tradition, for the three-hour exam. After I distributed the question sheets and the booklets, not a peep could be heard in the large, austere lecture hall. Within minutes, I was asleep, my head cushioned by my arms on the table in front of me.

Next thing, someone was tugging at my shoulder, barking in a starchy accent: 'Young man, young man, are you invigilating here?' Rubbing my eyes in wonder, I whispered, 'Pardon me.' A dowdy woman glared at me and repeated, 'Are you invigilating here?' Again I said, 'Pardon me.' The same sequence followed. Evidently a one-track mind, she persisted: 'I want to know if you are invigilating here.' With more than 100 African students listening to this breakdown in communication between a Yank and a Brit, I became embarrassed. What could she possibly mean?

Thoroughly confused, I decided that this whole business about invigilating sounded terribly crude. I stood up, to my full five feet five and five-eighths inches, and counterblasted: 'I assure you, ma'am, I would not do anything like that in public and surely not in front of students!' Instantaneously an uproar of laughter filled the room. My inquisitor stormed out, slamming the door behind her. What had I done?

UNDERSTANDING OTHER PEOPLE'S WAYS

During my first year in Uganda, the loneliest and most important period in my life, I discovered that social realities are not what they appear to be. On that initial occasion in the dining hall, I totally misread the behaviour of other students. That they focused their attention on me without initiating conversation had nothing to do with the colour of my skin. Later, many times over, I saw Makerere students relate to new

Ugandan students in exactly the same way they had received me. Makerereites are observant, and I had been ethnocentric: more than to most places, foreigners (myself included) come to Africa with specific notions about it. Having been raised in a *de facto* segregated city, I mistakenly projected racial preconceptions formed in the USA on to a different social reality. To be sure, there is racial prejudice in Uganda, but its causes and manifestations are unlike the pattern in the USA.

In contrast to the way in which my bigoted professor of political philosophy characterized Africa, I came upon a vibrant intellectual culture in Uganda, unhappily interrupted by Idi Amin's reign of terror. Much like Athenian democracy during the Age of Pericles, the Ugandan polis in the 1960s made strides towards melding knowledge and an active pursuit of the good life. The populace readily welcomed accomplished intellectuals who engaged in open political debate, a favourite pastime of Ugandans in the early years after independence. Compare the tradition in the USA where, despite near universal literacy, intellectuals are suspect in politics. The rule of thumb for the intelligentsia who enter American politics is either to come clean and bear the stigma of being an egghead, as did presidential candidate Adlai Stevenson, or to play down your PhD and credentials as a former professor, as did George McGovern, who also sought the presidency.

My experience administering an exam at Makerere taught me that understanding societies which encompass a myriad of cultures is a complex affair. Not only was I immersed in an African culture, but I also learnt to decipher a host of distinctive local societies as well as an overlay of Asian and European customs. In Kampala I encountered a medley of Bantu and Nilotic ethnic groups; refugee communities from nearby states, some of whom had arrived in the country as long ago as the late nineteenth century; many religious denominations, including a sect of Ugandan Jews established at the beginning of the twentieth century; a diverse lot of Indians and Pakistanis whose forebears built a railway from Lake Victoria to the Indian Ocean; and Europeans, who ruled for but a brief interlude in the history of East Africa. Thus one must unravel a cultural tapestry in order to truly understand the workings of institutions in postcolonial Uganda, as I discovered in the educational system.

When I told my tale about the testy woman rabidly yanking my shoulder, bemused English friends explained that invigilation means keeping watch over students at an examination. Asked what it is called in the USA, I said that we normally use the term proctoring, a construction which my friends, rightly or wrongly, insisted is a distortion of the English language.

DELVING DEEPER THAN POPULAR BELIEF

Intrigued by such cultural differences and intellectually drawn into African history, there was no turning back. I was hooked on debates over development and simmering social issues in multi-ethnic societies as well as on new-found cuisine and the delights of language learning. Following my second tour in Uganda, when I taught at the university, an unforgettable period punctuated by Amin's rise to power, I faced a crossroads: should I establish a home base where I could make sense of my experience, or should I join an international band of gypsies straying from one far-off berth to another? Among these gypsies are my fascinating and talented cohorts from Makerere, whom I still repeatedly encounter in the novels and short stories of V.S. Naipaul and Paul Theroux.

My wandering took me to liberated zones amid anti-colonial wars in southern Africa, republics lorded over by tight-fisted dictators in Latin America, and the states which have inherited the mantle of great civilizations in Asia. Reminiscent of the personal journey described by the philosopher René Descartes in the seventeenth century, as a young man I had resolved to seek knowledge beyond the world of books. I found great profit in becoming acquainted with other people's customs. But something was missing. I realized that the observation of experience did not satisfy me. So too for Descartes who, frustrated with the indeterminacy of book learning, had given up his studies in search of experiential knowledge only to detect just as much difference of opinion among the general populace as among men and women of letters. As described in his *Discourse on Method*, nine years passed before Descartes decided to stop his peripatetic ways and 'to lay the groundwork of a philosophy more certain than popular belief'.

Similarly, in my youth, I made up my mind to draw on two sources, experiential knowledge and the great books, in order to understand the promise and predicaments of the Third World. At that time, I set my sights on two problems: the historical puzzle of how people get embroiled in underdevelopment, and the practical question of how whole societies can escape it. As a scholar and as a practitioner working for international development agencies, these two questions have engaged me ever since.

I believe that it is crucial for all concerned people to re-examine the traditional lore about the Third World. Insofar as the Western public is concerned about this segment of the globe – which includes three-quarters of humankind – attention is centred on the wrong issues and neglects major questions. The media typically transmit a random accumulation of facts without regard for tenets behind practical policies. In bombarding us with information, reporters largely cover the activities of politicians, thus allowing government to set the bounds of what the public thinks about. In my view it is wrong to accept these inhibiting parameters of inquiry.

My concern in this book is to raise different questions about Third World development for an informed but non-specialist audience open to critical reflection. This project first took shape in my mind as an undergraduate course on 'The Political Economy of the Third World'. In searching for readings to assign, I discovered that the basic issues about the causes of, and solutions to, underdevelopment had not yet been presented in any satisfactory fashion. Neophytes seek an account that demystifies the issues, while many experts write about what their fellow experts say about the topic, which presumes that the audience has a prior familiarity with the literature. Rather than attempting to negotiate the demands of these two constituencies, this book deals with the issues *per se*, not how individual authors explain the issues. Above all, I try to assign and derive personal meaning from structural, or impersonal, processes.

Unhappily, the abstract ideas in scholarly works are tough going. Academic inquiry needs to be brought to life. In this volume, the discussion of heavy-duty concepts will be kept to a bare minimum (to be found in Part II). Without considering them, a treatment of concrete issues would be a mere exercise in storytelling. A country-by-country narrative – the Marco Polo approach of marching from one land to another – would perhaps be entertaining. However, its deceptive simplicity would render a disservice to readers.

Running through this book is a reappraisal of conventional and critical thinking. Versions of both ways of thinking are defective, yet some central themes seem to withstand critical scrutiny. Observers of the Third World must think about long-term prospects, and re-examine capitalism's fortunes and misfortunes over the last century. Then we can discern the basic motor forces behind global capitalism and fathom why peoples succeed or fail in the quest to achieve societal goals. Equipped with this knowledge, we are prepared to answer the practical question which ranks with the menace of war as the major social theme of our time: what works in the Third World?

My core argument is that underdevelopment is not inevitable. It is caused by identifiable processes. Underdevelopment may be best understood in terms of the interplay of capital accumulation, the state and class forces. The relationship among these factors defines the strategy of development adopted in a given historical context. The three typical strategies of development are joining global capitalism, withdrawing from the world system, and balancing the ties of dependency. Each option offers its own promises and risks. Moreover, each strategy must be seen in a realistic, non-romantic and highly problematic manner.

1988
Denver

JAMES H. MITTELMAN

Preface to the Second Edition

Since the publication of the first edition of this book in 1988, the world has changed fundamentally. Most notably, the disintegration of socialist regimes in the Soviet Union and Eastern Europe altered the global context for development. The ensuing wave of liberalization loosened repressive structures, opening the way for an explosion of cultural pluralism – a reassertion of historical forces – in many countries. So, too, have globalizing tendencies increased cross-border flows, blurring spatial markers among states as well as giving scope to intricate and fluid networks of social relations. In short, there are now many mediating factors that intervene among hitherto more stable positions in society.

In our view these changes, however sweeping, do not consign the conceptual framework advanced in the first edition to obsolescence. On the contrary, its explanatory power remains valid after the Cold War and in a globalizing world: the basic options for *overcoming underdevelopment* are still *joining, leaving* or *weaving*, all within the dynamics of global capitalism. Necessarily selective, the framework, however, requires broadening to account for new conditions. Students who read this book provided the most helpful comments that informed the revisions of the second edition. Like all books should be, *Out from Underdevelopment* is a work in progress, for there is no end to history, no finality in human affairs.

First of all, it is essential to update all chapters in the 1988 edition. Next, to account more fully for the strategy of 'joining global capitalism', we are adding a chapter on the 'Newly Industrializing Countries'. To examine linkages between various countries and globalization, we have eased, even more than before, the distinction between the internal and external dynamics of varied experiences with development. Fourth, the enduring concept of class forces is retained – though it may be unfashionable in the aftermath of the Cold War – since one of the responsibilities of scholars is to criticize today's conventions in order to help achieve a better tomorrow. Still, in this edition, we look more thoroughly at the relationships between class and non-class forces. The new edition represents an attempt to thread the themes of gender and environment into the analysis, especially in the case studies, where we expose the peril of borrowing from our children's future. If in the conclusion we are bold enough to present some modest principles about development choices, it follows from what is said here that one of the greatest challenges is to balance not only the apparent political and economic structures of dependency, but also the underlying *cultural* components.

This effort represents an extended collaboration between the co-authors. Indeed, in the single-authored first edition, Mittelman acknowledged Pasha's many substantive contributions to the book. Now, the 1996 edition includes a postscript by the second-named author, parallel to the preface to the first edition, indicating, from a very different vantage point, how he came to view the problems of the Third World.

As for editorial matters, we continue to draw on personal experience – vignettes – as a way to make abstract concepts accessible. Unless specified otherwise, use of the first person singular refers to Mittelman, not Pasha, save in the postscript written solely by the second-named author. To avoid any confusion in this regard, the author's initials are indicated after the pronoun 'I' in parentheses in Chapter 1–9 and the postscript.

Mittelman had primary responsibility for the first draft of all chapters save 6 as well as the revisions for Chapters 1, 2, 5 and 8; Pasha wrote 6 and revised 3, 4, 7 and 9. More important, we each provided information for, and made suggestions on, the entire book. This division of labour was designed to bring our varied backgrounds to bear on understanding the interactions between the global and local aspects of underdevelopment.

JAMES H. MITTELMAN
MUSTAPHA KAMAL PASHA

1995
Washington, DC

Acknowledgements

In my efforts to combine first-hand experience and researched analysis, I have had considerable help from others. Robert Ostertag (an undergraduate at the City College of the City University of New York) and Glenn Adler (a postgraduate student at Columbia University and now a Senior Lecturer in the Department of Sociology at the University of Witwatersrand, South Africa) gathered and wrote up basic research information for Chapters 5 and 7, respectively. They are excellent colleagues whose substantive contributions were invaluable. Marlene Guzman and Stanlie James – while at the Graduate School of International Studies, University of Denver – provided enormous assistance with editing, updating materials and verifying information.

Several scholars gave me unusually thorough and thoughtful criticisms on the entire manuscript. Although I may not have answered all their questions or followed all their suggestions, I am indebted to Mark Anikpo, Robert W. Cox, Kenneth Grundy, Joel Samoff, George Shepherd, Jr, and Linda Yarr. As the revisions progressed, I was guided by George Houser, Haider Ali Khan, John McCamant, Christopher Nwodo, Richard Sandbrook, Timothy Shaw, Peter Van Ness and Kristin Pelzer. Their ideas and queries on individual chapters have deepened my understanding.

The case studies in Part III of this book are based on official documents, secondary sources and visits to Brazil in 1970, the People's Republic of China in 1986 and 1988, and Mozambique in 1971, 1975, 1978 and 1981. For arranging travel and access to information, I am grateful to the China Centre for the International Exchange of Personnel in Banking and Finance and the African Studies Centre at Eduardo Mondlane University, Mozambique, whose director, the late Aquino de Bragança, was a purveyor of consistent encouragement and a fountain of knowledge.

My appreciation also goes to Sherle Schwenninger of the World Policy Institute. A grant from the Transnational Academic Program of the World Policy Institute supported the preparation of this manuscript. My thanks go to the staff at the Graduate School of International Studies, University of Denver – Arline Fink, Diane Reed, Asma Barlas and Diane de Rose Libero – for lightening my administrative load and typing and retyping many drafts. In addition, Queens College of the City University of New York – especially Helen Cairns, Sandra Carbone and Florence Friedman – assisted in the completion of the first edition of this book.

Prompted by my friend and series editor, Timothy Shaw, I agreed to prepare a revised and expanded edition of *Out from Underdevelopment*, and invited Mustapha Pasha to be co-author. The incentives for taking this assignment were the continuing need for an up-to-date book of this sort and the always pleasant working relationship with my publisher in London, Timothy Farmiloe, Gráinne Twomey, Keith Povey and their able aides at Macmillan.

The second edition bears the mark – meticulous research assistance – of Meliton Salazar, a PhD candidate, for whom no question was too big or too small. Another PhD student, Lilian Duarte, contributed importantly to the revisions on the Brazil chapter. A graduate assistant, Ashwini Tambe, rendered valuable information and advice in the final stages of preparing the manuscript. My home institution – the School of International Service at American University – facilitated the completion of this project. Special thanks go to the Director of Budget and Personnel, Joseph Clapper, and staff members Rana El-Khatib, Rebecca Saxe, Nina Smallwood and Sheila Wise.

An award from the Professional Staff Congress of the City University of New York and two grants from the World Society Foundation made possible research trips to some of the Newly Industrializing Countries (NICs). Especially productive was my affiliation with the Institute of Southeast Asian Studies in Singapore, where I was a Visiting Fellow in 1991.

While preparing the second edition of this book, I benefited enormously from working on two research projects sponsored by the United Nations University (UNU). One of them, 'Multilateralism and the United Nations System', was directed by Robert W. Cox. The other, on 'The New Regionalism', under the auspices of the World Institute of Development Economics Research (a centre within the UNU), was coordinated by Björn Hettne in collaboration with András Inotai and Osvaldo Sunkel. I am thankful for what I have learnt from the participants in these programmes: Richard Falk, Stephen Gill, Helge Hveem, Yoshikazu Sakamoto, and others. Above all, it has been a privilege to know Robert and Jessie Cox in many contexts.

To my wife, Linda, and our children, Alexandra, Jordan and Alicia, for being towers of strength and sources of inspiration, I am most grateful of all.

JAMES H. MITTELMAN

Thanks, first and foremost, to Jim Mittelman for inviting me to collaborate on this project, for steering it, and for providing encouragement and advice with grace and good humour. To Timothy Shaw, personal gratitude for providing support when needed. I am also indebted to Tyler Attwood, Meena Shah, Francesca Vassallo and Christine Chin for their valuable assistance. To the wonderful staff at the School of International Service, especially to Joseph Clapper, Rana El-Khatib and Rebecca Saxe, many thanks. Most of all, to Ritu Vij, enormous gratitude for her inspiration and confidence which made work on this project possible.

MUSTAPHA KAMAL PASHA

List of Abbreviations

ADB	Asian Development Bank
AID	Agency for International Development
ANC	African National Congress
ASEAN	Association of Southeast Asian Nations
CCP	Chinese Communist Party
CIA	Central Intelligence Agency
COMECON (also known as CMEA)	Council for Mutual Economic Assistance
DBCP	Dibromochloropropane
ECLA	Economic Commission for Latin America
EDB	Economic Development Board
EPZ	Export Processing Zone
FDI	Foreign Direct Investment (also Direct Foreign Investment)
FNLA	National Front for the Liberation of Angola (*Frente de Nacional de Libertação de Angola*)
FRELIMO	Front for the Liberation of Mozambique (*Frente de Libertação de Moçambique*)
G-7	Group of Seven
GDP	Gross Domestic Product
GNP	Gross National Product
IBM	International Business Machines
IMF	International Monetary Fund
ITT	International Telephone and Telegraph Company
MAT	Mutual Aid Team
MFN	Most Favoured Nation
NACLA	North American Congress on Latin America
NAFTA	North American Free Trade Agreement
NGO	Non-governmental Organization
NIC	Newly Industrializing Country
NIEO	New International Economic Order
NSSM	National Security Study Memorandum
OMM	Organization of Mozambican Women (*Organização da Mulher Moçambicana*)
OPEC	Organization of Petroleum Exporting Countries

OTM	Organization of Mozambican Workers (*Organização dos Trabalhadores Moçambicanos*)
PAP	People's Action Party
PRE	Economic Rehabilitation Programme (*Programa de Reabilitação Económica*)
PRI	Institutional Revolutionary Party (*Partido Revolucionario Institucional*)
RENAMO	Mozambique National Resistance Movement (*Movimiento Nacional de Resistência de Moçambique*)
SADCC (renamed SADC)	Southern African Development Coordination Conference (subsequently known as Southern African Development Community)
SOE	State-Owned Enterprise
TNC	Transnational Corporation
UAE	United Arab Emirates
UNCTAD	United Nations Conference on Trade and Development
UNDP	United Nations Development Programme
UNESCO	United Nations Educational, Scientific and Cultural Organization
UNITA	National Union for the Total Independence of Angola (*União Nacional para a Independência a Total de Angola*)
UNU	United Nations University

A Note on Style

For the sake of brevity and clarity of style, we prefer not to encumber the text with footnotes. Our sources and key references for each chapter are indicated in the Notes and References section at the end of the book. This section includes both the selective bibliography used in the preparation of this work and suggestions for further reading. Although our publisher has introduced British conventions of style, we have agreed to use billion in the US sense of thousand million (rather than million million, as is usually the practice in the UK).

JAMES H. MITTELMAN
MUSTAPHA KAMAL PASHA

1995

Part I

Introduction

1 Public Platitudes and Unfounded Attitudes

From listening to commentators on television and reading the newspapers, you may have the impression that many, if not most, non oil-exporting Third World countries are mired in poverty, ignorance, superstition, hopelessness and underdevelopment. Nowadays the media frequently refer to such countries as Bangladesh and Haiti as 'basket cases'. Some of these have been assigned to the 'Fourth World'. In its innocence, this could mean the bottom of the barrel: then *Time* magazine even suggested that we must distinguish a 'Fifth World'.

Is this gloomy view warranted? Or are the past successes of the oil cartel, new-found industrialization and the growth of manufacturing portents that the Third World may escape the doldrums?

Any assessment of the prospects for development must, of course, turn on the questions asked. A crucial task, then, is to determine what are the essential features of development and underdevelopment. This is a complicated business which this book seeks to unscramble. After exploring competing arguments over what ails the Third World, we will show that aspects of one interpretation – political economy – offer a master key to explaining historical trends and current realities both in Third World countries and in the world at large. Of overriding practical importance is to eliminate underdevelopment by devising alternative strategies of development. This task is especially challenging in the context of globalization. The panorama is huge, but obfuscations can be avoided if we pinpoint questions targeted at the heart of the controversies over development and underdevelopment.

AMERICAN RITES

The difficulty in getting a grip on fundamentally different ways of thinking about history and politics was apparent in a 1979 interview with President Fidel Castro. Speaking on national television in the USA, ABC News Correspondent Barbara Walters posed several penetrating questions which the Cuban leader answered with much grace and aplomb. Castro, however, was dismayed when the line of questioning dwelt on his personal life. It is instructive to quote the interview at length:

Walters: You are a man of great mystery to us. First of all, why the mystery? You come from nowhere, you seem to disappear, we hear you have no one home, you are a man of secrecy and mystery.

Castro: So then we could say we are facing the theory of mystery. So I ask myself, I'm the first to ask myself, where is the mystery? Because, well, there are certain things that we had to do since the beginning of the Revolution. That is, if a trip is made why should we tell the CIA [Central Intelligence Agency] and the terrorists that we are going to make a trip?

Walters: Do you have a house where you live? No one seems to know where it is.

Castro: Yes, of course and I even have a bed where I sleep.

Walters: Are you married?

Castro: What marriage do you mean, what do you call marriage?

Walters: What do I call marriage?

Castro: Marriage in the bourgeois type? No.

Walters: Wait, wait, many of your people, your brother is married in a bourgeois way. You were married once in the bourgeois way, you have a son.

Castro: Yes, I married once.

Walters: And are you divorced? Many people in this country are married. You considered them all bourgeois people?

Castro: No, no. Well, there are many interpretations about all this. That is, there are marriages with a different feeling also. There is no longer the girl that became educated to marry a millionaire. There are differences. But I am going to make a question.

Walters: Why not an answer?

Castro, somewhat puzzled by this emphasis, continued to respond politely, albeit with uncharacteristic reserve. Still, Walters inquired about romance and his family:

Walters (voice over): We advanced the oft-voiced opinion that his closest companion was Celia Sanchez, first secretary of the Communist Party, and one of the women who served with him in the mountains. He wouldn't affirm or deny this. We then asked about his sister.

Walters: You have a sister, Juanita, who lives in the United States.

Castro: Yes . . . ?

Walters: She has been very critical of you, she has even written to President Carter about you...

Castro: Yes...

Walters: I have two questions...

Castro: Don't you think it is monstrous that a sister says something like that about a brother?

Walters: Yes, I wonder why.

Castro: Well, I can tell you the following: we are children of course from the same father and the same mother, we have the same blood but we have different ideas. I am a socialist, I am a Communist, although her, in her passion, even gets to the extent of stating that I am not a Communist. She has different political ideas, she is an enemy of socialism, she is an enemy of communism. Actually an error is made, a mistake is made in trying to identify Castro as the symbol of all the evil things in the world. But, anyway, that is not the fundamental question. I am a citizen of this country, a country with nine-and-a-half million inhabitants. I would say the following very much according to my convictions: I have nine-and-a-half million brothers. I have a different vision of the world. My family is very large, my family is not only Cuba. My family is the Angolans, the liberation movements in Africa, my family is made up by all progressive and revolutionary peoples of the world. But a sister who attacks me because we are revolutionaries, that does not eliminate my honor, that does not even hurt me.

Walters: I have one final personal question. Will you ever shave off that beard?

Castro: As an exchange for what? The ceasing of the blockade? (Laughs)

Barbara Walters would have none of this blend of reticence and frivolity. She persisted in probing the Cuban's private life on the ground that the public is interested in a 'man of secrecy and mystery', whereupon Castro retorted: 'What is the importance of my being married or not and who cares whether I'm married or not? These are totally my problems. They do not belong to the international public opinion, they belong to me.' Punching home the point, he added: 'I can tell you the following: I'm a man that is totally free and that owns my own life. The rest is detail, untranscendental details that have nothing to do with the Revolution nor politics.' Undaunted by this appeal to talk further about affairs of state, the interlocutor said: 'Aha, but also,... you know the expression [marriage].' Then, Castro stoutly asserted that they should discuss love and marriage on another occasion and not in front of a large public audience.

This impasse epitomizes the gulf between the way of thinking of a stellar television interviewer and a structural perspective of international affairs. In the USA, from an early age and in our schooling, we are trained to think in terms of discrete events and individual personalities. Customarily in high school history courses, many of us were required to regurgitate long lists of dates and battles in the American Revolution and the Civil War. When it came to the test, I (JHM) could never recall the bulk of them and received a grade showing as much despite (or because of) light-hearted attempts at memorization the night before. The traditional lore was and still is a tale of superexcellent deeds by peerless superheroes. Clearly the 'great man' explanation of history is the basis of the general American view that, through the accomplishments of individuals and hard work, the USA earned its material abundance.

Unlike the libertarian view, a structural perspective, more pronounced in European education and in some quarters in the Third World, emphasizes underlying social forces and impersonal processes such as trends in population growth and movement, changes in patterns of consumption, and the relative mobility or immobility of labour. A structural perspective is grounded in theory – a dirty word to many practically minded North Americans – and takes a long range view of history.

In foreign affairs, large numbers of US citizens believe that Castro and other Third World leaders are hostile to the USA because they want what we have attained on the basis of our own initiative and resources. There is the feeling that the demands for a new international deal thinly disguise a desire to take away the unparalleled achievements of the people of the USA, whose only crimes are to allow political liberty to flourish and to start up mighty engines of economic growth.

What has rankled Senator Daniel Patrick Moynihan, a former US ambassador to the UN, for instance, is the attempt by small-time dictators in the Third World to claim what rightfully belongs to the USA. For cudgelling his pro-Third World critics, Moynihan gained a tremendous national following. 'There are those in the country,' he argued, 'whose pleasure, or profit, it is to believe that our assailants are motivated by what is wrong about us. *They* are wrong. We are assailed because of what is *right* about us. We are assailed because we are a democracy.' Moreover:

We repudiate the charge that we have exploited or plundered other countries, or that our own prosperity has ever rested on any such relation. We are prosperous because we are – or were – an energetic and productive people who have lived under a system that has encouraged the development of our productive capacities and energies. We also consider that we have been reasonably helpful and generous in our dealings with other countries.

That statement may be a fair summary of a cross-section of US public opinion concerning the Third World.

The ordinary citizen in other countries may be no more open-minded than Americans, but the USA is so powerful that its values affect virtually all nations. To a huge majority in the Third World and Europe, American perceptions of international relations are provincial in the extreme. This much was acknowledged by Adlai Stevenson who, as US ambassador to the UN, reportedly quipped that the technology Americans need most is a hearing aid. The inability to grasp other people's beliefs reflects misconceptions sown in our minds.

MISGUIDED ATTITUDES

Global processes are often seen as chaotic, complex and remote from daily life. Most people recognize that in comparison with national and local governments, international institutions are lacking in power and the ability to exact compliance. The branches of a national government enact and effect the rule of law, whereas the UN Security Council and General Assembly pass lofty and unenforceable resolutions; the Secretary General has neither a mandate nor a standing army to make these pious pronouncements binding, and the International Court of Justice has a docket ordinarily uncluttered by cases.

The differences between the national realm and the international sphere are fairly palpable. What is less evident, though, is the effort of government officials to foster the image of world disorder. Zbigniew Brzezinski, US national security adviser under President Jimmy Carter, described the challenge of formulating a sound foreign policy thus: 'My overwhelming observation is that history is neither the product of design nor of conspiracy but is rather the reflection of continuing chaos.' Rejecting the charge that the Carter administration failed to pursue a consistent foreign policy, Brzezinski insisted on the importance of the inherent 'complexity' of the modern world. 'The question I find meaningful,' he underlined, 'is not whether it is possible to pursue a consistent policy, but whether it is possible to pursue a *complex* policy.' What Brzezinski overlooked is a keystone of a democratic polity: the principle that matters of public policy are comprehensible and open to the influence of the ordinary citizen. Never mind, he seemed to imply: comprehension of international relations, intricate as it is, is beyond the ken, as well as the reach, of the common people.

The image of global affairs as chaos and confusion is accurate, but only as far as it goes. It omits structural processes – regularities and patterns – in the world system. What must be taken into account is hierarchy and the global division of labour. The pecking order ranges from the upper echelon in the most powerful nations and their local accomplices in the Third World, to the teeming downtrodden in a multitude of countries whose life chances are seemingly nil.

Ingrained images of the Third World have been forged by mass publications, the subject of Catherine Lutz's and Jane Collins' 1993 study of *National Geographic*, the magazine with the third largest number of subscribers in the USA. Founded in 1888, *National Geographic* commands the attention of nearly 40 million people every month. From its headquarters in Washington, DC, the magazine issues glossy pictures and captions that bring the Third World into the living rooms of Westerners.

As cultural anthropologists, Lutz and Collins turn the tables on *National Geographic*, displaying the practices and customs of the magazine itself. It has few black employees, and 96 per cent of its readers are white. Scrutinizing 600 randomly selected photographs published from 1950 to 1986, the authors find that *National Geographic* portrays the Third World as naturalized, idealized and exotic. In far-flung lands, peoples are seen as enjoying strange rituals and submerged in the sacred realm: marriage feasts in New Guinea, shamans in prayer in Tibet, and bejewelled women adorned in gold-embroidered saris in India. For the most part, the poor, the ill and the hungry do not appear in these photographs. It is largely a world unblemished by hardship and violence. Absent are suffering and responsibility.

In this image, Third World peoples are not only beautified but also sexualized. The photos of naked black women – the magazine's centrepiece – play to Western myths about their sexuality, namely that a lack of modesty places them closer to nature. Almost all of the breasts represented are black skinned, Lutz and Collins say. Meanwhile, it is men – white men – who risk their lives to conquer nature and bring modernity to the comforting madonnas and their children in the Third World.

Implicitly, a hierarchy of race is suggested. Progress is linked to skin colour, the continuum running from white on top, brown in the middle, and black on the bottom. The message conveyed by the photos and captions assigned to them does not ascribe emotions, motivations and personalities to the dark-skinned, smiling subjects. To the extent that whites can identify with these hapless peoples, they are thought to be victims of social Darwinism and thus in need of help from the West.

If popular magazines such as *National Geographic* give the impression that traditional culture is safe and orderly, the media offer a more sobering icon of peril with potential for contagion emanating from the non-Western world. While striving to present a balanced treatment of foreign affairs – to be sure, a difficult task – the media in the USA have come under fire from various quarters. The former Soviet Foreign Minister, Andrei Gromyko, usually a dour, melancholy sort, was asked his opinion of an article about him in the *New York Times*. 'About half is true and half is false,' he answered. 'Since The Times is a balanced newspaper, that is to be expected.'

When an outbreak of fever known as the Ebola virus began in Kikwit, Zaire, in 1995, fascination in the Western media and on the Internet had a Cuisinart effect, blending imagined scenarios from films and authoritative news accounts. Sensationalist reports warned: 'It could be in the United States within 24 hours.' At the same time, the World Health Organization repeatedly stated that the disease, spread primarily through contact with the blood or bodily fluids of an Ebola victim, is not very contagious or highly transmissible. Contrary to lurid headlines that fanned fears, Ebola does not travel through the air to infect people. Nevertheless, ABC's 'Nightline' and other news programmes even interspersed scenes from the fictional movie 'Outbreak' with footage from Zaire, bending the facts to put viewers on the edge of their seats. A dramatic episode in which a person infected with a deadly virus contaminates other people in a cinema by coughing and sneezing – a virtual impossibility with the known strains of the virus – was a source of misinformation, part of the mythology about Ebola.

It is no exaggeration to say that the media and films have traditionally fostered racist images of Third World peoples: Tarzan was the strongest man and Jane was his idealized companion in the African jungle. Whites portrayed superior beings, while blacks played subordinate roles. The impression of *exoticism* lingers because it is a simple and convenient technique for imposing intellectual order on an unknown Africa and a veiled Orient. So, too, *Islamic fundamentalism* is a label to tag diverse phenomena; religion is surely the idiom but not the basis of political protest in the Middle East. Similarly, *tribalism* is a term that conjures up images of primitive behaviour and an incapacity to manage the affairs of state.

Why should Nigeria's Ibo, Yoruba and Hausa-Fulani be stigmatized as tribes while the numerically smaller Basque, Flemish and Welsh are dignified as nations or ethnic groups? Furthermore, in explaining the outcome of an American election, say, a mayoral race in Boston, one of the first questions routinely asked is: who got the Irish, Jewish and African-American vote? Taking a cue from *The Federalist Papers*, American schools teach that myriad loyalties are the basis of counter-vailing sources of power which offset the relentless passions of human-kind. Publius, a composite of the three authors of *The Federalist* (John Jay, Alexander Hamilton and James Madison), warned that mortal feuds between factions spread uncontrollably and weaken a body poli-tic. But a proper balancing of interests could stem this paroxysm, ar-gued Publius. More than two centuries later, the image of a promised balance is rather tarnished as a result of the realities of racial strife. Even so, it is still widely believed that multiple forms of identification are a sign of health in a pluralist democracy, yet Americans often re-gard such ties as a pathology elsewhere in the world.

In today's Third World, tribal loyalty – ethnicity is a preferred term – is as much a product of colonialism as it is an aspect of indigenous cul-tures. It was the divide-and-rule tactics employed by the European powers which gave Third World peoples the incentive to identify along ethnic lines. In the early colonial period in south-western Uganda, for example, British administrators found rural dwellers – Americans would call them rugged individualists – who farmed the irregular banks of steep slopes. They belonged to clans and shared religious practices but did not truly coalesce until the British, or their local agents (drawn from the Baganda, the heartland ethnic group), offered tangible rewards – bore holes for water, modern medicine and mission schools – for estab-lishing the type of political structures favoured by the colonizers. These structures were in fact a means of installing political control.

It would be a grave error to deny that ethnicity is a major *form of* conflict in contemporary Africa. When a Langi, one of former Presi-dent Milton Obote's kin, gunned down a Kakwa, a compatriot from Idi Amin's home area, the motive may well have been tribal animosity. But it is tautological to reckon that Tribe A fights Tribe B because of tribalism. Properly understood, tribalism is an ideology moored in the history and social structure of a people.

Tribalism is not the lens through which crises in the Third World ought to be viewed. The American media's harping on tribalism during the Congo crises of 1960 and 1964 misled the public, and this slant is still the order of the day. The Western press continues to ask us to swallow a naive and prejudicial notion of tribal confusion. In a peevish magazine article whose title, 'Misunderstanding Africa', does ironic justice to its content, correspondent Xan Smiley encapsulates this unfortunate tendency: 'tribalism is incorrigibly stronger than a spurious nationalism based on recently drawn colonial boundaries, and remains by far the most important power in politics throughout the continent'. The antidote to tribal impulses, says Smiley, has been adopted by a 'brave band of sub-Saharan countries – Senegal, Gambia, Zimbabwe, Nigeria, Botswana, Mauritius – that have allowed their people a measure of pluralist choice'. In effect, his prescription is none other than the Western model, the same old institutions and procedures which failed to take root in Africa during that continent's first stage of decolonization: the transfer of political power which ushered in a climate of disillusionment in the 1960s and 1970s.

This is one of the central themes in *Petals of Blood* by Ngugi Wa Thiong'o. Ngugi, Kenya's foremost novelist, chaired the literature department at the University of Nairobi until the government stripped him of his position and placed him in detention. For a time the authorities had tolerated his biting novels about postcolonial Kenya. They were written in English, which many Kenyans do not read, and sold at around $5 per copy, a steep price by local standards. But his plays, composed in Kikuyu, a local language, and enacted by villagers, provoked the ire of the government.

In *Petals of Blood*, the protagonists are soured, their lives in total disarray, because of the authorities' betrayal of the struggle for Kenya's independence. As Wanja, an enchanting and reflective prostitute, puts it:

> They [the big men] want to encourage the formation of various tribal organisations. Each tribal union would have its oaths binding its members, on point of death, to an absolute loyalty to the group. Then the leaders from all the unions would form a National Front …It would be the duty of each union to eliminate disloyal elements under the pretext that such elements were betraying the tribe and its culture and its wealth to other tribes.

But what has caused this to happen? Her companion asks what is the basis of leadership? In a word, Wanja responds: 'Property'. The wielders of power fan the flames of tribalism in order to deflect attention from the *underlying causes* of conflict, thereby maintaining their own position on top of the heap.

Ngugi's compelling novel reflects an acute appreciation of the under-pinnings of social conflict in the Third World. Clearly such an apprecia-tion does not provide operational answers to the problems stalking underdeveloped countries, but it does lead one to pose fruitful ques-tions and to avoid certain traps.

One such trap is the widespread belief that it is a gap that sets apart the Third World from the advanced countries. Certain countries, the ar-gument runs, have fallen behind in their historical development. They are said to be caught in a vicious circle: poverty begets more poverty. A mounting population eats up economic growth.

The influential 1980 Report of the Independent Commission on International Development Issues, chaired by Willy Brandt, takes as a cornerstone of its study the premise that the gap separating rich and poor countries is so serious that human beings are divided into differ-ent universes. Numerous documents compiled by international organi-zations provide statistical indicators to show the severity of the gap. According to World Bank figures issued in 1993, the high-income economies have less than one-fifth of the world's population and four-fifths of its income, whereas the low- and middle-income economies, including China, hold more than four-fifths of the globe's population and one-fifth of its income. The *Human Development Report 1993* indi-cates that in the industrialized countries, life expectancy on average is 74.5 years, more than 10 years greater than the average for all develop-ing countries, and more than 20 years above that in the least developed countries. In 1990, in all developing countries, more than 12 million children died before the age of five; there were 200 million malnour-ished children under five; and about two in five adults were illiterate. Furthermore, 1991 income per person in the high-income economies was approximately 20 times that of the low- and middle-income econo-mies as a whole. The United Nations Development Programme (UNDP) reports that in the 1990s, 1.3 billion people in developing countries live in absolute poverty. Despite its static quality, the 'human development index' – a composite of life expectancy, literacy, and gross domestic product (GDP) per capita – reinforces the general picture of a basic gap between the rich and poor countries (see Table 1.1).

Beneath the aggregate statistics lay an important story. It would be a mistake to allow global data to jumble the wide variation among coun-tries. So, turning to national figures assembled by the World Bank, let us look at two indicators of the gap between countries: average income and average energy consumption. In 1991, per capita income in Tan-zania was $100; Bangladesh, $220; India, $330; and China, $370. The

Table 1.1 Human development index, 1992

Country	Life expectancy at birth	Adult literacy rate (%)	Real GDP per capita	Human development index 1992
Canada	77.4	99.0	20 520	0.950
Japan	79.5	99.0	20 520	0.937
USA	76.0	99.0	23 670	0.937
France	76.9	99.0	19 510	0.930
Sweden	78.2	99.0	18 320	0.929
Germany	76.0	99.0	21 120	0.921
UK	76.2	99.0	17 160	0.916
Hong Kong	78.6	91.2	20 340	0.905
Rep. of Korea	71.1	97.4	9 250	0.882
Argentina	72.1	95.9	8 860	0.882
Singapore	74.8	89.9	18 330	0.878
Venezuela	71.7	90.4	8 520	0.859
Russian Fed.	67.6	98.7	6 140	0.849
Mexico	70.8	81.5	7 300	0.842
Thailand	69.0	93.5	5 950	0.827
Malaysia	70.8	81.5	7 790	0.822
Brazil	66.3	81.9	5 240	0.804
Tunisia	67.8	62.8	5 160	0.763
Botswana	64.9	67.2	5 120	0.763
Saudi Arabia	69.7	60.6	9 880	0.762
Algeria	67.1	57.4	4 870	0.732
Jamaica	73.6	83.7	3 200	0.721
Peru	66.0	87.3	3 300	0.709
South Africa*	62.9	80.6	3 799	0.705
Philippines	66.3	94.0	2 550	0.677
Indonesia	62.7	82.5	2 950	0.637
Egypt	63.6	49.1	3 540	0.613
Nicaragua	66.7	64.7	2 790	0.611
China	68.5	79.3	1 950	0.594
Guatemala	64.8	54.2	3 330	0.591
Zimbabwe	53.7	83.4	1 970	0.539
Pakistan	61.5	35.7	2 890	0.483
Kenya	55.7	74.5	1 400	0.481
India	60.4	49.9	1 230	0.439
Zambia	48.9	75.2	1 230	0.425
Nigeria	50.4	52.5	1 560	0.406
Bangladesh	55.6	36.4	1 230	0.364
Tanzania	52.1	64.4	620	0.364
Uganda	44.9	58.6	860	0.329
Mozambique	46.4	36.9	380	0.246

*Preliminary update of the Penn World Tables using an expanded set of
international comparisons, as described in Robert Summers and Alan Heston,
'Penn World Tables (Mark 5): An Expanded Set of International Comparisons,
1950–1988 ', *Quarterly Journal of Economics* 106 (1991): 327–68.
Source: *Human Development Report 1995* (New York: Oxford University Press,
1995), pp. 155–7.

Table 1.2 Structures of production, 1993

Country	GDP in millions	Distribution of GDP (%)			
		Agriculture	Industry	Manufacture*	Services, etc.[†]
Canada	477 468	n/a	n/a	n/a	n/a
Japan[‡]	4 214 204	2	41	24	57
USA[‡]	6 259 899	n/a	n/a	n/a	n/a
France[‡]	1 251 689	3	29	22	69
Sweden	166 745	2	31	26	67
Germany[‡]	1 910 730	1	38	27	61
UK	819 038	2	33	25	65
Hong Kong	89 997	0	21	13	79
Rep. of Korea[‡]	330 831	7	43	29	50
Argentina	255 595	6	31	20	63
Singapore[‡]	55 153	0	37	28	63
Venezuela[‡]	59 995	5	42	14	53
Russian Fed.	329 432	9	51	n/a	39
Mexico[‡]	343 472	8	28	20	63
Thailand[‡]	124 862	10	39	28	51
Malaysia	64 450	n/a	n/a	n/a	n/a
Brazil	444 205	11	37	20	52
Tunisia	12 784	18	31	19	51
Botswana[‡]	3 813	6	47	4	47
Saudi Arabia[‡]	121 530	n/a	n/a	n/a	n/a
Algeria	39 836	13	43	11	43
Jamaica	3 825	8	41	18	51
Peru	41 061	11	43	21	46
South Africa[‡]	105 636	5	39	23	56
Philippines[‡]	54 068	22	33	24	45
Indonesia[‡]	144 707	19	39	22	42
Egypt	35 784	18	22	16	60
Nicaragua	1 800	30	20	17	50
China[‡]	425 611	19	48	38	33
Guatemala	11 309	25	19	n/a	55
Zimbabwe	4 986	15	36	30	48
Pakistan	46 360	25	25	17	50
Kenya	4 691	29	18	10	54
India	225 431	31	27	17	41
Zambia[‡]	3 685	34	36	23	30
Nigeria	31 344	34	43	7	24
Bangladesh[‡]	23 977	30	18	10	54
Tanzania	2 086	56	14	5	30
Uganda	3 037	53	12	5	35
Mozambique	1 367	33	12	n/a	55

*Because manufacturing is generally the most dynamic part of the industrial sector, its share is shown separately.
[†]'Services, etc.' includes unallocated items.
[‡]GDP and its components are at purchaser values.
Source: *World Development Report* 1995 (New York: Oxford University Press, 1995), pp. 166–7.

corresponding amount for Sweden was $25 110; Germany, $23 650; the USA, $22 240; and France, $20 380. In 1991, energy per capita consumption in Tanzania was 37 kg of oil equivalent; Bangladesh, 42 kg; India, 337 kg; and China, 602 kg. For the purpose of comparison, consider 1991 data for the advanced countries: Sweden, 5901 kg; West Germany, 3463 kg; the USA, 7681 kg; and France, 3854 kg. Table 1.2 on structures of production offers a more comprehensive picture of the productive sectors of the rich and poor nations. This table, nonetheless, presents only a snapshot of the different economies, not a picture of *structural* capacity.

It is not necessary to cite more statistics, nor to belabour the obvious implication drawn from this way of thinking: the overriding need is to close the widening gap between the rich and the poor.

The existence of the gap is an indisputable datum. But that is not the heart of the matter. The point is that the gap between the advanced capitalist countries and the Third World is a *symptom*, not a *cause*, of what ails the world political economy. The manifest problems cannot be solved without remedying fundamental causes. The situation is much the same as treating a medical condition such as a chest pain. Before a prescription is given, it is essential to diagnose what is causing the ailment. The cure for indigestion is altogether different from the treatment for a heart attack. And an accurate diagnosis takes into account an individual's medical history, for what afflicts one part of the body affects the health of the entire organism. So too the position of a Third World country must be seen as a single limb of the whole, an organic segment of the world political economy.

If the challenges facing the Third World cannot be understood symptomatically, we must look beyond what meets the eye. If solving the problems of the Third World simply required closing a gap, the oil-exporting countries would now be advanced countries, given the massive transfer of capital and technology to them. Yet the member states of the Organization of Petroleum Exporting Countries (OPEC) have been unable to digest the inflow. Clearly the matter is more involved than narrowing a gap.

Some observers say that the trouble in the Third World is the erratic, win-all-lose-all political process there. In many countries, coups beget counter-coups, with no end to this spree in sight. Political instability, it is believed, obstructs national development, especially when self-serving military juntas give priority to lavish expenditures on 'defence' and security.

This argument, like the other ones reviewed, is plausible. The difficulty with it lies in the distinctive experiences of certain heretofore

stable countries like Zambia and Morocco. Politically stable countries
in the Third World have on the whole fared no better at development
(if we dare use the word before defining it) than have politically unstable countries. Consequently, factors other than political stability and
instability must be considered. Politics is not an autonomous sphere of
activity. In politics the critical issues are heavily economic, as illustrated
by an unhappy incident in southern Africa.

POLITICAL ECONOMY

Since it was likely that Ian Smith's bombers would attack guerrilla
camps that night, I (JHM) urged my driver to cover the distance between Chimoio, a town on the Mozambican side of the Rhodesian border, and the coastal city of Beira in the shortest time possible. At dusk
we had a flat tyre. The driver was momentarily amused by my instructions to change it. 'There are no spare tyres in Mozambique,' he explained. I then understood that the parked vehicles strewn along the
roadside had been abandoned. Suddenly my musings were interrupted
by planes nose-diving overhead. Fear knifed through me. I felt utterly
helpless. Would I become a hapless victim of the convulsions shaking
the Third World?
   The predicament in which I found myself provides a starting-point
for understanding what ails the Third World. I was imperilled in rural
Mozambique essentially because the sputtering economy lacked foreign
exchange to import tyres. The reasons for Mozambique's chronic
balance of payments problems lie in the intermeshing of politics and
economics in the subcontinent of southern Africa.
   Exactly what is the nexus between politics and economics? Controversies over this are legion. In the eighteenth and nineteenth centuries,
an extraordinary lot of writers – among them Adam Smith, David Ricardo and John Stuart Mill – considered themselves political economists. Karl Marx, who wrote *A Contribution to the Critique of Political
Economy*, was a part of this tradition. For these classical thinkers, political economy was the practical aspect of the study of moral philosophy. It developed as a single field of inquiry centring on the dynamics
of civil society, including the social relations of production and the
distribution of income. The classical writers primarily investigated
national rather than international issues.
   In the last quarter of the nineteenth century, economics became separated from political economy. Mainline economists became increas-

ingly concerned with price and market theory, and less occupied with political phenomena. They focused on marginal techniques for making rational choices in a situation of market equilibrium.

In neo-classical economics, as this avenue of inquiry is called, the ideal is a perfect market, the allocator of scarce resources. Against this standard, market defects are gauged and explained. The manipulation of quantitative price models is an important element in this tradition. The concerns of classical economists with production relations and the conflicting interests of classes have been dismissed.

Meanwhile, in the twentieth century, political scientists have elaborated their own abstract models, chiefly concentrating on how social systems cohere and treating political behaviour as an activity separable from economics. They have sought to attain the high standard of empirical rigour characteristic of neo-classical economics, but have diverged sharply from the substantive concerns in that discipline. Whereas the two fields draw on a common fund of data and share research findings, they continue to formulate different sorts of questions in their compartmentalized areas.

Emblematic of this decoupling is the fact that the most recent edition of the highly touted *International Encyclopedia of the Social Sciences* contains not one entry under political economy. At the appropriate place for political economy, going by alphabetical order, there is an article on the familiar topic of political culture, after which the reader is referred to various other orthodox headings: culture, government and socialization, especially political socialization. Mention is made of related articles on modernization, national culture, political anthropology, political sociology and societal analysis. The index lists a single book on *Political Economy*, by a contemporary author, Oscar Lange, who taught at the University of Chicago before taking a senior position in the government of Poland. (Reviewing Lange's work for the *Encyclopedia* was a Polish immigrant to the USA who chaired Columbia University's heavily neo-classical Department of Economics.)

Now there are forces pushing economics and politics back together, but analysts disagree over the meaning of political economy. In attempting to predict fluctuations of output (unemployment and business cycles), neo-classicals have developed a sophisticated understanding of market mechanisms. Nevertheless the limitations of deducing phenomena, such as the marginal efficiency of capital and the propensity to consume, from statistical observation of past behaviour are patent.

Added to this, in the aftermath of decolonization it has become increasingly evident that a host of factors, not least cultural practices, has considerable bearing on economic development. That the capacity to organize economic development is a political matter could no longer be denied. And of utmost importance beginning in the 1970s, world-wide economic tremors rekindled interest in the field of political economy.

The mainstream is at present storing a vast armoury of knowledge on the political dimensions of economics and vice versa. Politics and economics are said to be 'interdependent'. For, following John Maynard Keynes, who sought to substitute a steady level of employment for the historical pattern of boom-bust, recession-inflation, governments regularly intervene in the economy through their policies of taxation, nationalization, agreements over prices and wages, and so on. It is also widely recognized that the strength or weakness of an economy may seal the fate of a particular government or administration. Given this acknowledged interplay, conventional political scientists and economists have adopted parallel procedures, but are loath to meld what they still see as their distinguishable spheres of professional activity.

Unlike many liberal political economists, Marxists have steadfastly emphasized the social context of their studies: class *and* power. They have stuck to a holistic analysis. For Marxists, economics, politics and ideology are integrated levels of social structure. All three levels are deemed vitally important in history, economics being the major yet not the sole determinant in the capitalist mode of production. It is true, as its detractors claim, that some versions of Marxism are economistic. The crass view has it that 'politics is all economics'. Marx himself railed against this brand of reductionism, and the large majority of contemporary Marxists go to great lengths to scotch this vulgar way of thinking.

In keeping with the classical authors, then, political economy involves the social processes that differentially allocate produce among proprietors, holders of capital and labourers. It entails the governance of production, distribution and consumption of goods. Thus, a political economy analysis must take into account the workings of the state, especially its ability to employ force against enemies, to broker class struggles and to exercise ideological hegemony. In sum, political economy is a discourse over the ends and means of public policy. It is a reflection on the human condition. Various elements of this definition will be examined in subsequent chapters (especially Chapter 4). But now it will be helpful to specify the object of the political economy analysis in this book: the Third World.

HOW MANY WORLDS?

The Third World is easier to characterize than to define. In barest out-line: labour-intensive economies, mixed with some capital- (but rarely technology-) intensive sectors, abound. Typically, a large part of the population is engaged in agriculture. This sector is usually marked by low levels of productivity and fails to meet the wants of the domestic market. The economies are oriented to the satisfaction of external needs, namely those of the advanced countries. Hence priority is often given to the production of cash crops – not food crops – and the extrac-tion of raw materials for export. Technologically innovative industries are exceptional, although some countries have shown possibilities in this area: most notably, four in Asia (South Korea and Taiwan, plus the city-states of Hong Kong and Singapore). Foreign trade predomi-nantly centres on a few advanced capitalist countries. The direction of trade is paralleled by the movement of skilled human resources, which is a major transference of wealth from the Third World to the West, though some of it returns home in the form of migrants' remittances.

Equally important to consider are social elements. In most parts of the Third World, the receding colonial power sought to graft Western parliamentary and party institutions on to indigenous cultures, which are based on other historical realities. This implantation often aggra-vated existing class and ethnic rivalries. The apparent forms of conflict have varied enormously. Which issues rent the social fabric – religion, language, regional disparities, and so forth – depended on the distinc-tive history and culture of a particular area. In all but a few cases, the replicas of Western polities could not withstand the swirl of these cen-trifugal forces. Soldiers often step into the political breach only to for-get their promises to return willingly to the barracks. Not surprisingly, there have been quite a few instances where politics have been awash with repression and no party systems, not to mention bulging bureau-cracies. Popular discontent may then be vented in the form of riots, in-surgency, secessionist movements and civil wars.

Beyond a brief mention of the broad characteristics of the political economies of the Third World, generalization is hazardous, lest one oversimplify a multifaceted phenomenon to which different definitions are assigned. As defined by the French authors who coined the term, the Third World – an analogy to the Third Estate before the French Re-volution – meant specific strata not belonging to either of the most pri-vileged groups of the day, the nobility and the clergy. The Third Estate was led by a non-commercial and professional bourgeoisie. Supported by the peasants, the Third Estate, unlike the other two orders, advocated vote by head. Even so, the deputies elected by all three orders argued that only men of property could qualify, thus excluding women of all stations and the common men.

A somewhat different notion assimilates the Third World to poverty in general. In World Bank parlance, the Third World comprises low-income countries. These may be subdivided according to gross national product (GNP) per person, but this definition is replete with empirical contradictions. Kuwait has a higher average per capita income than does the USA, and there is a greater incidence of poverty in Harlem than in many parts of the Third World. Furthermore, at stake is a qualitative, not a quantitative, condition. From yet another angle, the term 'Third World' means the proletarian nations. It suggests the existence of states that are exploited and of others that are exploiters. The designation of proletarian and bourgeois nations has a certain cachet in some leftist quarters. But surely no present-day society is without classes; no social formation is composed entirely of the exploited masses or of their exploiters.

In common usage, the Third World encapsulates all countries not included in the First World and Second World. The First World alludes to the Western capitalist countries plus Japan, Australia and New Zealand. This grouping often finds room for Israel and South Africa as well. Until the demise of the Soviet Union and its allies in Europe, the Second World consisted of the socialist countries of the East. These were sometimes called the Soviet bloc, but that rubric did not cover Albania and the former Yugoslavia. The *Third World encompasses the nations of Africa, Asia and Latin America, most of them former colonies which to varying degrees lack power in the global political economy.* This is true, for example, of the oil-exporting countries. Unable to imbibe massive inflows of capital, these countries invested the lion's share of it in Western financial institutions. The banks recycled much of this capital in the form of commercial loans to oil-importing nations of the Third World. The oil importers are now repaying, on top of principal, staggering debt-servicing charges to Western moneylenders.

The ambiguities associated with the term 'Third World' are manifold. The term appears all too comprehensive. It can shroud the differences between and within the three continents in a mist of deceptive simplicity. Another complication is the role of oppressed peoples elsewhere in the world. Are African-Americans part of the Third World? Native Americans? Australian aborigines? With immigrant workers in mind, Alain Geismar, a leader of the 1968 student uprising in France, asserted: 'The Third World starts in the suburbs.' (The suburbs around

Paris are working-class districts.) Relatedly, ethnocentrism may be detected in assigning first place to the countries that rank ahead of the others according to an economic and technological yardstick. The Third World would be first if the criteria were the chronology of the human species (which begins with Africa) or total population.

Yet another snag is the disagreement over whether China belongs to the Third World. The Chinese position during the early 1970s, called the theory of three worlds, held that the USA and the Soviet Union made up the First World. The other developed countries formed the Second World. With the exception of Japan, the whole of Asia, Africa and Latin America comprised the Third World. China proclaimed itself to be a socialist nation and part of the Third World, for it has suffered from imperialism, was not a superpower and shared common tasks with other oppressed nations.

Beijing's view of the matter was not endorsed by Third World leaders. Despite all the accolades given to China for supporting Third World causes, hesitation to enlist her stemmed from the perception that while China may not qualify as a superpower, a country with 1.2 billion people, bountiful natural resources and nuclear hardware is, by any means of accounting, a big, big power. Hence, at meetings of non-aligned nations, China had been an onlooker, not an invited participant. During the late 1970s, as China's economic and political relations with Japan, Western Europe and the USA expanded, references to the three-worlds theory declined. By the early 1980s, with the growing emphasis on modernization, the theory practically disappeared from foreign policy pronouncements.

Ambiguities aside, some observers reject the term 'Third World' altogether. The Brandt commissioners, among others, preferred a dichotomy, as indicated by the nomenclature of their report: *North-South: A Program for Survival.* The differentiation is between two hemispheres, the northern nations being more economically advanced than are their southern counterparts. The North includes well-to-do nations south of the equator: Australia, New Zealand, and more problematically South Africa. Located in the northern hemisphere, too, are India, with 866 million people in 1991 – 16 per cent of the world's population – the rest of South Asia, most of south-east Asia, the Caribbean, Central America and the northern tier of South America.

However, the North-South distinction is not the only way to divide the world in two. In the twilight of his career, Kwame Nkrumah, Ghana's flamboyant head of state from 1957 to 1966, held that 'the "Third World" is neither a practical political concept nor a reality. It is merely a misused expression which has come to mean everything and nothing.' For him, the differentiation was ideological, tied to capitalism and scientific socialism. But surely this view is too rigid. It makes no allowance for different forms of capitalism or transitions in history. No attention is given to the process whereby nationalism spawns or converts to an alternative strategy of development. In Nkrumah's vision, socialism is seemingly a magic remedy for all the ills of capitalist life, without any consideration of the specific forces which might give it expression.

Another viewpoint is that the world is one. To wit, former Indian Prime Minister Indira Gandhi claimed that it is wrong to slice up the world and to deny its unity, adding: 'We are responsible not to individual countries alone, but to peace and prosperity of the whole world.' A worthy goal that is! Yet Mrs Gandhi's imagery is devoid of power relations and social conflict, aspects of human existence that cannot be wished away simply because they are monstrous.

In a perceptive book, *The Capitalist World-Economy*, sociologist Immanuel Wallerstein also makes the entire world his unit of analysis, reasoning that there is a single world economy and it is capitalist. Like the Trotskyites who dismiss 'socialism in one country' as an impossibility, Wallerstein believes that an alternative to capitalism requires a new world system, which in turn necessitates a world government. The analysis that follows from this presupposition is useful in that it alerts us to an important dialectical process: while globalization stirs unevenness among and within countries, it also acts as a homogenizing mechanism reducing national distinctiveness. On the one hand, economies (and sectors) develop and underdevelop at dramatically different rates. On the other, outside elements weighing on the Third World increasingly standardize commodities (witness consumption goods such as Coca-Cola and blue jeans); transnational corporations (TNCs) invite – even command – a large measure of uniformity in their management agreements as well as royalty and technology contracts; and international monetary institutions prescribe the same basic conditions, politely called 'adjustment policies', for diverse economies. The danger, however, in overemphasizing the broad strokes lies in omitting the fine detail, which is precisely what in substance must be discerned.

So where does this leave us? With one, two, three, four or five worlds? The division of the world into three components is a reality. But they are changing. Most important in a post-Cold War era is the disintegration of the Second World. Moreover, the global political economy is increasingly differentiated, with important distinctions between the first generation of countries to have penetrated Japanese and Western markets, possible competition from a second generation of NICs, and, at the other end of the spectrum, sub-Saharan Africa, which is the most marginalized region in the mosaic of globalization. Rather than nullify the concept of the Third World, these changes suggest that there is a 'new Third World' comprised of all the countries that have graduated above the mid-point on the scale of global competitiveness (Brazil, China, Korea, Taiwan, and so on) and an 'old Third World' made up of all the rest. Some members of the old Third World have attempted to industrialize but are not competitive, and others (especially the ones in sub-Saharan Africa and the Caribbean) have not even entered the Industrial Revolution. Yet, with market reforms and the plethora of problems unleashed by the upward mobility of the new Third World – varying degrees of social polarization, regional imbalances, corruption, crime, environmental degradation, and so on – this grouping could well be tomorrow's old Third World.

The Third World is a metaphor for a structured hierarchy. Some of the participants in the global division of labour and power have shifted positions, mostly at the margins. But this movement has not eclipsed the basic idea, sometimes pivotal in such forums as the UN. It is also an association of states, albeit not a unitary entity. However, to the extent that the Third World is a geographical category referring to the three continents, it is not an analytical concept. The drawback to Third Worldist thinking is sentimentality, the tendency to romanticize the struggles waged by 'the wretched of the earth'. A Third Worldist perspective gives the impression that only the advanced countries are the oppressors, neglects important differences within underdeveloped nations, and ignores the role of the locally dominant strata in these nations. In this book we will nonetheless continue to use the term Third World as a convenient shorthand to describe a critical and varied phenomenon. Despite its pitfalls, the convention is better than the other options. The phrases 'emerging areas', 'modernizing societies', 'developing nations' and 'less developed countries' are hollow euphemisms. The language adopted ought not to be allowed to mask the struggles within societies, or to deflect attention from class and other alliances emerging within civil society, cross-cutting and transcending national borders. But what is the reality lurking behind what we choose to call the Third World?

LEARNING FROM OUR CHILDREN

The question of terminology raises major substantive issues that form the core of this book. For now, we simply want to introduce the basic themes in this undertaking.

Volumes have been written about the meaning of development and underdevelopment. Within this compass are the master works of antiquity. Plato's *Republic* is a utopian schema for engineering distributive justice, and Aristotle conceived the polis as an agency to develop to the utmost the potential of humanity. According to the Greek doctrine *physis*, humans are in motion from a primary natural condition to a formed and finished completion. We will, says Aristotle, one day look back on the historic process, and observe the growth of institutions to discover their course and ultimate state. To this end, the philosophers of antiquity took it as their task to make value judgements about what constitutes the good society and about the institutions and processes through which the good life can be achieved.

Over the centuries the inherently ethical aspects of the development debate have endured. There is the story of the English administrator serving overseas in the early days of empire. He stumbled upon a 'native' lolling beside a lake and decided to do the chap a good turn. The colonizer gave the local a swift kick to the ribs, awakening him from a deep sleep, and demanded: 'Why are you idling with a dozen or so fish beside you instead of catching more?' The lackadaisical response was: 'I have caught all the fish that my family can eat today.' Unperturbed, the Englishman didactically informed his acquaintance: 'My good man, if you net another string of fish, you can sell it in the market place.' The local repeated his point: 'But we already have enough to eat.' So the English official persisted: 'With the proceeds of your sale, you can employ other fishermen.' By this time, the local was feeling quite dumbfounded. He asked: 'What then?' 'Why,' said the Englishman, 'then you can retire and sleep all day along this lovely waterfront.'

This apocryphal story not only raises the crucial ethical question 'development for what?' but also suggests deeper socio-economic processes. Clearly Third World producers are drawn into the cash economy in many ways. Demographic changes due to conquest or migration, the imposition of hut and poll taxes, the introduction of cheap manufactured goods, and the advent of wage labour flush peasants into production for exchange. All the same, the story reminds us to be aware of our values in arriving at judgements about development and underdevelopment; one must indeed guard against ethnocentrism. To do so in an area of inquiry which stirs sensibilities and emotions requires us to confront our own values. This leads to self-clarification and self-definition. In studying other cultures, we are the primary beneficiaries because we come to a better understanding of ourselves.

However, moral indignation, while understandable, will not solve the fundamental problems of underdevelopment which are deeply embedded in the political economies of the Third World. Let us avoid misunderstanding about the concept of underdevelopment. As employed by political economists, it is not an invidious term insinuating cultural deficiencies; neither is it virtually the same as undevelopment: objective shortfalls in production, organizational competence, technological know-how, and so on.

More properly, *underdevelopment* refers to the blockage which forestalls a rational transformation of the social structure in Third World countries: rational not in the commonsensical meaning that the options are deduced from reason alone, or in the bureaucratic sense of a neat adjustment of means to ends. Rather, rational in that the interests and needs of the majority are increasingly dominant. What blocks development is an internal and external constellation of power and privilege.

Development entails but is not synonymous with economic growth. In our usage, *development* is the increasing capacity to make rational use of natural and human resources for social ends.

To create more goods and services, all peoples have sought to alter their relations with the environment. Thus development is a universal process, but the rates of development are highly uneven. Added to this, there is marked inequality in distribution.

In precapitalist, communal societies, economic productivity was of course low. The technological aspects of production were rudimentary. Property belonged to the collectivity, and work was done in common. People produced for their mutual needs, not for exchange with others. Commodities were not bought and sold on the market. There were social differences between the sexes and between elders and juniors. With growing specialization in production and the advent of long-distance trade, social differences became more pronounced. These undeveloped societies increasingly, albeit slowly, expanded control over their environment. The reversal of this condition through the withdrawal of the benefits of nature's bounty and human labour constitutes underdevelopment, a historical process which will be examined more fully in subsequent chapters.

Nowadays the most vexing matter, the terminus of the journey undertaken here, concerns the transition from underdevelopment to development. Third World – hereafter also called underdeveloped for reasons that will be explained – countries, from Afghanistan to Zimbabwe, are all grappling with the question of how to engage the transition. Definitive answers are nowhere to be found. Yet novel experiments and new ideas warrant careful examination.

These new forms are a response to the profound structural metamorphoses marking our era. It became a cliché during the mid-1980s to note that the power of the USA had taken a nose dive. There was more to this than the well-known reasons for the USA's economic troubles, beginning with the collapse of the Bretton Woods monetary system and depreciation of the dollar in the 1970s. In 1984, the US trade deficit reached $108 billion. By the end of 1985, the USA turned from being the world's major creditor into the largest debtor nation, borrowing over $100 billion in that year alone, larger than the total Brazilian debt. The US share of total world output was less than one-quarter by 1991, down from one-third in 1950.

These woes cannot be chalked up solely to misguided government policies, for not only the US but the entire capitalist world has been beset by deep-seated ills. However, it is important to note that in the early 1990s, when most industrialized countries continued to struggle through a recession, the USA was making significant economic gains. In 1990, US workers were the most productive in the world, surpassing their German and Japanese counterparts. In addition, the country's share of exports by industrialized countries, which shrank to 10 per cent during the 1980s, climbed back up to 14 per cent. Today, the USA exports steel to Seoul, transistors to Tokyo, and cars to Cologne.

As a whole, however, in the Western countries the level of unemployment, gains in productivity and the rate of profit are causes of considerable concern. Restructuring in the West edges into the Third World in a shrinkage in the volume of exports of primary commodities, while the price of most imports continues to mount. Meanwhile, the mature capitalist countries have lent the underdeveloped world over half a trillion dollars. Debt service of all Third World countries expanded from 13.3 per cent of exports of goods and services in 1970 to 20.4 per cent in 1990. The greater the burden of debt service, the more the borrower's capacity to repay diminishes. Current borrowing continues at a gallop just to defray the cost of old loans, let alone to meet present needs. For many underdeveloped countries, continued access to needed external financing required the implementation of structural adjustment programmes. Faced with huge balance-of-payment and budget deficits, most countries had no choice but to acquiesce to conditions set by international institutions.

Is there a common thread to help us disentangle all this? A clue may be found by turning to children's ways. Children are intrigued by products discarded by the adult world: empty cartons, food containers, corks from wine bottles and so on. Not infrequently a young child prefers the box in which a present is packaged to the present itself. Children are known to have profound insights. However, much of this profundity is lost precisely because the socialization process hammers it out of existence. Then again, maybe not all qualities should be redeemed: children are often egocentric, intolerant and downright selfish.

We adults also waste products which ought to be preserved. We should rehabilitate some of the wisdom lost from our intellectual heritage. Discarded alternatives may be detected in the classical theory of capital accumulation and usefully applied to fathom the political economy of the contemporary Third World. The key is to go back to the classical tradition in order to go forwards from it. Then we can adapt the old concepts to new problems, albeit ones for which they were not intended. To be sure, new problems require new answers. Eternal verities are not engraved in 'the great books', but these works do indicate a general direction in which to move and provide positive guidance.

This guidebook will stress that underdeveloped countries are in no sense helpless, mired in a hopeless situation. Underdevelopment is not an immutable fact. The foremost difficulty in attempting to snap out of this condition is to dismantle the mechanisms that reproduce it. Built-in features of the global political economy regenerate underdevelopment. This argument redoubles upon itself, for underdevelopment is renewed as ideology as well. Until now orthodox doctrines of development have been part of the problem. Our job here is to present an interpretation that will be part of the solution. Thus in Chapter 2 we will clear away some of the dead wood before charting another course.

Part II

Ideologies and Structures of Accumulation

2 Sources of Received Ideas about the Third World

The Acholi, a Nilotic people in northern Uganda, are wedged in a stretch between Zaire, Sudan and Kenya. The standard maps do not identify their locale as Acholi-land. I (JHM) first encountered them when a fellow student invited me to his home, a mud-thatched hut, one among many surrounded by a makeshift thicket fence erected to keep out intruders, human or otherwise. Afterwards I discovered that the plight of the Acholi is told in a moving tale, *Song of Lawino*, by the late Okot p'Bitek, an Oxford-educated poet and novelist who directed the National Cultural Centre of Uganda. Indeed, the personal meaning of the changes stalking the Acholi, and the bulk of the Third World, is encapsulated in the lives of two fictional Ugandans; Lawino is a perceptive uneducated woman who cries out in anguish over the new-found ways of her husband, Ocol:

> My husband
> Has read at Makerere University.
> He has read deeply and widely,
> But if you ask him a question
> He says
> You are insulting him;
> He opens up with a quarrel
> He begins to look down upon you
> Saying
> 'You ask questions
> That are a waste of time!
>
> He says
> My questions are silly questions,
> Typical questions from village girls,
> Questions of uneducated people,
> Useless questions from untutored minds.
>   . . .
> Ocol says
> He has no time to waste

Discussing things with a thing like me
Who has not been to school.
He says
A university man
Can only have useful talk
With another university man or woman.
And that is funny,
That he should stoop so low
Even to listen
To my questions.

Ocol's altered attitudes are evident in his scorn for his people's religious practices, which he no longer observes.

My husband wears
A small crucifix
On his neck,
And all his daughters

Wear rosaries.
But he prohibits me
From wearing the elephant tail necklace,
He once beat me
For wearing the toe of the edible rat
And the horn of the rhinoceros
And the jaw-bone of the alligator.

A large snake
Once fell down from the roof
Of the cold hall!
The Nun who was teaching
The Evening Speakers' Class
Grabbed her large crucifix
And pressed it on her bosom,
Closed her eyes
And said something
We could not understand.

My husband says
The cowry shells.
The colobus-monkey hair,
The dog's horn charms
Are all useless things.

> He says
> Only foolish backward folk
> Uneducated simple fellows
> Who live in the shadow of fear
> Carry these dirty things!

In the end, Lawino, grief-stricken, mourns the loss of her man. He has been mortified by wisdom, by the weighty knowledge of books. He is no more than a stump, thoroughly emasculated.

> He borrows the clothes he wears
> And the ideas in his head
> And his actions and behaviour
> Are to please somebody else.
> Like a woman trying to please her husband!
> My husband has become a woman!
>
> Then why do you wear a shirt?
> Why do you not tie
> A sheet around your waist
> As other women do?
> Put on the string skirt
> And some beads on your loin!
>
> Bile burns my inside!
> I feel like vomiting!
>
> For all our young men
> Were finished in the forest,
> Their manhood was finished
> In the class-rooms,
> Their testicles
> Were smashed
> With large books!

When Lawino asks whether she must share her bed with a woman and whether the son of the Acholi can recapture his manhood, she does not plead for going back to the old ways. Rather, she implicitly raises the central question of how to escape the unsettling conditions in which her people are trapped. In fact, Lawino's lament is a condensation of the most basic human dimensions of development and underdevelopment. It is a clue for interpreting the whole.

In order better to understand the single instance, let us turn to the world of ideas and search for the precipices of new knowledge. Paradoxically, we are ultimately able to derive the utmost meaning from individual conditions by initially moving from the specific to the general. There are certainly different ways to traverse this course. The best known path has been staked out by liberal reformers who view modernization as, above all, a shift from a parochial fund of *traditional values* to an array of *new norms*.

LIBERAL REFORMISM

In the years immediately following the Second World War, a presentation of a thoroughgoing statement of the foremost theorizing about development and underdevelopment would not have required much space. It could have only been an embellishment of what the master philosophers had written about equality and inequality among peoples.

In the time of Plato and Aristotle, the Greek city-states increasingly came into contact with people who differed from the Hellenes in physique and culture. The leading minds of Athens attributed these differences not to race but to the effects of distinct environments on a stable human nature. In Greek eyes, it was the facts of geography that caused the tremendous variation in human culture.

For aeons the primary economic and social divisions of the world were understood as expressions of natural differences in climate, soil and rainfall. The eighteenth-century philosopher Montesquieu, for example, maintained that the immutability of culture and the low levels of income in southern nations result from a climate that saps the body of vigour and strength. Excessive heat, he argued, precipitates faintness of the mind. Under such conditions there is no enterprising spirit, no curiosity. Behaviour is passive. In India, even the children born of Europeans become indolent and lose the courage distinctive to their own climate, argued Montesquieu.

In the nineteenth and twentieth centuries, Western observers dismissed the environment theory and substituted a race theory to explain the diversity of humankind. It has been believed in some quarters that inherent differences among human species, identifiable in terms of skin colour, distinguish the achievements of societies. This way of thinking is so well known that we need not dwell on its tenets. A few graphic examples will suffice.

In a televised lecture delivered in 1963, Hugh Trevor-Roper, the Regius Professor of Modern History at Oxford University, maintained: 'Perhaps, in the future, there will be some African history. . . But at present there is none; there is only the history of Europeans in Africa. The rest is darkness, . . . and darkness is not a subject of history.' Similarly, Eric Severeid, the senior scholar of American television news, claimed: 'The truth is that there is very little in most of the new African and Asian nations worth anything in twentieth century terms that was not put there by westerners.' Adding to this, he commented: 'The truth is that in spite of talking about returning to their own cultural roots – remember Africanization – what they want to be is what the west already is.'

Such arrogance has often been carried over into American foreign policy. For example, in 1969 Henry Kissinger presented the then President, Richard Nixon, with five policy options in southern Africa, and Nixon chose the wrong one. He adopted the now famous Option 2, embodied in NSSM-39 (National Security Study Memorandum-39), based on the supposition that the liberation movements would fail: 'The whites are here to stay and the only way that constructive change can come about is through them. There is no hope for the blacks to gain the political rights they seek through violence, which will only lead to chaos and increased opportunities for the communists.' NSSM-39 Option 2 called for expanded communication with the white minority regimes. In practice, the policy meant closer economic and military cooperation.

Any remaining doubt about Kissinger's attitude toward the Third World was removed in the same year, when Gabriel Valdés, the foreign minister of Chile under the Eduardo Frei government, informed Nixon that Latin America was remitting $3.8 for every dollar in American aid. When Nixon questioned the statistic, Valdés pointed out that the figure had been borrowed from a study undertaken by a bank in the USA. The next afternoon Kissinger requested a private meeting with Valdés. Kissinger opened the session with a salvo:

Mr. Minister, you made a strange speech. You come here speaking of Latin America, but this is not important. Nothing important can come from the South. History has never been produced in the South. The axis of history starts in Moscow, goes to Bonn, crosses over to Washington, and then goes to Tokyo. What happens in the South is of no importance. You're wasting your time.

'I said,' Valdés recalls, 'Mr. Kissinger, you know nothing of the South.' 'No,' Kissinger answered, 'and I don't care.' Seymour M. Hersh, from whose book on Kissinger this illustration is drawn, concludes:

'The Valdés incident showed the White House attitude: like a child, Latin America was to be seen and not heard.'

The foregoing incidents are not harmless or isolated examples. They represent public or official behaviour by prominent scholars affiliated with top universities, Oxford and Harvard, an influential television commentator, and a former secretary of state. It is true to say that, nowadays, their statements run counter to a great deal of commentary in the media and a flurry of literature which attacks the race theory. Attitudes such as Kissinger's view of the Third World have come under fire on the grounds that they are factually wrong and morally repugnant. Contemporary liberal thinkers contend that it is not race but a lack of capital and technology that explains why the developing countries are lagging behind. External inputs, primarily investment and technical assistance, it is widely believed, are needed to modernize the flagging nations.

The term 'modernization' gained currency when it was trumpeted by American foreign policy makers as part of President Harry Truman's 1949 Point Four Program, which included assistance to transmit scientific and industrial knowledge to the underdeveloped countries. The term came into general usage in the age of decolonization, when most of the countries in Africa, Asia and the Caribbean graduated to political independence. The doctrine of modernization offered a palatable explanation for America's burgeoning role in the Third World. Its icy, analytical language called for a new world order, seemingly one without exploitation.

It is worth recalling that the naive optimism of the modernization school contrasted sharply with the canny *weltanschauung* touted in the old days before imperialism became a dirty word; the authors of imperialism had spoken unblushingly about a world of power. In 1895 Cecil Rhodes said:

> I was in the East End of London [a working-class quarter] yesterday and attended a meeting of the unemployed. I listened to the wild speeches, which were just a cry for 'bread, bread!' and on my way home I pondered over the scene and I became more than ever convinced of the importance of imperialism... My cherished idea is a solution for the social problem, i.e., in order to save the 40,000,000 inhabitants of the United Kingdom from a bloody civil war, we colonial statesmen must acquire new lands to settle the surplus population, to provide new markets for the goods produced in the factories and mines. The Empire, as I have always said, is a bread and butter question. If you want to avoid civil war, you must become imperialists.

For the architects of imperialism, power was empire, and empire was conquest. The vanquished, they claimed, would be better off living under the regency of the civilized rather than left to their own devices.

In time revolutionary nationalism increasingly challenged imperial doctrine. Battered by its Western critics as well, it slowly lost legitimacy. A theory was needed to replace the discredited notion of the 'white man's burden' and the *mission civilisatrice*. Attuned to the metamorphoses in an international system racked by two world wars, modernization theorists offered a vision of a restructured global order based upon universal processes of development. The alternative etched by these thinkers – most of them Americans – would be made possible by the spread of US economic muscle and military might. The new world powerhouse was portrayed as liberal, progressive and truly international. It had put in train international organizations – the UN and the Bretton Woods twins, the International Monetary Fund (IMF) and the World Bank – bent on curbing global war and helping all free nations to develop peacefully.

An avalanche of books and articles released by the acolytes of the modernization school descended upon our universities and libraries in the 1950s and 1960s, tunnelling the vision of an entire generation of thinkers, some of whom stepped into leading policy making positions. This much was brought home to me almost two decades ago when I (JHM) was standing on the steps of the library at the London School of Economics engaged in lively conversation with a distinguished African writer and activist. In mid-sentence he nudged me and muttered, 'Look there.' I noticed a doting old man in a tweed jacket supported by a cane. My companion, a graduate of the London School of Economics, said, 'That chap set me back in my thinking by 20 years.' The old man was his former mentor, a specialist in the field of international development. The topic of conversation then shifted to an assessment of the foremost thinking about modernization conveyed to students and filtered to the general public.

Needless to say, as with other schools of thought we will examine, there are different versions and major debates among authors working within the compass of the modernization framework. Bibliographies and distinctions among individual writers, however, would be burdensome to follow and need not detain us. Our concern here is to identify the mainstream of modernization analysis, not the tributaries.

In brief, modernization theory is an attempt to establish a model for understanding universal patterns of change. The starting gate for all nations embarking on a fast modernizing track is traditional society. In this stage, humans exercise little control over their environment. Traditional people lack the traits of modern individuals, whose culture is urban, literate and participant. Traditional society is not inscribed by political consciousness or active involvement in attempting to shape the future.

Not only can nations be distinguished in terms of the dichotomy between tradition and modernity, but also segments of a society and sectors of an economy reflect this split. The same duality is evident in the ambit of technology, where there is a change-over from age-old methods to the applications of scientific knowledge; in agriculture, a conversion from subsistence farming to the commercial production of crops; in industry, a turnabout from reliance on human labour and animal power to the use of machines; and in human ecology, a transformation from rural and village life to urban settlements. In all realms, tradition is staid and inhibiting, whereas modernity is vigorous and creative.

All societies progress through distinct phases on the road to modernization. In one formulation, the sequence consists of five categories: traditional society is said to be one with limited production functions based on pre-Newtonian science and technology, with a ceiling on attainable output per head. The second stage of growth satisfies the preconditions for the take-off to a modern economy: in a context rocked by the expansion of world markets and international competition, the insights of modern science are translated into increased production both in agriculture and industry. Then, in the third stage, comes the great turning point in this sequence. The take-off is the period when the obstacles to growth are transcended; the new technology becomes predominant in society and growth becomes self-generating.

In the drive to maturity, the economy converts to more refined and complex processes: for instance, from coal, iron and the heavy engineering industries of the railway age to machine tools, chemicals and electrical equipment; it moves beyond the original industries which propelled the take-off to absorb and to develop a wide range of resources. Finally, we reach the age of high mass consumption. The leading sectors of the economy now produce durable consumer goods and services. The advancement of modern technology is not the sole objective, for at this ultimate stage societies choose to allocate additional resources to social welfare and security.

All societies, it is worth repeating, are thought to traverse this path. The progression is fixed and linear. The early modernizers (the Western countries) piloted the way; the late-comers will follow the same unswerving course.

What touches off the stirrings of modernization? Clearly no single element or agent spawns this process. Modernization is multidimensional, pluralist to the core, entailing a syndrome of impulses: as societies become increasingly complex, more specialized roles emerge. No longer does the chief represent the political executive, legislator and judge. Elaborate institutions evolve gradually. There are distinctive activities and functions to be carried out in order to solidify the nation-state; the gulf between castes, tribes, regions and religious groups must be bridged. Forging a national identity necessitates moulding new attitudes which centre on individual achievement and empathy for fellow citizens.

At the heart of modernization theory is evolutionary optimism. A fundamental premise is that this multifaceted process will correct the lag in development. This whole genre of thinking is permeated by a nineteenth-century belief in progress. Change is change for the better. The end point of the modernization vision approximates the traits of the present-day Western nations. The terminus of the journey is liberal democracy, a goal which all nations can attain.

This intellectual framework has had an enormous impact. To illustrate its practical consequences, consider the following application: in Bukoba, a district in north-western Tanzania, *matoke* bananas (the staple food) and coffee are interplanted because land is in short supply; the majority of producers, poor peasants, do not have access to sufficient acreage to grow the two crops in separate areas. The government's agricultural extension officers, however, have advised the small farmer to cultivate pure-stand coffee, since interplanted bananas draw nitrogen and water from the soil and shade the coffee crop. This advice is based on experiments performed under laboratory conditions. It benefits only the minority of well-to-do farmers with enough land to segregate bananas and coffee. The large land holder cultivates under conditions that resemble those of the research station. In addition, he (rarely she) is likely to mingle with the government experts in a social milieu that facilitates communication and hence adoption of the proposed changes.

The poor peasants resist the innovations suggested by the research team because its recommendations are useless or harmful to them. They have been known to fry cotton seeds before putting them in the ground or to plant cassava cuttings upside down. The government officers in turn regard the peasants as traditional: the stereotypical description is backward, irresponsible, lazy and stupid. The modernization thesis is then invoked to justify supporting the agents of change. These are deemed to be the rich farmers. The whole argument about modernization is often used to legitimize coercing the so-called traditional peasants.

This is not a random case. It typifies the way this armoury of knowledge is deployed. In fact, modernization theory informed US policy throughout Latin America during the 1960s. Known as the Green Revolution, it called for a large dose of foreign assistance to increase agricultural yields. Most observers believe that contrary to the rhetoric of the US Agency for International Development (AID), the overall impact of the policy was to entrench the powerful and the wealthy landowners in the Latin American countries at the expense of the small farmer.

Although the modernization school has contributed importantly to social science by extending its focus beyond the West to the Third World, there are a number of problems embedded in this way of thinking. To begin with, modernization theory is too general, too abstract, and without adequate grounding in history. The modern world, of course, did not come out of nowhere. The Western countries experienced a protracted and painful process disrupting older ways of life. In Britain in the eighteenth and nineteenth centuries, the enlargement of the market and the fanning out of wage labour entailed untold human suffering, including widespread violence and extensive pauperization. True, what was rational for an inventive bourgeoisie severed persistent bonds of exploitation, namely feudal servitude. But it is foolish to regard this process as progress for everyone and to sanctify its dynamics as the essential features of a model applicable to the development of the entire world.

Furthermore, the division of the world into traditional and modern societies implies that all peoples were alike at one stage. Thus bands of nomadic hunters, classical Greek city-states and bureaucratic empires of feudal times are placed in a single category. To term all of them traditional not only obscures the differences among them but also denies the unfolding history of peoples in the premodern, or precapitalist, era.

More problematically, modernization thinking lacks an explanation of the causes of underdevelopment. It is not that modernization theorists are wrong about the causes of underdevelopment: they do not even raise the question. They lead one to believe that underdevelopment is an original condition akin to original sin, and must be due to chance or bad luck.

The notion that underdevelopment can be chalked up to an (indeterminate) incapacity ingrained in Third World cultures gives the impression that these countries are autonomous, and that their leaders can really make fundamental decisions about their own destiny. This premise underrates external constraints on leadership and the forces of globalization; it is blind to the ways that Third World economies are tethered to the world market. This model of development, which defines Western values as universal values, deflects attention from the links between the underdeveloped countries and the mature capitalist countries.

These links are of course deeply rooted, going back to slavery, plunder and forced trade. Horrific tales of the kidnapping of about 20 million Africans, pillaging silver and gold from Latin America's ancient civilizations, and opening Asia's ports at the point of a gun are well known. What must be kept uppermost in mind is that the drain of resources from what is now called the Third World has fuelled the engines of capital accumulation in the advanced countries. An important aspect of this process was the enterprising ethic of a creative bourgeoisie in Europe. This ethic, dubbed an orientation to achievement, has been projected on to the Third World by modernization theorists.

An entrepreneurial spirit is indeed integral to an ideology of inequality wielded by the privileged. In the final analysis, modernization theory is an ideology of capitalist accumulation. We do not live in a modernizing world but in a capitalist world. What makes this world tick is not the need for achievement but the drive for profit. In the quest for profit, ideology poses as science. The primary targets for the ideas and symbols of modernization are the working class and peasant producers in the Third World. These ideas and symbols are transmitted by government programmes, bilateral aid projects and international lending agencies. Rationalized as the doctrine of modernization, government policies reinforce and extend inequalities, shoring up a way of life in which certain groups predominate. Today, however, modernization theory is widely held in disrepute because of the bruising charges levelled by its critics and its failures in practice.

WHERE HAVE ALL THE MODERNIZATION THINKERS GONE?

Stung by criticism from a variety of quarters, modernization theory no longer knows what to make of itself. That modernization thinking is fundamentally flawed is widely acknowledged, but liberals refuse to choose among other options. All things considered, the conventional approach finds itself at an impasse.

Modernization theory's intellectual crisis has engendered a more empirical approach. The grand theory of the 1960s and early 1970s, initially dominated by the work of the US Social Science Research Council's Committee on Comparative Politics, gave way to a move towards greater policy relevance and a rediscovery of the importance of economics. Concepts like 'decisions', 'choice' and 'development management' came into vogue in the 1970s. Theorists have often failed to articulate what they mean by policy studies, but they refer to values and social consequences as well as to processes and choices. Sometimes policy is regarded as a synonym for state activity. Like modernization theory's emphasis on elite maintenance, the focus of policy studies is on the ruling elite who are deemed to act on behalf of the general citizenry.

Such attempts to amend modernization theory have provoked much discussion. Both strands of analysis fail to account for the dynamics of globalization: a compression of the time and space aspects of social relations. With new production systems and technologies, especially in communications and transportation, computers, fax machines and so on speed transactions among peoples, thereby reducing geographical constraints and benefiting some groups more than others. Modernization theory and its progeny moreover neglect the underpinnings of state power and class formation. In fact, public policy decisions reflect the efforts of elements within a social structure to allocate state resources for their own or allies' benefit. In this sense, policy analysis is thoroughly antiseptic and structurally blind. Eddies in the mainstream have not achieved a breakthrough but rather carry with them the flotsam of problems of modernization theory.

In practice, the drive to modernize has been converted into neo-liberalism: an opening of markets, liberalization, and privatization. This reform programme – sometimes known as the three Ds (denationalization, deregulation and devaluation) – has been widely adopted. Take Sri Lanka, known previously as Ceylon. This country has done everything in the economic realm that modernization theorists-cum-neoliberal reformers could hope for. The government, championing the virtues of free enterprise, abolished import and exchange controls, unified the exchange rate, established free trade zones, opened the economy to foreign banks and gave wide latitude to market forces. Domestically, the authorities reduced food subsidies, scaled down the rate of unemployment and developed energy sources. Meanwhile, on the international market, rubber prices plummeted while petroleum costs soared. Textile manufacturers encountered protectionism abroad, resulting in a cutback in Sri Lanka's development programme. Between 1980 and 1991, the country's external debt grew from $1.2 million to $5.7 million.

As a percentage of GNP, its external debt increased from 46 per cent to 73 per cent. During the same period, official development assistance and food aid in cereals also rose; food production per capita declined.

Recognizing that without substantial foreign *financial flows* countries such as Sri Lanka would sink, many influential commentators now claim that the modernization vision can never be more than a pipe dream for most of the developing world, save a small number of NICs (an issue to which we will return). By and large, a mood of despair about the prospects for most of the Third World has set in. The unbridled optimism of the modernization school was supplanted by profound pessimism, as evidenced by the dependency approach.

THIRD WORLD RADICALISM

With the debate over the liberal paradigm came the search for other modes of inquiry. If Western liberal thought was marred by ethnocentrism, why not turn to the Third World itself for novel directions in building an analysis of underdevelopment? Could the Third World explain its own dilemmas?

In the 1950s and 1960s a new outlook, known as the dependency school, emanated from Latin America. The dependency perspective, while not monolithic, initially drew its inspiration from a UN agency, the Economic Commission for Latin America (ECLA), established in Santiago, Chile, in 1948. The technocrats and intellectuals staffing ECLA offered a blistering critique of mainstream economics, arguing that its emphasis on the theory of prices and general equilibrium failed to recognize the built-in features of the global economy which disadvantage the underdeveloped countries. In particular, ECLA highlighted the unequal terms of trade between the exporters of raw materials and the exporters of manufactured goods, resulting in chronic balance of payments problems. The first general secretary of ECLA, an Argentine economist named Raúl Prebisch, held that Latin America needs to industrialize behind high protective barriers. He called for state planning and a common market to achieve economies of scale. Most importantly, he proposed an inward-oriented development path known as import-substitution industrialization, which is based on manufacture to satisfy demand previously met by imports.

In addition to drawing on the work of ECLA, the dependency perspective gained strength as a result of the blossoming of leftist movements in the 1960s and 1970s. The Cuban Revolution, China's Cultural

Revolution, the election of the Marxist government of Salvador Allende Gossens in Chile and the American debacle in Vietnam seemingly lent credibility to a radical analysis. Moreover, this was an era of aggressive economic nationalism in Latin America, creating a greater appreciation for the external constraints on development.

In Peru a nationalist military clique ousted the constitutional government of President Fernando Belaúnde Terry in 1968. The generals immediately extended state control over the economy. The government took over 75 per cent of banking, partially nationalized industry, organized an extensive agrarian reform programme and established procedures to give workers a 50 per cent share of their companies. But when the officers, led by President Juan Velasco, expropriated the holdings of the International Petroleum Company, a subsidiary of Exxon, and forced foreign concerns to relinquish mines that were not being developed, Peru entered a period of relative economic stagnation. There was little new private investment for five years. Although Washington officially denied placing a credit squeeze on Lima, the US government naturally sought to advance the interests of foreign investors. Hence the US Export-Import Bank provided no low-interest loans for projects in Peru. A number of loans from other sources were shelved until Washington and Lima reached an accord known as the Greene Agreement: the Peruvians were to pay $150 million in compensation to expropriated firms, $76 million to be allocated by Washington and $74 million to be distributed to companies by Lima.

Such examples are legion in the Third World. Many governments have initiated acts of economic nationalism only to erode the confidence of private investors and to set the nation on an unnavigable economic course that, in the end, is capped by a military incursion into politics or the assassination of the head of state.

Against this background, radical intellectuals in Latin America further refined the dependency approach. Their starting point is imperialism, viewed as an amalgam of economic expansion and political domination. Under imperialism, capital accumulation is based on the export of capital from the advanced countries to underdeveloped areas. Political and military might is used to assert control over the means of production in foreign lands, benefiting a segment of the citizenry in the advanced countries and their partners overseas.

Thus dependency denotes the effects of imperialism on underdeveloped countries. A special form of domination and subordination, dependency's defining characteristic is vulnerability: the limits on a collectivity's ability to determine its own response to social forces within the world order. External forces, the economies of the 'centre' (advanced capitalist nations), 'condition' the responses of the 'periphery' (Third World countries), narrowing the options for independent development.

A country is dependent when the accumulation of capital cannot find its own dynamic within the national economy. The capacity to increase the scale of capital requires the creation of new technologies and the expanded production of capital goods (machinery and equipment). But peripheral economies are unable to alter the basic features of production because of the structure of relations between social groups within the underdeveloped countries. The groups holding the reins of power are the chief beneficiaries of their ties to the centre and would be threatened by a realignment of political power. They have established through the political process a form of production consistent with their interests and objectives.

Clearly the dependency approach differs in essential respects from modernization thinking. Dependency analysis emerges from an explicit political position. And like Marxism, it takes the dynamics of capitalism to be the key to understanding development and underdevelopment.

The major contribution of the dependency approach is to pinpoint the process whereby imperialism has incorporated Third World countries into global capitalism, thereby underdeveloping the internal socio-economic structures within these countries. Theoretically, *dependentistas* have mounted a biting and effective critique of the modernization concept. For instance, they have debunked the dualist thesis, which holds that Third World economies are divided into a capitalist sector and a subsistence sector. On the contrary, commercialization and accumulation do occur in peasant enterprises and backward rural areas are yoked to the national economy as well as the world market. Practically, *dependentistas* helped to muster support for liberation struggles in Indo-China and Africa.

Although *dependentistas* have assailed modernization authors for their lack of historical analysis, dependency writing itself tends to be historically weak. The centre-periphery distinction is based on existing market imbalances, not on unfolding social relations in the production system; thus, the concept of unequal exchange concerns trade between nations and does not address the question of class conflict. It is unclear how the imagery of centre and periphery is linked to class forces. Many writings within this framework say surprisingly little about the changing relations between peasants and workers on the one hand, and the dominant classes on the other, in a specific historical context.

One would like to know precisely which countries are dependent and which ones are not. President Charles de Gaulle, it will be recalled, charged that the USA was a neo-colonial power subjecting France and other European countries to a subordinate position. More recently, Canadian officials have been galled by US dominance of their economy and, some say, of their culture and polity as well. In 1992, 77 per cent of Canada's exports went to the USA, while 65 per cent of its imports came from the USA. Between 1983 and 1992, the US accounted for 64 per cent of direct investment in Canada, which has more foreign ownership of its industries than any other country, according to a study by Bruce Wilkinson.

Given the imbalance in trade and investment between the two countries, is it proper to assign dependent status to the USA's northern neighbour? If so, is Canada therefore an underdeveloped country? Are dependency and underdevelopment one and the same? Obviously not, but what differentiates these concepts is murky.

Added to this problem are major omissions in the dependency framework: in the capitalist world economy, what role did the socialist countries play? After the collapse of the Soviet bloc, where do states such as Cuba and North Korea fit into a world of central and peripheral countries? Not only do *dependentistas* neglect this issue, but they also fail to come to grips with how to eliminate dependency relations: how permanent and stable are these patterns? What is the way out? Seemingly the choices are either continued dependence or revolution. Some proponents of revolution also call for a strategy of self-reliance: an attempt to delink from the world economy and to follow a path of national autonomous development. But this strategy (which will be discussed in Chapter 7) engenders its own set of problems. There are no instantaneous solutions.

BEYOND ORTHODOXY

Clearly there is a wide choice in models of development, ranging from modes of analysis that are overly optimistic to avenues of inquiry that are unduly pessimistic. Notwithstanding the drawbacks to each model, the debates in recent years between divergent schools of thought are a significant advance beyond older, encrusted ideas which attribute a lack of development either to climatic factors or racial differences.

To recapitulate the key points: underdevelopment is not primarily a quantitative phenomenon (such as statistical measures of poverty), not merely falling behind and not by any stretch of the imagination an original condition; it is foolhardy to think that some countries suffer from a curse. Rather, underdevelopment may be best understood as a single chapter of the whole world political economy. Underdevelopment is a historical process. The same forces which generated development in the West engendered underdevelopment in the Third World. True, some aspects of a country's position in the global political economy, such as its resource endowment, have nothing whatsoever to do with external or social causes. But in the main the root problems of under-development are not attributable to nature: they are manmade.

When Europeans first penetrated Africa, they encountered a medley of civilizations which were in no sense stagnant. In West Africa, there was a vigorous trans-Saharan trade, an exchange of scholars with North Africa, a gradual expansion of some centralized political systems, such as the Ashanti kingdom, and the extension of economic ties among previously disparate peoples. Similarly, in India the early Western explorers found highly advanced skills among artisans as well as soph-isticated crafts. The colonizers introduced manufactured products, destroyed rural home industries, wielded superior military technology, and practised divide-and-rule tactics, pitting ethnic groups against each other. Some Third World peoples submitted to the indignities of imperialism, others actively collaborated and still others waged fierce resistance struggles.

In all cases, precapitalist economies changed dramatically. Indigen-ous skills were substantially eliminated. Cash crops were implanted, often replacing food crops, consequently altering dietary habits. To market these products new classes emerged, extending social differ-ences. An ascendant merchant class played a vigorous role in corroding the home economy and paving the way for capitalist relations of pro-duction, in the absence of which it would have been impossible to in-stall industrial capital. The colonial economy became increasingly oriented to export, rather than to local needs, catering as it did to the vagaries of foreign markets.

For centuries production and consumption had been in harmony but not unchanging. Subject to the precapitalist class structures and the limitations of their resource endowment, local peoples produced what they consumed and consumed what they produced. With the injection of imperialism, however, production and consumption were disjoined. Hence nowadays local peoples largely produce what they do not con-sume and consume what they do not produce.

The Third World was undeveloped but not underdeveloped before the advent of imperialism. Imperialism reversed ongoing processes of precapitalist development in the Third World, contributing to class formation and hampering productive accumulation. In order better to comprehend the mechanisms that sustain imperialism in our time, let us briefly consider the transnational institutions which use to their advantage the ideas emerging from modernization and dependency analysis.

3 Received Ideas and International Institutions

Years ago, an African reminded fellow diplomats of the practical limitations of the UN in dealing with conflicts which the contestants do not wish to resolve: 'When there is a dispute between small countries,' he said, 'the dispute in question disappears. When there is a dispute between a large country and a small country, the small country disappears. When there is a dispute between two large countries, the United Nations disappears.'

The inability of the UN to solve such crises as the Indo-China War, the Nigerian-Biafran clash and strife in former Yugoslavia has prompted much criticism of the organization, which goes to the heart of the nature of international institutions. What role do they really play in the global political economy? What do they institutionalize? Insofar as they bear upon resource transfers, who benefits and who shoulders the burden?

INTERNATIONAL ORGANIZATION

For over a decade, various US permanent representatives to the UN hurled a volley of attacks against the Third World voting majority in the General Assembly. Thus in 1974, President Nixon's representative to the UN, John A. Scali, warned that when majority rule becomes 'the tyranny of the majority, the minority will cease to respect or obey it'. Similarly, William F. Buckley, Jr, a US delegate to the twenty-eighth General Assembly, argued that the irresponsibility of the smaller nations of the world in the General Assembly is making the UN 'the most concentrated assault on moral reality in the history of free institutions'. Similarly, another US delegate, Daniel Patrick Moynihan, commented: 'the United Nations has become a locus of a general assault by the majority of the nations in the world on the principles of liberal democracy'. Numerous US ambassadors intoned that it was hypocritical for Third World delegates to lash out at South Africa's policy of apartheid while turning a blind eye to genocide in their own countries.

In the face of this challenge to the world organization, compounded by the rhetoric of various US administrations and the 1984 decision to pull out of the UN Educational, Scientific and Cultural Organization (UNESCO), liberals rightly maintain that sovereignty does not lie with the organization but with its 185 member states. The main problem with the organization, the argument runs, rests in Washington and the other capitals of the world, not at UN headquarters. Inasmuch as the cause of the world body's limited capacity to carry out the mandate inscribed in its charter is sovereignty, the solution frequently proposed by liberals is reform, particularly in the veto provision that permits any one of five powers to block action.

In the liberal perspective, the rationale for upgrading the UN, particularly its humanitarian activities and development programmes, centres on the important role the organization plays as a forum for exchanging ideas and learning from others' experiences. An oft-repeated justification for UN conferences on the environment, population, women and so on is that they help to raise people's consciousness about public issues and make politicians aware of their responsibilities. Even if the high-flown resolutions adopted at such conferences are unenforceable, it is said, these pronouncements educate the public and legitimize worthy goals set by the representatives of the majority of humankind.

The positions staked out by both conservatives and liberals are correct as far as they go: voting in the General Assembly is dominated by Third World countries, and in the implementation of Security Council decisions there is no way to override the will of the great powers. While bemoaning the gap between General Assembly resolutions and likely action, observers of varying hues frequently overlook the fact that international institutions are intended to distort the status quo. If they merely mirrored the distribution of power among member states, there would be little need for them. The key question – and a controversial one – is whether decisions made in the UN affect existing differences positively or negatively.

The claim that the gulf between lofty resolutions and effective implementation is due to automatic voting majorities or a hegemon's heavy handedness underplays the responsibility of individual member states to honour the expressed will of the world body. It is not only those resolutions adopted at the behest of small states contrary to the intentions of the great powers that remain unimplemented. In the case of UN action against Rhodesia, for example, in 1968 the Security Council unanimously adopted Resolution 253 calling for mandatory sanctions. Yet the USA, a permanent member of the Security Council, and hence with primary responsibility for the maintenance of international peace and security, wilfully violated sanctions by importing Rhodesian chrome.

The implications of the double-standards argument are unclear. Would the UN be in a better position if it did not take a stand on burning social issues? The response of most member states is that certain affronts to human dignity and well-being – namely, genocide including variations of ethnic cleansing – are so fundamental that the UN must seek to establish a climate of opinion favouring change, even if it is unable to provide a solution.

Going further, the UN's special conferences on women, the environment and so on have been important occasions for non-governmental organizations (NGOs) to share information, communicate their concerns, and mobilize transnationally. The UN is thus not only an arena of struggle, but also has created political space for counterhegemonic groups to forge links. Doubtless, too, a source of opposition to the UN after the Cold War represents an attempt to restrict or close down this space.

Arguably, as the UN's detractors point out, the contention that the organization's chief contribution is standard setting can be stretched too far. The beauty of the claim is that standard setting is an infinite process, one that is never completed, for there are always new objectives which avoid curtailment of the institution's programmes. The danger in the claim is that it can give the illusion of progress where there is none and deflect attention from the essential issues. The main point is that to make international institutions more viable, one must first understand history in terms of global processes.

Since capitalism encompasses the entire globe, its architects require a universal vision, a picture of a globally conceived society, to join classes in different countries. The task of international organizations is to institutionalize global capital accumulation by setting general rules of behaviour and disseminating a developmentalist ideology to facilitate the process. Some international agencies in the UN system, such as the UNDP, still reflect the precepts of modernization thinking, whereas other agencies like the United Nations Conference on Trade and Development (UNCTAD) have, at least until they succumbed to neo-liberal forces, transmitted the dependency perspective. All of these agencies, however, maintain the dominant world order by promoting globalizing tendencies.

Changes in global production and politics are reflected in the ideology of international organizations. They disseminate values and norms that contribute toward redesigning the global political economy. From the height of the Cold War to the more recent concerns of globalization, international institutions have absorbed the realities of global political economy and its contradictions. Imbued with neo-liberal doctrines, the current remedy for all ills is the market. Keynesian policies are being abandoned in favour of market-based solutions for both accumulation and distribution. The thrust of neo-liberalism is the weakening of the welfare capacity of states, while increasing their links to global capital. The recent wave of democratization facilitates the implementation of neo-liberal policies, for some elected leaders enjoy more political legitimacy than their predecessors. With the delegitimation of state planning, the bandwagon of economic liberalization looks respectable. First practised under authoritarian regimes, neo-liberalism is acquiring unprecedented momentum under the guise of democratization or the development of civil society. Foreign capital faces fewer barriers from state controls. Deregulation lifts curbs on the socially disruptive and polarizing aspects of economic growth. Environmental concerns, becoming a fetter for unbridled private accumulation, are often sacrificed on the altar of neo-liberal globalization.

Above all, the social contract between labour and capital is being redrawn or scrapped altogether. Globalization of production weakens the bargaining power of established workers, whose gains after protracted struggles extracted social protection from society, but are now negated. Note the growth of financial services and production services, often combined under merger, on the one hand, and the availability of unprotected workers (women, temporary, seasonal and other migrant labourers), on the other. Capital is less compelled to respect either national boundaries or politicized trade unions. Top-down multilateral policies, for all practical purposes, institutionalize systemic features of the global political economy. Paradoxically, however, neo-liberalism produces a greater need for global welfare, for the postcolonial state and some other forms of state are stripped of their capacity to provide social protection. The contradictory nature of world development could not be more transparent.

The main business of the international development establishment, therefore, is partially to fill the void of neo-liberal policies by attending in a limited fashion to the welfare aspects of global capital accumulation, but also to ensure compliance with the procedures codified in agreements among states. This broad claim can be best defended not by theoretical argument but through concrete investigation of foreign aid, technology, TNCs and international banking.

FOREIGN AID

At one time, welfare, sometimes known as aid, was a key element in global negotiations over a projected new international economic order

(NIEO), originally proposed at the Algiers Conference of Non-aligned Countries. Special sessions of the UN General Assembly promulgated the ideology of the NIEO in 1974 and 1975. The avowed purpose of the NIEO was to initiate processes of growth and diversification in Third World economies. It was to facilitate net inflows of real resources through trade and aid. In brief, the package of global reforms included the removal of tariff and non-tariff barriers against imports, the expansion of the Generalized System of Preferences (temporary and limited safeguards to promote exports from underdeveloped countries), price indexation agreements, commodity management and stabilization schemes, the enlargement of processing and manufacturing for export in underdeveloped countries, the transfer of technology to low-income areas, product sharing and specialization arising from complementarity among Third World economies, and an increased official development assistance target.

Advocates of these resource transfers counsel that power and decision making within international institutions must be shared more broadly to reflect greater sensitivity to Third World problems. Various international commissions have called for an enlargement of 'mutual interests' of North and South, based on a common perception of the complex 'interdependence' in the contemporary world. This ideology is reflected in two reports, issued in 1980 and 1983, by a team of prominent commissioners headed by former West German Chancellor Willy Brandt:

> The valuable and unprecedented basis for consensus in the UN system, for communicating between North and South and between East and West, must be preserved. It is vital to get the best out of it, to strengthen it, and to build on it, utilizing the experience of the last three decades and the benefits of wide participation. An increasingly interdependent world must organize itself for the different and more difficult tasks of the future, which will call not only for political will and wisdom, but for a framework of institutions and negotiations which can convert policies and ideas into action.

The work of such commissions is useful inasmuch as it spotlights the external constraints on local initiatives in underdeveloped countries.

The calls for concessions to meet the demands for global reforms focus on market mechanisms. To be sure, if the international market operates more smoothly, the world economy will be more robust. Underdeveloped countries stand to gain from greater purchasing power and increased savings. Even if state bureaucrats and large-scale traders were to consume much of the gains from tariff reductions and other aspects of a NIEO, there would still be an increment to feed into production. Gains in productivity may in turn filter down to the masses, thus contributing to capitalist development. The extent to which transfers of international capital actually augment production is contingent and varies from one context to another.

Whether such gains are deemed significant hinge on how the underlying problem is defined. If one posits, as does the Brandt Commission, that the root problem in 'North-South relations' is imbalance in the world economy, it follows that the solution is to establish balance. The problem may then be meaningfully addressed at the level of distribution (or redistribution) of wealth. But if one premises that a political economy analysis must spring from the level of production, then the redistribution of wealth, however far-reaching, cannot erase the structures of global inequality. As long as the social relations that underpin these structures remain intact, pouring capital and technology into underdeveloped countries, as the proponents of the NIEO prescribed, would at best be a palliative. The wealth funnelled into highly inegalitarian social structures has, in some countries, improved social services, but also has inflamed political tensions and has worsened economic polarities on the local level, thus deepening underdevelopment.

An ideology that espouses 'an increasingly interdependent world' diverts attention from the world economy's built-in biases which sustain underdevelopment. To issue moral injunctions is to ignore the limits to international reform. To call for 'power sharing' is to wish away differences and conflicts. To call for consensus through global negotiations evades the point that the negotiators would be statesmen (or stateswomen), most of whom have built their careers on forestalling fundamental change. It is preposterous to think that the Mubaraks (Egypt), Bhuttos (Pakistan), de Leons (Guatemala), Mobutus (Zaire) and Mois (Kenya) of this world – those who have the most to lose from basic change – are going to restructure the global economy in the interests of the poor and downtrodden.

The ideology of the NIEO and other such reform measures blend elements of the modernization school and dependency thinking. They are a hodgepodge. There is little that is new; many of the elements have been tried, unsuccessfully, in the past. Against the transformations in the global political economy, notably in the past two decades, the hopes of a NIEO had run out of steam. In the 1970s, several developing nations began to shift from import substitution to export promotion. De-industrialization in the advanced capitalist countries, but more fundamentally, the stirrings of globalization changed the vector of opportunities and constraints for the developing world. Foreign debt soared, presenting many Third World economies with new conditions to restructure their global economic ties. Financial and market discipline unleashed by neo-liberal policies in the 1980s, in turn, undercut the possibility of forging united fronts against the developed world. Key to the fall in a united front strategy was the systematic dismantling of OPEC as an axis for NIEO supporters. Availability of alternative sources of energy, conservation and mistrust amongst OPEC members undermined the organization, but also confidence in Third World coalitions. Advances in technology made geographic specialization somewhat redundant. New production systems – especially the advent of post-Fordist strategies of flexible accumulation, with emphasis on sub-contracting, off-shore and semi-processing, and niche marketing – foiled the NIEO design predicated mainly on established patterns of international specialization among nations. Cross-border migration flows also contributed to a diminution of a strategy emphasizing relative advantages of local production. In a word, globalization eroded the foundations of the NIEO programme by intensifying patterns and injecting novel elements in the global political economy.

Foreign aid, or development assistance, was viewed as the solution to the Third World's problems in the late 1950s and the 1960s. It was thought that if the Marshall Plan had helped to put Western Europe back on its feet after the Second World War, why not do the same for the postcolonial countries? Today, this idea is outmoded if not downright naive. The purpose of the Marshall Plan was to strengthen Europe as a bastion against the Soviet Union, and the recipients of aid obtained non-repayable grants, not loans conditioned on bankers' criteria of creditworthiness. Donors know that debt-ridden borrowers are unlikely to repay new loans. And no one seriously believes that aid is a disinterested gift.

We understood the pitfalls of technical assistance in Uganda shortly after political independence in 1962. Ugandans, who in a short time had their fill of international experts, told the story of the two bulls. A young bull and an old bull eyed a herd of cows. The young bull said to his companion, 'Let's run over and get one.' The more experienced bull replied, 'No, let's walk in and get them all.' In this tale, the brash bull is the American bull who wants to charge forward and take over; the subtle bull is his British counterpart who knows how to control the situation.

In fact, many white settlers stayed behind after independence in East Africa. International aid agencies hired some of them because of their familiarity with local conditions. The 'experts', so-called local expatriates as well as foreign nationals, are often seconded – sent as technical assistants – to government ministries where they act as advisers and supposedly train counterpart personnel. But as numerous inter-agency reports show, few technical assistance projects actually build local institutional capacity; the experts rarely leave behind indigenous people with the know-how to carry on.

As a consultant to an international agency, I (JHM) was asked to evaluate a UN project designed both to strengthen training in international law and to set up a doctoral programme in this field at a university in the Third World. By preparing students for teaching or work in such ministries as Foreign Affairs, Commerce, and Industries and Finance, the university would provide for the needs of the country as well as those throughout the region. Due to the time required for the university to select one of the three candidates named by the international agency, the expert, a professor of international law from Holland, started later than foreseen.

From the outset, problems impaired the implementation of the project. The dean of the Law Faculty who had initiated the project, an expatriate, left the country three days after the arrival of the Dutch expert, forgetting to consult the Faculty Board. The new dean, an indigenous scholar whose priorities fundamentally differed from his predecessor's, had major reservations about the orientation of the project. He suggested that the expert, an abrasive sort by all accounts, teach legal disciplines other than international law, a proposition that the expert was reluctant to accept. The dean's view of legal education reflected political and intellectual changes taking place in the faculty, leading to innovative approaches to teaching and research.

The expert's tenure was a stormy period, for other faculty members maintained that he was transmitting the very ideology which perpetuates underdevelopment. Under these trying conditions, the expert did accomplish the project's primary objective: the establishment of a postgraduate programme in international law. The expert also contributed to classroom teaching, developed syllabuses and course materials for the LL M and PhD degrees, and helped to obtain from his agency the equipment and books that an international law programme requires. The main shortcoming, however, was the failure to train a counterpart. When the expert departed, no qualified national was available to replace him. At the close of the project, the options were to hire another foreign expert, again with the mandate to prepare at least one full-time, local counterpart, or to abandon the programme altogether.

Typically, there is inadequate coordination between international agencies and local training institutions. What needs to be ingrained, or restored, is local capacity for solving problems, implementing and evaluating projects, generating data, and analyzing research findings. Central to these tasks is the development of training facilities.

The psychological effects of foreign technical assistance can be debilitating. A pervasive attitude in some parts of the Third World is that if a job is to be done properly, it must be assigned to outside experts. When skills and equipment are imported from one particular country, there is a tendency to continue to depend on that same source for future projects. In the long run, since technical assistance personnel implant certain practices and institutions, those ways of doing things become customary. Aid engenders reliance on foreign experts. It becomes a matter of habit.

Meanwhile, technical assistance personnel bring their life-style to the host country. By introducing their market habits, they transfer consumer tastes. For instance, grocery stores in impoverished countries sell kosher foods, exquisite imported wines and books on how to prepare French cuisine. Other examples of taste creation are skin lighteners, cosmetics, soft drinks and powdered baby formulas. The tourism industry creates economic opportunities in the service sector for drivers, waiters, bellboys, guides, and the producers of artefacts facetiously known as airport art, but fails to build a resilient economy. A downswing in the metropolitan economies can have a devastating impact on a country dependent on tourist trade. Moreover, the wholesale importation of foreign customs can dilute the local culture and offend sensitivities. Cultural conflicts have arisen over Western ways such as nude bathing and, on the beaches of Gambia, the procurement of young male prostitutes by Nordic women: this conduct is regarded as distasteful by most people in the host countries.

Tourism may bolster a country's economic infrastructure by channelling foreign investment into airports, roads, hotels and so on. It does not, however, augment directly productive activities. Diverting development efforts from production-oriented to local needs, and pumping capital into projects designed to show 'profitable' returns in the short run, is unrelated to, or antithetical to, long-run solutions.

The problems frequently encountered with external aid are apparent in Tanzania, the recipient of $3 billion in foreign largesse during the 1970s. In the decade after Tanzania pledged a policy of socialism and self-reliance, its foreign borrowing increased by a multiple of 21 and surpassed the domestic component of total development spending. Aid accounted for about two-thirds of Tanzania's development budget. There was a huge crop of economic blunders, often cultivated by foreign-aid agencies. So pervasive are the agencies that, as one US AID official told me (JHM), they simply divided the country among themselves, one taking Arusha Region, another Mwanza, a third Iringa, and so forth. When former President Julius Nyerere announced a policy of decentralization, the regional offices of government, lacking expertise in development planning, called on the international agency personnel based locally to help design the plan and thus to decide on basic priorities. In other words, the foreign experts do more than advise. They frequently make policy in such key ministries as planning. In 1986–87, development assistance equalled 15.2 per cent of GNP in Tanzania. Government expenditures as a percentage of GDP stood at 20.9 per cent. Development assistance was roughly the equivalent of three-quarters of government expenditures.

Many aid projects only compound underdevelopment, for they lack a basis in the economy. Specifically, Tanzania does not produce spare parts for heavy-duty machines and equipment imported from abroad. Without foreign exchange, one cannot purchase these goods. Even so, to distribute food and other essential commodities, it is essential to maintain the transportation system. Tanzania's trains, buses and trucks come from such countries as Britain, Hungary and Norway. In an effort to keep these vehicles running, much of the aid that flows into Tanzania goes right back to the donor countries to pay for repairs, contractors, material and petroleum.

Britain agreed to build a $110 million highway in south-western Tanzania. London pledged to spend only $12 million locally and to employ a *total* of eight Tanzanians on the job. A rail project, funded by Canada, was to provide 205 cattle cars and oil tankers, all from Canadian manufacturers. Meanwhile, a Dutch official remarked that he expected $51 million of Holland's $73 million in annual expenditure of aid to be remitted to Amsterdam.

Probing such loan agreements, a British economist uncovered the conditions for establishing a fully automated bread factory in Tanzania. Funded by the Canadian International Development Agency, the new factory would employ 60 workers and produce 100 000 loaves per day. There were several complications. One was that the cost far exceeded the original expectations. Critics of the project pointed out that 10 compact, semi-mechanized bakeries could each produce 10 000 loaves of high quality bread per day for much less. More than five times as many people would have worked in the small bakeries. With small units, the baking industry would have been less vulnerable to breakdowns. Since many of the spare parts for the automated factory are made only in Canada, Dar es Salaam's bread supply is subject to total disruption. The large bakery makes Tanzania dependent on a Canadian machine supplier and expertise; small-scale bakery equipment could have been produced in Tanzania. Because much of the wheat, which provides the flour used in baking the bread, is imported, the foreign exchange implications of the project are considerable. (Wheat, of which Canada is a major exporter, is a luxury food item in a maize-growing country.) All told, the decision to establish one large, foreign built, foreign maintained, and foreign supplied baking industry was directly contrary to the government's professed intention to nourish grass-roots self-reliance.

Given the drawbacks to foreign aid, should it be terminated or merely reformed? There is no doubt that such aid flows as refugee relief and food assistance are useful stopgap measures, particularly under emergency conditions. Development assistance can be improved through reforms, especially if greater emphasis is given to training local personnel. However, foreign aid does not begin to tug at the roots of underdevelopment: the blockage in the social system that limits the potential for advance. In fact, development assistance, granted to those who control state power, may strengthen locally dominant classes, thereby deepening underdevelopment. Thus foreign assistance can either facilitate in a very marginal way or impede the escape from underdevelopment; but aid flows are not an essential component of a strategy of eradicating underdevelopment.

More recently, NGOs, not host governments, have been touted as the vehicles of development. This shift corresponds to less emphasis on the state and more on civic associations to create new opportunities, both in the economic and political domains. International aid to NGOs provides more lucrative arenas of employment, chiefly for skilled personnel. The salaries and benefits offered by internationally-financed NGOs is disproportionately higher than in the state, and sometimes even then in the domestic private sector. Despite their apparent autonomy, the NGOs are an object of state patronage. International aid through these NGOs makes its way to already privileged members in developing societies. Sons and daughters of several elite families in Pakistan, for instance, have found internationally-financed NGOs a prized avenue for employment.

TECHNOLOGY

Like foreign aid, technological change has a mixed character. It may either accelerate or hamper development. Technology is not a neutral element for attaining societal goals. Rather, it is both a commodity bought and sold on the world market and a cornerstone of the ideology of modernization.

One architect of the modernization school, W. W. Rostow (whose 1960 book, *The Stages of Economic Growth*, influenced a whole generation of scholars and policy makers), held that the fundamental turning points of history are the times of new scientific discoveries. As noted in Chapter 2, traditional society is said to be based on pre-Newtonian attitudes; it stands in sharp contrast to a Newtonian world subject to knowable laws and capable of systematic 'productive manipulation'. The central feature of traditional society, Rostow adds, is an upper limit on the level of attainable output, which reflects the absence of modern technology.

A widely accepted notion in modernization theory and neo-classical economics is the 'natural mobility of productive factors' within but not between nations: each national economy is to specialize in the production of goods for which it is endowed with the more abundant factor (labour, capital or natural resources). All partners in exchange then share equally in the benefits of international trade. Dependency writers, however, reason somewhat differently. They emphasize the imperfect conditions in the international market for technology. The advanced countries account for 96 per cent of the total research and development of new technologies, according to a 1994 UNESCO study. As a percentage of GNP, developed countries spend 2.92 per cent while developing countries expend only 0.64 per cent. There is mounting sensitivity over who controls the technology, for Western-based transnationals hold over 95 per cent of the patents on new technology.

In the face of rising Third World nationalism, increasing attention has been given to the transfer of technology. Transfer connotes the movement of knowledge, skill, organization, values and capital from the point of generation to the site of adaptation and application. There are several modes of transfer. One is direct foreign investment (FDI), the injection of technology with other critical inputs; another is purchasing machinery and other capital goods which embody technology; a third is licensing and related contractual arrangements with foreign governments.

To correct the imbalances in the international economy, the proponents of modernization have stressed the importance of sharing knowledge. There has been no dearth of proposals: mechanisms for the exchange of scientific and technological information, international and regional centres, evaluation techniques and so on. International organizations have called for technical cooperation among developing countries, workshops, consultancy groups and codes of conduct. Integral to many UN recommendations is the idea that technological development requires building capability for the utilization of new knowledge.

Unfortunately this way of thinking is often confined to narrow problems and highly specialized issues concerning technical innovations. A technicist point of view is one that overemphasizes technical factors at the expense of non-technical considerations. Technology, after all, is a process, not a fixture: more like learning carpentry than purchasing a new drill. If one does not develop the skill to use the tool adeptly, and if one does not understand how one particular stage relates to other stages of production, one's product will be inferior and not sell. All stages of a technological venture are inter-related and must be comprehended. As two professors at Harvard's Graduate School of Business Administration put it: 'If the technology is imported from another company, even if the developers come with it, but the necessary support systems and understanding do not exist, then it is likely that the new products will be rejected as the human body rejects a heart transplant, though it is necessary for survival.' For technology to take root, it must become integrated in, or emerge from, the existing society. Social relations are more than a seedbed of technical processes. Changes in social relations have a reciprocal, or at times a decisive, influence on the course of development. Technological innovation requires that social relations be altered to allow for the potential for economic advance.

If technology does not exist in a free state, but is understood as a commodity like other commodities, then one should avoid the trap of technological determinism, the belief that changes in technique are the key to overcoming underdevelopment. This is a fallacy. There is no quick fix for the problems of underdevelopment. A technological fix does not address the underpinnings of underdevelopment.

It is frequently said that an appropriate technology is one that contributes the most to meet the objectives of development. The idea of the appropriateness of technology can help to expose the failings of a technology policy. Typically, commentators claim that too much emphasis is given to high-powered goods and services while the bulk of the population needs plain conveniences, such as pulleys for drawing water and simple stoves. But the criterion 'what technology?' must be linked to a consideration of 'technology for what?' Ultimately, this is a matter of 'whose objectives are to be met within a society?' Thus the appropriateness of a technology should be defined in relation to its social, economic and ecological context. In the end, science and technology must be understood in relation to educational and production systems. It is research and production that have the primary institutional capacity for learning and innovation.

As mentioned, investments in research and development are predominantly made by the advanced countries. Nonetheless it is true that TNCs originating in the USA, for example, do spend around 1 per cent of their total research and development expenditure in the Third World. These transnational-driven research and development efforts are concentrated in a handful of countries, most notably Brazil and Mexico. Another facet of corporate-generated innovation is dumping old or obsolete equipment on the Third World. A changing global division of labour assigns higher technological tasks to the advanced countries and lower technological functions to the underdeveloped countries. Generally speaking, these functions involve the processing of goods and certain aspects of manufacturing, especially assembly operations.

In India, Brazil and East Asia, there have been real technological advances in textiles, steel and shipbuilding. India even exports consulting services and engineering goods. A country that is capable of producing its own engineering goods has extensive technological capacity. There is no doubt that local capital in the underdeveloped world has an internal dynamic. Capitalism in the Third World is not all externally driven. But once again the objectives of an underdeveloped country's technological capacity limit innovation. In India, a major concern with national prestige and regional competition with China and Pakistan put a premium on production of the atomic bomb, missiles and other military hardware. Also, India's industries imitate the consumer patterns of Western societies. Locally generated technology in the villages has been outstripped by Indian and foreign large-scale producers in such industries as soap, cooking oil, eating utensils, building materials and tyres. The great bulk of the technological system is not immediately relevant to the needs of most Indians.

Technological innovation in the Third World, while to some extent genuine and certainly important, should not deflect attention from the overall pattern: not only is the lion's share of research and development carried out within TNCs (supposedly the conduit of technology transfer), but most technological knowledge remains within the corporations themselves. The putative flows between countries are really flows from corporate headquarters to the premises of a subsidiary. Innovative capacity is not transferred. In reality, the so-called transfer can become a substitute for innovation by indigenous people. Also, a bona fide transfer of the highest and most sophisticated technology can be at odds with the interests of the dominant classes in the heartlands of global capitalism. The transfer of technology, to the extent that it actually occurs, is nothing other than leakage from TNCs.

TRANSNATIONAL CORPORATIONS

It is sometimes claimed that TNCs are a Trojan horse for neo-colonialism, betraying the promises of political independence in the underdeveloped world. On the other side of the ideological fence, TNCs (the bearers of capital and technology) are likened to Prometheus bringing light to the impoverished countries. As these images make clear, prevalent views of the impact of the large firms are highly polarized and, to avoid moral posturing, it is important to demythologize the issue.

The first step is to recognize that to abstract TNCs from their historical context would be a grave error. Properly understood, today's TNCs are but one facet of world industrial organization, a global structure in which the entrepreneur of yesteryear, the jack of all trades, is an anachronism. Formerly industries consisted largely of single function firms, usually controlled by one owner or a small family who made all the decisions. More recently, multidivisional business, often a vertically integrated industry with a general office, hierarchically organized from top to bottom, carefully plans and coordinates the growth of corporate capital on a global scale. A firm which operates according to the principles of vertical integration joins under its auspices different phases of the production process, potentially ranging from sourcing raw materials and crude processing to marketing the final commodities.

As such, the TNC is neither villain nor hero, as its detractors and apologists claim. True, as shall be shown, it is sometimes involved in crimes but, as with other types of criminal activity, one must search for both manifestations and underlying causes.

The TNC is both an agent in and the result of the process of capital accumulation. It embodies the inner logic of the capitalist enterprise. So, too, it is an expression of the globalization of production, a worldwide phenomenon which allows the politics, culture and ideology of one country to penetrate another. The dynamic is one of amassing capital, not of creating equality, and the benefits accrue unevenly.

From where do TNCs derive their power? Despite all the talk about free enterprise, TNCs seek to preserve a monopoly of technology. In theory, free competition would mean the perfect diffusion of technical information; every producer would have open and free access to technical innovation. In reality, technical knowledge is now a commodity produced by institutionalized activity, known as research and development, inside the big corporations. The ideas that scientific workers generate are owned by capitalists, whose patents help to ensure monopoly profits. What is more, TNCs seek to confine technological innovation to their home offices and plants, forestalling centres of innovation outside their immediate control. To do otherwise could reduce the profits garnered from the spread of their products and operations.

Another basis of transnational power is sheer size. The capital, market knowledge and access of the corporate giants are formidable assets compared with the resources commanded by an underdeveloped country. In some cases, the coffers of a single firm are much larger than the treasuries of entire countries. Moreover, the scope of TNCs has increased astronomically since 1960. Revenues of the top 200 firms rose ten-fold, from about $200 billion to over $2 trillion in 1980. Total revenue of the top 200 firms, doubling between 1980 and 1994, has reached $4.6 trillion. Mega-mergers and acquisitions – the corporate catchwords are 'restructuring' and 'maximizing shareholder value' – have become commonplace. The subsidiaries of huge companies now dispense entirely different product lines, with profits shifting from one to subsidize another so as to underprice competition. Hence, using its profits from Marlboro cigarettes, the parent firm, Phillip Morris, adopted a strategy of low pricing and massive advertising to transform Miller, a small brewer it had purchased, into the second largest beer producer in the world.

Amid this concentration of capital, the position of US firms has declined. In 1960, 127 of the top 200 TNCs were US-based, accounting for 72.7 per cent of the group's revenue. Twenty years later, of the top 200 firms, 91 had their headquarters in the USA, their revenue share having dropped to 50.1 per cent of the total. By 1994, US-based transnationals accounted for only 56 of the top 200 firms and 40.8 per cent of the total revenue.

Equally striking is the ascendance of Japanese-based TNCs in the top 200, increasing from 5 to 20, with sales up from $2.9 billion in 1960 to $155.2 billion in 1980. The growing prominence of Japanese firms has continued into the 1990s. Sixty-three Japanese firms, with revenues of $501 billion, were included in the 1994 top 200 list. France, too, has moved up, its companies numbering 19 in 1994 in the top 200, as against 7 in 1960. Their revenues have soared from $3.5 billion in 1960 to $495 billion in 1994. (See Tables 3.1 and 3.2.) Clearly this increasing concentration of capital does not entail a reduction in competition. A multitude of disputes over international trade – the question of US protectionism against the influx of Japanese vehicles, a so-called pasta war to bar Italian products from the US and so on indicate that the global capitalist economy still fosters rivalries between corporations and between governments.

The globalization of production means that TNCs swiftly deploy resources across economic sectors and national boundaries. Companies manufacture parts of a commodity in one country, assemble it elsewhere, put on the finishing touches in some other locale and sell it in

Table 3.1   Top 200 companies by country, 1960–80

Countries	1960			1980		
	Number	Sales ($ billion)	Percentage of total sales	Number	Sales ($ billion)	Percentage of total sales
USA	127	144.6	72.7	91	1080.4	50.1
W.Germany	20	13.4	6.8	21	209.0	9.7
UK	24	19.6	9.9	16.5	199.5	9.2
France	7	3.5	1.8	15	161.0	7.5
Japan	5	2.9	1.5	20	155.2	7.2
Netherlands	3	6.4	3.2	5	89.6	4.2
Italy	3	1.9	0.9	4.5	69.5	3.2
Canada	5	2.6	1.3	5	32.5	1.5
Switzerland	2	2.0	1.0	4	31.9	1.5
Belgium	1	0.5	0.2	2	14.5	0.7
Sweden	1	0.4	0.2	2	11.0	0.5
Rep. of Korea	–	–	–	2	10.0	0.5
Others	2	1.1	0.5	12	91.1	4.2
Total (excluding USA)	73	54.4*	27.3	109	1074.8	49.9
Total	200	199.0*	100.0	200	2155.2	100.0

*The figures presumably intended here are 54.3 and 198.9, respectively.
Source: Calculated from *Fortune's* listing of leading industrial corporations by John Cavanagh and Frederick F. Clairmonte, 'From corporations to conglomerates: a review of multinationals over the last twenty years', *Multinational Monitor*, January 1983, 17.

Table 3.2　Top 200 companies by country, 1994

Countries	Number	Sales ($ billion)	Percentage of total sales
USA	56	1879	40.8
Germany	22	646	14.05
UK	10	348	7.57
France	19	495	10.77
Japan	63	501	11.00
Netherlands	5.5	117	2.54
Italy	5	161	3.5
Canada	1	16	0.34
Switzerland	7	164	3.56
Belgium	0.5	19	0.41
Sweden	1	20	0.43
Rep. of Korea	4	88	1.95
Others	6	142	3.08
Total (excluding USA)	144	2717	59.2
Total	200	4596	100.0

Source: Calculated from *Fortune*'s 'Global 500: The World's Largest Corporations', *Fortune*, August 7, 1995, pp. F1–F4.

yet another. To move goods along this production line, TNCs often rely on joint ventures, licensing and subcontracting agreements, and free trade and export processing zones. Their market power derives from the mobility of capital, but also from the relative immobility of labour. For as capital encircles the globe in search of cheap labour and other favourable conditions, Third World countries must vie with each other. If workers protest the conditions of capital or go on strike, TNCs either pull out and dip into another labour reservoir or simply threaten to relocate. Either way, the postcolonial state will attempt to crack down on its labour movement, for those in power and their allies would be hurt the most by the withdrawal of their patrons.

More specifically, what is the impact of TNCs on underdeveloped countries? The relations between transnational and national interests have changed since the companies' initial incursions into the Third World, and now range from consensus to conflict over control.

When American corporations went abroad, many of them for the first time in the 1950s, they were an awesome force. Nationalist leaders – Jawaharlal Nehru of India, Gamal Abdel Nasser of Egypt, Kwame Nkrumah of Ghana – accused American firms of interfering in local politics. It was no wonder. The big oil companies reportedly helped to topple Iranian Prime Minister Mohammed Mossadegh, in 1953. Many observers claim that the United Fruit Company's quarrel with Guatemala's leftist head of state prompted the US-backed invasion there in 1954. And it is generally believed that, in the early 1970s, International Telephone and Telegraph Company (ITT) paved the way for a coup against Salvador Allende Gossens, Chile's socialist president.

The boldness of ITT's alleged venture shocked even the establishment in Washington, causing the Senate Foreign Relations Committee to investigate the influence of US TNCs on foreign policy. It will be recalled that Allende had been elected on a platform of nationalizing much of Chilean industry, especially copper, a sector controlled by a handful of firms such as Anaconda and Kennecot Copper. American firms operating in Chile accumulated huge profits: during the 1960s Anaconda made $500 million on a $300 million investment. ITT, with $200 million in diversified investments in Chile, urged the Nixon administration to safeguard US holdings there. The New York-based corporation's high-powered board of directors, which included the former head of the CIA, John McCone, found a sympathetic ear in Washington, where Kissinger exercised tight control over the intelligence agencies. Presented with a plan for anti-Allende activities, Kissinger remarked: 'I can't see why we need to stand by and watch a country go Communist due to the irresponsibility of its own people.'

Evidence compiled by investigative journalist and Pulitzer Prize winner Seymour Hersh, as well as by other researchers, suggests that the Nixon administration's policy against Allende was conditioned by an overriding concern for the future of American corporate assets in Chile. After much consultation, Nixon gave Richard Helms, the director of central intelligence, *carte blanche* to destabilize the Allende regime. All the while, McCone, an intermediary between ITT and Kissinger and Helms, relayed ITT pledges of assistance for getting rid of Allende. Acting independently, ITT subsidized members of the Chilean opposition, waged a propaganda campaign, and sought to convince Chileans that Allende's policies would mean economic chaos. There followed the killing of Allende during the military overthrow of his Marxist-oriented government in 1973.

Such marked divergence between transnational and national strategies of accumulation is unusual, however. The norm is for TNCs to reinforce local accumulation and to support the existing power structure. Broadly speaking, the partnership between transnationals and local entrepreneurs is based on a common interest in profits and accumulation. After all, the corporations are invited into host countries by the state and national capital, which expect to benefit materially from the connection. Within this framework of consensus is secondary conflict over the extent of local control.

Transnational drug firms, for example, have been pressed to decentralize their operations so that host countries retain a larger share of the profits. This has not caused a major problem. A sizeable portion of pharmaceutical production vested in TNCs now takes place in the Third World. But they still keep the generation of knowledge at home. Pharmaceutical executives claim that the environment in such countries as Brazil is unsuitable for research. They say that important economies of scale in research mean that shifting technologically innovative activities to another location would diminish efficiency.

Meanwhile, Third World peoples pay for a large portion of these research costs, often indirectly in the form of exorbitant promotional fees. According to a 1977 report prepared by a British physician, Dr. John Yudkin, the 147 drug company representatives working in Tanzania, a country with 600 doctors, spend £1.07 million per year, more than the country's sole faculty of medicine's annual budget, to persuade these doctors to prescribe the company's products. Spending on drugs in Tanzania accounts for 22 per cent of the national health budget, a proportion twice as high as Britain's.

Drug purchasing in Tanzania is in the hands of a small group of people beset by drug sales representatives offering free gifts, parties, drug samples, help in ordering and support for medical research and equipment. In a variety of Third World countries where legislation is inadequate and medical literature scarce, Dr. Yudkin notes, some companies suggest that 'potentially hazardous drugs be used for minor modifications and they play down the risks of side effects'. Central medical stores have enough drugs to last from 5 to 50 years, whereas their shelf-life is less than two years and may be no more than six months under tropical conditions.

Kumariah Balasubramaniam, former pharmaceutical advisor to UNCTAD, asserts that the Third World is subsidizing research and development costs for the developed world by buying drugs from transnationals which fix medicine prices based on their level of research spending. It is estimated that no more than 4 per cent of the total pharmaceutical research budget is devoted to medical problems specific to the Third World. Nevertheless, by purchasing over 4 per cent of the drugs produced by the transnationals, the Third World is contributing more to the research and development budget than it is receiving. This problem is compounded by double standards in marketing practice. Drugs designed for restricted use in the country of origin can often be legally marketed for alternative uses and without warning information on labels. One example is Organon's Durabolin, used for treatment of osteoporosis in post-menopausal women and aplastic anaemia in the UK. The same drug is marketed in Pakistan for malnourishment in children despite the risk of causing premature puberty in girls.

Pesticides developed and marketed by transnational chemical companies and utilized by American-based food growers in the Third World have resulted in a legacy of health problems and environmental damage. Dibromochloropropane (DBCP), developed by Dow Chemical and Shell Oil, was linked to sterility in 1977 and withdrawn from use in the continental USA after being rated a probable human carcinogen. However, US laws did not prohibit the export of DBCP to Third World countries, requiring only that the pesticide be properly labelled with warnings and directions for workers to use protective gear. This reliance on labelling to protect Third World labourers presumes the availability of safety equipment and shielded wear as well as the ability and desire of the state in underdeveloped countries to safeguard its workers.

Notwithstanding known risks, American-based growers continued to use DBCP in the Third World; for example, DBCP was applied in Ecuador until 1981 and in the Philippines until 1986. When the large chemical companies halted their exports and many growers ceased to purchase the fumigant directly, its use did not stop. Instead, smaller manufacturers entered the market and paid royalties to the original producers. The fruit companies simply required that the local farmers who wished to sell their bananas to them utilize the pesticide to produce fruit of the appropriate quality. In the mid-1990s, some of the victims of this hazardous pesticide, 25 000 workers from 12 countries, are suing the manufacturers and fruit growers who employed it. The lawsuits, however, will face formidable obstacles given the inexperience of Third World court systems in liability cases and the considerable economic influence of the TNCs.

In the face of the drug companies' anti-social tendencies, host countries have adopted legislation to regulate, though not ban, the firms. A growing number of underdeveloped countries have initiated policies aimed at curbing the excesses of pharmaceutical companies and attaining control over the health care sector.

Still, there is a broad range of unresolved problems concerning local regulations, monitoring, education, cultural differences and corporate behaviour. The tragic leak of poison gas from a chemical plant in Bhopal, India, in 1984, killing more than 2000 people and injuring 200 000, brings these issues into sharp relief. The Union Carbide plant did not meet American standards and had not been visited by auditors from headquarters for $2\frac{1}{2}$ years. It is not clear whether the company violated local laws, but many experts believe that corporations have a responsibility to live up to high standards, especially where the workforce is unskilled and the populace unaware of the risks presented by such plants. For the most part, the law in underdeveloped countries is not yet equipped for high technology. Regulation in these nations lags behind the introduction of new technologies. In the absence of an industrial culture, the testing practices prescribed by Union Carbide could not be used. Workers memorized what they were supposed to do without understanding the reasoning involved in safety procedures. Maintenance people signed what they could not read, and critical pressure gauges for toxic chemicals were in disrepair. Training and education programmes were lacking and sorely deficient in respect to cultural differences. In fact, in some parts of the world, pesticides are widely regarded as medicine because they kill worms and insects and help subsistence farming. Thus workers in Latin America have been known to come home with their woollen parkas soaked with pesticides and to sleep in them.

Most recently the emphasis on controlling transnationals has changed to channelling FDI into designated sectors or areas. Many Third World countries now offer the transnationals such incentives as low taxes, import privileges and market advantages. At the same time, they set performance standards, including the establishment of training programmes, the development of forward and backward linkages, export percentages and import ceilings. Notwithstanding the companies' interventions in local politics and the questions posed by the Bhopal disaster, underdeveloped countries are increasingly trying to attract external capital and, in some cases, allowing more generous terms for foreign enterprise. In this context, industrial capital and loan capital go hand-in-hand, the latter often securing the conditions for the former.

In the era of globalization, the Third World state has become a facilitator of transnational activity. Regulation of TNCs is not only replaced by incentives, but the state is eagerly seeking access to global capital. China's Export Processing Zone (EPZ) strategy, for instance, reflects the new attitude towards the TNCs, which often prefer strong state regulation in the areas of labor control and discipline. This marriage between foreign companies and an authoritarian state is pronounced in countries like Singapore, as we shall notice in Chapter 6.

TRANSNATIONAL BANKING

David Rockefeller and other financial tycoons insist that ideological considerations do not determine their loan policies, but conservative business practice dictates that funds for Chile dry up when an Allende is in power and are plentiful for undemocratic regimes such as General Augusto Pinochet's. Quite clearly the political power wielded by the moneylenders is formidable. Like other transnational organizations, the banks eagerly dispatch their representatives to pursue Third World clients. Flush with OPEC deposits, they finance such strongmen as Zaire's General Mobutu Sese-Seko, a large measure of the monies going into the hands of his corrupt accomplices and their private accounts in Switzerland.

The growth of international lending to underdeveloped countries is a phenomenon of only the last two decades. Before the onrush to independence in Africa in the 1960s, market surpluses and deposits mobilized locally were stored for safekeeping in Europe and far exceeded the volume of loans to the colonies. By lending money to the colonizers, the colonies helped to finance development in Western Europe. Similarly, the private banks did not channel loans to Latin America before the mid-1960s. Historically, the movement of gold and silver flowed in the opposite direction. However, large-scale industrial expansion in Latin America in the 1950s and 1960s, the rise of Euromarkets accompanied by the search for new customers and the oil shocks of the 1970s all made overseas borrowing a booming business.

In 1971 the lion's share of the outstanding debt of the Third World came from governments, while most credit from private sources emanated from commodity suppliers, not banks. At the end of 1980, loans from official sources had dropped to 37 per cent of unpaid debt, and bank loans had jumped to more than 60 per cent of uncollected private credits. Since 1990, there has been a surge in private capital flows to developing countries. Unlike the 1970s and early 1980s, a substantial part of inflows are non-debt-generating capital with FDI playing a critical role. A major cause of this shift is neo-liberalism's emphasis on prying open economies and privatizing them.

In fact, the banks have become so highly exposed that it is difficult for them to avoid involvement in political crises in the Third World. Through the mid-1980s and projected into the 1990s, aggregate net resource flows showed a trend towards higher shares for official sources in debt financing. For instance, in 1991, the official share (most official non-concessional loans) of net flows stood at 60 per cent while FDI investment and portfolio flows accounted for the bulk of the private flows.

In the face of a trillion dollars' worth of Third World debt to private foreign banks, governments and international agencies, no one really believes that the principal will be repaid. It is widely recognized that interest payments are a political problem within underdeveloped countries, not strictly a technical economic matter. To expect Third World countries to make huge debt payments each year, to achieve economic growth, and to maintain political stability – all at the same time – is utterly unrealistic.

The immense debt owed to the banks is a storm cloud that threatens to burst. Each of the nine largest US banks has more than 100 per cent of shareholders' equity at risk in four countries: Mexico, Brazil, Venezuela and Argentina. Taking a single bank as an example, Citicorp, with $250 billion in assets in 1994, serves 100 locations around the world. It earns the bulk of its before-tax income from overseas operations. The bank's statements note that its loans to Brazil in one year exceed the total equity of the Citicorp's shareholders. Now, what would happen if the four superdebtor countries defaulted on their payments? Obviously the banks would have negative net equity, requiring their shareholders to absorb the losses. In the USA, as well as in other Western countries, the state would then have to choose between allowing the major banks to collapse or intervening to keep them afloat. Notwithstanding their neo-liberal, anti-statist ideology, the Republicans in Washington could be compelled to support a *de facto* nationalization.

How did the banks, presumably expert at assessing risk, let loans to underdeveloped countries reach gargantuan proportions?

The crisis of indebtedness emerges from a mix of causes. With massive injections of petro-dollars, the banks sought new customers. Third World countries promised high interest returns. As competitors, the banks did not share information with each other about the level of lending to the debt-laden countries. Deregulation in the USA pushed this tendency to an extreme, impelling the transnational banking industry to evade the strictures of federal agencies. Besides, the regulatory agencies could not keep up with the quickening pace of lending. The bankers did not understand the root cause of the problem, for they were part of it. At bottom, the crisis reflects the *incoherence* of Third World economies. When the debt piled up in the 1970s, the bourgeoisies of the Third World thought that they could rely on external loan capital to sustain accumulation. There followed not an accumulation of capital but an accumulation of errors. The contradiction between the consumption patterns of the bourgeoisie and the need for the internal generation of savings is glaring. So drained are Third World economies that debtor countries borrow just to repay a portion of the interest due. Prior indebtedness thereby eats up current export earnings. The debt-ridden countries are caught between the demands of their overseas creditors and the needs of ordinary people at home.

The banks are also in a fix. They must provide new money just so that their borrowers can pay interest on old debt. The problem redoubles upon itself: if a bank wants to stay on the top echelon of world finance, it must continue to attract deposits; yet the crisis in the world economy has limited the number of creditworthy countries capable of generating these deposits.

Impaled on the horns of this dilemma, some private banks seek relief through a multibillion dollar secondary market which enables them to swap the troubled loans or to sell them. An investor, for example, can buy a Bolivian loan for about 20 cents on each dollar of face value or an Argentine loan for around 70 cents on the dollar. Most of this discount purchasing is done by corporations with business interests in a particular country, by investors who thrive on risks and by the debtors themselves who reclaim their loans at a discount. Volume on this market, believed to have begun in 1982 during the Falklands War, was fairly small: about $3 billion in 1984. Trading of developing country debt increased considerably during the period 1988–91, reaching an estimated volume of over $100 billion in 1991. This increase was due to a rise in debt-equity swaps, primarily in the form of bonds. Eighty per cent of the trading in 1991 was concentrated on four Latin American countries, Argentina, Brazil, Mexico and Venezuela.

In March 1989 the US Treasury Secretary, Nicholas Brady, came up with a plan to reduce commercial-bank debt of Third World nations, especially in Latin America. The Brady Plan was designed to favour nations willing to implement IMF-led structural adjustment. They would receive partial debt forgiveness from commercial banks and new financial resources would also be made available to them. Under this plan, debt-ridden Bolivia was permitted access to apply borrowed resources to buy back a substantial part of its commercial-bank debt at 11 per cent of the face value. Several other countries, including Mexico, Venezuela, Costa Rica, Uruguay and Argentina benefited from the Brady Plan, provided they were willing to accept IMF discipline. One implication of the Brady Plan was that a portion of Latin America's Third World debt became a proxy for US debt and the debtor nations promised to privatize their economies.

In the context of the globalization of finance, vulnerable economies face the uncertainty of volatile speculative markets. The peso crisis in Mexico illustrates the hazards of growing financial integration on a world scale. Less than a year after the signing of the North American Free Trade Agreement (NAFTA), on 20 December 1994, the Mexican government decided to devalue the peso, causing a blitz among foreign investors to convert pesos into dollars. By mid-1995, the value of the peso had fallen to half its original value. Mexican living standards tumbled drastically, as did the fortunes of foreign creditors and speculators. Alarmed by the possible impact of the peso crisis, the Clinton administration quickly put together an $18 billion package, later boosted to $52 billion in US loan guarantees, to restore the peso and to help the Mexican government repay government debt to bondholders, mostly US-based investors.

The bail-out was, in effect, designed to help the investors responsible for the crisis in the first place. Signs of the peso crisis had been visible for some time – ignored by investors – including an abnormally high current account deficit (8 per cent of GDP in 1994) and surplus foreign capital inflows, considerably greater than domestic capital outflows. The inflows were directed to short-term government bonds and speculation rather than productive investment. With mounting political uncertainty in Mexico, in large part fuelled by an armed uprising in the southernmost province of Chiapas, foreign investors decided to shield their risks by inflating interest rates, demanding shorter maturities on their loans and payment in dollars. These short-term market fluctuations put the Mexican economy in gyration. Critical to financial certainty were the Bank of Mexico's foreign currency reserves. From a high of almost $30 billion in February 1994, these reserves fell to $5 billion in December as the bank used up this scarce resource to buttress the peso. Convinced that devaluation would daunt foreign investors while raising the cost of imports, President Ernesto Zedillo's government postponed the inevitable until December.

The effects of the peso crisis were distributed unevenly among social strata, with the poor bearing the brunt. An austerity plan was put into effect in March 1995, directly hurting ordinary Mexican consumers and businesses. Fuel prices rose by 33 per cent, residential utility rates by 20 per cent, the federal value-added tax from 10 to 15 per cent, and interest rates on consumer credit by 125 per cent. With hikes in the minimum wage restricted to 10 per cent against expected inflation rates, purchasing power fell by 18 per cent. With hikes in food prices, the hardest hit were the very poor. The Mexican minimum wage could buy one-third of the minimum basket of goods.

While the Mexicans were forced to pay dearly for the financial crisis, the bail-out benefited Wall Street speculators and affluent Mexicans and politicians. The peso crisis points to the risks of neo-liberal market reforms in economies unable to withstand financial shocks.

The private banks have forged a symbiotic alliance with international monetary institutions. The commercial banks increasingly rely on the IMF's 'stabilization program' for assurance that a country is a good credit risk. To Citicorp, Chase Manhattan and the other transnational banks seeking an outlet for their surplus petro-dollars, the IMF seal of good housekeeping on the financial policies of a member state indicates that the debtor country has accepted the fund's stringent formula. For the borrower, the IMF imprimatur means that private bank loans and development assistance, of a magnitude far larger than the fund's largesse, are likely to flow.

To comprehend the fund's current impact on underdeveloped economies, it is essential to recall why it was established and how it has evolved. The IMF was launched at the 1944 Bretton Woods monetary conference in order to encourage free trade and investment between capitalist countries. The vast majority of underdeveloped countries were colonies in 1944 and hence were not involved in designing the IMF. Based in Washington, DC, near the US Department of Treasury, the Fund was organized to allow an American veto on any major policy issue. A lender of last resort, it was created to provide short-term financing for temporary balance of payments relief, not to redress deep-seated ills in the world economy.

Since 1944, almost all of the underdeveloped world has gained political independence and has joined the IMF. Nowadays the deficits of the underdeveloped countries differ in essential respects from those of the developed countries: most underdeveloped economies are structurally weak, subject to declining terms of trade and afflicted by wild fluctuations in the prices for their commodities on the world market. The very attempt to restructure an economy – to develop – is likely to create a deficit because of inevitable short-term dislocations. The IMF was not set up to deal with this *development deficit*.

Increasingly the financially strapped members of the IMF require emergency loans. The Fund, however, does not command huge resources. Rather, its power stems from its role as a coordinator among the advanced capitalist countries and as a go-between with the underdeveloped economies. To secure an IMF loan, a borrower must accede to a set of conditions: policies which ensure reliance on market mechanisms and which impose austerity measures. Specifically, the Fund's standard formula, known as conditionality, calls for retrenchment in the public sector, including cuts in social programmes and the reduction or elimination of subsidies (on food, for example) to diminish government expenditure further and to heighten use of the market; increases in taxes so as to decrease the overall deficit and to hold down consumption; restrictions on domestic credit and money supply, particularly in countries that produce a great deal of currency; devaluation, which raises the prices of imports to local consumers and lowers the cost of exports for foreign buyers; and higher interest rates, which put a damper on borrowing, deflate the economy and constrain imports. The objective is to liberalize capital flows and to promote export-oriented growth.

The problem with this prescription is that there is little evidence that it works. In terms of balance of payments, growth, savings and investment, the economic performance of Third World countries with IMF programmes was no better than for the countries without them. This is apparent even if the criterion is the Fund's own targets, as shown in careful research by the Canadian economist John Loxley. Why else would there be a multitude of debt reschedulings for IMF members who borrow heavily? Although official creditors claim that they will negotiate debt relief arrangements only when a debtor country is in a state of 'imminent default', postponements have become increasingly frequent. According to the State Department, the USA participated in 76 multilateral debt negotiations from 1956 to 1983, 24 of these reschedulings in the period 1980–3. From 1990 to 1994, the USA rescheduled $20.58 billion owed by 47 countries.

Borrowing countries apply for IMF loans because they lack other sources of foreign exchange. But if a debtor enters a pact with the fund, it must take the pain along with the cash. The burden of adjustment is borne unevenly by local classes. It falls most heavily on urban wage earners. The belt-tightening exercise administered by the state invites social protest, often followed by a wave of repression. So-called IMF riots have swept such countries as Peru and the Dominican Republic.

The effects of adjustment are also distributed unevenly across gender. As secondary workers, women are often in low-wage jobs. In times of retrenchment, as one World Bank study reveals, women have been forced to take on a heavier burden, raising children and working long hours to make ends meet. To illustrate, women's representation in the work-force increased from 40 to 52 per cent in a low-income urban community in Guayaquil, one of Ecuador's largest cities, between 1978 and 1988 (a period of considerable economic fluctuation). Even the diet was affected with a decline in the consumption of milk, fish and fresh fruit, and meals were restricted to breakfast and supper. In 1988, 80 per cent of the children there suffered from malnutrition. The indirect effects of adjustment included an increase in drug use and domestic violence, often the consequence of conflict over household expenditures, and teenage vagrancy among boys.

Perhaps prosperous societies that have developed social security and unemployment insurance can make the sacrifices mandated by IMF structural adjustments. Underdeveloped countries, however, do not have the socio-economic infrastructure to relieve the destitute who are called upon to reduce their standard of living.

The IMF's export-oriented model accentuates the problems endemic to disjointed, outward-looking economies originally fashioned by colonialism to meet the needs of the metropolitan market. This is how the seeds of indebtedness were planted in the first place. IMF interventions cannot remedy the crisis, for the fund's framework reflects a view of modernization, nowadays under the banner of neo-liberalism, that is a product of the advanced capitalist countries. The concept of squeezing local demand in order to force production into exports may achieve the goals set by policy makers if the factors of production are highly mobile, or can be mobilized, in response to monetary manipulation. But the mobilization of factors of production is problematic in most, though not all, underdeveloped economies. As noted, one cannot count on the willingness of rural dwellers to adopt a sophisticated technology to increase production. The explanation pertains to the dynamics of social structure at a level that does not enter into the IMF framework. Insofar as fund interventions permit the local ruling class to consume loan capital and require that peasant surplus flows back to the advanced capitalist economies in the form of interest on old debt, the direct producers will actively or passively resist IMF policies.

Although the IMF was designed to bridge short-term problems of an imbalance of payments, the crisis in underdeveloped economies is not of a short-term nature. It is structural; a worldwide financial crack-up is a real possibility. All the great banks of the world are involved, and the structure of debt cannot be effectively tackled by ramshackle arrangements. Bail-outs and infusions of more money – global welfare – do not go to the heart of the problem. Resolution of the world economic crisis lies outside institutional control. The story of debt is no more and no less than the problem of underdevelopment itself. Patchwork measures beg the question, 'In whose interests will the international monetary system be reformed?' Adjustments will continue but, in the end, what will be left to adjust? In this vein, former Brazilian President João Baptista Figueiredo's 1984 comments give pause. He reportedly declared: 'When I took office in 1979, Brazil stood at the brink of an abyss. But in the last five years, we have taken a great leap forward.'

Like Brazil, many Third World countries have encountered the predicament of how to generate capital accumulation at home while participating in the global political economy, a network of structures (some of them enshrined as formal institutions) that disadvantage the underdeveloped world: upward mobility is evident only at the margins. International institutions embody the rules of the game. One of the main functions of international organizations is to look after the welfare aspects of global capital accumulation. Owing to the effects of superpower competition during the Cold War, supplanted by hegemonic leadership, the importance of UN security provisions pales in comparison.

Fifty years after the founding of the Bretton Woods system, a number of voices are challenging the nature and role of the World Bank and the IMF. Development economists, environmentalists and other Third World activists who seek reform or the abolition of these powerful institutions have numerous grievances against them: charges of secrecy, misallocation of funds, disregard for poverty reduction, and promotion of socially disruptive and ecologically harmful projects. Some critics claim that an unelected and unaccountable global cohort is entrenched in the commanding heights of these institutions, callous to the pangs of the world's poor. Others contend the World Bank and the IMF have outlived their usefulness. Initially set up to promote international commerce and infrastructural development, the goals of the two institutions have radically changed to incorporate more fully the poorer nations into a world economy driven by expansive market forces. Third World countries enjoy little influence on these institutions, especially in the areas of debt relief. They primarily serve capital in industrialized nations, and to a lesser degree at home.

Another line of criticism focuses on structural adjustment programmes, often proposed by neo-liberals in the IMF to remove budget deficits, but with far-reaching consequences for underdeveloped countries. As noted, adjustment 'packages' call for privatization of the economy, reducing the size of public enterprises which provide employment to large numbers, devaluation of currencies to promote exports, and trade and investment promotion. The main consequence of these packages is a reduction in the social security net for disadvantaged segments of the population, not only the urban poor but also people on fixed incomes, including state employees. Inasmuch as rich sectors of society rarely practise austerity, the real casualty of IMF-sponsored structural adjustment programmes are those who are least capable of withstanding a diminution in their income. In the face of such biting criticism, the Bretton Woods organizations remain wedded to the dominant power structure of the global political economy. The web of international organizations, aid agencies, technological agreements, TNCs and banking concerns presents a formidable challenge to the Third World: how to amass an investable surplus while reducing global inequality?

4 Back to the Nineteenth Century for New Ideas

Saudi Arabia's royal family is trying to spearhead an advanced industrial economy while inoculating against a social upheaval. Given the surge in the price of oil from about $3.50 a barrel in 1973 to a peak of $34 in 1981 and 1982, billions of petro-dollars were made available to plough back into development projects and private industry. The sum accumulated in one year alone (1981) – a $30 billion excess of income over expenditure – was truly colossal.

Buttressed by these oil revenues, Saudi Arabia embarked upon an ambitious developmental programme to bring the kingdom, one-quarter of the size of the continental USA with only 17 million people (including foreign nationals), into the twentieth century. Through the mid-1970s and early 1980s, the signs of material growth were evident everywhere in the desert kingdom. A flashy superhighway – leading to no apparent destination – sweeps by a clatter of donkey carts, herders and their camels. A glittery airport (the world's largest), massive bulldozers, and burly cranes decked the landscape around Jeddah, the ancient port on the Red Sea. Jutting boldly out of the sand the elegant edifices of Jubail and Yanbu shot up, fledgeling industrial cities built by the government. With the worldwide oil glut, the boom was quickly turning into a mirage. Production, up to almost 10 million barrels per day during 1980–81, fell to about 2 million barrels per day in 1985. Oil prices fell to $13.15 per barrel in 1989; and they hovered just below $17 a barrel in 1993. The onset of the Gulf War further aggravated Saudi woes of an economy super-dependent on the vicissitudes of world oil prices.

State involvement in the economy is extensive. Bloated state agencies are responsible for the construction of roads and housing, electrification and the establishment of private companies, particularly in agribusiness. Public agencies provide subsidies for food and free medical care, and offer many types of interest-free loans. During the happy days of massive oil revenues, these agencies could dole out $300 per month to university students to supplement lavish stipends which covered the full cost of books, tuition, and room and board. The gush of oil was so prodigious that income tax was deemed unnecessary.

The state is attempting to inaugurate a work ethic. A network of recently constructed schools is trying to speed the training of locals to replace foreign nationals, nearly 4.6 million, in order to increase Saudi influence. The teachers propagate new values centred on success and mobility. In rural areas nomads are given incentives to settle down and farm according to the prescribed procedures.

Yet the obstacles to development are formidable. The economy still remains susceptible to oil prices, with oil accounting for more than 75 per cent of the country's exports and nearly 75 per cent of state revenues. Five per cent of the population are nomadic, spread across a gigantic sandbox. Twenty-seven per cent of males and 52 per cent of the female population is illiterate. The ten-fold hike in oil revenue did not commensurably buoy the non-oil sectors of the economy. The theocrats-cum-business executives who run the show are forcing rapid social and economic change but, as the Iranians found out, there is no sure-fire way to control it: a swift shift in the mode of social relations can unsaddle an entire political system.

This brings us to the crucial recognition that development and economic growth are not identical; while economic growth is essential to development in the Third World, it does not guarantee it. Economic growth refers to change in one dimension of society, specifically the economy; development, on the other hand, refers to change in a society taken as a whole in its social, economic and political aspects. Just as the whole is never the sum of its parts nor coterminous with a predominant part, development entails more than economic growth. In fact, just as growth in one sector of the economy need not necessarily result in the growth of the entire economy, so too economic growth need not parallel social and political change, as already noted in the case of Saudi Arabia.

In light of the upward spiral of fierce competition in the national marketplace, what haunts many Saudis today are the prospects for their own rockbottom economic survival. There is tremendous pressure to dodge the throng, to avoid being obliterated by the rash of new companies spawned by the state, and above all to accumulate capital.

Saudi Arabia is an exceptional case in that it is the world's largest oil-exporting country. Still, even in the poorest countries, a *surplus product* – the end-result of human labour expended for goods which are not immediately consumed – is available for productive investment. Typically, what is in dispute are the uses of the surplus product: how are savings for investment disposed in new methods of production? This is not simply a question of economic allocation, determined principally by economic factors alone. On the contrary, the process of deciding how the surplus is to be reinvested is a highly political one mediated by the nature of the social structure of particular societies. This question gives rise to contending ideas about how to achieve development. These ideas in turn help to shape the policies aimed at conquering underdevelopment. Thus if *the current challenge in the Third World is to eliminate poverty, the first step is to create new knowledge to build the capacity to develop natural and human resources.*

In this chapter we turn to the key building blocks for analyzing development and underdevelopment in particular countries. The place to begin is with the cornerstone of all strategies of development: capital accumulation as it relates to the state and social forces.

CAPITAL ACCUMULATION

Why is capital accumulation the port of entry to understanding the dynamics of the Third World? First, in most contemporary Third World societies, the primary political debates do not only or primarily concern formal institutions – elections, representation in Parliament, party responsibilities, and so on – but also the politics surrounding the generation and allocation of capital: how to wrench limited resources from the existing units of production and channel them so as to uplift the national economy? From whence is a surplus product to be roused if a country is going to industrialize? Will the peasant sector permit a transfer of resources to the more advanced sectors of the economy? In the countryside, what units of production – privately-owned estates, state farms, cooperatives, communes or families – merit government support so that a nation can feed itself and not drain precious resources from other worthy activities or go into hock to international banks?

Second, notwithstanding the passionate tug-of-war between them, Marxists and non-Marxists alike regard the question of capital accumulation as central to economic development. In the mainstream view, capital accumulates when some quantum of current income is saved and invested in order to elevate further outputs and income. New factories, machinery, plants and equipment augment the 'capital stock' of an economy, making it possible to expand output. These are investments in 'directly productive' activities. They must be accompanied by investments in 'infrastructure', which facilitate other economic measures. Infrastructure has both social (for example, health care and education) and economic (for example, feeder roads, railways and harbours) components. Whatever the form of investment, and irrespective of the type of resources, capital accumulation involves a trade-off between present and future consumption: sacrificing something now for more later.

In the classical Marxist view, capital accumulation is the process of profit making and reinvestment. A successful capitalist enterprise gathers a portion of its profits and pumps it back into production in order to enlarge the scope and improve the efficiency of the operation. A well-known tenet in Marxism is that a capitalist economy must expand; it cannot stand still. (As Walter Wriston, who reigned for 14 years as chairman and chief executive officer of Citicorp, the biggest banking organization in the world, gleefully expressed his Darwinian philosophy of how business works: 'You either move forward, or you die; it's true in all biology.') A stalled capitalist enterprise will be devoured by large, dynamic corporations. Moreover, continuous expansion is forced by labour market competition; collective working-class actions have resulted not only in labour unions but also in organized political activity.

To come to grips with accumulation in a Third World country, it is essential to inspect the system of production. *The starting point is production* because consumption is necessary for human life, and to consume, humans must produce: goods must be produced before they can be distributed and converted to use. However, a system of production presupposes a specific alignment of social forces. This simply means that for a *capitalist* system of production to ensue, society must be divided between those who own the means of production and those who own nothing but their capacity to labour. The first refers to those who have access to resources in excess of what they need to survive; they can invest a part of their resources in plant and equipment, and hire others by paying them a wage. Without this group of persons willing to invest their resources in production for profit, a *capitalist* mode of production would not obtain. Equally important are those who own nothing but their capacity to work and must contract their labour-power to someone in the former group so that they may subsist. Marx referred to this as labour that is free in a double sense: free from bondage to another (as in slavery and serfdom), and free from the ownership of any means of production. In order to gain access to resources necessary for his or her survival (food, clothing, and so on), the factory-worker is compelled to voluntarily sell his or her labour-power to the factory-owner not because the latter coerces him or her to do so but because the worker has no other means of livelihood. Without the division in society between these two groups and the voluntary exchange of labour-power for wages, a capitalist system of production would not exist.

Production, distribution, exchange and consumption are inter-related aspects of a cycle. The sequence among them is crucial, as the following parable shows. Isaac and Levy own jewellery stores opposite each other. Isaac buys a decorative pearl necklace for only $10. He shares the news with Levy, who is spellbound. 'Sell me this necklace,' he pleads, 'I was just promising one like it to Rebecca, my wife. She'll love it. Here's $11.' Isaac gives in. Later he informs his wife, Sarah, about the deal. 'At 10 this morning,' he says, 'I bought a necklace for $10, and five minutes later I sold it to Levy for $11. A dollar made in five minutes!'

'You idiot,' answers Sarah. 'It's always the same with you. If Levy paid you $11 for that necklace, it was because he realized it's worth much more. Hurry up and buy it back from him.'

A few hours hence, Isaac visits Levy. 'Levy,' he implores, 'if you are a friend of mine, sell me back that necklace. Sarah made one of her scenes about it ... Here is $12.'

Levy hands it over, and at dusk tells Rebecca about it. 'This morning Isaac came over to sell me a necklace for $11 and this afternoon he bought it back from me for $12. I made a dollar without stirring from my counter.'

'You idiot,' declares Rebecca. 'It's always the same with you. If Isaac came in to see you again, to buy back that necklace for a dollar more than he sold it to you, it must have been because he'd found out meanwhile that it's worth much more. Go and get it back from him.' Next day, Levy proposes $13 for the necklace and takes it back to his shop. Then Isaac recovers the necklace at a cost of $14 and on they go.

Two weeks later, the necklace had gone up in price to $24 and is on Isaac's counter. Levy comes in and slaps down $25. 'The necklace,' he commands.

'The necklace isn't here any more,' Isaac responds. 'Last night, just before I closed, an American woman looked in. I offered it to her for $30, and she bought it.'

Levy falls into a chair. 'You've sold our necklace? But, you idiot, thanks to that necklace we were quietly, easily making a dollar a day each. And you've sold it – our livelihood.'

There is something amusing about this story. But what? It seems absurd to think that someone makes money without adding value to a product. This is precisely the point. First goods must be produced before they are worth swapping. Then a profit is realized in exchange between buyers and sellers, as on the stock exchange. A profit accrues to an individual when he (or she) outsmarts competitors by buying cheap and selling dear. This activity occurs in the orbit of circulation. Society as a whole has not gained, the commodity has only moved about. In order for society to gain, production must mount. (This assumes a single national economy. In the context of the global political economy, however, the picture is obviously more complex. As we shall see, by virtue of their location in the international division of labour, some countries – specifically NICs – have benefited immensely simply by serving as facilitators of *circulation*. Hong Kong, for instance, has achieved rapid rates of economic growth not primarily by producing commodities but by becoming a major hub for international finance and trade. Whether a country can accumulate capital in the long term without increasing production cannot be ascertained independent of its roles in the global political economy.)

Now production, an interchange between humans and nature, must be considered in terms of both its physical and social facets. The *physical organization of production* means the technical units and instruments (tools or machinery) applied by human labour to transform nature into commodities for distribution and consumption. The *social organization of production* refers to the relations between groups of people in the national, international, and global divisions of labour. By knitting together the physical and social aspects of production, one avoids adopting a mechanical and overly economic view of capital accumulation. Crucial to political economy is to know who controls production and to what end. In turn, how owners and actual producers relate to other social forces in society also impinges upon the developmental process. The existence of a particular structure of patriarchy, for instance, can have a major impact on the form of surplus extraction. Barriers to women's participation in the work-force due to culturally sanctioned norms can stifle social development. A gender-based work-force can allow capitalists greater flexibility in hiring or firing employees. The existence of a substantial female work-force can also promote greater wage differentials. Also pertinent to production broadly understood, the depletion of the environment resulting from fast-track industrialization can undermine long-term developmental possibilities. A failure to pay attention to bio-diversity is likely to generate permanent health risks to living species, and diminish productivity.

The social aspects of the expansion of capital are bound up with the whole question of the *exploitation* of labour. In common parlance, exploitation means utilization for profit. Whether exploitation is sinister is not at issue here. Ethics is an important aspect of political economy, but moralizing about societal ills is not the purpose here, for our objective is to understand social forces. Exploitation may take many forms and may be sanctioned by law. The following vignette, related by one of the first Zimbabweans to go abroad for military training during the anti-colonial campaign, graphically illustrates one form of exploitation.

The main issue giving rise to the armed struggle in Zimbabwe was land hunger among the rapidly growing black population. Peasant producers were deprived of their land by the colonial state, especially after the Second World War, with the large influx of white farmers, who cultivated only a tiny portion of the areas reserved for Europeans. In 1951, when the Native Land Husbandry Act (which reduced Africans' entitlement to land and cattle) was passed, a young herder who was to become a guerrilla received one shilling in return for a cow which had been a gift from his father. Thereafter, the father repeatedly asked his son whether the shilling had turned into a larger sum, and the boy, puzzled by the question, answered that it had not. This procedure continued for weeks until the father explained that the shilling had not expanded in value because Africans were oppressed. Meanwhile the cow, now the property of the white man, was producing calves and hence wealth for the farmer, but the shilling would remain a shilling, the father added, for the Act was simply a means to impoverish Africans and enrich Europeans. The father rightly perceived that expansion is the key to exploitation. Although exploitation in the economic sense is crucial to understanding the nature of domination in capitalist societies, it is equally important to recognize that exploitation is always *embedded* in social relations and their legitimation. This means that economic exploitation usually takes place in the context of other forms of social discrimination, frequently expressed in terms of religion, ethnicity and gender. The structure of exploitation and domination thus results from parallel, overlapping and mutually reinforcing processes. For example, in India, the rigid hierarchies of patriarchy and religion render women of the lowest caste in Hinduism – the shudra or untouchables – the most economically disadvantaged.

However, the central question in political economy is, expansion of what? Not of cows, as in Zimbabwe, but human labour, which is a source of value. That being the case, capitalist exploitation may be regarded as the value added by the worker beyond the sum needed to cover his (or her) means of subsistence. The incremental value is wrested from the worker by the capitalist in the process of production.

This principle is a bedrock of the trail blazed by Karl Marx. An understanding of the major tenets set forth in *Capital* can provide a solid foundation for grasping political economy. Examining Marx's theory of capitalism is the basis for resurrecting the concept of capital accumulation as well as for considering reformulations and extensions of this theory in respect to the Third World.

THE ENIGMAS IN MARX'S VIEW OF HISTORY

The young Marx became embroiled in the great philosophical debates of his day. At the universities of Bonn and Berlin, the radical current in German philosophy turned the tide in Marx's life. He chose a revolutionary path, leading him into exile. This bearded foreigner lived a spartan existence in one of London's darkest slums. Marx, his wife and children were often gravely ill. Hounded by bill collectors, he beseeched his lifelong friend and collaborator Friedrich Engels for assistance from his family's textile industry. There were times when this strange man in tattered clothing could not go to his work-place, the British Museum, to pore over tomes of documents and statistics because his shoes and overcoat were at the pawnbroker's. Poking his nose out one day, he aptly commented: 'Never has anyone written about "money in general" amidst such total lack of money in particular.'

Throughout his life, Marx was preoccupied with the question of the interplay between economics and society. First and foremost, he viewed people as productive creatures. Production is the expenditure of labour power, the capacity for work. Production creates the objects which correspond to human needs, whereas consumption satisfies these needs. Between production and consumption are distribution and exchange. Distribution divides social products, and exchange further apportions the shares to individuals.

A familiar tenet in Marxism is that, in the development of a society, its mode of production is decisive. A mode of production is a combination of forces of production and social relations of production. Forces of production means the mode of appropriation of nature; relations of production, the mode of appropriation of labour. For Marx, appropriation entails 'transformation'. Tools, for example, are used to transform natural substances into value.

Of course Marx was not primarily concerned with stringing together definitions. Rather, by enlisting the power of abstraction, he unfurled a bold working hypothesis to explain emerging historical patterns: people are always adapting their relations of production to their forces of production to suit their needs.

One of these elements, by itself, cannot constitute a mode of production. Machines and the other means of production are instrumentalities but not a social process. Marx recalls the experience of Mr. Peel, an English manufacturer, who set out for Swan River, West Australia. No mere tourist was he. Mr. Peel brought with him means of subsistence and of production to the tune of £50 000, as well as 3000 working-class men, women and children. As soon as he reached Australia's bountiful shores, Mr. Peel no longer had a servant 'to make his bed or fetch him water from the river'. 'Unhappy Mr. Peel who provided for everything except the export of English modes of production to Swan River!' In effect, he found himself without a class of wage labourers. In England, Mr. Peel had owned and controlled the means of production. In budding Australia, however, labourers could accumulate for themselves. They were no longer for hire. The old social relations of British capitalism did not obtain.

Capitalism differs from other class societies in one vital respect: exploitation takes the form not of bondage or serfdom but wage labour. The surplus coaxed out of labour is surplus value, which is partly realized as profit and is systematically ploughed back into production.

The concept of surplus value is based on a distinction between two types of value, use value and exchange value. A commodity's use value is simply its utility, its usefulness. Use value is realized only through the consumption of a commodity. But a commodity is produced not only for use but also for exchange for another use value. Put differently, commodity production has both a qualitative and a quantitative dimension.

The quantitative relation between things is in reality only an outward form of social relations. What is embodied in the commodity is human labour. Both living labour and dead labour are congealed in machines and materials. Under capitalism, the qualitative transformation of use value is replaced by the quantitative expansion of exchange value as the object of production.

The capitalist buys the proletariat's labour power at its full exchange value. All the while members of the proletariat are deluded into thinking that they are free because they can sell their labour power to whichever capitalist employer they choose. The capitalist class as a whole administers the use value of the labour power it has purchased. This useful labour creates an exchange value of the labour power contracted. Here lies the key to profit making.

Surplus value cannot derive from lifeless materials, and neither can it arise from a mere exchange of commodities: as we have seen, if everyone were to attempt to land a profit by hiking prices 10 per cent, what one gained as a seller would be lost as a buyer. Hence the expansion of capital springs only from the value that labour imparts.

For his (or her) contribution, the labourer expects to receive a wage. The actual wage depends on the number of working hours the labourer needs to subsist. If it takes five hours of labour per day to keep the worker alive, his (or her) worth is $5 (at $1 per hour). But a whole working day is not five hours. At present it is eight hours. Hence today's labourer provides eight hours of value a day, although he (or she) is paid for merely five hours. Wages cover subsistence and not more (in the absence of collective working-class action). Meanwhile, the labourer has sold the value which he (or she) produced in an entire working day. This differential is the source of surplus value.

Inasmuch as the value of the labourer's wages, computed in hours of labour time, is less than the number of hours the labourer works for the capitalist, the labourer surrenders a share of his (or her) creative power. This is surplus value: the overall value churned out less the wages paid to the labourer.

Thus the capitalist skims additional value in the production process. No one is swindled. These are the rules of the game. The capitalist appropriates surplus value not because of greed or an innate profit 'motive'. The non-labour components of the production process must be purchased, and the capitalist must receive compensation. Moreover, the capitalist makes decisions within a structure of accumulation over which an individual exercises little control.

All the choices concern how most profitably to redirect a chunk of surplus value in production in the form of capital. The capitalist may convert a portion of surplus value into means of production, referred to by Marx as *constant capital*, or may designate a larger or smaller segment for the means of subsistence (wages), which Marx termed *variable capital*. In so doing, the capitalist can hire additional labourers or intensify the pumping out of surplus value from labourers whose labour power has already been contracted. A combination of these techniques is the structure of accumulation characteristic of capitalism.

It is possible to accumulate a limited amount of capital without converting surplus value into additional capital. This may be accomplished by extending the length of the working day or by increasing the productivity of labour through an improvement in technology (exclusive of a supplementary outlay of capital). Not surprisingly, the capitalist will try to jack up the number of hours which the labourer spends producing surplus value relative to those required to generate subsistence wages. Over the long haul, however, the restless forces of accumulation, driven by inter-capitalist competition and the labour-capital conflict, necessitate the conversion of surplus value into productive capital. With the appropriation of more and more surplus value, accumulation brings about a concentration of wealth in the clutches of the capitalist class. The owners of capital extend the scale of their operations, speeding, amplifying and homogenizing the accumulation process. In the meantime bigger units of capital devour smaller ones. Acting in their individual capacities, the captains of the rail industry, for example, could not have sent their steam engines whistling around the globe in the nineteenth century. Centralization of capital, along with technical know-how, made this feat possible.

The further application of machinery to the labour process means, by definition, that constant capital expands faster than does variable capital. Capitalism provides more labour power than it can absorb, thus establishing an 'industrial reserve army of labour'. The reservoir of labour performs a double service for the capitalist. It furnishes both a potential pool of labour power and pressure on the proletariat in the form of a lever to lessen wages and heighten exploitation.

If surplus value is extracted from an ever-declining amount of variable capital, relative to the amount of constant capital, then the rate of profit is likely to fall. This is a tendency, not a law. There is a host of countervailing factors. These include cheapening the elements of constant capital, intensifying exploitation, depressing wages below their value, making adjustments in foreign trade and investing capital abroad where rates of profit are higher than at home. Even if an individual capitalist enterprise adopts techniques such as speed-up and stretch-out to augment exploitation, its competitors have recourse to the same methods. Hence the rate of profit may fall irrespective of the will of the individual capitalist. To counteract this tendency, and to replenish the reserve army of labour, capitalism periodically erupts in crises. Typically, capitalist production then inclines towards further centralization and concentration while readying for the next crisis. Once again, productive forces are spastic and expansive. Labouring producers are rendered increasingly superfluous. The technical calibre of production exceeds the capacity for social control.

This logic led Marx to deny the possibility of infinite capitalist expansion, but he failed to map the intricacies of the breakdown of capitalism. Moreover, he had limited knowledge of economically and technologically backward areas outside Europe. By current standards, relatively few sources of information were available to him. This is especially true with respect to Africa. It will be recalled that Marx wrote before the partition of Africa at the Berlin Conference of 1884–5. And unlike the pattern in Europe, the capitalist mode of production did not completely replace precapitalist modes in the Third World. The low level of productive forces in Africa would not permit class formation along the lines of European feudalism. Owing to a lack of advanced technology and the insubstantial productivity of labour, there was a meagre surplus for an African appropriating class.

Although Marx studied the period of primitive accumulation in which the Western bourgeoisie amassed capital by plundering Africa, Asia and Latin America, he nevertheless had little to say about underdevelopment. Moreover, his central supposition about it was wrong. Marx foresaw not underdevelopment but development in what is now known as the Third World. In the *Communist Manifesto*, he seemed to anticipate that advanced capitalism would spread throughout the world. He expressed this theme in the following terms in 1867 in the preface to the first edition of *Capital*: 'The country that is more developed industrially only shows, to the less developed, the image of its own future.' But as we know, this is far from what actually happened. Advanced capitalism did not replicate the European, North American and Japanese pattern whereby surplus generated in agriculture is reinvested internally to stimulate the growth of industry and hence to elevate demand for the production of mass consumption goods and capital goods. Rather, it created dependent, export-oriented economies in the Third World.

There have been many transcendental developments thoroughly unforeseen by Marx. Capitalism is remarkably adaptable. Today, many savants are returning to the unsettled questions in political economy. In particular, they are bringing to light the nature of the state and contemporary class conflict. Rather than copying the paragons of the nineteenth century, the task before us is to enrich these concepts creatively.

BEYOND CLASSICAL AND NEO-CLASSICAL THOUGHT

Capital accumulation, the state, class, and non-class forces are interwoven aspects of the political economy of development and underdevelopment. They are themes suffused throughout classical political economy. We might visualize their relationship as a triangle much like that shown in Figure 4.1.

The internal space delimited is development and underdevelopment. The opening allows for specific conditions: social dynamics cannot be fully explained without reference to particular cultures and historical

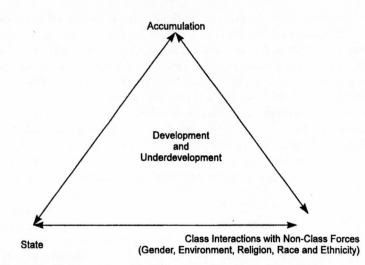

Figure 4.1   The dynamics of development and underdevelopment

trajectories. A new accumulation strategy corresponds to a realignment of class and non-class forces. A reconfiguration of social forces means an alteration in state power. An alteration in the social composition of the state is the basis for an innovative policy of accumulation. Yet no state is reducible to only the dominant classes. The latter are often aligned with strata elsewhere, both inside and outside the state. Fractions of the 'middle class' removed from direct material production provide crucial support or opposition to the production process. Elements of this 'class' can afford a critical political basis for directing society in particular avenues. Imbued with interests and ideas, non-class forces may sink or swim by aligning themselves to pro- or anti-industrial development. In many Third World nations, the obstacles to development often originate with alliances between a landed aristocracy and bureaucratic groups within the state, impeding industrialization. In turn, rent-seeking states, those which thrive on using state machinery to extract already existing social surplus, prevent accumulation. New capital remains hostage to cumbersome state intervention.

In several Third World settings, the ideological orientations of non-class forces help set parameters of political discourse with real effects on development. Islamicists in the Middle East and South Asia have development in these countries. Judicial debates over the legality of capital interest in Muslim society have created a maze of regulations which, though nominal, have slowed down investment.

Despite these qualifications, thinking of development primarily as a strategy of capital accumulation, submerged in its social and political context, has prima-facie plausibility. Contemplate the acquisitiveness of capitalist culture in the West, which is familiar to all of us. In addition, mull over the crass materialism in many Third World countries. For example, Nigeria during its period of oil opulence was awash with a surfeit of commodities. Even with the tightening of the spigot, there were so many vehicles in Lagos that the authorities adopted a licensing system to reduce traffic; each private vehicle was permitted on the road only on alternate days. It was still impossible to travel at more than a snail's pace, making midtown Manhattan's gridlocked streets look like expressways in comparison. Driving to the airport in Lagos, one was solicited by a horde of aggressive entrepreneurs hawking their wares, a surprising stock of goods pirated from the far reaches of the earth: Japanese radios, Italian shoes, American tool kits, French linens, English sweets, and so on.

At government officials' homes, a visitor's request for water was greeted by the sound of popping corks released from champagne bottles. Some of these houses have upwards of 20 bedrooms and are adorned with Victorian antiques galore imported directly from London. The owners believe that they are living in mansions, but they are fooling themselves. In fact, the huge, surrounding cement walls laced on top with broken glass give the impression of prisons.

At a gala luncheon at the home of a former vice-president of Nigeria, a chief dressed in a snazzy Western business suit was seated opposite me (JHM). Asked his occupation, he said, 'A real estate agent'. It seemed reasonable to presume that the dapper gent traded in expensive property in Ikoyi, a swanky section of Lagos. 'No,' he responded, 'I deal in Beverly Hills, Scarsdale and Kensington.' Overheard at the same state function was a warm personal greeting, meant flatteringly, exchanged among officials: 'You smell of money.'

So it seems safe to say that the theory of accumulation passes the inter-ocular test: it hits you right between the eyes. But we have seen the limits of commonsensical explanations of social behaviour. Clearly, accumulation in the present day Third World is of a different order from that in the time of Karl Marx.

For one thing, industrialization is firmly implanted in such countries as China, South Korea and India. This entails a complex division of labour and gains in productivity. Second, foreign capital is heavily involved in local manufacturing, as in the case of the NICs. Foreign interests may indeed be a decisive political element. Third, the state plays a major role in organizing the local economy. In most parts of the under-developed world there has been a neo-liberal restructuring of state power in recent years, with the economic ministries taking priority over the agencies charged with responsibility for social policy. State power has often meant only executive power, and is thus increasingly challenged by pro-democracy movements.

Whereas the state is a set of political institutions, it is not most useful to describe these institutions. Rather, the telling question is, whose interest does state power serve? In the liberal view of things, the state supposedly acts in the interests of society a whole. It is a referee, a neutral arbiter, among competing groups. The state ought to pursue policies which benefit the bulk of the citizenry, widening the middle classes and providing stability, a vital condition for economic growth.

From a decidedly more critical perspective, the state is an agent of capital accumulation. Officeholders seek to consolidate the accumulation process. They erect a bureaucracy and a civil and military technocracy to smooth the process. Political institutions are thus a means whereby dominance is maintained. Rarely is there dominance by a single class. Typically in Latin America, domination is maintained by the allied interests of the *latifundia* (large landed estates), the Church, the army, local industry and TNCs. Just as the capitalist state unites these diverse elements, so too it disunites the groups at the bottom of the heap, namely workers and peasants.

Given its pivotal position in organizing and disorganizing class conflict, the state is a prize contested by competing groups. It is also an arena of political struggle, the site at which major societal conflicts are fought out. But it seldom comes down to all-out class warfare.

Societal conflict cannot be understood in class terms alone; in fact, it may be more accurate to say that class warfare is itself mediated by the larger cultural context in which it is situated. Caste, for instance, has dominated social conflict in India. The battlelines between the 'higher' and 'lower' castes have transcended class polarization. In other instances, caste and class are interlaced; privilege is the outcome of birth.

In a number of Third World countries, several new social movements have arisen aligned on a non-class basis, including gender, environment, religion, race and ethnicity. South Asia is the home of many women's groups seeking equality in the work-place and in society. Responding to neo-liberal policies, self-help organizations promote women's empowerment. Though often located among women workers, leadership of these groups comes from the middle class, members not directly engaged in production. Similarly, environmental groups promote consciousness-raising and responsible development strategies in nearly all developing nations. Members of these groups are usually drawn from middle-class strata. In some Muslim countries, the failure of Western-directed neo-liberal policies, and the inability of other states to preserve 'core' religious values, have spawned Islamic movements. These are directly implicated in challenging state-sanctioned development or filling in vital areas left untouched by 'national' development. From schooling in religious centres to short-term economic relief to rubbish collection, Islamicists are active in 'development'. Linking these realities to the globalizing tendencies of ascendant transnational capital, market fundamentalism in Africa and some other parts of the Third World, often under the banner of structural adjustment, has not meant political and economic development. It has, rather, pushed people back on cultural identities, a resurgence of precolonial bonds for survival.

The proliferation of social movements in the Third World has weakened the efficacy of trade unions. Class polarization appears less transparent in contexts in which religious solidarities, gender conflict, and particularistic identities inform the daily practices of social actors. Sometimes as an idiom of class conflict, elsewhere as an alternative set of cleavages such as religion and gender, as well as those forming around the environment, race and ethnicity, stratify populations along lines other than class. Yet, structurally speaking, class continues to serve as an enduring divide in Third World societies and a focal point of identification and action. The precise relation between class and non-class social forces cannot be determined a priori, but is subject to historical verification and analysis.

How does the pervasiveness of non-class forces condition the state? Consistent with our earlier discussion of the centrality, though not primacy, of classes to explaining material production, the state is comprised of a condensation of class and non-class forces. However, to the extent that the state is a pivotal actor in society, its character reveals the dominance of class forces proximate to production and the reproduction of society. Non-class forces rarely enjoy autonomy from dominant classes. During those brief moments when they are relatively independent, they need to reconstitute new alliances if the social order is to endure. Typically, the state does not resort to draconian measures because it projects an ideology to legitimize the interests of the dominant classes. These interests are presented as the interests of society as a whole, or the national interests, which is a device for muting class

conflict. The state furthers the position of its dominant classes by melding consensus and coercion.

A telling example of this use of ideology may be drawn from Henrik
Ibsen's *An Enemy of the People*. The play centres on a small town economically dependent on tourists who are attracted to the area by
springs with reputed curative powers. The town's doctor discovers that
the water supply is infected by organic matter from a nearby tannery,
also a mainstay of the local economy. The mayor – the doctor's brother
– warns him not to disclose this information couching the issue in
terms of 'moral authority', while imploring: 'The public doesn't need
new ideas – the public is much better off with old ideas.' Having failed
to persuade the town elders of the impending danger, the doctor appeals to the public to take decisive action. In the end, the liberal press
and the townspeople, along with the business community and the politicians, heap scorn upon the doctor. Dominant interests and the
collective ideology are one.

The process portrayed in Ibsen's native Norway is similar to what
transpires in the Third World. The leadership propounds an ideology
of 'modernization', which, the general public believes, serves the
national interest. Politics in Mexico, for instance, is dominated by the
Institutional Revolutionary Party (PRI). This party controls the main
positions within the federal, state and municipal governments. The
PRI is a corporate organism enveloping organized labour, peasant associations and the so-called popular sector, which includes congeries
of small landowners, teachers and state employees. The leading elements of the PRI form a coalition of major private interests, powerful
groups within the state and foreign capital. (This is not to overlook secondary conflicts among them.) The dominant sectors of national private capital are highly concentrated: vertically integrated industries,
commercial houses, transportation firms and financial institutions.
Ownership is in the hands of an oligarchy of about 2000 wealthy
families. The state guides the accumulation process, commanding
resources and key sectors, investing directly in industries such as
chemical and iron and steel, and establishing tariff and fiscal policies
which channel the inflow of external capital.

Meanwhile, the PRI brooks no opposition from left-wing movements.
The left is either coopted or repressed. Cooption, the preferred option,
is largely an ideological process. The PRI claims the legacy of the Mexican Revolution of 1910. The state vaunts the image of defender of the labouring and marginalized classes as well as opponent of the privileged
classes and the monopolies. To maintain their image, state agencies dif-

fuse populist ideas and practices. These are rituals thoroughly detached from their original historical significance.

To the extent that subtle forms of social control fail, outright repression is used. The armed forces are unleashed to enforce 'law and order' and to neutralize dissident groups. In an acute crisis of accumulation, the soldiers are apt to move into politics and topple the civilians who hold the reins of power. Ordinarily it makes little difference which are the officers staging the coups. There are numerous reshufflings among military officers that change the style but not the substance of politics. In Guatemala, for example, rightist generals ran the country for three decades. General Efraín Ríos Montt came to power in March 1982 by a coup supposedly because he and his supporters regarded that year's presidential contest to be rigged. Yet he refused to schedule elections for the presidency in 1983, postponing them until 1985. His sad human rights record drove the economy near bankruptcy. The apparent potential for instability troubled foreign investors. Also bothersome to the small crew of rich landowners, military men and conservative bureaucrats who really dominate the country was General Ríos Montt's religious fanaticism. A born-again Christian from a small California sect, the Church of the Word, he openly aided the campaign to proselytize within Catholic Guatemala. He lectured Guatemalans about repenting their sinful ways, and gave unintelligible interviews to the media. Hence it was not surprising when he was ousted in April 1983 by Brigadier-General Oscar Humberto Mejia Victores.

The coup was launched because Guatemala's leader had come to be seen as a liability to the landowners, officers and bureaucrats who sought to establish a propitious climate for foreign investment and social stability. There and elsewhere, the soldiers' underlying mission in seizing state power was to stabilize the process of extraction and investment of surplus. Military intervention, however, did not solve Guatemala's problems. In 1985, the military rulers were replaced by civilians. The new regime continued to terrorize the society by brutal repression, disappearances, torture and murder. Today, Guatemala's human rights record is still marred by flagrant abuses.

The role of the state in the underdeveloped world is of course not precisely the same as it is in the West. In the Third World, political power is a major means of appropriation of surplus. In countries resistant to democratization, there is a win-all-lose-all philosophy because political power is the route to the accumulation of wealth. The modern state did not appear in the Third World as an embodiment of indigenous societal development. Colonialism shaped the coercive apparatuses of the state to provide new channels for creating hegemonic forces. The preponderant role of the military in many countries, for instance, is the consequence of several factors, including colonial practices, poorly delineated 'national' borders, Cold War politics, and the recent appetite of men (rarely women) in uniform to hold on to wealth and privilege in the name of unity or security or both. In turn, the impoverishment of civil society in colonial and postcolonial times (which of course varies greatly from one context to another) has left the state as the primary avenue for acquiring power, wealth and status. Finally, the constrained nature of Third World political economies gives the above mosaic a structural character. Failure to accumulate wealth is not simply an internal affair, but also influenced by the global political economy. However, the site where the state meets class is best analysed at the local level.

The attitude that the state is a route to wealth is vividly dramatized by Chinua Achebe, one of Nigeria's best-known novelists, in *Man of the People*. The corrupt politician Nanga shrewdly understands that the voters will respect his self-interest if he honours his promise to benefit them. Odili, a young intellectual bitterly opposed to the element personified by Chief Nanga, summarizes its outlook:

> We ignore man's basic nature if we say, as some critics do, that because a man like Nanga had risen overnight from poverty and insignificance to his present opulence he could be persuaded without much trouble to give it up again and return to his original state.
>
> A man who has just come in from the rain and dried his body and put on dry clothes is more reluctant to go out again than another who has been indoors all the time. The trouble with our new nation... was that none of us had been indoors long enough to be able to say 'To hell with it.' We had all been in the rain together until yesterday. Then a handful of us – the smart and the lucky and hardly ever the best – had scrambled for the one shelter our former rulers left, and had taken it over and barricaded themselves in. And from within they sought to persuade the rest through numerous loudspeakers, that the first phase of struggle had been won and that the next phase – the extension of the house – was even more important and called for new and original tactics; it required that all argument should cease and the whole people speak with one voice and that any more dissent and argument outside the door of the shelter would subvert and bring down the whole house.

Speaking through Odili, Achebe articulates the frustrations of the first postcolonial generation in Africa. He recounts the large sums of money piled up by a government of corrupt politicians and their betrayal of the dreams of independence. But dreams cannot suffice.

If independence is to become a reality, one must begin with an acute understanding of the social forces which are expressed through the political realm. The key factor is the nexus between social forces in the establishment of a system of accumulation.

Class is an elusive concept, one that has been subject to much dispute. Marx did not assign a formal definition to it. The critical last chapter of volume 3 of *Capital*, entitled 'Classes', was interrupted by Marx's death. The chapter breaks off just where he begins to elaborate the concept. To this day, there are several unsettled questions about class precisely because it is a dynamic construct: since classes are always being born and are always dying, they defy precise boundaries.

There are a number of common confusions about the concept. One is to view class as merely a statistical category. The press in the USA, for example, uses the term class to designate an income level or a conglomerate of occupations. Thus 'the middle class' is frequently employed as a residual, catch-all of everyone between the very rich and the very poor. In this usage, description is a low-grade substitute for explanation. Second, class is often understood in strictly economic terms. The trouble with this singular way of thinking is that the class struggle is ultimately fought out by political means. And as we have seen, classes propagate ideologies. Ideologies can convince people to embrace a position that does not correspond to their interests. Workers, for instance, sometimes espouse a bourgeois position, as did the 'hard hats' (a term derived from the helmets worn at construction sites in the USA) who supported the war in Vietnam. Third, and closely related, class is not primarily a matter of social origins. In contrast to belonging to a class, caste membership is ascribed by birth. You cannot switch from being an untouchable to being a Brahmin. But if you are born into the working class, you can become a capitalist.

While there is some mobility, class membership is not primarily a matter of individual experience and choice. For an overwhelming majority, class place is determined by underlying societal conditions. That a minority escapes its social origins legitimates the ideological myth 'from rags to riches'. Even if all the individuals who comprise classes were to switch places overnight, fundamental social structures would still remain. Only the members would change. Irrespective of whether the owner of a firm is a Rockefeller or someone born in a ghetto who then 'made it big', class exploitation is a basic dynamic of capitalistic life.

Properly understood, class is a grouping of agents who occupy a definite place in the social division of labour. In other words, classes must be seen in reference to the means of production. And it makes no sense to speak of a single class. The concept denotes opposition. Classes must be discerned in regard to their ever-changing relations with each other.

Non-class forces are also pivotal to understanding the nature of social relationships in the Third World. By non-class forces, we mean those groups in society that transcend class lines. Most important among them are religious, ethnic or gender-based groups as well as single-issue social movements (for instance, the environment). Whereas in the West, particularly in the USA, class, race and gender provide the matrix through which social phenomena are analysed, in most Third World countries the interplay of religion and ethnicity with class and gender is crucial to understanding social phenomena. For instance, the uneven impact of the 'Green Revolution' in India – benefiting high-caste Punjabi farmers in Northern India more than the lower-caste Biharis of central India – cannot be understood without taking into account the interplay of caste differences rooted in religion, ethnicity and class.

The interactions among class and non-class forces, the state and a strategy of accumulation suggests a basic set of relationships. A coalition of local propertied classes, the military and transnational interests supports an authoritarian state, supplanted by more democratic forms, bent on a dependent, subsequently neo-liberal, strategy: massive government intervention in the economy, severe exploitation of the labour force, and a substantial inflow of foreign investment accompanied by the outflow of national capital. Alternatively, in the afterglow of a revolution, a worker-peasant alliance spawns a bureaucratic ruling class whose strategy of accumulation emphasizes autonomous national development and withdrawal from the world capitalistic economy. A worker-peasant alliance can also bequeath state power to its agents. Labourers, bureaucrats and revolutionary intellectuals imperfectly represent the alliance and manage the ties of dependency by simultaneously bolstering and undermining global capitalism. In all instances, non-class forces qualify societal conflict. But what are the successes and failures of each strategy? What are the trade-offs? Who benefits and who loses?

The varying relationships among class, non-class forces, the state and accumulation rivet our gaze on efforts to remove the blockage which is at the core of underdevelopment. This explanatory framework requires continuous updating. What is needed is creative and original thinking in different historical contexts. In the next five chapters, we will see the extent to which distinct strategies adopted by Third World countries have lifted or reinforced the blockage restraining development.

Part III

Strategies of Accumulation

5 The Conventional Route, Joining Global Capitalism: Track 1 – Brazil

Formulating a strategy of development requires looking back over the trails Third World countries have already trod in their quest to accumulate capital. The real choices in the current global political economy are quite limited. One is to join the lane of traffic headed for capitalist development. (Tracks 1 and 2 distinguish the different conditions traversed by this outward-bound lane.) A second is to leave the mainstream, join the incoming traffic and aim for another destination. Third is to weave through the congestion, exploring an alternative passage, forcing an opening to the other end of the tunnel. Each route is a risky venture.

On the main thoroughfare, the police are tough; they are strict about enforcing the highway code, imposing it on all travellers. For those who choose the exit option, there are the twin dangers of coming up against a dead end and being run off the road by police with licence to patrol any territory. The other possibility, mindfully threading through dense traffic in search of an uncharted diversion, may wind up as a circuitous and harrowing path back to the capitalist lane. These journeys mark the entire range of options. *The choices are joining, leaving, or weaving.* Each one leads to distinctive fortunes and misfortunes, as Chapters 5–8 on Brazil, the Asian NICs, China and Mozambique illustrate.

BRAZIL IN THE LIMELIGHT

In 1975 two businessmen met in a posh New York hotel to strike a deal which would allow an American firm to distribute the ambrosial coffee beans produced by a Brazilian enterprise. One of the men, well heeled and expert in the ways of high finance, sensed that his counterpart was in a weak position, his company ripe for the taking. Flush with himself after the meeting, the urbane financier confided in an associate, 'I'm going to buy this company.' Within one year, he made good his pledge!

A typical case of *yanqui* imperialism quenching its thirst by lapping up the resources of the Third World? Not at all. Corpersucar, a Brazilian-based multinational titan, had swallowed up Hills Brothers, the fourth largest coffee producer in the USA. When the deal was consummated, Brazilian well-wishers let fly a barrage of telegrams deluging the offices of the financier who had made the purchase. The local press treated the transaction as a sign of Brazil's destiny: a Latin American powerhouse among the handful of industrial countries that dominate the world of international capital.

Indeed, observers have dubbed Brazil's meteoric rise to fortune and fame in the period 1968–74 as nothing less than a miracle. The country's performance during those years is often touted as a model for other nations aiming at rapid economic development. By any standard, Brazil is an extraordinary land, a mosaic of African, native American, Lusitanian and other European cultures. The largest country in Latin America and the fifth in size in the world, Brazil has a population of 150 million: one out of every three Latin Americans is a Brazilian. Its borders touch all the South American countries save Chile and Ecuador. Not only is its economy the ninth largest in the world, but its resource endowment is truly colossal: 16 per cent of the world's reserves of lumber; 25 per cent of the iron ore; and 60 per cent of the niobium, which is used for making jet engines, gas turbines and rockets. Compared to other national producers, Brazil ranks number one in its stock of tin, and number three in bauxite and manganese, the latter being an essential ingredient in the manufacture of warships, tanks and armour plating. Much of these resources are found in the Brazilian Amazon which covers 4 million square kilometres or 58 per cent of the country's territory. Brazil is also the world's top exporter of coffee, orange juice and soyabeans; the number one producer of sugar; and the second largest source of cattle and cocoa. Additionally, earnings from industrial exports exceed proceeds from raw materials and the sale of some state enterprises represented an important revenue stream in the mid-1990s.

Given its strategic importance and vast resources, Brazil's chances of pulling out of the quagmire of underdevelopment are seemingly greater than are those of other Third World countries. If the state capitalist model of development – widely adopted in the underdeveloped world – is to make good anywhere, it should score a success in Brazil. The fate of the Brazilian model has major implications for dozens of nations, if not for all of us.

Stripped to its essential features, the Brazilian strategy of development is to embrace global capitalism; tighten monetary and fiscal policy while accelerating privatizations and easing state monopolies so as to gain revenue; accumulate capital from above and outside in order to expand the stock of machinery and other productive equipment; exploit natural resources to sell on the world market; and concentrate income in the fists of the upper echelon of society and major foreign investors while promising that wealth will ultimately percolate down to the needy. Of course this development strategy cannot be properly understood without reference to how present patterns came to be.

THE BACKDROP

From the advent of Portuguese colonialism in the sixteenth century until the world depression of the 1930s, a bevy of local landowners and large merchant concerns, mainly English firms, dominated the economic and political life of Brazil. The planter oligarchy exported primary products – sugar, precious metals and coffee – to the burgeoning European market and imported manufactured products. These were mostly luxury goods. In the mid-1600s, for example, one-quarter of all profits generated from the export of Brazilian sugar was spent on imported wine.

The plantation owners and the European merchants sought to thwart the emergence of a manufacturing sector in Brazil and forestall diversification of the local economy. Both groups wanted to ensure a steady supply of cheap labour and the flow of inexpensive goods from overseas. To meet their needs, the colonial government allowed slave traders to import between four and five million Africans and banned the manufacture of products which would be competitive with finished goods produced in Europe.

The lion's share of the capital accumulated in Brazil was ploughed back into the production of primary goods for sale in overseas markets. Export earnings were used either for luxury consumption or the purchase of manufactured goods. A large share of the profits from the turn of the century rubber boom, which represented the beginning of the economic exploitation of the Amazon, was spent lavishly on luxury items and public buildings. Coffee, Brazil's major export crop, is especially susceptible to the vagaries of the international market. A rapid downturn in the price of coffee coupled with slack foreign demand could cripple the Brazilian economy, since the domestic market is too scant to cushion external shocks.

When the big shock came in the 1930s, the worldwide depression jolted the social order of Brazil. The economic convulsion set loose new class interests. A nascent, profit-minded, urban-based bourgeoisie had already sunk its savings into maiden industries. Railways were an especially lucrative investment given the interest of the planter oligarchy and merchants in transporting coffee to the ports. The entrepreneurs who built the railways required the services of an expanded proletariat, for which they had to compete with a lingering class whose strength had waned. The heady days of the planter-dominated agro-export economy were over.

With the industrialists in the driver's seat, the old economic vehicle was abandoned and replaced by a more dynamic model of capital accumulation. The new model, known as import substitution, was designed to develop Brazilian industries capable of producing basic manufactured items previously purchased abroad. Locally produced goods were to substitute for foreign imports, thereby lessening Brazil's reliance on external markets. Multinational corporations would provide the capital and technology to establish modern industries. The state was supposed to regulate these activities in order to ensure that foreign capital would not stall domestic capital accumulation.

Whereas local industrialists stood to gain the most from the new system, they could not ignore the demands of other classes. The rural bourgeoisie had not been totally disarmed. It tacitly agreed to go along with import substitution as long as the state maintained the price of coffee and pledged not to upset the system of land tenure from which the landlords benefited so handsomely. The urban petty bourgeoisie received government jobs and positions in public enterprises. The industrial proletariat was coopted by state-run unions and through fringe benefits, mainly social services and retirement packages. The huge mass of rural labourers continued to produce agricultural goods for export without deriving any concessions from the new corporate order.

An authoritarian regime ushered in import substitution during the 1930s and 1940s. Although the pro-fascist politicians were ousted from office following the Second World War, their populist successors similarly promoted rapid industrialization, quadrupling Brazil's production of manufactured goods in the period from 1930 to 1964. Also notable during this period was the expansion of the state's role in the economy. The government sought to channel foreign and domestic capital into designated sectors and to reserve critical areas for direct public investment. Government incentives channelled through the Superintendency for the Valorization of the Amazon, for example, led to the appropriation of land and investments in new agricultural and ranching activities by Amazonian merchants and traders, large landholders and southern industrialists.

To achieve success, an import substitution policy must foster capital accumulation based on a growing internal market and must increase the production of domestically manufactured goods. Yet in Brazil, the rural bourgeoisie's dogged control over an exploited work-force, combined with the political weight of an industrial bourgeoisie whose rate of profit hinged on keeping wages at a subsistence level, deformed and constricted the domestic market. Added to this, the decision to rely on foreign investors to 'rev up' the fledgeling industries put multinational corporations in a dominant position in some of the most dynamic sectors. By the late 1950s, Volkswagen, Mercedes, Willys, Ford and General Motors had established motor vehicle manufacture as the leading industry in Brazil. Bethlehem Steel began to exploit manganese deposits in the Amazon. Other foreign firms set the pace in the production of refrigerators, locomotives, radios and washing machines.

The industries which sold the bulk of their goods in the advanced capitalist countries realized the highest profit margins. The external orientation of industries driven by capital-intensive technology plus cheap labour reinforced the tendency of an underdeveloped economy to satisfy the wants of the well-to-do rather than the needs of the people of humble origins. This conjunction of interests was not the result of conscious political decisions, but rather reflected the logic of the market. Since the poor had no money, capitalists could not profit from producing for them. All in all, an import substitution policy caused some inefficiencies, stimulated a rising rate of inflation, created relatively few jobs, and stymied the growth of the domestic market. The policy was, however, proceeding into investment in capital goods, the technologies required to turn out finished products. This important move was interrupted by the economic crisis of the early 1960s. Triggered by a drop in prices for raw materials on the international market, the crisis coincided with political instability in Brazil.

The populist presidents of the post-1945 period rode to power on the back of multiclass electoral alliances. To form winning coalitions, the populist leaders made honeyed promises, all of which could not possibly be honoured. The pledge to provide price supports and to fund industrial projects laid excessive claims on the Treasury. The professed commitment to increase wages on a par with the rate of inflation could not be reconciled with the economic stabilization measures enjoined by both domestic and foreign industrialists.

Brazil's leaders postponed a political breakdown for two decades, adroitly combining economic growth, partly based on a chronic trade deficit, and high inflation rates. But one impresario after another found it impossible to run the show. Getulio Vargas committed suicide in office in 1953. His successor, Juscelino Kubitschek, completed a full term but bequeathed a major crisis to Jânio Quadros, who resigned after only eight months at the helm. Three years later João Goulart, formerly Quadros' vice-president, was deposed in a military coup.

THE STAGE IS SET

At a historic rally in Rio de Janeiro on 13 March 1964, President Goulart stood nervously behind a speaker's platform. Facing him were 150 000 workers flanked by several rows of plumed fighting cocks: white-helmeted army officers, their machine guns at the ready. Goulart was apprehensive because he feared the day of reckoning his predecessors had so resolutely postponed.

Perhaps the president briefly contemplated the course of events that led him to the dais on this day: the economic engine serving as the motor force of the populist programme had run out of steam. The only real option was to ask Washington to provide the means to rejuvenate Brazil's efforts to achieve industrialization. But the IMF and the USA, wary of a president who was a wealthy rancher but soft on 'the Communist threat', had laid down harsh terms for a loan. Stung by the monetary fund's conditions, Goulart then contemplated walking out on the talks and declaring a unilateral default.

There was no easy answer to the question he undoubtedly pondered: was the government's popular base sufficiently large and adequately organized to enable the regime to weather the political storm which would erupt if Brazil refused to take shelter under the IMF's umbrella? Brazilians of various ideological hues called for a clear-cut decision: either cope with the tumultuous elements generated by the international market or pay the price and pull out of the storm. When faced with this dilemma, Goulart vacillated. He played for time, initially agreeing to the conditions set by the IMF and later balking at implementing them. Consequently, in March 1964, enraged foreign creditors curtailed assistance to Brazil. At the same time, all parties to the populist pact impatiently demanded that the government honour its end of the bargain. Everyone knew that the cupboard was bare, but nobody was prepared to walk away hungry. Goulart had to decide whose stomach to feed.

At this point, perspiring profusely, the president grasped the dais. The enthusiastic applause of the assembled workers rose to an earsplitting crescendo. Goulart dramatically signed two decrees that buried Brazil's post-war *modus vivendi*. The first one called for the nationalization of all private oil refineries operating in Brazil. The second bill announced the expropriation of large tracts of land, the oligarchy's massive holdings. In addition, Goulart proposed to enfranchise illiterate workers and *favelados*, the inhabitants of sprawling slums and jerry-built squatter settlements, massive appendages of untold misery and human despair surrounding Brazilian cities.

These moves irrevocably violated the class truce of the last two decades, burning the regime's few remaining bridges to international capital and alienating domestic capital, especially the rural bourgeoisie. Some military officers already favoured deposing the president. He had antagonized officers by siding with subaltern ranks in a dispute with their superiors. Thus the military establishment claimed that Goulart was an enemy of the constitution; he had initiated the take-overs and land reform measures by presidential decree, not by legal process. Dutifully noting their responsibility to defend the constitution, the armed forces promptly ousted the civilian-politicians.

With hindsight, it is clear that Goulart played the card he should have held for another hand. He gambled on the poorly organized and deeply divided working class against the allied forces of domestic and international capital, which put their money on the odds: the Brazilian armed forces. Goulart made a fool's bet. The soldiers, holding all the aces, marched on the capital unopposed. Having tempted fortune, a bad wager under the circumstances, Goulart made his last move as president when he slipped over the border into exile in Uruguay.

SAME CAST, NEW CHARACTERS

Central to the Brazilian drama was the Johnson administration's decision to cut off all financial assistance to the national authorities (but not to politically acceptable state governors), deeming the Goulart government to be 'the most serious problem for us in Latin America – more serious in fact than Cuba since the missile crisis'. Thus when the generals staged the coup on April 1964, US naval and airborne units were immediately mobilized to support their fellow soldiers. Although foreign military intervention was not required, the USA opened the economic pipeline, pumping aid as quickly as the spigot had been turned off. The US AID dished out $50 million to the new regime within hours of the soldiers grabbing state power. From the vantage point of policy makers in Washington during the Cold War era, not only was Brazil the strategic linchpin of the South Atlantic, but also the soldier-politicians' ideological outlook dovetailed with the American national interest.

The generals called for a rapid expansion of industry driven by a massive infusion of FDI and foreign borrowing. A system of incentives was established to steer capital into areas and regions deemed important by the state. Low wages and high productivity could ensure substantial profit rates in the new industries. Admittedly, this strategy would not remedy the perennial problem of the constricted internal market. Although the economy would maintain its export orientation, the low cost of labour would convince investors that Brazilian exports could be priced competitively in world markets. Export earnings would be used to repay the debts incurred in the new wave of industrialization, leaving Brazil with a modern industrial base and placing the economy in a strong position in the global pecking order. At that point, wages could be raised so as to allow all Brazilians to share the growing wealth. The curse of underdevelopment would be but a relic, a legacy shorn of its most odious aspects.

Realizing the vast potential of the untapped resources of the sparsely populated Brazilian Amazon, the military regime also adopted an aggressive strategy to exploit these resources. The Amazon contained 79.7 per cent of the country's lumber resources, 81 per cent of its fresh water, half its iron ore deposits, 93 per cent of its aluminium, almost all of its tin deposits, and the largest source of rock salt in the world. To encourage private investment in the region, the Superintendency for the Development of the Amazon was thus created in 1964. The regime established incentives and provided subsidized credit for land acquisition. Significantly, foreign corporations were now eligible for these benefits. Various decisions and decrees by the military government, for example, reversed a nationally stringent mineral code. This paved the way for the exploitation of iron-ore deposits by Hanna Mining Company in southern Brazil and by US Steel in the Amazon basin. In 1968, to take advantage of the new incentives, King Ranch of Texas established a 180 000-acre cattle-ranch.

In this script, each class was cast in a specific part. Playing a premier role, the military provided ideological leadership, forging cohesion in the new order, partly by embellishing their self-seeking policies with modernization lingo. The coup was not a coup but a 'democratic revolution'. Bureaucrats were not bureaucrats but 'technocrats'. Hard political choices were to be made not through political competition but by the 'scientific methods' deployed by technocrats who would render 'fair and impartial' judgements in a backward society lacking 'the discipline' to advance itself. Although the power behind the technocrats was evident, the ranking officers were said to be 'above politics', representing no one class or faction but rather 'the national interest'.

If the populace failed to understand the logic of modernization, there were other ways to convince people of their true interests. The military found Brazil's labour law, a copy of Mussolini's, a handy instrument. It was basically unchanged since Vargas had introduced the legislation. Under its provisions, military rulers unleashed repression against rural organizations. Additionally, the Ministry of Labour exercised close control over union operations. Worker organizations outside official structures were banned. In deciding upon union recognition, the ministry stressed social welfare programmes, not the unions' role in representing workers' interests. Budgets were monitored and strike funds proscribed. The ministry reserved the right to approve slates of candidates for office. It supervised the election process and vetoed winners whom it deemed unacceptable. The ministry took over the administration of unions, seizing monies and occupying labour organizations' headquarters. If these techniques were unsuccessful, the military politicians relied on brute force. Amnesty International reported that the Brazilian authorities frequently inflicted torture: electric shocks, near drownings, simulated execution, *Pau de Arara* (hanging from a parrot's perch or rack), sexual abuse and detention in refrigerated cells.

On the front stage, too, the multinational corporations were supposed to provide essential ingredients in the Brazilian strategy of development. The legacy of import substitution under the populist government was a demonstrated capacity to produce manufactured goods but not capital goods. Brazil needed computers for automation and quality control in mass production as well as state-of-the-art mechanisms for extraction in the country's huge petrochemical industry. The multinational corporations were the only possible source of these much sought-after capital goods, technologies whose utilization require skills usually furnished by foreign experts. Powerful corporations generated the capital to finance the technology and skilled personnel, both directly through the investment of their own funds and indirectly by their very presence in Brazil, which the big banks viewed as a green light to go ahead. Added to this, corporate collaboration facilitated access to foreign markets: an essential element in the government's plan to sell the new products abroad. Without participation by multinational corporations, this whole scheme would have been unworkable.

Although Brazilian capitalists were to be among the main beneficiaries of the miracle plan, they were assigned a supporting, not a starring, role. Their part was to provide practical information about the political and economic climate in their home country and to whip up popular enthusiasm for the performance. In Brazil, as elsewhere in the Third World, nationalist sentiment against multinational penetration runs high. In fact, Brazilians of diverse classes have backed legislation enacted to control the multinational firms, though with the worldwide move towards neo-liberal globalization in the 1990s, the civilian regime headed by Fernando Henrique Cardoso put out the welcome mat for transnationals which, by then, were no longer described as multinationals because holdings merged, circumventing territorial borders and largely escaping regulatory frameworks. Notwithstanding military might, whether in the background or foreground, economic policies without a veneer of nationalist respectability are politically unwise. Nationalist appeals, nonetheless, have their limits since they may spotlight social inequalities.

The working class was cast in the role of the fall guy. Punished by wage cuts, the chosen weapon in the fight against inflation, workers were required to produce goods cheaply enough to guarantee the nation's export earnings. Moreover, the regime banned working-class political activity because it could threaten the stability needed to attract foreign investors. The generals sought to silence the workers by promising to house and feed them if they would only sacrifice current consumption for a secure future.

In this wave of industrialization, more Brazilian working women participated in the formal sectors of the economy. However, women workers were concentrated in low-wage, low-status, unskilled or semiskilled work. This sexual division of labour meant women received lower wages and were subjected to harsh working conditions. In São Paulo, according to a 1980 survey, 73.5 per cent of women industrial workers earned less than twice the minimum wage. In the De Millus lingerie factory in Rio de Janeiro, set production targets required more than eight hours of work per day, yet women received no extra money for overtime. In an attempt to reach production targets, women were permitted to go to the toilet once a day and restricted to a 20-minute lunch break.

Backstage, the rural bourgeoisie would go along with the show provided that the large agricultural estates were left intact. The deal struck by the landlords in the 1930s was still in effect. Behind the scenes as well, the *favelados* were marginal to the political economy of Brazil.

They produced little and consumed less. Even more marginal were the Amazonian Indians, regarded as 'culturally retrograde and as obstacles to progress'. Inasmuch as colonization of the Amazon constituted an invasion of ancestral lands, the Indians were direct victims of the plunder of the Amazon. The new highways and related state projects affected the territories of 96 groups. Migrants introduced malaria, measles, and influenza to previously isolated indigenous peoples. Pacification efforts – for example, paving the way for the Trans-Amazon Highway – led to an influenza epidemic among the Parakanân Indians. Highway workers were also reported to have raped Indian women. In other areas, government-authorized mineral exploration and prospecting activities brought sickness and death. In 1972, a report by a French physician noted that over 60 per cent of the Surui contracted tuberculosis. A World Bank study documents that 'diseases transmitted by the new settlers have decimated whole tribes'. Invasions of indigenous people's lands continued during the 1980s, when 13 000 Indians were within the area delimited for the Greater Carajás iron-ore project. Thus, when the curtain rose on the Brazilian miracle, the underclass was decidedly off-stage and was assigned no role in the prepared script.

ACT ONE: THE DRAMA UNFOLDS

After a marked slump from 1964 to 1967, when policy makers crafted a new strategy, the Brazilian economy inaugurated a remarkable six-year boom. Showered with accolades, government planners were dubbed 'wizards' and Brazil was touted as 'the Latin American darling of the international business community'. Academic pundits celebrated the technocrats' policies, sanctifying them as a general economic doctrine and proliferating theories on why military rule lends itself to conquering underdevelopment.

There is no mistaking Brazil's economic achievements during the period 1968–74. The GNP ballooned at a rate of 10 per cent per year, the highest in Latin America. The industrial sector enlarged even faster, 11 per cent per year. The agricultural sector increasingly focused on production for foreign consumption. Agriculture-based exports, excluding coffee, grew at an average annual rate of 22 per cent between 1965 and 1977. True, the full-throttle expansion of international investment and the carefree disregard for society's poor made the meekest observers a bit queasy, prompting one journalist to comment ruefully, 'The Brazilian economy has grown... in much the same way as a Brazilian drives his car. That is extremely fast, disregarding everyone else on the road, narrowly avoiding accidents, and not stopping to consider whether his passengers have been left behind.' But during the miracle years, such criticism was rarely heard.

The government barred open questioning of the rocketing foreign borrowing. Acting without scrutiny by the press, the flamboyant Minister of Planning, Antônio Delfim Netto, repeatedly expressed unwavering conviction in his own course of action: 'We know 100 per cent of the population are getting 100 per cent of the national income: the distribution is not important.' This posture, characteristic of Mr. Delfim's aggressive personality, led local commentators to quip that the minister's spherical physique illustrates that the distribution of national income is no problem for at least one citizen.

Turning to the evidence for Mr. Delfim's claims: under military tutelage, the authorities stepped up domestic production of weapons. Brazil, which has the Third World's biggest arms factory, exceeded the $1 billion mark in export sales per year. Government patronage extended into this realm and others as well. The state served as a forum in which local and foreign capital could set the terms of joint ventures. To the extent that Brazilian capitalists lacked the muscle to vie with multinational corporations, the government served as the primary Brazilian participant in these ventures. The state, drawing on the country's vast resources, acted as an agent of capital accumulation.

High-tech, high-profit enterprises spawned by the alliance between state and multinational capital quickly outstripped the capacity of Brazil's creaky infrastructure. The state reacted by expanding its direct investment in basic industries, especially steel, fuel and power as well as in such related activities as communications and transportation. Ungrudgingly, the military-politicians and bureaucrats abandoned their conservative notions of free enterprise, sanctioning instead government ownership of a major portion of the assets of the 100 top firms in the country. In 1972, the state controlled 46 per cent of the assets of the largest 100 non-financial corporations in Brazil; foreign companies accounted for 31 per cent, and local private interests held 23 per cent.

In the 1970s a welter of state companies was established with catchy titles usually ending in 'brás', signifying Brazil in Portuguese: Electrobrás, Portobrás, Siderbrás, Nuclebrás, and a few hundred others. These state companies have consumed the largest portion of the federal budget. In the 1980s, their payrolls carried 1.4 million employees who enjoyed lifetime job security. The ranks of the state-run enterprises are filled with retired military officers who are offered bonuses for showing up for work and a share of annual profits even in firms which generate no profit. Researchers have found that Brazil's state-run corporations are 50 per cent as efficient in their use of capital for productivity and job creation as are private domestic and foreign firms.

Massive state involvement in the economy made some business people squeamish. The head of one foreign concern regretted that Brazil had joined the socialist camp. Another executive, who also confounded socialism and statism, remarked: 'It's like doing business with the Russians: you have to play by their rules.' These misgivings, however, were uncustomary. US-based multinational corporations increased their direct investment in Brazilian manufacturing from $846 million in 1966 to over $2 billion in 1973. Large investments poured in from West Germany, France, England and Japan as well.

By the late 1970s, multinational corporations held predominant interests in over half of Brazil's 100 largest private manufacturing enterprises and accounted for about 50 per cent of manufacturing sales. Forty per cent of Brazil's biggest corporations were subsidiaries of multinational concerns. These concerns controlled all of Brazil's production of automotive materials and rubber goods, 94 per cent of pharmaceuticals, 55 per cent of machinery, 32 per cent of foodstuffs, 32 per cent of aluminium, 32 per cent of pulp and paper and 80 per cent of chemicals.

From the vantage point of the state, what the multinational corporations did with their profits was their own business. Tax regulations drawn up by the generals left the state with a small cut. Foreign investors remitted the lion's share of the profits to their home countries. There was no legal requirement to do otherwise ever since the military government nullified a law enacted during Goulart's tenure stipulating that foreign concerns must plough a large measure of locally earned profits back into the host economy. Thus in the mid-1970s, the Brazilian Congress reported that the 11 multinational corporations most active in the country had invested a total of $238 million in the economy over the last half-century and had exported $744.5 million in profits during the past decade.

The Brazilian capitalists with a foot in the door of the massive multinational and state projects reaped something of a bonanza. Their compatriots who retained control of their own operations also cashed in on the booming economy. But many small and medium sized businesses went bankrupt. In an attempt to drive down inflation, the state adopted tight credit policies, which took a toll on all but the largest entrepreneurs.

Local business people could have questioned the extensiveness of foreign capital in the Brazilian economy, but to raise doubts about the legitimacy of the multinational corporations would have meant challenging the very basis of the generals' development strategy and indeed of the regime itself. Rendering such demands effective would have required mobilizing a constituency to support them. The working class was the only candidate for this role. Yet the spectre of a mobilized proletariat rallying against the big corporations was as frightening to Brazilian capitalists as it was to their foreign counterparts.

The development of the Amazon during this period followed a *latifundia*-based model which entailed the monopolization of large tracts of land for commercial farming or cattle-ranching. Operation Amazonia provided both tax breaks and crop subsidies for those investing in agribusinesses in the Amazon interior. Between 1966 and 1969 alone, the number of livestock projects increased from four to 162. In a time of increasing unemployment and landlessness, cattle-ranching contributed little. One job was created for every 2000 head of cattle. As the Amazonian *caboclo* [peasant] says, 'Where cattle move in, we move out, cattle mean hunger.' In addition, according to figures prepared by the Brazilian Institute of Forestry Development, cattle ranching and highway construction were to blame for the deforestation of approximately 60 per cent of the total area divested of trees between 1966 and 1975. By itself, cattle-ranching projects undertaken with government fiscal incentives accounted for 33.6 per cent of the area. The Amazonian Indians who survived malaria, measles and influenza experienced the erosion of their traditional land rights, and were integrated into the regional economy as a reserve labour force.

For the common people, conditions worsened considerably during the miracle years. By 1970 the real minimum wage had plummeted to 50 per cent of its value of a decade before. Nearly 60 per cent of Brazilians working in industry received only the official minimum wage or less. And they had little to consume. Despite the profusion of such luxury items as passenger cars, the production of staples – rice and beans, the bulk of the working-class diet – declined precipitously during the early 1970s. Moreover, the diminishing amount of affordable food had to be divided among more people: Brazil's population was growing at the brisk pace of 3 per cent per year.

In greater São Paulo, the largest industrial centre in the country, the proportion of houses with access to piped water fell from 61 per cent in 1950 to 56 per cent in 1973. After six years of military rule, 52 per cent of Brazilians suffered from malnutrition: an increase of 7 per cent from the time of the coup. In addition, the infant mortality rate rose a staggering 45 per cent in the period from 1960 to 1973, climbing to a level exceeded in Latin America only by that of Haiti. In terms of its social effect, the miracle years meant that the majority of Brazilians were hungrier, sicker, dying younger and paid less than in the placid days before the wonder plan.

Another trend was the increasing incorporation of women in the wage labour force. As Sonia Alvarez notes, 'While the official discourse of Brazil's military rulers extolled the virtues of the family and traditional womanhood, the regressive economic policies of the new regime destroyed working-class families' survival strategies and thrust millions of women into the work force.' The number of women in the total labour force increased from 13.5 per cent in 1950, to 20.8 per cent in 1970, and to 27.4 per cent in 1980. Middle- and upper-class women entered the job market as professionals. Meanwhile, a rising cost of living left little choice for women in impoverished families who had to search for work. Responsible for the welfare of their families and hence their communities, women were driven by the continuing decline of the conditions for Brazil's poor. Consequently, women were burdened not only with traditional duties, but also with the task of augmenting family income by participating in the formal labour market. Women unable to find work in the factories had no other alternative than to turn to domestic service or prostitution.

At the same time that its inadequate standard of living declined, the working class was stripped of its political rights. Apart from exercising tight control of electoral politics, the military brought organized labour to heel by dismissing union leaders and handpicking new ones. The government unilaterally determined wages. Negotiations between workers and management were proscribed. Workers who sought to spark 'illegal' strikes were incarcerated for a minimum of four years. We have already noted what a labour organizer could expect during the period of incarceration.

ACT TWO: A FAILED MIRACLE

Suddenly, in 1974, as quickly as the economy had boomed six years before, the growth rate declined. Domestic consumption plunged and inventories piled up. A mounting deficit in trade and in balance of payments caused financial loans to dwindle. New international loans failed to pick up the slack. In 1975 inflation rose 20 per cent and the cost of living index climbed 32 per cent. When the curtain dropped on the miracle period, a former cabinet minister uttered: 'We are at a dead end, trapped, and so is [President João Baptista] Figueiredo, even if he doesn't know it.' There is no doubt about how quickly the tide turned, but what explains the sudden ebbing?

The greater the expansion of the pace-setting sector during the boom – upgraded technology, high-profit manufacturing – the greater the need to import capital goods. Brazil could pay for capital goods only by exporting its manufactured products. But Brazil's finished products – television sets, for example – are sold in highly competitive markets. Not only did an export-oriented economy generate an increasing need for imported technology, but also many of Brazil's leading enterprises, subsidiaries of foreign-based corporations, transferred abroad mushrooming profits made on the sale of export products. The need for foreign exchange was also an incentive for the continued and increased exploitation of the nation's natural resources, mainly commodities for export.

A sky-high growth rate, which attracted foreign investment and loans to cover the mounting deficit, was the glue which held the whole lopsided package together. In a heady economic climate, government planners envisaged a happy future in which strong demand and easy credit would be around forever. Their projections came to naught, however. The onset of the world recession in 1975 restrained the customers who purchased Brazilian goods and slammed the brakes on domestic economic growth. Policy makers debated how to compensate for the shrinkage of worldwide demand.

The obvious solution was to offset the contraction of foreign markets with increased domestic sales. But to stimulate domestic sales, a nation's industries must produce goods which satisfy the needs of the people. In addition, wages must be sufficient to enable the masses to buy these goods. In Brazil in the mid-1970s, the realization of one or both of these conditions would have knocked the legs out from under the entire development strategy. After all, the shopping basket from which Brazilians could choose their goods was not the result of mere happenstance. The economic menu served up to society at large reflected the tastes of Brazil's upper crust and the appetite of foreign capital. The delicacies gobbled up by these prosperous consumers were obviously not the common people's pickings. Wages were depressed expressly to court foreign investment and to fetch high profits in export markets. In effect, the allied interests of the locally dominant classes and international capital formed an economy dangerously exposed to external shocks.

In the late 1970s Brazil's foreign exchange reserves dipped to perilously low levels. The rates of inflation and unemployment soared. Many businesses folded. The generals' only real option was to enter secret negotiations with the US government and the IMF. Finally, in November 1982, an official from the central bank of Brazil visited Washington to deliver a letter of intent to the Fund. In such a document, the sending government indicates the steps that it is prepared to take to set its economic house in order. Adoption is contingent upon the application of stiff austerity measures. If IMF officials deem the proposed measures adequate, a rescue package is normally provided.

Two weeks after Brazil filed its letter of intent, the US President, Ronald Reagan, sought to add a touch of personal warmth to the already cosy relationship between the two countries. He visited Brazil, meeting President Figueiredo, the country's fifth consecutive military ruler. In the midst of a sumptuous feast at a formal state dinner, Mr. Reagan rose, lifted a glass of Brazil's finest wine, and invited those present 'to join me in a toast to President Figueiredo and the people of Bolivia'. When an aide discreetly pointed out his gaffe, Mr. Reagan corrected himself: 'That's where I'm going.' Wrong again. His itinerary included Bogotá, the capital of Colombia, not Bolivia.

No matter. The president was preoccupied with other business. He announced that the USA would grant a jumbo loan of $1.2 billion to keep the Brazilian economy afloat during the coming weeks. But he did not mention that negotiations over the loan had begun in October and had been hushed up so as not to embarrass the military regime before elections were staged. Instead, he applauded the government's pledge to institute austerity measures – a reduction in the spending of state-controlled enterprises, slashes in social programmes, increased taxes and further restrictions on wages – in exchange for an injection of international finance.

At the close of the state dinner, President Reagan again hoisted a glittering wine glass and offered to allow a Brazilian astronaut to ride on a US space shuttle. The offer startled his hosts since there are no Brazilian astronauts. A local commentator twitted the politicians, suggesting that planning minister Delfim Netto should be the first Brazilian put into orbit. Had he not sent Brazil's inflation rate, then over 100 per cent, skyrocketing? Had he not launched the foreign debt, already $83 billion, into outer space? Coming down to earth, a practical observer noted that a relaxation of US import controls on Brazilian shoes would make the people happier than a free ride on a guided missile.

A fortnight after Mr. Reagan's goodwill mission, the store of funds supplied by the US government was depleted. Brasilia immediately announced that it was seeking an additional $1.5 billion in emergency loans. The *New York Times* declared that Brazil was on the verge of financial collapse. Similar crises in Mexico and Argentina had shaken the confidence of the international banks in investment in Latin America. No loan officer, explained the *Times*, wanted to be the last one to extend credit to Brazil before the country went bankrupt.

After a spree of negotiations dragged on for two months, the international banking community mounted a massive rescue operation. Finished in late 1983, its dimensions were staggering. Designed to put Humpty Dumpty together again, a cornucopia of loans, credits and refinancing provided Brazil with an infusion of over $30 billion. The agreement called on Brazil to implement a stiff austerity programme, cut its budget deficit in half by 1984, and again divide it by a factor of two in 1985.

The IMF declared that the crisis was resolved, but for many Brazilians it meant climbing down to the bottom of the ladder. Typical is the deteriorating situation that Luiz Antônio Pereira and his wife Vinhais have faced. They live in a *favela* in Rio de Janeiro with their two sons, aged 10 and 12. Still employed as a delivery man, Mr. Pereira is more fortunate than many of his compatriots. Galloping inflation, however, has changed the Pereiras' lifestyle dramatically. 'We're restricting ourselves to staples,' Mrs. Pereira told a *Wall Street Journal* correspondent. 'Last year our main dish was soup. We can't do that anymore,' she added. The interview in the *Journal*, however, did not recount what remained on the table when soup was beyond the family's means.

Also worrisome for the Pereiras is medical care. To pay for emergency dental treatment, Mrs. Pereira sold her sewing machine. Root canal work and glasses for the children are out of the question. Yet unlike most *favelados*, Mr. Pereira is bringing home some money. His job is all that separates the Pereira family from the untold misery and abject fear that haunts the teeming mass of unemployed Brazilians.

The Pereiras and their cohorts on the lower rung of the social ladder immediately felt the effects of the austerity formula prescribed by the IMF. Two months after the deal with the Fund had been sealed, the unemployment problem reached explosive proportions. Out of a total work force of 5.2 million in São Paulo, for example, 800 000 people were jobless. Each week 1500 more workers joined the ranks of the idle. Added to this, the rate of inflation rose to 210 per cent in 1983.

Against this background, desperate groups of homeless persons seized public lands in Rio de Janeiro, housewives in areas adjoining

Brasilia burned utility bills, and frustrated youths in Rio and São Paulo stoned and axed public buses. The political climate was increasingly feverish. President Figueiredo rushed a note to Delfim Netto asking, 'Is it possible to endure this?' According to *Time* magazine, what perturbed the president was not the inflationary spiral or unemployment but the climbing interest rates, which upset the business community. The April 1983 march of unemployed workers lit the fuse that ignited a keg of political dynamite. Hordes of disgruntled labourers romped through the streets, pillaging shops and desecrating hallowed symbols of authority, including a governor's mansion. Storming major arteries in city centres, the rioters chanted, 'Stop unemployment or we will stop Brazil.' A European ambassador, possibly recalling President Reagan's difficulties in uncurling the names of American countries, offered to translate the grievance to outsiders: 'The riots could be a message from the people that they're not willing to accept the conditions that foreign bankers and the International Monetary Fund are imposing on the country.' Not only the downtrodden but also the well-to-do chafed on account of the economic crisis. As a prominent Brazilian lawyer put it, 'Before, every Brazilian was an expert on soccer; now we've become a nation of economists.' For Brazilians of all classes, the suture joining hunger and international capital is not an imperceptible stitch sewn into the minds of a long-haired intelligentsia but a nasty scar apparent to all save the most undiscerning bystanders.

ACT THREE: IN SEARCH OF A NEW MIRACLE

To sustain the marriage between the state and global capitalism, Brazil continued to borrow heavily from both international public and private banks. In 1964, the Brazilian foreign debt came to $3 billion; by 1974, with the onset of the world petroleum crisis, it reached $17 billion. By 1982, the debt oscillated between $80 billion and $88 billion. Nine years later, in 1991, the debt stood at $123 billion. Complicating matters was a spiralling inflation rate which rose from 34 per cent in 1974 and 1975 to almost 300 per cent in 1986. The average inflation rate for the 1980s was 284 per cent. In 1992, inflation soared to 1500 per cent, an improvement from 7000 per cent in 1990. Behind these aggregate figures, the Brazilian people continue to suffer.

A wide range of solutions has been attempted. The Cruzado Plan of 1986, a heterodox approach to the problem of inflation, imposed a general freeze on the prices of goods, an upward adjustment of wages, then wage restraints. The Summer Plan of 1989 was a return to a more orthodox formula: a temporary price freeze, an emphasis on collective bargaining, a credit squeeze, and reductions in the government bureaucracy and spending. But the problems mounted and inflation continued to rise. To cope with the country's growing external obligations, in-house technocrats favoured the voluntary renegotiation of the debt to allow breathing space. Some economists held that Brazil should reduce its economic dependence on foreign markets by adopting a modified model of expanded domestic consumption of agricultural and industrial products. Members of the opposition party discussed the possibility of the wholesale cancellation of foreign debts, claiming that the advanced capitalist countries have exploited the Third World and have recycled the profits in the form of loans. Taking this logic one step further, critics called for the creation of a debtors' cartel to prevail upon the North for easier repayment terms.

In response to growing resistance to its austerity programme, in 1983, the state began to ignore parts of its agreement with the IMF. The fund consequently suspended payments of a second tranche. Brazil was forced to come up with a new fiscal programme to present to the IMF. The relationship between Brazil and the Fund continued to follow this zigzag pattern of recrimination and rapprochement through the 1980s. Subject to increasing domestic tensions, the Brazilian state would ignore policies set forth in letters of intent. The IMF would then withhold new loans. In 1986, riots erupted in Rio de Janeiro and Brasilia over the latest adjustment efforts. Soon thereafter, Brazil initiated a debt moratorium. Faced with the possibility of a cancellation of loans, the state returned to the fold in 1987, only again to suspend payments in 1989.

To contend with the tilt towards the conventions of international finance, a government must exercise an ironclad political will and enjoy the unwavering support of the popular classes. It must rest assured of its ability to inspire the masses to withstand a Niagara of pressure. The ability of a government to mobilize the general populace implies deliberate and effective mass organization, which is a far cry from the actual situation that prevailed in Brazil. Until a regime with these attributes comes to power, the vaunted debt threat emanating from this potential strongman in the Third World was nothing more than a pipe dream.

In the meantime traditional plans for bailing out Brazil were untenable. If the government actually played the game by the bankers' rules, the stiff conditions for debt repayment would have mired Brazil in deeper recession. Short of revamping the debt structure itself, Brazil's foreign debts would not peter out, and whether it would ever be cleared up appeared to be a $100 billion question. No one was more acutely aware of the intractability of the problem than were the foreign bankers. On the one hand, they reaped whopping profits in Brazil: up 126 per cent from 1981 to 1982, including 20 per cent of Citibank's worldwide net earnings in the latter year. On the other, the banks themselves were trapped in this debt structure. Citibank and some other large US banks increased their loan loss reserves in 1987. In fact, this policy represented an internal transfer of funds, and did not relieve the burden on the debtor countries. The banks still attempted to recover the interest and principal outstanding on their loans.

Thus in the revised script, we were witness to – nay, actors in – an unfolding drama of debt peonage in which the big banks and multi-national corporations portrayed the plantation owner, the Brazilian bourgeoisie was the foreman, and the labouring classes were the serfs. The *dénouement* was a failed miracle, a modern day Third World tragedy. It was a melancholy conclusion to an economic *tour de force* once touted as a magic cure for the ills of underdevelopment.

More specifically, the difficulty was that Brazil's tight-fisted military rulers turned a blind eye to the nation's domestic market, taking at face value the World Bank's claim that export earnings could filter down to all reaches of society. This strategy was shipwrecked on the torrents of external markets and the government's own miscalculations, particularly overinvestment in glamorous, state-run and inefficient development projects. Aware of the shortage of fuel, Mr. Delfim tried to stoke these enterprises, but Brazil's economic furnaces would not heat up. The country was caught between high interest rates and weak overseas demand. Hectored by his critics, Mr. Delfim, not one to mince his words, angrily snapped:

> Of course we have a neo-capitalist economy – no denying it – with all of its errors and all its faults. It's an unstable economy and, what is more serious, no mechanism is provided for redistribution of national income. But I would like to know in which capitalist country things are any different.

CURTAIN CALL: THE DEBT NOOSE TIGHTENS

Whatever the shortcomings of Brazil's economic performance, Mr. Delfim should be given a fair hearing. The government's chief planning expert never looked upon development as the national use of resources for the benefit of the majority. His is a narrower concept centring on sheer economic growth. Judged on this basis, Brazil's rapid industrialization is a truly impressive feat. Under Mr. Delfim, the miracle plan certainly did achieve six years of real growth averaging 10 per cent per annum. One facet of this growth is the export of national capital to other countries. Brazilian construction firms have established subsidiaries in Africa and the Middle East, and a government-owned petroleum corporation is active in oil exploration abroad. What is more, Brazil's new-found capacity to produce steel outstrips domestic demand. Siderbrás steel company is negotiating to export semi-finished steel slabs to corporations in the USA despite the objections of American labour and the doubts of Washington.

Brazil's economic accomplishments during the miracle period suggest that, in the underdeveloped world, the most expedient way to accumulate capital rapidly is to woo foreign investment and to exploit thoroughly the domestic labour force. This strategy is usually the work of the military and the propertied classes led by a non-popular client state. This species of capitalism is propagating, nowadays most often under civilian regimes, displacing the old-fashioned neo-colonial regimes, and supplanting socialist projects.

In the dependent statist variant of capitalism, accumulation has fallen more to the public sector. Compared to Chile and Guatemala, Brazil relied heavily on gigantic state-owned enterprises and the regulation of much of the economy. To be sure, Brazil sustained respectable growth rates after the miracle period. In 1985, the country's first civilian president in 21 years took office, and the economy grew at an astonishing rate of 8 per cent, the world's fastest. The recovery, however, was accomplished by inflationary means: a vast increase in the money supply, a hike in the government's internal debt (what it owed to Brazilians), and high interest rates.

In its attempt to amass funds to service a huge foreign debt, an externally-oriented economy must rely on its export earnings. The logical move is to make exports cheaper in order to increase sales. This is achieved by devaluing the currency. Devaluation, however, causes imports to become more expensive. The rub is that imported goods are essential to production. Falling production levels lead to diminishing revenues. Then when the value of the currency drops, debt servicing is more expensive. The debt noose tightens as a result of a policy designed to loosen it.

Another noose slowly tightening around the country is the continuing degradation of the environment. Faced with larger bills to pay, there is an even greater incentive to exploit the export potential of the Amazon. The Greater Carajás Programme, an iron-ore mining project, for example, entailed the partial or total deforestation of an area larger than France and Britain put together. Foreign funds financed ecologically damaging projects, such as the World Bank-supported Tucurui hydroelectric dam which flooded 21 600 hectares and displaced 5000 families. According to the World Resources Institute, in the 1980s, not only was Brazil the Third World's largest debtor, it was also the biggest deforester. In addition, pollution in industrialized centres such as São Paulo is a major concern. As the country struggles to live up to its external obligations, it is slowly eating into its stock of natural resources. Without cutting the structural cords of underdevelopment, the more a Third World country thrashes about trying to escape, the tighter the knot.

Is there a way to slip out of this noose? With a resolute political will, which would require a different social configuration in power, Brazil could seriously challenge its creditors. Of critical importance are the country's bounteous resources, the scale of the economy (as noted, the ninth largest in the world), and a surplus between its exports and imports ($31 610 million versus $22 959 million in 1991). In the event of a moratorium, Brazil produces almost everything it needs except oil. Even a lack of oil could be overcome, for the country's sugar plantations are providing alcohol, which is already being used as fuel, and other Third World countries would continue to sell petroleum to Brazil.

THE CONTINUING SAGA

The 1990s have witnessed Brazil's experiment with a transition to democracy, allowing competitive elections if not opening political access to different socio-economic interests. As finance minister and then president, Fernando Henrique Cardoso, formerly a leftist professor of sociology, brought down inflation quite substantially, at least temporarily. To mop up its $120 billion foreign debt, Brazil, still the largest debtor in the underdeveloped world, completed a 1994 agreement with its creditor banks. Although without an approved economic programme from the IMF, the Brazilian accord is part of the Brady Plan. This novel arrangement permits Brazil to repay much of its debt with special bonds – 'Brady bonds' – backed by US collateral. The debt-reduction agreement cut Brazil's outstanding foreign debt to commercial banks by $4 billion, to $45 billion, and reduced interest owed by an additional

$4 billion. In return for a reduction in its burden due to 750 creditor banks and guarantees on payment, Brazil committed itself to an even more open economy. The National Privatization Programme called for competitive bids for some of the subsidiary companies of major state monopolies. In 1995, the Chamber of Deputies approved a constitutional amendment that would end the distinction between Brazilian companies constituted by national capital and those by foreign capital, paving the way for overseas companies to operate in more sectors of the economy. In line with this opening, Brazil looked increasingly towards developing a hemispheric free trade area founded on the principles of neo-liberal globalization.

Neo-liberal reforms, however, carry a cost. Brazil's income distribution, already one of the world's most unequal, continued to widen. The World Bank's statistics indicate that in the 1980s, the percentage of Brazilians living on less than $2 per day increased from 34 to 41. In the 1990s, the poorest 10 per cent of the country's population held less than 1 per cent of its wealth. In comparison, the richest 10 per cent commanded 49 per cent of the nation's wealth. These data are drawn from Brazil's most recent census, and it seems fair to ask: who was included, and who was excluded?

Problems in taking a census are notorious. Undercounting of certain segments of the population is a frequent occurrence. To the extent that regions and different groups bitterly compete for resources, counting is a highly politicized process. What is more, remote regions – such as the interior of the Amazon Basin – are not the favourite spot of census takers, often regarded with suspicion and as government agents.

Although Brazil's 1988 constitution contains enlightened sections on Indian rights, many indigenous lands – 11 per cent of the country's area – have not been demarcated and most have not received presidential confirmation. To make free-market changes in policy, President Cardoso depends on votes from Amazon congressional representatives, who staunchly oppose setting aside the land and favour halting all new demarcations of reservations. Local politicians' interests in mineral or timber extraction become worthless if an area is delimited as Indian land. These politicians back invasions by farmers, wildcat gold miners and loggers. Inasmuch as local police refuse to become involved, the Brazilian army is keeping an uneasy peace in locales where there is little protection of human rights.

The issues of undercounting Brazil's poor and the protection of human rights converge over the question of land. Quite clearly, land reform is not part of the neo-liberal package. In Brazil, land holdings are among the most unequal in the Third World. Nearly 80 per cent of the land is owned by 10 per cent of the farmers. Some estimates indicate that two million families are in search of land. These migrants are often forced on to poor land, and some of them end up as modern-day slaves.

As a result of the sting of economic pressure in the late 1980s and the 1990s, there has been an upsurge in slavery, abolished in 1888 in Brazil, the last country in the Americas to do so. A similar trend is apparent in Peru, Haiti, the Dominican Republic and elsewhere, where land-owners continue to exploit cheap labour by developing means to bind the poor who are forced to incur unpayable debts at company stores or canteens. Able to document only a fraction of the total cases in Brazil, the Pastoral Land Commission, a group sponsored by the Roman Catholic Church, presented evidence of an increase from 597 known victims in 1989 to 16 442 in 1992. The commission defines modern-day slavery as luring workers with false promises. Soon after they arrive at camps hundreds of miles from home, workers find that they are already in arrears for bus transportation, meals and the use of tools. They are subject to imprisonment and coerced into staying with their employers.

In this situation of debt peonage, workers are sometimes intimidated by armed foremen or stranded on remote ranches without a way to leave. Reduced to working only for food, the victims are found in isolated rural settings such as sugar cane plantations on the Atlantic Coast, and gold mines and charcoal industries in the Amazon, where foremen have been known to chain workers at night and kill those who have tried to escape.

Citing the revival of slavery, Carlos Eduardo Barroso, a Rio de Janeiro prosecutor who has investigated labour law violations in his country, remarked: 'In the nineteenth century, the chains were metal. Today, the chains are debt – the worker has to repay his transportation, his tools, his food.' His metaphor for debt peonage is apt, and can be rightfully extended to large segments of the population. It would seem that the chains of neo-liberalism manacle not only these victims but also many Brazilians of varying hues.

6 The Conventional Route, Joining Global Capitalism: Track 2 – the Asian NICs

On the conventional route's high speed track, only the more daring have managed to navigate the main thoroughfare. Fast-tracking runs greater risk of collision, but also offers the passengers greater rewards, at least in the short term, should they survive the deadly traffic. Both dismal failures and spectacular successes have been recorded.

A new orthodoxy, spawned by the achievements of a handful of countries, show-cases the Asian NICs as success stories, suggesting that they are worthy of emulation by the laggards of the South and providing free-market advocates with an occasion to promote the virtues of unbridled capitalism: private initiative and open-door policies. Prescribing high velocity integration into the global political economy as the most efficient way for the Third World to escape underdevelopment, the neo-liberal orthodoxy calls for the dismantling of road-blocks to global capital.

In terms of high growth rates and equitable distribution of wealth, the Asian NICs, or Four Tigers (Taiwan, South Korea, Singapore and Hong Kong), have done exceptionally well as producers and exporters of industrial goods and services. The economic performance of these countries relative to the rest of the Third World is remarkable, renewing faith in its faster track. If countries following this course can graduate from underdevelopment, what can prevent others in the Third World from doing the same?

A closer understanding of the NIC phenomenon reveals a less sanguine picture. The NIC experience is embedded in a specific configuration of time and space and, for reasons that will become clear, not replicable elsewhere. Yet non-NIC countries, which comprise the majority of the Third World, can still draw a few worthwhile lessons.

'MIRACLE' ECONOMIES

'In 20 years,' prophesied Lee Kuan Yew, senior minister and modern Singapore's founding father, 'the influence of the west on our lifestyles, foods, fashions, politics will drop [from 60] to 40 per cent and Asian influence will increase to 60 per cent.' Such rhetoric from the Third World might be easily dismissed but, as reported in the prestigious London-based *Financial Times*, a statement from the leader of an Asian 'tiger' with $60 billion in foreign exchange reserves and the fourteenth highest GNP per capita in the world (above that of Italy, the UK and Spain), usually merits serious attention. Lee's remark captures the new-won confidence of having achieved the prized status of NICs, a small tier of upwardly mobile countries on the cusp of development yet still feeling the pangs of underdevelopment. New winds seem to be blowing and Asia is seizing the initiative long held by Western powers to affect the ebb and flow of the global political economy.

With average GDP growth rates between 8 and 10 per cent for nearly two decades, wage increases and record low unemployment, the Asian NICs have substantially reduced poverty and have improved many aspects of the physical quality of life. In addition, life expectancy is higher, infant mortality is down and literacy has increased at a record pace during the past three decades. Unemployment and underemployment, until their recent reappearance, have dropped significantly. In Hong Kong, as early as the 1960s, there were no signs of unemployment, and Taiwan managed to cut its unemployment rate to a mere 2 per cent between 1968 and 1982. South Korea, too, was able to attain full employment by the 1980s, compared to an unemployment rate of 9.5 per cent in 1963. Singapore had achieved as much by the early 1970s relative to an unemployment rate of 9 per cent in 1966.

With only 240 square miles and a population of just 2.8 million in 1993, Singapore has virtually no natural resource endowments, yet it has a GNP per capita of $19 850. As the tenth largest export market for the USA in 1993, $15 billion larger than those of either Italy or Spain, it boasts one of the most rapidly growing economies in the world. A gateway to south-east Asia, Singapore absorbs state-of-the-art data processing machines, electronic components, chemicals, and aircraft parts from the USA. Hong Kong, another city-economy, enjoyed a GNP per capita income of $18 060 in 1993: clearly not a picture of an impoverished Third World nation. In only one generation, Taiwan has transformed itself into a trading powerhouse, holding one of the largest foreign exchange reserves in the world ($96 billion in 1994). For 15 consecutive months Taiwan can afford not to worry about its import bill, for these international reserves would suffice. Samsung, Hyundai and Daewoo are household names across the globe. Their home base, South Korea, is the seventh largest trading partner of the USA. By all accounts, the economic growth of the Asian NICs has been astronomical, anointing them as 'miracle' economies. How does one account for the so-called NIC phenomenon? Is it generalizable across time and space? Can Asian NIChood be the future of other benighted nations?

The term 'NICs' was initially invented to baptize Latin American countries such as Brazil, Argentina, Mexico and Venezuela, which had chosen import substitution strategies to create their own miracle with considerable foreign assistance and blessings from their mighty northern neighbour. But it is the Asian economies that are most frequently bracketed under that title. There is no consensus among the experts as to what constitutes a NIC, though different meanings are often assigned to the category. A shorthand for countries that have scaled the industrial ladder since the end of the Second World War, the term 'NICs' is applied to countries that have emerged from the changes in the global division of labour, especially since the 1960s. On this latter criterion, second-tier NICs, such as Malaysia and Thailand, may also blaze a pathway for others, given mutations in the world production structure. The World Bank and IMF use the term in a third sense, in which statistical criteria, including per capita income, savings ratios, levels of manufacturing and a physical quality of life index characterize a typical NIC economy.

Economic and political analysts have long debated whether the growth rates in the Asian NICs are a result of domestic cultural, social and economic conditions or propitious global circumstances, such as strategic links to the USA or a favourable international economic environment. The most frequently encountered explanation among policy intellectuals holds that at bottom, an outward-looking, export-oriented strategy, augmented by generous inflows of foreign capital and technology, lies at the basis of the Asian 'miracle' economies. Within the family of conventional accounts, there is also reference to a high rate of crude factor accumulation (factors are the inputs into the production process: land, labour and capital) which may have spurred growth rates, making the economic performance of the NICs appear less miraculous. In either case, the market is accorded the accolades for catapulting the Asian economies up the world hierarchy within a mere 30-year period.

Without question, relative to other regions, Asia has registered rapid growth. A so-called 'NIC model of development' is now an established category for international policy makers. But Asia (excluding the Middle East and Central Asia), not even considering the Third World in its entirety, is quite heterogenous, with at least four groups of economies: Greater China, which includes the People's Republic, Hong Kong, Macao and, politically more problematic, Taiwan; the Four Tigers; the four larger members of the Association of Southeast Asian Nations (ASEAN-4), namely, Indonesia, Malaysia, Thailand and the Philippines (usually termed second-tier NICs, though the last lags behind the other three); and the South Asian nations of Bangladesh, Bhutan, India, the Maldives, Nepal, Pakistan and Sri Lanka. But what is the basis for this *Asian* miracle and 'near miracle' in Indonesia, Malaysia and Thailand, with the Philippines tagging along?

There is no dearth of elements that need to be systematically tied together to explain the NIC phenomenon. A favourable global environment; human 'capital' endowments, especially an educated and disciplined work-force infused by a quasi-Confucian ethic; 'correct' macro-economic policies of trade and investment; the role of an authoritarian state; these are all often mentioned as the leading factors. Japanese economists, following Akamatsu Kaname's writings in the 1930s, have talked of a 'flying geese' pattern of growth, emphasizing a harmonious transition to industrialization: starting with one country, followed by others: from labour-intensive export-oriented to more sophisticated industrial production. The pattern has been more uneven, sporadic and asymmetrical, but Japan is usually held as the pioneer blazing the Asian way.

To inter-relate these disparate factors, analysts advance three theses: neo-classical, cultural and statist arguments. Neo-classical authors stress an outward economic orientation as the key to the NIC phenomenon. Embodying in full the workings of the law of comparative advantage (a country has the comparative advantage of the production of a good when it can be produced at a lower cost in terms of other goods than it could be in another country), the NICs developed the ability to produce cheap manufactures, thereby facilitating an optimal response to opportunities presented by the international economy. Especially in Hong Kong and Singapore, trade and exchange-rate policies, despite state intervention, have been left to the market. According to neo-classical economists, the Asian economies are market-based and subject to less regulation than are their counterparts elsewhere. Private initiative is encouraged, and the state is generally predisposed towards market solutions. An outbound industrialization strategy allowed NICs to successfully exploit the world market, carve out greater shares of manufactured exports, and move up the industrial ladder with changes in patterns of world production.

For other observers, it is culture that separates the NICs from the pack. On this view, Confucian values of temperance, individual sacrifice for the collective or national good, social harmony, an emphasis on order and the subordination of the individual to the collectivity, a work ethic and obedience to authority give the Asian NICs a competitive edge. All four 'miracle' economies share the so-called Confucian value of *Chung hyo* (loyalty to the state, filial piety and harmony). Respect for hierarchy provides, in the words of Lucian Pye, a 'strong ethical-moral basis of government – that both sets the limits on the pragmatic uses of power and requires that authority act with compassion for the people'. An authoritarian state can make virtue out of this principle, and capital can overcome the stark reality of conflict with labor. Echoing Max Weber's theme of the affinity between a Protestant ethic and the rise of Western capitalism, culturalists lay the so-called Asian 'miracle' at the feet of a Confucian ethos. Seemingly dormant for several centuries, lately the ghost of Confucius has possessed East Asia and the results have been more than an apparition.

Too easily ignoring the argument once made – that Confucian values serve to impede, rather than facilitate the emergence of a modern economy – the facile reduction of the East Asian economic success to a Confucian ethos serves more to obfuscate than illumine the causes of success. Culture is, after all, neither static nor homogeneous. A blend of Confucianism, Buddhism, Taoism and Christianity, East Asian cultures should neither be treated ahistorically in static terms, nor dismissed altogether as irrelevant to a comprehensive explanation of the NIC phenomenon. While recognizing the role of culture in creating a work-force more readily persuaded by the ideology of the 'national interest', the role of the state in mobilizing these cultural resources under given conditions must also be accounted for.

A third position departs from both neo-classical and culturalist explanations, emphasizing the contributions of a development-centred state *à la* Japan, mostly insulated from particularistic interests. Taiwan and South Korea are often used to illustrate the efficacy of the state in pursuing national goals. There, institutional arrangements, namely the existence of a centralized, meritocratic bureaucracy, autonomous from societal interests, facilitated long-term economic policies with little interference or interruption. A talented managerial class gave direction to society and advanced mutually reinforcing interests of both capital and the state. Unlike other developing nations that are marred by factionalism, the political leadership in the NICs drove the economy to expand. Providing stability, 'administrative guidance' for infrastructural investment and development of strategic sectors, the developmental state is seen as the author of 'miraculous' economic growth. The state's role was particularly efficacious in integrating the agricultural sector into the national economy. The proverbial thorn in the side of developing economies, the disjuncture between the growth of the agricultural and industrial sectors serves to constrain the overall rate of economic growth. By successfully incorporating the rural economy, the NICs could maximize the level of efficiency, specifically in the distribution of resources between the rural and urban sectors.

Making sense of the NIC experience, against the complex of so many disparate factors, is quite problematic. In this mix, what relative weights can one assign to 'domestic' in relation to 'external' factors? Is it possible to abstract a uniquely 'NIC' strategy of growth given the vast changes a Singapore or a Taiwan has undergone? Given the historical embeddedness of the developmental process, is it possible to isolate discrete elements? Only at the most basic level can factors be classified, causes grouped, and connections made.

THE LEGACY

East Asian specialist Bruce Cumings correctly notes that 'if there has been an economic miracle in East Asia, it has not occurred just since 1960; it would be profoundly ahistorical to think that it did'.

Fortuitous historical circumstances no doubt provide a central backdrop to an understanding of the NIC phenomenon. Neither Singapore nor Hong Kong, for instance, is a typical Third World country either in terms of geographical and population size or the complexity of social structures other larger nations embody. Both are offsprings of particular colonial policies, which in other contexts left a trail of underdevelopment. An outward orientation seemed quite natural, given the entrepôt status of these two cities. Lacking in natural riches, they have eschewed an import substitution strategy which often entails the establishment of large domestic markets. Singapore aggressively sought an outward-bound pathway with wholesale reliance on foreign trade and investment. An ex-colony of Britain and a major port even in colonial days, Singapore has long depended on foreign trade, worth three times the country's GDP in 1993.

Only six years after purchasing Singapore, Britain combined Singapore, Penang and Malacca in 1830 to establish the Straits Settlements, a peripheral outpost of the British East India Company. By 1867 the Straits Settlements had been transformed into a major British Crown Colony. Subsequently, in 1946, Penang and Malacca were united in a single British Crown colony to form the Federation of Malaya. A self-governing territory, Singapore became an independent city-state in 1965. It was conjoined with Malaya, Sabah and Sarawak (the last two were former British Borneo territories) to form Malaysia. After a protracted dispute between Singapore and Kuala Lumpur, Singapore separated from Malaysia to become an independent republic.

Like Singapore, Hong Kong has no natural wealth, and this 400 square-mile British colony has also relied on its links with the outside world to support its six million people. After the Chinese Communist Party's (CCP) triumph on the mainland in 1949, a large Chinese population emigrated from China to Hong Kong, building much of the territory's current industrial prowess.

More recently, the Cold War served as a relevant point of compass for economic growth in both South Korea and Taiwan. These countries benefited disproportionately from the superpower rivalry, given Washington's perception of their geopolitical importance. Security arrangements and the rewards that strategic arrangements made possible helped create a psychosis of insecurity and allowed authoritarian regimes to channel national resources towards the overriding goal of growth. Access to Western markets normally denied other Third World nations was also made available.

LAND REFORM AND INDUSTRIALIZATION

Without exception, transformation of relations on land is a necessary prerequisite for industrialization. Before industrialization is possible, the social structure must allow new actors to realize their potential. Countries that manage to undo the old agrarian structure may succeed; those that cannot dismantle the erstwhile structure fail to remove impediments to the creation of an investible surplus.

Hong Kong and Singapore had no agrarian remnants of consequence to begin with. Without land reform, Taiwan and South Korea would possess a substantial landed class to imperil industrialization. However, collaboration with the Japanese undermined the social standing of this group and the removal of tenancy practices with land reform paved the way for wholesale industrialization. Towards the end of land reform, owner-cultivators would constitute 90 per cent of the labour force. With no intermediaries to support, the state would be able to extract vital surplus to spur industrialization without impoverishing the rural economy.

With an area of 35 981 square kilometres (14 000 square miles) and a population of 20 million, Taiwan is one of the leading Asian economies, recording a growth rate averaging 9 per cent between 1952 and 1993. Three-quarters of the Taiwanese population can trace their ancestry to Chinese immigrants from the mainland provinces of Fujian and Guangdong, who arrived in the eighteenth and nineteenth centuries to escape economic pressures. A colony of Japan, Taiwan was ceded to Tokyo by weakened Qing rulers after the first Sino-Japanese war in 1895. (About 330 000 aborigines, found in the mountainous regions of central and eastern Taiwan, belong to Malayo-Polynesian groups.) After the CCP's triumph in 1949, another two million people arrived in Taiwan in 1949 from all parts of the mainland. Since its 'secession' from the mainland in 1949, Taiwan has experienced high-speed industrialization and has emerged as a major trading power. How did this island economy attain its present status?

During colonial rule, a significant portion of arable land was controlled by Japanese landlords. With their departure, the path was paved to implement drastic land reform in three major phases. In the first one, beginning in April 1949, rent on the main agricultural crop was reduced substantially, from one-half (sometimes two-thirds or above) of total surplus to 37.5 per cent. Initially, there was poor compliance, but that changed subsequently. In the second phase of the reform, land owned or controlled by Japanese authorities or citizens (nearly one-fifth of total cultivable land) was put up for sale to Taiwanese.

By the end of this phase in 1953, 35 per cent of public lands had been sold to the actual cultivators, 24 per cent was under lease to private farmers, and 41 per cent came under public control. The third phase of the reform, implemented in 1953 and 1954, was characterized by a land-to-the-tiller programme which allowed tenant land to be bought by the state and sold to existing cultivators. An ingenious mechanism was devised to finance these purchases by sales of stocks and bonds. Consequently, this cut the tenancy rate to 15 per cent. Compensation was provided to big landowners in the shape of commodities certificates or stocks in state-owned enterprises (SOEs), mainly in light industry which was the propellant of Taiwan's industrial take-off. Four big SOEs – in cement, mineral, paper and forestry products – became outlets for the land owners. The barter ratio between fertilizer and rice also became an important mechanism to compensate displaced landlords.

The main beneficiaries of land reform were cultivators, but the programme also allowed for the rise of Taiwan's vanguard industrialists.

Unlike other agricultural societies, where landlords continue to block accumulation, farmers in Taiwan became owners and their rent contribution was also significantly curtailed. Both direct and indirect results followed. Farmers became the mainstay of agricultural modernization, which transformed the rural economy, enhanced productivity, released agricultural surplus for industrialization, and established the basis for equitable income distribution. One major effect of land reform was the elimination of parasitic layers in society predisposed to rent-seeking behaviour.

If land reform established the foundations for transforming Taiwan into an industrial economy, the crucial external factor was foreign investment. Embracing Taiwan as an independent power from its inception, the USA was Chiang Kai-Shek's main benefactor as foreign investor and military protector. Taiwan's strategy relied on labour-intensive export production in the 1960s, succeeded by industrial upgrading in the 1970s and 1980s, and an expansion of the domestic market, especially the service sector, and infrastructural modernization in the 1990s. Statistics from Taiwan indicate that for this small nation, investment from 1952 to 1989 totaled $10.9 billion. The US share of foreign investment was 28 per cent, or $3.1 billion, one of the largest for US allies in the developing world.

Despite Taiwan's insistence on domestic ownership as an essential ingredient of foreign presence – unlike Singapore's or Hong Kong's policy – the authorities in Taipei managed to attract FDI with considerable facility. Somewhat similar to South Korea where joint ventures and minority ownerships have been the norm, or unlike Singapore where foreign concerns enjoy majority or whole ownership in the host economy, Taiwan is more restrictive in regulating FDI.

Despite neo-classical claims of 'free-market' reign, the state in Taiwan has been a key to economic growth, not only orchestrating an aggressive land reform programme, but spearheading industrial production. Investments in education, for instance, produced a 92 per cent literacy rate in Taiwan by 1990.

With mitigated challenges, the state was able to fuel labour-intensive industrialization. An important aspect of state intervention in Taiwan has been the establishment of EPZs to pull foreign investment in several sectors, including consumer electronics, textiles and agrofood. To diversify industry, the state actively promoted capital- and skill-intensive industries in the 1970s. In the 1980s, new 'strategic' industries, especially information, electronics, bio-technology and machinery, were stressed while SOEs as well as shipbuilding and aluminium smelting industries were downgraded in anticipation of overproduction. One-third of the economy is still dominated by large SOEs in areas as diverse as banking, transportation, electricity, water, steel, petroleum products, sugar, cigarettes and alcoholic beverages. But SOEs accounted for only 15 per cent of total manufacturing output in the 1980s compared to 50 per cent in the 1950s. Nevertheless, seven of the 10 largest industrial enterprises are still SOEs. Credit and interest rate policies have been designed to favour small and medium-sized enterprises, producing lean companies with an equity basis. For instance, out of Taiwan's 90 000 industrial companies, over 90 per cent had fewer than 30 employees.

High tariffs in key sectors continue to 'distort' prices. The state has periodically applied financial and fiscal instruments to induce economic growth in specific directions. Reform of the exchange rate regime has been used to encourage import of sophisticated foreign machinery. Conversely, financing has been provided to exporters of industrial raw materials.

Access to US markets, aided by security interests, has been central to Taiwan's explosive economic growth. Taiwan not only possesses a formidable 550 000-strong military, which absorbs 5 per cent of the GNP and 28 per cent of the central budget, it is the recipient of the latest US military hardware and know-how. As the largest trading partner, the USA takes 36 per cent of exports and 23 per cent of Taiwanese imports. With a highly skilled, disciplined labour-force, Taiwan has made foreign trade the chief engine of its growth. Resource-poor, with over 92 per cent of its energy imported, Taiwan has become a major exporter of industrial goods (95 per cent of total exports), especially electronics, which receives the largest proportion of US investment, and textiles. Total trade increased five-fold in the 1960s and ten-fold in the 1970s. Though the pace slackened in the 1980s, trade still tripled in the same decade. Textiles constitute the second biggest industrial sector in Taiwan, but the economy has been diversifying. Other important export industries include machinery, sporting goods, footwear, plastics and toys. Several small- and medium-sized Taiwanese firms have also benefited from original equipment manufacturer arrangements, giving them the right to produce cheaper goods under established foreign brand names, including IBM, Texas Instruments, K-Mart, Hewlett-Packard, J.C. Penney and Sears.

One key dimension in the NIC experience is continuous industrial upgrading. Capturing a niche in the world market is part of the strategy; to be able to adjust industrial production is another. Taiwan has been successful on both counts. Although Taiwan has elevated sectors of its economy to a capital-intensive stage, a number of factors, including a 55 per cent currency appreciation between 1985 and 1989 (which made Taiwanese exports more expensive), labour shortages and soaring labour costs represent impediments to higher performance. One option for climbing higher up the value-added ladder is off-shore relocation of production and, in the 1990s, Taiwan (despite receiving handsome foreign investments) has sought to invest overseas, especially in nearby south-east Asia.

COMMAND CAPITALISM

As in Taiwan, land reform – implemented in two phases, active state intervention in the economy, and the shadow of Cold War politics – played a vital role in South Korea's rise to economic stardom.

Korea's past has been turbulent, characterized by invasions and foreign influence. In 1910, it was annexed by Japan and Tokyo exercised stiff control over the peninsula for the next 35 years, including efforts to impose its own culture and language. The division of Korea at the end of the Second World War left much of the nation's mineral and hydroelectric wealth and Japanese-built industrial base in the North. Lacking natural resource endowments, South Korea, with an area of 98 500 square kilometres (38 000 square miles), inherited an agrarian economy. Beginning in the mid-1950s, it was able to transform itself into 'Asia's next giant' after Japan. From 1963 to 1978, real GDP increased at a rate of nearly 10 per cent per year. Throughout the 1980s, Korea has maintained steady growth rates. South Korea's remarkable economic prowess also began with the transformation of its agrarian structure.

Land ownership in South Korea, even more than in Taiwan, was highly skewed under Japanese colonial rule. For instance, merely 3 per cent of landowners, mostly Japanese, controlled 64 per cent of the land on the eve of Japan's surrender to the USA. Though the initial motivation of US military commanders was political, namely to thwart communism, they served an important economic role in redistributing land and laying the basis for industrialization. Following US occupation, Japanese-occupied land, nearly 15 per cent of all arable soil, was redistributed among 35 per cent of farmers. By 1964, with reform, small land-ownership became the norm in South Korea as a result of legislative steps allowing the state to expropriate absentee land, plots without self-cultivators and any parcels exceeding 3 hectares. Self-cultivation increased from 16.5 per cent in 1947 to 71.6 per cent in 1964, and tenancy declined from 42.1 per cent to only 7 per cent during the same period.

Compensation to landlords was offered in the shape of discounted government bonds exchangeable for industrial ownership, but several landowning families found it expedient to make a transition into industry, which was augmented by compulsory grain purchases by the state.

Coterminous with land reform, the state intervened at all stages of industrialization in virtually every strategic area of the economy. Alice Amsden points out that South Korea's late industrialization was based on learning from earlier innovatory nations. The capacity for State intervention in the economy emanates from the country's militaristic past, the existence of a meritocratic civil service (a colonial legacy), and raw material scarcity which necessitated careful expenditure of resources. Over time, the state, in Amsden's words, 'usurped the domain of the traditional private entrepreneur by making milestone decisions about what, when, and how much to produce'.

The presence of US forces on the peninsula was also instrumental in driving Korean authorities towards 'developmentalism' with the aim of reducing dependence. From providing low interest 'policy loans' to enforcement of discriminatory regulatory policies to strategic targeting of future industries, the state has always taken the lead. Even at the micro-economic level, prices of many products have been controlled. Credit was allocated according to firm size and the state approved all bond and stock issuances. Nearly all overseas capital flows were also firmly circumscribed. Domestic competition to the *chaebol* (large corporate cartel) was discouraged through investment and product safety regulations, which also worked against foreign competitors. Consequently, FDI in South Korea has not been very high relative to even the second-tier NICs, ranking only ninth among Asian economies. High tariffs were systematically used to protect domestic industries and only when these industries were strong enough to withstand the threat of competition were they lowered.

A core feature of the Korean economy since the early 1960s has been a series of five-year economic plans which have allowed the state to direct the economy in specific avenues. The major shift in 1964, from an import substitution strategy to export-led industrialization, was premised on targeting strategic industries (mostly textiles and consumer electronics), providing special access to credit. Via exchange rate reform, the state manipulated the incentive structure in favour of export and intermediate goods producers. Beginning in 1973, South Korea's successful transition from labour-intensive to capital-intensive industries, especially steel, shipbuilding and electronics, was also a brainchild of the state. Aggressive investments in research and development, and worker retraining shaped industrial upgrading, including moving upstream on the value-added chain.

While consumer imports have been traditionally given restricted entry into the domestic market, vital raw materials and capital equipment have been granted favourable access. Confidence in the national economy has allowed trade liberalization in all areas since the mid-1980s, except in the agricultural sector. But in order to protect domestic industry, the state reserves the power to levy 'emergency tariffs' as high as 100 per cent on imported goods. Additionally, the state can apply 'adjustment tariffs' to neutralize the effects of trade liberalization. In the public consciousness, imports are still regarded as luxury goods. Periodic 'frugality campaigns' have been launched in the name of 'overconsumption' to discourage imports. Domestic industrialists have often tried to sway government officials against foreign companies. In 1993, a curious instance of such pressure was a campaign, also joined by the media, against foreign cosmetics, which were allegedly taking too much floor space in department stores. Custom officials used audits and investigation of their import procedures to put pressure on these companies.

One strategic area of state intervention was in education, measured by the fact that in 1990, adult literacy was 96 per cent in South Korea. Moreover, education has been designed to abet the economy, especially in engineering. But the key point here is direct intervention in the economy.

The state has also applied tax audits and fiscal authority to keep *de facto* control over industry. A major actor, SOEs also play a prominent role in the economy. A total of 133 SOEs account for about 10 per cent of the GNP. Despite lagging efficiency and productivity, the SOEs remain important avenues of state privilege and patronage.

Imbued with a developmental logic, discipline over business as well as labour, Amsden suggests, was the key in the initial stages of industrialization which produced the possibility of extensive foreign borrowing. Organically connected to the state, the *chaebol*, a Korean version of the Japanese *keiretsu*, normally purchase their inputs from 'family' suppliers; and in awarding public contracts, the state promotes these transactions (what it calls 'localization' of production and technology transfer). Over the decades, relations between officials and businesses have been quite close. Not willing to imperil a firmly ensconced relationship between foreign firms and *chaebol*, small and medium-sized suppliers refrain from dealing with outsiders.

One outcome of the state's patronage of the *chaebol* is a concentration of capital and industrial output in a few hands. For instance, the top 30 *chaebol* account for 28 per cent of total manufacturing capacity and 45 per cent of the total capital of the domestic financial sector. Relative to Taiwanese firms which tend to be small, family establishments, Korean companies have been quite large. In 1981, for instance, gross receipts of Korea's largest *chaebol*, Hyundai, were $10 billion, three times the size of the total gross receipts of 10 of Taiwan's largest private companies, estimated at $3.5 billion. Big, even debt-based, companies were given privileged access to credit on low interest rates.

In addition to land reform and the role of an activist state, South Korea's strong military and economic ties to the USA were central to providing an environment to pursue export-led industrialization with guaranteed access to Western capital, markets and technology. Designed to help defend South Korea against aggression from Pyongyang, the security relationship with the USA was enshrined in the 1954 US-Korea Mutual Defense Treaty. For over four decades, the USA maintained thousands of armed personnel in Korea, currently about 37 000 uniformed men and women. Many *chaebol*, such as Daewoo, became suppliers of goods to the US military before their metamorphosis into global firms. During the Vietnam War, Korean industry received a boost, owing to its close links to the USA. In the 1950s and 1960s, US aid was instrumental in generating productive capital. During the Vietnam War, contracts with local firms and purchasers, as well as tourism from American GIs, played an important role. For Hyundai and Daewoo, work for the US military provided the initial foreign contracts.

Foreign borrowing was not inconsequential to South Korea's industrial upgrading in the late 1970s and early 1980s. In 1985, external debt had soared to $47 billion, which was subsequently reduced. Faced with tough competition from second-tier NICs, labour unrest, rising labour costs and political instability, Seoul, like Taipei, is moving away from export-led industrialization to an expansion of domestic demand, rebuilding its infrastructure, regionalizing and globalizing its economy. The rise of a middle class in South Korea gives domestically-oriented development a social basis. In the next decade alone, $100 billion is expected to be spent on scores of new infrastructural projects. To improve competitiveness, Korean leaders are calling for a globalization drive, which includes investments overseas, especially in the newly emerging Pacific Basin Region.

CITY-STATE TO GLOBAL CITY

A major factor accounting for the NIC phenomenon is that of historical conjuncture: the interface of particular 'external' events and specific constellations of 'domestic' social forces. To abstract from history a simple formula of economic growth is to overlook the inter-related dimensions of time and space. City states such as Singapore and Hong Kong are archetypal examples of how a certain location within the global political economy can lend economic significance disproportionate to size. Viewed in isolation from the global political economy, one is likely to embellish economic achievement or place the burden of success exclusively upon individual attributes, cultural or otherwise. The invocation of Confucianism or an equivalent Asian achievement principle as an explanation for the rise of Asian economies recycles this erroneous logic. This is not to disregard 'domestic' social or cultural elements, but to contextualize them.

In the postcolonial period, Singapore has emerged from being a mere trading post to becoming one of Asia-Pacific's and the world's leading finance centres. With a high per capita income second only to Japan in Asia, Singapore is a regional financial power. As one of the most densely populated countries, with 4231 persons per square kilometre (10 961 per square mile), and possessing few natural resources, Singapore has also managed to make important advances in computer-related technology and electronics. In the social sector, an emblem of Singapore's achievements is that 83 per cent of its citizens own their own housing, while the majority of the Third World's inhabitants is without decent shelter. The mainstay of this remarkable pattern is Singapore's ability to play the global card.

The main plank of Singapore's growth is the marriage between foreign investment and an authoritarian state. There are over 3000 TNCs with investments in Singapore, including 900 US companies and some 3600 US companies with representatives in the city-state. In 1993, foreign investment constituted nearly 80 per cent of total investment, or $1.8 billion. Singapore has exacted no taxes on capital gains and places no restrictions on foreign ownership with the exception of banking and insurance, stock-broking, legal services and engineering services. With seven free zones for either manufacturing or storage and repackaging, Singapore is one of the global political economy's most attractive economic centres.

However, it is misleading to infer that Singapore is free of regulation. By 1990, for instance, Singapore's commitment to education had yielded a literacy rate of 88 per cent (compared to 90 per cent in its sister city-state, Hong Kong). In the financial sector, the Monetary Authority of Singapore grants only 'offshore' licences to foreign banks that assign local retailers a minor position. Also, in economic activities requiring large capital investment due to the risk factor, the state has played a central role in sponsoring state-companies. The Economic Development Board (EDB), a quasi-state agency which identifies sectors with high potential, helps design eonomic policy. Resources are channelled accordingly to direct the future course of industrial upgrading. The EDB has been instrumental in creating tax and fiscal incentives to stimulate foreign investment. Both foreign and locally owned firms are assisted in manufacturing new technologies, automate, and promote product development.

Though restrictions on foreign trade and investment have been slight, the state's role is critical. A number of strategic industries, including shipbuilding, oil refineries and iron-steel have received privileged treatment. In 1983, 450 companies were SOEs, either wholly or partially, with $2.4 billion in paid-up and $18.2 billion in fixed capital. Employing only 5 per cent of the total labour force, the contribution of these SOEs, however, was 21.4 per cent of sales in the manufacturing sector.

The strategy of facilitating transnational activity with locally inspired initiative in unfamiliar economic climes has resulted in making Singapore a hub for light industry, oil refining and financial services. Over the years, Singapore has positioned itself as a centre of global finance by developing state-of-the art infrastructure, including the world's finest airport, according to various business magazines, and the largest sea port. Excellent road links, an ultra-modern subway and superior telecommunications have interfaced with reliable public utilities to attract finance. Regular refurbishing of infrastructure is made possible by research and development efforts, in part bolstered by a major national university. Few import duties or non-tariff barriers to trade are levied. The state has also tried to keep the national economy competitive by concentrating on high value-added activities, given a constricted labour market, and overseas investment, especially in East and South Asia.

Singapore has become a regional trading hub, as shown by the fact that more than 32 per cent of Singapore's total imports are re-exported, mostly to neighbouring countries. Hence Indonesia, Malaysia, Thailand, Vietnam and the Philippines are major recipients of goods from Singapore. Total trade in 1993 reached $160.7 billion, of which $86.0 billion were exports and $74.7 billion were imports. An exporter of refined petroleum products and electronics, Singapore has emerged as the largest supplier of computer disk-drives in the world with nearly 50 per cent of total output. Computer-related products, likely to remain in high demand, are also exported in large quantities. Accounting for 46 per cent or $25 billion of manufacturing output, electronics is Singapore's chief manufacturing industry and employs 34 per cent of the labour force.

With globalization, Singapore has sought to extend industrial upgrading and its regional outreach. In 1993, Singapore's Changi Airport provided links to 108 cities, servicing 58 airlines with over 2100 flights each week. By the year 2000, Singapore is likely to emerge as the pivotal point for the entire Asia-Pacific region. Like Hong Kong's Kai Tak, Changi Airport can handle 24 million passengers each year. One ambitious plan envisages Singapore as an 'intelligent island' by the year 2000. The state already has blueprints to connect every home, factory, office and school via optical fibres. Given Singapore's political system, an Orwellian world does not seem far away.

Recognizing internal limits to growth, the idea is to create an 'external wing' for the economy as part of an extensive regionalization drive. In addition to value-added re-exports, Singapore aims to be a key player in constructing major industrial parks in the burgeoning economies of China, India and Indonesia. Singapore invested in over $4 billion in joint ventures in 1990 alone, with one-fifth going to Malaysia. Trading companies with close family and business ties are quite prominent in extending Singapore's outreach into south-east Asia.

If foreign investment has been the central 'external' element in Singapore's rise to NICdom, it is the authoritarian state that has been the pivotal 'internal' factor propelling growth. Nominally a parliamentary republic, Singapore has been a one-party dominant system since its inception as an independent state. Political stability, enforced by draconian laws and stringent enforcement, is Lee Kuan Yew's legacy to Singapore. Lee vacated the office of Prime Minister in 1990 in favour of Goh Chok Tong, but has wielded paramount power by taking the title of senior minister as well as retaining his presidency of the People's Action Party (PAP), the pre-eminent party. In the 1991 elections, PAP received 77 out of the 81 seats, a measure of the absence of any viable political opposition in the city-state. With stringent internal security laws, the police exercise vast powers, communist activity is banned and dissidence is ruthlessly crushed. Lee's order, serviced by repression and periodic appeals to Confucian values, has helped create a well-disciplined labour force of 1.64 million (supplemented by 360 000 foreign, mostly unskilled, workers). Since 1978, there has only been one strike in Singapore.

Constant industrial upgrading remains Singapore's strategy of growth. After the attempt to restructure its manufacturing base was abandoned with the first oil shock, in 1979 a new scheme was put into effect. Increasing reliance on immigrant workers and higher wages led to a downgrading of labour-intensive activities as well as a payroll tax and a Skilled Development Fund levy on employers of unskilled labour. A shift towards more skill- and more technology-intensive activities, microprocessors and other sophisticated electronic products replaced much of the traditional manufactures.

LAISSEZ-FAIRE TO MARKET-LENINISM?

With virtually the whole city-state comprising a free trade zone, Hong Kong, like Singapore, has thrived by making itself a centre of exports and re-exports. Offering complete banking services, Hong Kong's 172 fully licensed banks, like Singapore's, are a magnet for global finance. Cultivating international links, this small territory represents the eighth largest trading economy in the world.

Open links to the outside world are the result of Hong Kong's historical legacy. A by-product of the notorious opium trade in the nineteenth century and Britain's unequal treaties with China, Hong Kong was chartered under a 99-year lease in 1898. In 1949, after Mao's victory on the mainland, a large influx of Chinese emigrated to Hong Kong and became the mainstay of its industrial and commercial activity. An entrepôt from the start, by the late 1960s Hong Kong had already established an industrial base. Sensitive to changes in world production patterns, its labour-intensive industries were flexible enough to change with the times.

Hong Kong's excellent location and infrastructure have allowed business to flourish. The world's tenth largest merchandise exporter and the main entrepôt for mainland China, Hong Kong is the site of the world's finest natural deep-water port, a first-rate communications structure and an educated work-force. This has allowed Hong Kong to become a major transit point for both exports and re-exports, the latter constituting three-quarters of total exports. (Re-exports is the official term for foreign goods that enter Hong Kong's custom territory for shipment onward to other countries, either to China or North America,

Europe, or the rest of Asia.) In 1992, 100 million tons of cargo went through Hong Kong. In 1993, Hong Kong imported goods worth $139 billion, with China as the leading supplier (37 per cent). Japan provided 17 per cent of imports the same year; Taiwan 9 per cent; the USA, 7 per cent. Measured in per capita terms, US imports to Hong Kong averaged almost $1845 in 1993. USA-Hong Kong trade was worth $20 billion in 1993.

Like Singapore's economy, Hong Kong's could not thrive without international commerce. One indicator of the importance of foreign ties to Hong Kong's prosperity is the presence of 900 US companies which belong to the American Chamber of Commerce in Hong Kong and 30 000 US current residents. During its years as a British colony, Hong Kong has pursued an open-door, export-oriented economic strategy, led by private capital. Capital gains are exempt alongside dividends and interest. But lacking in anti-trust regulation, the economy is marked by oligopolistic practices. Like South Korea, giant conglomerates loom large over the economy. Interlocking links bind commercial and industrial companies.

With China's mercurial rise as an industrial giant, Hong Kong's geographic proximity, cultural affinity and infrastructural links to Guangdong Province in the People's Republic have facilitated close economic ties. Anticipating political integration under the 'one country, two system' formula, which would allow Hong Kong to maintain economic autonomy for a minimum of 50 years following its incorporation into China in 1997, Beijing and Hong Kong are virtually integrated in a vast subregional economy. Industrialization in southern China continues to benefit Hong Kong. Sixty per cent of Chinese exports pour through Hong Kong, and China is becoming a leading investor in its would-be 'special administrative province'. On the other hand, China's impending take-over of Hong Kong in 1997 has also been the primary catalyst for the exodus of skilled and professional personnel. In 1993, nearly 70 000 people emigrated, with the majority headed towards Canada.

The structural shift from domestic exports to re-exports is largely a product of Hong Kong's economic relations with the mainland. Hong Kong-owned companies are a key component in manufacturing in . southern China, while Chinese companies utilize Hong Kong's developed infrastructure to extend their reach. Cheaper land and labour costs are crucial to the relocation of production for Hong Kong-based firms in the toy, watch and consumer electronic industries, as are Hong Kong's marketing and financial links important to China's open door. Authorities in Hong Kong see technological upgrading as a significant vehicle to meet changing regional conditions. Despite attempts to diversify its economy, Hong Kong remains the world's major textile and apparel exporter. These two industries constituted 40 per cent of Hong Kong's domestic exports (or $11.4 billion) in 1993 and employed 42 per cent of the total manufacturing labour-force.

Since the 1980s, Hong Kong has been afflicted by labour shortages in almost every sector of the economy, including construction, manufacturing and some service industries. Land speculation has made Hong Kong's real estate among the most expensive in the world. Compared to what has transpired in Singapore, industrial upgrading in Hong Kong has been less significant than the development of a regional service economy, focusing on China and south-east Asia as colossal markets. More than one-third of total domestic exports or three-quarters of Hong Kong's GDP consists of services, a sector that employs nearly two-thirds of the work-force. While textile and apparel still predominate, tourism, with $7.7 billion (1993 figures), is the third largest earner of foreign exchange. Close to two million tourists, including 1.8 million from Taiwan alone, visited Hong Kong in 1993. In the context of globalization, Hong Kong's changing role is apparent from the volume of cargo and number of passengers at Kai Tak (second and fourth in the world, respectively). Over 24 million passengers and 134 000 aircraft movements used this single-runway airport in 1993.

Yet Hong Kong's economic future remains uncertain. China's 'market-Leninism' offers both possibilities and perils for its long-term growth. One scenario sees Hong Kong's continued centrality in China's southern strategy. But with other industrial centres developing on the mainland, it is conceivable that Hong Kong may lose its past prominence.

THE UNDERSIDE OF GROWTH

Celebration of Asia's 'miracle' economies is not universally shared. Many critics point to the social cost and the political underside of economic growth. Some of them regard the environment as a major casualty of climbing the industrial ladder so quickly. Still others find these economies in crisis, having peaked or unable to promote self-sustaining growth. Critics also suggest that the social compact built around economic growth appears to confront new political and social tensions. Shifting from an industrial economy to an innovation-driven growth strategy, in turn, may open the political economy of the Asian NICs to unfamiliar democratic pressures.

Several factors are cited to support these claims. Whether it is Singapore, where local businesses have sought an end to special treatment for foreign capital, or Taiwan, where cries for 'ecological balance' are shadowing growth concerns, or South Korea, where a more restless middle class is demanding more equitable income distribution, the structural planks of the NICs have begun to give. Inflation, world recession and domestic transformation portend trials for the NICs.

Increases in wealth, as displayed in consumer spending, produced inflation in all Four Tiger economies. Asian Development Bank (ADB) data for 1981–90 indicate average annual inflation rates of 8.2 per cent for Hong Kong and 6.2 per cent for South Korea, but only 2.3 per cent for Singapore and 3.1 per cent for Taiwan. Though considerably lower than inflation levels in many other countries in the developing world, the above rates were somewhat greater than the average for some Group of Seven (G-7) economies which are also the major importers of NIC products. In a period of slow growth and neo-mercantilist protectionism among major economic powers, export-dependent development bears its risks. Yet it is political change, propelled by new social forces, that may pose the greatest challenge.

The political ground is shifting in the NICs, as revealed in growing worker unrest. Clashes between the state and workers increased in the late 1980s. Repression, weak unionization and state interference in labour organizations produced low wages, lengthy work-hours, and many industrial accidents. Workers appear to be less pliant today. Some highly educated Singaporeans are also protesting, but in another way. Fearing reprisals, they have sought a quiet exodus to avoid a ruthless one-party system and policies favouring, they believe, foreign over domestic capital.

In an era of globalization, Asian NICs are also likely to be less effective in designing statist policies. Pressures to pry open the domestic economy, especially for South Korea, are going to be greater. Administered prices may face market coercion. Access to credit, state subsidies, and investment incentives – crucial to early industrialization – may also shrink. Furthermore, trade surpluses with the USA, quite significant in nourishing market expansion, have to be reconciled with massive deficits with neighbouring Japan. Finally, there is the challenge from neighbouring Asian nations, ready to compete with the Four Tigers by offering both cheaper labour and land costs and industrial upgrading.

An open secret of NIChood is the employment of women workers and their exploitation by the institution of patriarchy consecrated by

Confucianism. The rapid expansion of the work-force in all the NICs is due largely to the participation of women. The role of women has been critical, especially in the early phases of the industrialization drive, but as industrialization has proceeded, women's participation has not diminished. In Singapore, for instance, the proportion of women grew from 17 per cent in the late 1960s to almost one-half of the labour force in the early 1990s. In Taiwan's three EPZs, 85 per cent of the workers were women.

Both implicit and explicit advantages have been considered in bringing women into the labour-force. Women workers can be paid considerably less than their male counterparts, as in Taiwan where the average female wage was 62 per cent of the male wage in the 1970s. Employers have seen women as being more adaptable for jobs requiring repetition, monotony and 'nimble fingers' (for example, in textiles and the electronic industries). But there is also the extra dimension of employing unorganized female workers, perceived as less troublesome. During South Korea's early industrialization, preference was given to unmarried women between the ages of 16 and 25. This also permitted employers to seek workers with a middle-school education and to preserve the male-dominated hierarchy of firms, with a male aristocracy situated in more capital- and knowledge-intensive positions. Hence, wage-differentials are promoted at the expense of low-wage 'factory girls', employed for long working hours to ensure Korean competitiveness in labour-intensive industries. Not only do women workers enjoy less job security; they are also more easily expendable in times of economic slowdown.

Confucian values of patriarchal dominance have been a key source of disciplining female labour. Often, there is a convergence between domesticity at home and docility in the work place, including company-provided housing, sanctified by liberal prescriptions from a culturally manipulated value-system. Women are also positioned in those sectors of the economy where the 'feminine' in societal consciousness serves stereotypical uses.

Compounding the human cost of high-speed industrialization, whether the exploitation of women workers or the destruction of the agrarian base, is an assault on the environment in all the NICs. For instance, Taiwan's strategy of export-led growth, an undervalued currency and cheap labour have been based on a mutually conflicting relationship between industry and the environment. Bello and Rosenfeld call Taiwan 'a poisoned paradise of free-wheeling capitalism', an appropriate designation for a country where the absence of environmental controls has had devastating consequences. Crops laced with pesticides and contamination of agricultural land by heavy metals are among the more glaring indices of unregulated growth. Taiwan's pursuit of industrialization saw the rural landscape turn into a waste dump. The urban scene offers little solace either, with air pollution levels that would be regarded as hazardous in the USA being designated 'safe' in Taiwan. One of the world's leading users of chemical fertilizers, Taiwan positions a sizeable proportion of its 90 000-factory industrial base in the countryside, giving the country roughly three factories per square kilometre, or 75 times the industrial density of the USA. Contamination is widespread, with heavy metals, such as mercury and arsenic, found in 30 per cent of the rice grown. Industrial waste pollutes 20 per cent of the farm land. Despite increases in life expectancy, cancer deaths have doubled in the last three decades and the rate of hepatitis infection is among the highest in the world. Only direct action like plant occupations by local residents has delayed further expansion of nuclear power and petrochemical industries.

The other super-NIC, South Korea, has its own environmental problems. Seoul's air contains record levels of sulphur dioxide concentration. Acid rain and contaminated water supply present major environmental threats. But the foremost risk comes from the nine functioning nuclear reactors (with two more under construction), which generate over 53 per cent of total electricity. With falling productivity, the agricultural sector in South Korea is also showing signs of great distress. In short, high-speed industrialization in South Korea, as in Taiwan, carries a steep price, making Seoul face the question of whether explosive economic growth is socially sustainable.

CONCLUSION

The major challenge to the NICs and to future contenders for NICdom arises not only from the actual and expected costs of high-speed industrialization, but also from globalization. Even if the Asian NICs were held up as worthy models of development for the rest of the Third World, their embeddedness in historical social and cultural structures would rule out replication.

Global restructuring is re-embedding the Third World in neo-liberal capitalism and creating fissures across national boundaries. Movements toward economic regionalism, massive migratory flows, and new political and social constellations make a linear pathway towards NICdom a dubious possibility. Above all, the state is being restructured to become more a facilitator of global capital than a guardian of the national interest. Regionalism is producing uneven channels to the centres of global production, finance and information. Against these developments, a NIC model of economic growth appears too abstract and static.

The Asian NICs managed to align their domestic orders to the global political economy in a period favourable to industrialization in the periphery. In the era of globalization, new strategies have to be conceived and implemented to attain economic growth.

Finally, in the absence of strong labour movements to win political and economic concessions, the projection of a 'common good' has been left to an authoritarian state. In the case of South Korea, Taiwan and Singapore, political power has been concentrated in a state committed to high-speed economic growth. The legitimacy of the state has been inextricably tied to rates of capital accumulation and economic growth. With persistently high growth rates, maintaining a docile labour-force was possible. This is changing, especially in South Korea, where the labour movement has grown much stronger. In the case of the Asian NICs, political will to bring different parts of society together was clearly based on authoritarian practices. In a period of democratic sensibility, Third World countries will have to follow an alternative route to establish a common purpose.

7 The Exit Option, Withdrawing from and Re-entering Global Capitalism: China under and after Mao

In recent years, the People's Republic of China, like many underdeveloped countries, has sought to industrialize and to sell more of its manufactured products overseas. Once isolationist, China is now one of the world's 10 largest trading nations, enjoying a surplus of nearly $25 billion dollars with the USA alone (which puts China second only to Japan in the size of its imbalance with Washington). And while the Western economies have registered recession or only mild economic growth rates, the Chinese economy seems to be on fire, recording an average growth of 10 per cent in the past decade. Attracting nearly $90 billion of FDI in the same period, China is poised to be the largest economy in the world by 2010 according to purchasing-power parity, a measure the World Bank uses to assess the real worth of the wealth of nations.

One effect of Chinese exports to the USA is the redundancy of American workers, especially in the textile industry. Pressure has mounted to restrict China's access to the US market, and Washington has responded by cutting Beijing's textile quotas. This has produced no dramatic changes in Chinese trade behaviour. With an eye to China's enormous market, Washington has often relented, granting Beijing Most Favoured Nation (MFN) status, despite major economic and political differences with Beijing; China is too important economically to push around. For now, American investors seem quite pleased with China's rise as an economic power, for they do not want to be left behind Japan and other developed powers vying for economic presence in the world's potentially largest market of 1.2 billion consumers. Weighing heavily in the political decision on US trade policy is a desire to outpace Western European businesses and Washington's determination to outflank Japan in the Asia-Pacific region. Notwithstanding basic tensions with Beijing over security, commerce, and human rights, trade privileges which are normally reserved for the other major Asian producers, all staunch members of the capitalist camp, have been accorded to China.

That China succeeded in winning concessions from the USA is striking, for the underdeveloped countries have triumphed infrequently in their economic dealings with the West. Not only is China's MFN status an emblem of China's re-emergence in the world political economy, but also it gives pause to consider that nation's industrial and agricultural development. Viewed historically, the contradictory nature of China's agricultural and industrial policies is the key to understanding the achievements and failures of an inward-looking development strategy and China's re-entry into the global political economy.

'THE EAST IS RED'

A shortage of arable land and extreme inequality in property ownership stalled capital accumulation in prerevolutionary China. Whereas landlords and wealthy peasants owned the best land, animals and tools, the bulk of the population rented their fields and implements or worked as wage labourers. In bad times peasants had little protection from the ravages of floods and droughts. In good times dilapidated infrastructure kept rural dwellers from marketing their crops save through unscrupulous merchants. Constantly threatened by indebtedness and foreclosure, peasants lacked the power and resources to develop rural society.

The condition of women was particularly desperate in the old China. Social and economic practices of feudalism marginalized women in virtually all walks of life. The Confucian adage that 'for a woman to be without ability is a virtue' defined the mental universe of rural China. One of the key effects of land reform under the New China was to make strides in the status and role of women. In the first decade of China's socialist experiment, the abolition of feudalism opened up greater opportunities for women's equality, though their condition in subsequent years was marked by the resurgence of patriarchy.

Urban industry was no more advanced than the agricultural sector. Fighting during the Japanese occupation of the Second World War and the Civil War between Nationalist and Communist forces devastated the budding industrial economy. In 1949, industrial output and grain production amounted to half of the prewar peak level. Transportation networks were destroyed. The Guomindang (the National People's Party that had ruled from 1928 to 1949) looted the state treasury, stripping the country of its foreign exchange reserves. The Soviet Union, seeking war spoils, commandeered over half of the industrial capital in Manchuria, a major centre of manufacturing and transportation. China's nascent manufacturing sector included a textile industry, electrical power plants and steel mills. Adept at absorbing foreign technology, a bevy of scientists, engineers and skilled workers spearheaded this small but vibrant sector. Concentrated in a few coastal cities, its products (mostly consumer goods) were largely for export. Clearly a miniscule export-oriented manufacturing sector, alongside rural impoverishment, could not sustain a national economy. The abject state of capital accumulation in China in 1949 was not only a catalyst for revolution but also a formidable challenge for the Communists who seized power.

OUT OF THE ASHES

At the time of the Chinese Revolution, the USA held a commanding position in worldwide production and trade. Washington sought to enforce 'a multilateral and competitive trading system in which American goods would enjoy the widest possible access'. Old policies on import controls and other protectionist measures were renegotiated through a new complex of international organizations to harmonize with US interests. Prerevolutionary China was to be part of this system: in 1948, the USA provided 48.4 per cent of China's imports, approximately 250 per cent more than in the years immediately before the war.

The USA had furnished large amounts of military and development aid to the Nationalist regime in prerevolutionary China. In 1950 the Truman administration decided to support the defeated Guomindang as the sole legitimate government of China. Moreover, the administration sought to isolate the new regime by adopting a two-pronged policy of international trade embargo and military containment. The USA had already applied extensive controls to the Eastern European countries and had attempted to ensure compliance by its Western allies. The Western powers followed suit but not always to the letter. Britain and Portugal, for example, maintained indirect contact with China through their colonies, Hong Kong and Macao.

To enforce the boycott against China and other socialist countries, the USA set up an international coordinating committee in 1952. The

Chinese Community Party(CCP), in turn, threatened to nationalize foreign holdings. Adamant in its stand, Washington showed no willingness to end the boycott and blocked Chinese assets in the USA. Beijing retaliated by seizing American property and assets in China. The USA repeatedly wielded its veto and influence in order to exclude China from the UN and other international agencies. Aid was denied, and China was barred from multilateral agreements on development, trade and finance. Meanwhile, the USA concluded a series of bilateral and multilateral military agreements in Asia. The Truman administration proclaimed its commitment to defend Japan, Korea, Taiwan and Indo-China.

Although some Western countries violated the trade embargo, China had already turned to the Soviet Union and Eastern Europe for economic assistance. In the military realm, China faced the US-led effort to subdue Korea's communist north. In October 1950, Chinese forces blocked General Douglas MacArthur's attempt to cross the thirty-eighth parallel, and then checked his campaign aimed at the Manchurian border. Three years of war had not ended nor weakened communist rule in North Korea and China.

Isolated from the West and assisted by the East, the CCP sought to convert China's weaknesses into strengths. As noted, the vast population was engaged in inefficient, labour-intensive agriculture, and the minute manufacturing sector was limited to a few urban areas. China lacked essential agricultural inputs, and a capital-intensive policy would surely have driven people from the land. The CCP therefore planned to utilize the existing basis of agriculture as a source of surplus. The state would buy grain from peasant producers and sell it at a higher price in urban areas. A large measure of the difference between producer prices and consumer prices would be channelled into the industrial sector and targeted according to the national development plan.

When the Soviet Union introduced a similar strategy in the period after 1928, the authorities often relied on coercion in the countryside. The Russian Revolution had originated in the cities, and the Bolsheviks lacked long involvement in the peasant sector. By contrast, the CCP had experimented with reforms to supplant landlord power in its northern China base areas, in some cases satisfying claims by poor peasants for redistribution without alienating middle peasants.

The CCP could not have adopted the coercive measures practised in the Soviet Union. Grain consumption in China after 1949 verged on bare subsistence. However meagre, the Soviet peasantry's standard of living in the 1920s hovered above subsistence, allowing the state to skim surplus for investment in industry. China had no such room for manoeuvre. A policy of cutting peasant consumption would have caused massive starvation. Internal capital accumulation required increasing the rate of savings by expanding, not merely redistributing, agricultural output. The problem, of course, was not simply to amass surplus but to generate it in the first place. The task was to increase peasant production, hold down consumption and deliver surplus to the state. For those in power, the key question was how to stimulate productive forces both in industry and agriculture in a manner that improved the material conditions of the working classes.

During the era of postwar reconstruction, vast new territories came under the control of the CCP, often in areas where the party lacked organizational structure. While the CCP faced the challenges of economic development, it had to lay its political foundations in central and southern China. Mobilizing its cadres, the party instructed the villages to sort the local populace into classes, separating the rich from the poor, the exploited from the exploiters, the landlords from the peasants. This process was meant to raise class consciousness and to establish the party's legitimacy by empowering the peasantry.

To generate revenue for the state, the CCP introduced tax reforms with exemptions for the downtrodden. The authorities kept average tax rates below the levels set by the Guomindang. In addition to cancelling all back rent owed to landlords and the credit institutions, the CCP reduced interest rates by 25 per cent. The new tax and interest rate policies were accompanied by land reform, a programme which aimed to sever feudal landlords' control of agriculture.

Government policy stipulated that all peasants had the right to work a plot of land without infringement by landlords. In some villages, however, there were no landlords. The overzealous implementation of government policy thus deprived rich and middle peasants of their land, alienating them from the worker-peasant alliance. In other villages, redistribution was carried out smoothly, but the amount of land transferred to peasant households was relatively small. In Hunan and Hupei, a family of five generally received between one and two acres.

At the same time that the CCP restructured rural property relations, it increased agricultural output beyond prewar peak levels and attained greater political legitimacy. One obstacle, however, was the lack of trained cadres to implement policy, particularly outside the party's base areas. New recruits, many of them unschooled in Marxism and without technical know-how, were responsible for instituting state programmes at the local level. Learning their jobs by trial and error, they provided leadership, channelled state policies to the village and conveyed information to the party hierarchy about local conditions. Partly owing to its weak foundation in many villages, the party allowed new recruits great latitude in interpreting policy. They were encouraged, for example, to launch bold attacks on counterrevolutionary elements. Not surprisingly, abuses of power often resulted. In such cases, the people were supposed to have recourse through 'rectification' campaigns: public criticism of the performance of party cadres, who could be held responsible for their action. These campaigns actually served as a group-pressure method of regulating behaviour within the party.

The political and economic reforms established new mechanisms for capital accumulation. Most importantly, the reorganization of the agricultural sector provided the conditions under which peasants could produce a larger surplus for investment. Without swelling government expenditure, this policy allowed the CCP to pump a small supply of capital into the industrial sector.

In industry, the state sought not only to complete the tasks of reconstruction but also to control private enterprise. Whereas the state took over large enterprises owned by 'bureaucratic capitalists' and the former government, it preserved a sphere for the market economy and permitted private concerns to do business. Even so, with the expansion of the state sector, an increasing amount of revenue flowed into public enterprise. State companies dominated trading in key commodities. The CCP nationalized extensively but steered clear of across-the-board expropriation and refrained from introducing wage and price controls.

In foreign economic relations, ties to the Soviet Union were crucial in the reconstruction period. Faced with Western intransigence, Beijing and Moscow signed a 'Treaty of Friendship Alliance and Mutual Assistance' in 1950, followed by agreements on long-term credits and defence. COMECON's (the Council for Mutual Economic Assistance) share of China's trade increased from 29 per cent in 1950 to 70 per cent in 1952, the end of the recovery period. Soviet loans, heavy industrial equipment and advisers played an increasingly important role in China's effort to overcome underdevelopment.

In 1952, prices stabilized, marking an end to the runaway inflation of the immediate post-war period. After three years of rehabilitation, annual output of grain and cotton rose 11.3 per cent and 53.6 per cent respectively over the prerevolutionary peak. Steel production jumped 46 per cent above the previous record. Coal increased 7 per cent above the highest preliberation level. Further, the state restored transportation networks, with all prewar rail lines in operation by 1951. Remarkably, China completed the reconstruction process while embroiled in the Korean War and in the throes of a rural transformation.

THE FIRST STATE PLAN

In 1952–3, Chinese planners prepared the First Five Year Plan. They faced awesome challenges in the countryside, where class antagonisms raged. Poor peasants were still insecure and feared that their land would be reclaimed. Centralized control over land could reverse egalitarian reforms and redound to the advantage of rich peasants. Similarly, in manufacturing, a capitalist class could rear its head and find new opportunities for accumulation. Various restrictions on business would probably hamper growth, but successful capitalist ventures could jeopardize socialism.

The First Five Year Plan, operative in 1953, gave new direction to China's development strategy. The plan called for increasingly advanced forms of cooperative farming. Typically, Chinese peasants cultivated fragmented plots far from each other. Noting the vast amount of nonproductive labour power devoted to transporting tools and workers, the state decided to consolidate agricultural units into larger and more rationally organized enterprises.

As a first step toward collectivization, MATs (Mutual Aid Teams, which were small units in which a handful of peasant households pooled their labour) encouraged peasants to help each other with the harvest, furthering what had previously been an informal practice in the countryside. While materially helping the poor peasants, the MATs roused the communal impulses of the peasantry without attempting to convert private land ownership. There was no attempt to collectivize in one fell swoop. The plan called for gradual change, with several phases in which each step followed on the heels of the previous one. Seasonal MATs were to be replaced by permanent teams, which would share land and tools. In time, teams would merge, forming larger work units and evolving into more comprehensive collectives.

The party envisaged that cooperatives would be the main vehicle for transforming the countryside. They were to mobilize labour for such projects as irrigation works and land reclamation. By amassing the savings of peasant households into a general fund, the cooperative could provide the basis for productive investment. Risk would thereby be spread, easing the burden of failure by individuals or enterprises. The cooperatives, each one encompassing a cluster of farms, would also offer economies of scale in the use of machinery, seed and irrigation schemes. Finally, the cooperatives furnished an improved social security system: a welfare fund to protect peasants when times were bad. Among the many problems in installing the cooperatives was the peasantry's ingrained attitude of self-interest. Smallholders with relatively good land were sometimes unwilling to pool their plots with those of poor peasants, since transfer of property disproportionately benefited the latter. Skilful farmers hesitated to work hard when their reward was commensurate with that of their less productive team members. At issue were incentives: how to persuade peasants to transcend self-interest for the common good?

Peasants would develop cooperative attitudes only if the new units could demonstrate their superiority as a system of agricultural production. This was a tall order: nothing less than new technology, improved management, reduced expenditures and higher levels of output. To entice peasants, a network of people's banks offered savings programmes and low-interest loans to the cooperatives, facilitating transactions with state trading companies. While granting preferential rates to the cooperatives and to poor peasants, the banks siphoned domestic capital, funnelling it to high-priority productive structures. The expansion of the banking system brought an end to the private moneylender market. The state's interlocking policies in the areas of price, trade and finance closed off unregulated private accumulation, but did not entail direct expropriation (save part of the property of the landlord class). In the peasant sector, one could no longer amass wealth by renting land, hiring labour, lending money or buying cheap and selling dear. Income would accrue only through expanded production. In theory, increasing numbers of peasants would prefer cooperative agriculture, because more surplus could be generated at less risk through joint efforts.

As before, surplus from the agricultural sector was to be diverted to urban industry, particularly to capital-intensive enterprises. In industry, the CCP squeezed private concerns. State enterprises sold their products below market value until competitors went out of business, levied exorbitant taxes on certain commercial activities and purchased shares in private companies. Thus government ownership of industrial enterprises snowballed from 34.7 per cent in 1949 to 67.5 per cent in 1956; the remaining firms in the latter year were joint (public-private) concerns. Under the First Five Year Plan, the state unswervingly directed over three-quarters of capital investment into a core of heavy industries, including a nucleus of 156 fully equipped factories imported from the Soviet Union. During the plan, agriculture contributed from 37 per cent to 46 per cent of total gross domestic profit but received only 8.6 per cent of total investment.

With the quickening pace of collectivization in 1954–5, agricultural output fell below the party's expectations. Despite the CCP's efforts to serve the interest of poor and middle peasants, the privileges of many wealthy peasants were intact, betokening renewed class conflict. Meanwhile, industrial output slackened. Worse yet, the imbalance between sectors caused unprecedented problems. Sluggish performance in the agricultural sector doubly threatened industry: lower agricultural output reduces investment and lessens peasants' capacity to purchase goods produced by local enterprises. This tendency is compounded when faltering industries are unable to provide the necessary inputs to fuel the agricultural sector. A decline in both sectors makes it even more difficult to motivate workers to meet production targets, for the people fail to reap rewards from the system.

By 1955, the Chinese economy was on a downward course. The First Five Year Plan called for 4.6 per cent growth per year between 1953 and 1957, but actual growth in 1953–4 came to only 1.7 per cent, a decrease from the previous year. In industry, growth in the production of consumer goods reached 26.7 per cent in 1953, then slipped to 14.2 per cent in 1954, and registered a negative percentage in 1955. Similarly in producer goods, 36.5 per cent growth in 1953 receded to 17.8 per cent in 1954 and to 14.5 per cent in 1955. These shortfalls were shocking because they occurred in the very sectors earmarked for substantial investment.

Equally troublesome was the repolarization of wealth in the countryside, weakening the position of the productive middle peasantry. The party sought to strengthen the relationship between this class fraction and the poor peasants, both indispensable elements in the effort to augment agricultural production.

According to Vivienne Shue's data on agricultural income in 1954, productivity per *mou* (one-sixth of an acre) of cultivated land was higher among middle peasants than among poor peasants. In fact, the average household income of middle peasants per *mou* approximated that of rich peasants. However, on average, rich peasants' overall household income far exceeded middle peasants' household earnings. The rich peasants generated a higher level of income less by elevating their rate of productivity and more by virtue of owning and controlling the means of production, especially land, tools and wage-labour. The relative deterioration of conditions for middle peasants thereby offset the state's egalitarian reforms and eroded the support of a key class fraction for the new agricultural policies.

In June 1955, Mao Zedong admitted the failings of agricultural policy and advocated a stepped-up pace of collectivization. Although his fellow party leaders and state officials in Beijing did not wholeheartedly embrace Mao's position, the bulk of the peasantry supported his initiative. Yet, as Shue notes: 'in the provinces and rural counties they [the local leaders] leapt at his words as the solution to their problems of rural investment capital seepage'.

The wave of collectivization swept through the countryside. In March 1955, only 14.2 per cent of peasant households belonged to Agricultural Producer Cooperatives. By May 1956, 91.2 per cent joined, manifesting the end of private agricultural production in China.

Mao repeatedly emphasized that channelling peasant resources into large units and developing them at a rapid pace would be the catalyst for a radical transformation in the countryside. Critics have assailed his policy on the ground that it marked both the abandonment of efforts to accommodate gradual transition and the denial of democratic participation in the socialist project. In response Shue explains that, 'Mao accurately perceived the precariousness of the shifting balance of power in the villages.' She adds: 'The peasant constituency for a swifter transition was clearly in place; the demand for it was voiced by a restless village cadre force.' Given the currents that backed collectivization, the difficulties with the policies emanating from the First Five Year Plan signalled the need for a dramatic change in the agricultural sector.

In industry, the wages of industrial workers rose 19 per cent between 1954 and 1956; however, feeble output prompted a review of policy. The difficulties may be traced to the organization of production at the factory level. China imported not only factories from the Soviet Union, but also borrowed Moscow's system of industrial relations, which tied rewards (wages and promotion) to performance. In nearly one-quarter of China's industries in 1956, wages were determined by piece-rate: the volume of a worker's output governed his or her remuneration according to standards set by managerial specialists. The system pitted line workers against managers; the former sought to hike wages by pushing for changes in rates. In the face of budding protests, the CCP installed small worker-administered teams to organize and discipline their cohorts. Management groups continued to determine wages according to piece-rate calculations.

The piece-rate system circumscribed the authority of the small groups, denying the party a base in the factories for motivating workers. Workers thus channelled their grievances to factory-level management, increasing the probability of factory-wide protest. Group leaders found themselves in an ambivalent position, upholding management policy and sympathizing with workers' grievances about piece-rates. These leaders were placed in a potentially adversarial relationship with workers and exercised little influence over the setting of rates. The reward system, according to Andrew Walder, 'directly undermined Party efforts . to establish political and social control in industry at precisely the time they were forced to extend it over a rapidly expanding state sector'.

In addition, the system of wage determination was ill-suited to the vagaries of an underdeveloped economy undergoing a radical transformation. Geared to worker effort, the piece-rate method provided no means to compensate workers when production halted through no fault of their own. The Chinese economy did not yet run according to plan: goods were frequently delivered late, in insufficient quantities, or in substandard condition. When machines broke down, spare parts were in short supply. The reward system could not respond to such complications, thus worsening other industrial problems.

In both industry and agriculture, discontent among the rank and file threatened to distance the party from its principal support base. Clearly the CCP had reaped the benefits of reconstruction and land reform. But following the redistribution of wealth, it was human labour that had to produce greater value. The CCP still faced the fundamental problem of how to build a self-sustaining economy.

'MASS PRODUCTION OF USELESS PRODUCTS'

Against a backdrop of a rapidly changing international environment, central planners reassessed the strategy of accumulation adopted under the First Five Year Plan. Imports from the COMECON countries cushioned China against the effects of the US-led trade embargo. With the recovery of the Western economies in the mid-1950s, an increasing number of European countries violated the embargo. Ultimately, the USA alone remained adamant about maintaining the boycott of certain commodities. Meanwhile, China developed ties with the embryonic non-aligned movement. Premier Zhou Enlai played a key role in the 1955 Afro-Asian conference in Bandung, and China promptly established diplomatic and trade relations with such newly independent countries as Ghana and Guinea.

In 1956 Nikita Khrushchev shocked the outside world by attacking Joseph Stalin's strategy of 'Industry First' and his abuses of power. Given their own experience with Soviet industry, the Chinese were famil-

iar with its shortcomings and wary of domination by a powerful neigh-
bour. While Moscow wanted Beijing to develop as part of a socialist
commonwealth, in which the Soviet Union was the senior partner,
China sought Soviet aid to boost national industrial development. Fol-
lowing differences over the impending offshore islands crisis and the
Soviet Union's hesitancy to bolster China's fledgeling industries,
Beijing moved towards self-reliance on defence questions in 1958.
Moscow then withdrew its atomic assistance in 1959. In addition, the
Soviet Union called home many advisers. Trainloads of Soviet equip-
ment and supplies were halted, slowing China's industrial recovery.

In the light of these international pressures and recurrent failings in
domestic economic policy, the CCP reconsidered the lofty growth targets inscribed in the Second Five Year Plan, which began in 1958. China
embarked on the Great Leap Forward: a mass mobilization to raise
industrial and agricultural production. This campaign emphasized the
simultaneous development of industry and agriculture, or 'walking on
two legs'. Age-old methods of production were to be used alongside
new technologies. The campaign was to be spearheaded by novel forms
of social organization, with renewed ideological consciousness.

The state would direct added inputs into agriculture and assign
priority to the mobilization of labour in the countryside. Central planners called for new vehicles to enlist underemployed and offseason
labourers. Thus peasant communes, established in the period 1958–60,
were to serve as the nucleus of administration and decision making in
rural areas. Planners reasoned that the communes could make extensive use of labour-intensive techniques and raise the level of productive
forces in the countryside without requiring vast inputs from the industrial sector. Then expanded agricultural output would produce surpluses for investment in the cities. Productivity in the agricultural
sector could be enhanced with little supplemental cost.

The revised plan also stressed small-scale industry. The party
exhorted peasants to expand local operations which provided inputs into
the farm economy: cement works, iron foundries, fertilizer plants and
so on. The urban industrial sector would maintain its large-scale, capital-intensive basis, fed by redirected farm surplus. The state aimed to
bring select industrial projects closer to the communes, in the locale of
raw materials and large markets, thereby spreading employment opportunities and reducing transportation costs.

Central planners believed that in one intense effort, a great leap,
China could realize its latent potential. They set new production targets
and, initially, the country's teeming population made impressive gains.

Steel production more than doubled, from 5.35 metric tons in 1957 to 11.08 metric tons in 1958. Total grain output rose from 191 metric tons to 206 metric tons during the same period. The targets, however, were later revised downwards because of falsified reporting at the beginning. Successive years of drought and flooding followed the excellent harvest of 1958. Equally nettlesome were the human errors of poor planning, overzealousness in the execution of policy, and breakdowns in communication. Although such difficulties were not new, the Great Leap Forward heightened uncertainty and accentuated tensions.

In the 1959–60 period, the economy entered a depression. While industry grew slightly, agricultural production dropped precipitously, reducing per capita grain output to its lowest level since 1949. Aside from the overall decline, the problem was that the party had established a new social structure of accumulation without eliminating powerful vestiges of the old structure. Within the worker-peasant alliance, conflicts developed between industrial labourers and factory leaders, between peasant and collective, and among fractions of the peasantry. As was to be expected, counterrevolutionary tendencies among former landlords and the capitalist classes were rife.

The party gradually consolidated power and extended its reach, but at considerable cost. Generally speaking, local leaders were creative, flexible and adept at matching the central government's policies with community needs. However, as the party sought to increase agricultural output and to appropriate surplus at higher, assured levels, central officials became less tolerant of partial compliance with their policies. The authorities in Beijing came to view local leaders as untrustworthy aides and as rivals. No longer was the rural party a basis for, and an extension of, central authority, bringing government to the people and facilitating communication with leaders at the top. Now the party sought to diminish the power wielded by local cadres.

Local leaders became increasingly guarded and less candid in dealing with the centre for fear that they would be blamed for deviations from policy. They began to regard their relationship with the government as competitive.

Similarly, in industry, the problems of planning and party power caused a shift in policy. In the late 1950s, the party instituted a work-group system to replace Soviet-style piece-rates. Under the new system, a small number of workers and a leader evaluated performance and determined rewards, including wages, promotions, food ration stamps and medical care. The work-groups considered not only output but also an employee's attitudes towards colleagues, the factory and socialism. This system reduced the power of technical personnel formerly responsible for setting piece-rate quotas, giving the impression of redistribution of power in the factory.

However, the redistribution was lateral, not vertical; group leaders assumed power in the factories. The new leaders dominated the evaluation process and hence the allocation of rewards. In sectors where work-groups were most important, principally in state-owned heavy industries, jobs were few and the remuneration generous by Chinese standards. Workers coveted these jobs, knowing that their economic standing hinged on maintaining employment in the same sector, which invariably meant in the same factory. Rewards were tied to one's performance evaluation by fellow workers and especially by the group leader. The locus of conflict over wages and working conditions thus shifted from the relations between labourers and factory-level management to the arena of small groups. This system enabled the party to prevent factory-wide and industry-wide opposition. Activist workers could be coopted by granting rewards tying the most articulate and politically engaged employees to the power structure; and disgruntled workers could be brought into line by actual or threatened sanctions.

The party paid a political cost for effective control of the shop floor. Factory workers were called upon to direct their grievances to the very individuals who determined their wages, thus impeding genuine communication. Leaders and workers engaged in a ritual wherein employees were supposed to raise criticism while the group sought to achieve consensus. This exercise was something less than democratic and participatory: while leaders attempted to enforce directives, workers conformed to standards during structured political activities. Like their rural counterparts, urban workers looked out for their own security and avoided politically sensitive issues.

The CCP exhorted workers to adopt innovative techniques which would enable Chinese industry to overcome the 'superstitions' of Western productive methods. Workers were to increase production without additional capital investment. The labour force thus responded by taking shortcuts to meet quotas. In steel mills, for example, workers cut heating time in half by doubling temperature. The new procedure had a disastrous effect on quality. Factories produced 'steel that was like butter' and machines that did not work. Such problems could not be candidly broached at group meetings, for workers feared receiving a poor evaluation.

A major casualty of this reckless strategy was environmental degradation. Premised on vast increases in wood and coal production to propel industrial production, Chinese planners unleashed an unprecedented assault on the environment. The effects of these practices continue to plague China today.

During the Great Leap Forward, the CCP dismissed technological constraints and proven engineering practices, applying instead untested production methods in vast areas without regard for differences in local conditions. In the new rural industries, unschooled cadres and inexperienced workers were unfamiliar with the notions of inspection and quality control. Industries lacked essential inputs, primarily because of recurrent shortfalls in the agricultural sector. Food supplies were inadequate in the cities and the countryside. In the face of impending famine and widespread opposition to the Great Leap Forward, the party again reappraised its strategy of accumulation.

READJUSTMENT

The failure of the Great Leap Forward demonstrated the futility of attempting to develop the agricultural sector without a sizeable investment in the countryside. Little uncultivated land remained, and the labour-intensive land reclamation efforts had apparently reached their limit. Further expansion of agriculture depended not only on mobilizing labour, but also on scientific advancement and substantial expenditure.

While internal sources failed to furnish an accumulation fund, tensions with Moscow continued to mount, culminating in the public expression of the Sino-Soviet split in 1960. That year 11 000 Soviet technicians went home, causing major disruptions in Chinese industry. Imports from the COMECON countries, which represented between 60 per cent and 80 per cent of total purchases in the 1950s, were drastically reduced.

In the period from its break with the Soviet Union in 1960 to Mao's death in 1976, China adopted a strategy known as self-reliance. In principle, this strategy entails an attempt to minimize participation in the global economy and to mobilize domestic resources. In fact, China's international options were limited, for it brooked opposition from both superpowers. China received no long-term commercial loans, foreign assistance or credit from international monetary institutions. The country by and large spurned tourism, private foreign investment, imported consumer goods and academic training in most Western countries. However, China did not totally withdraw from the international political economy. After an initial decline, foreign trade grew.

The trade profile changed: large quantities of grain, not inputs for heavy industry, dominated imports. Additionally, in its quest for self-reliance, China exported capital in the form of loan repayments to the Soviet Union and aid programmes for underdeveloped countries.

At home, in a startling reversal of policy in 1961, the CCP assigned priority to agriculture as the foundation of the economy. Next in order, light industry took precedence over heavy industry. Rejecting a strategy of rapid industrialization, planners held that the growth of industry would ultimately follow upon increasing extraction of raw materials in the rural sector. Although these shifts in policy were clearly articulated, there is little reliable information concerning actual allocations to respective sectors.

Without dismantling the infrastructure set up in the 1950s, the authorities decentralized communes so that smaller production teams would decide issues of management and decentralization. To provide incentive for increased production, the state relaxed grain quotas. Most importantly, the state invested substantially in new agricultural inputs, authorizing long-term, interest-free loans to stimulate the production of chemical fertilizer, tools and equipment such as electric water pumps.

Not only did the state invest in communes, but it also provided material incentives for individual peasant producers. Private plots, eliminated during the Great Leap Forward, were restored, allowing independent accumulation and household consumption outside the network of cooperatives. The state thus tolerated a very limited role for the market economy.

In the industrial sphere, planners called for the consolidation of all installations. The nucleus comprised factories inherited from the pre-1949 capitalist period, large plants supplied by the Soviet Union during the 1950s and small rural industries inaugurated during the Great Leap Forward. A major problem was the lack of linkages between these disparate industries. Now planners sought to lay the groundwork for the sharing of technical know-how and administrative skill. Unlike the old formula of expanding investment in industry with little consideration for quality, the new pattern was to synchronize and improve existing facilities.

Novel policies in agriculture and industry emphasized coordination, better management and streamlined administration. The economists and technical specialists demoted during the anti-superstition campaigns and the Great Leap Forward regained positions of authority in the planning process. In factories, the influence of technical experts increased relative to that of work-group leaders. Central officials assumed greater power over planning, provincial economic matters and even individual enterprises. They sought to impart discipline in industry by introducing austerity measures, closing non-competitive factories and restraining workers' wages to cut costs. Undertaken to promote efficiency, implementation of the new policies sometimes required the application of brute force. The state pushed educated, urban youth out of the cities into the countryside, thereby shifting the burden of supply to the rural communes.

The readjustment reforms effected some savings, but an inept swollen bureaucracy swallowed up surpluses, preventing the state from substantially building its accumulation fund through a range of policies. Enterprise managers, struggling to meet output quotas, adopted devious tactics. From a manager's vantage point, underproduction jeopardized one's position while overproduction caused the next quota to increase. Managers, therefore, concealed excess output. Goods were left unfinished in one production period so that they could be added to the quota in the next period. To avoid coming in under quota, managers hoarded spare parts and raw materials. Such practices enabled factories to achieve their targets, but the waste and inefficiency drained China's industrial sector.

To remedy similar problems, Eastern European countries introduced market forces in the state sector. Chinese officials in the 1960s, however, considered this course 'revisionist', and inveighed against the capitalist road.

CAPITALIST ROAD OR SOCIALIST ROAD?

The lesson Mao drew from the Soviet experience and the problems besetting the Chinese Revolution was that a one-sided emphasis on productive forces could not transform society. The greatest danger to revolution comes from above, Mao attested in 1966 on the eve of the Great Proletarian Cultural Revolution. He admonished leaders who failed to honour the principles and values of the revolution, dubbing them 'capitalist roaders', and called for the continuous involvement of peasants and workers in the management of their own affairs. Mao described the immediate aim of the Great Proletarian Cultural Revolution as the removal of the capitalist roaders.

The campaign to reduce bureaucratic privilege began with the promotion of egalitarianism in production units. All workers received 'supplementary wages' of about 5 *yuan* per month irrespective of how hard they laboured or what their group achieved. No amount of effort could increase their wages. Without the power to manipulate wage rewards, the group leaders relied on hortatory appeals, political education and group criticism. In place of work-group evaluations, study meetings and self-criticism sessions were supposed to provide collectivist incentives.

However, the living standards of industrial workers as a class did not improve during the 1960s. The state appropriated a large share of the margin between subsistence and total production as surplus for investment. Moreover, the changes in the incentive system introduced completely new forms of inequality. In the eight-grade scale of industrial wages, workers at the top earned three times as much as those at the bottom. Whereas in the past increasing seniority meant higher wages, the abolition of upward wage adjustments ended remuneration for seniority. However, the termination of adjustments meant that a worker who had received periodic bonuses now collected double or triple the wage of a recently hired worker equally skilled at the same job. The skilled worker recruited after the adoption of the new policy had no hope of closing the gap. Similarly, employees enlisted under the new policy in the 1960s earned the same amount as novices hired in the 1970s. The older worker was likely to have a family to support, but drew the same wage as a young, single employee. In wholly unanticipated ways, the new system failed to promote egalitarianism among workers. Apart from changing the incentive system, the state reduced the power of technical experts in industry. As many as 80 per cent of them were cut in some plants. These technicians received new assignments as production workers on the shop floor. Power devolved to line managers, who gained control over the allocation of resources in individual shops. The problems that afflicted management at the factory level – hoarding of spare parts, working to quota and avoiding novel experiments – contributed to a worsening performance on the shop floor.

The campaign against bureaucracy backfired, contradicting the plans of its architects. Faced with unprecedented levels of inefficiency in the 1970s, the state finally reinstated many technical experts, but the political cadres who had assumed responsibility for technical tasks during the 1960s often remained in place. Bureaucracies thus snowballed in size without any real change in incentives for direct producers.

The Great Proletarian Cultural Revolution failed to alter the basis of capital accumulation. There was not a great deal of rural mobilization, and the displacement of party leadership in the countryside fundamentally disrupted agricultural production. The shift from material incentives to intensified political education and appeals to Maoist values did not motivate peasants to increase output. At the local level, the shift engendered confusion, resistance and overzealousness. In one case, village elder Old Guo saved his family from starvation by selling a steady supply of duck eggs. The brigade leader viewed the private ownership of ducks as a 'sign of rotten capitalism', and he ordered Guo to cut the tail of capitalism by slaughtering the six ducks. Guo could either do as told or appear at a criticism session before the commune. He risked being branded as an opponent of the will of Mao, a grave offence. The old peasant put up a spirited defence and defied the brigade leader. 'Do you know whose ducks these are?' Guo asked. 'These ducks are Chairman Mao's ducks. One is for Old Liang, to repay my debt to him. But I'm sending the other five to Peking for Chairman Mao to eat. And whoever is crazy enough to kill my ducks, well, he's the one opposing Chairman Mao.'

Not only in Old Guo's village but in the rural areas generally, the Great Proletarian Cultural Revolution exacerbated the problems it was supposed to solve. The attack on bureaucracy failed miserably. The authority of central planners remained intact. Despite changes in institutional forms, the idea that workers could gain control over their own lives proved illusory. Not surprisingly, the Great Proletarian Cultural Revolution abruptly ended in 1969.

In the post-Cultural Revolution period, a crack soon appeared in the edifice of self-reliance. In 1972, Premier Zhou Enlai and President Nixon issued the Shanghai Communiqué, which pledged that China and the USA would work toward the normalization of relations. Chinese planners knew that they had to relieve pressure on peasant production. They sought to purchase grain, technical inputs and even industrial plant from the USA.

From the close of the Great Proletarian Cultural Revolution to 1975, agriculture and industry registered moderate growth. But the real wages of industrial workers in 1975 remained at the same level as in 1956, and the population continued to increase by about 2 per cent per year. The effort to build an accumulation fund still hinged on the appropriation of surplus from workers who lived at a near-subsistence level. Notwithstanding the reorganization of production and the development of productive forces, the mass of Chinese experienced little material improvement in their lives during the period from 1957 to 1976.

MAO'S LEGACY

Inasmuch as underdevelopment means the blockage that restrains the rational transformation of a social structure, the CCP did make some swift strides by eliminating China's old alignment of Nationalist power and feudal privilege. From the end of the Civil War in 1949 to Mao's passing in 1976, China underwent a metamorphosis in relations of production as well as in industry and, to a lesser extent, in agriculture. Inflation remained low. The party achieved structural change through land reform, collectivization and industrial control. At the same time, Mao avoided incurring a sizeable external debt and minimized dependence on foreign technology and raw material inputs. Faced with the cancellation of Soviet aid and a Western boycott, China formulated an inward-oriented strategy. By no means a blanket withdrawal from the world political economy, this strategy significantly reduced reliance on external market forces.

On the other side of the ledger a large number of economic policies were introduced, only to be reversed later. The reversal of policies took a toll, for any citizenry's tolerance for experimentation is not without limits. Mao's policies entailed extensive coercion and bloodshed. The rights of direct producers in a society under the weight of an elephantine bureaucracy were not protected. Top-heavy governmental structures and ritualized participation forestalled political competitiveness. All in all, China in 1976 was, and still is, a one-party state dominated by a bureaucratic class. In the final analysis, China under Mao was unable to solve the problem of underdevelopment through policies designed to generate internal accumulation and (though not entirely by choice) to constrict external sources of capital accumulation.

CHINA UNDER DENG

After a brief interlude of continued Maoist fervour between the waning years of the Cultural Revolution and the fall of the Gang of Four (the Maoist faction virtually in charge of Chinese affairs after Mao's death), China took perhaps its sharpest ideological turn in 1977–8. The emergence of Deng Xiaoping, previously twice purged for 'rightist' ideas, as China's paramount leader and his pro-capitalist cohorts began what can be regarded as China's Second Revolution. 'Black cat or white cat, it's a good cat if it catches mice', Deng's 1979 statement, captures his pragmatic thinking on post-Mao China. Initiating the Four Modernizations in agriculture, industry, national defence, and science and technology, China under Deng embarked upon an ambitious programme to catch up with the developed world by shunning inward-looking policies of development and self-reliance. Re-entry into the global political economy via an 'open door' policy, with acceptance of foreign trade, aid and investment, long regarded as taboo under Mao, was embraced as the manifesto of the new strategic design for China. China's 'socialist market economy' would take market principles as a basis for guiding economics. Personal acquisition would substitute for socialist values of egalitarianism, following Deng's pronouncement, 'it's glorious to get rich'. Satellite television, stock markets and Western management techniques would quickly become the new symbols of post-Mao China, though the public sector and planning would still loom large, giving China's developmental strategy a hybrid character. Contradictions of market socialism would also appear on the horizon and introduce unfamiliar problems to Chinese society.

Radical economic reform has been the lodestar in China since 1978, but especially after 1982. Special Economic Zones, inviting foreign investment with the carrot of investment incentives and cheap labour were set up in Shenzhen, Shantou, Zhuhai, Xiamen, and later in Hainan. Fourteen coastal cities and several free ports were also earmarked to provide special tax and investment incentives to erstwhile 'foreign devils', a Chinese epithet reserved especially for Westerners and the Japanese. Concentrated in southern China, close to capitalist parvenus Hong Kong and Taiwan, with Chinese populations known for their closely knit entrepreneurial networks and a hunger for extending their economic reach to the mainland, the 'open door policy' has grown to affect other areas as well, both in urban and rural regions of China. Public ownership has continued to be the norm, but increasingly ownership and management over the means of production are parting company. Once the 'socialist market economy' has entered its mature phase of development, the goal for central authorities is to get rid of socialist ownership altogether. In reality, two systems – public and private – have come to co-exist, often colluding and colliding to give central planners economic power and unexpected political troubles, while producing a spectacular rate of economic growth.

If ideological purity was the apparent guiding principle in the Mao years, Deng's reforms are premised on the elementary logic of letting the genie of self-interest lead China into the twenty-first century. With the economy in shambles after the massive dislocations of the Great Leap and the Cultural Revolution, Deng Xiaoping has sought legitimacy for the CCP in economic prosperity. Betting on the expectation that this new principle, rather than the proddings of ideology, would shake China out of its economic slumber, Deng put China on an uncertain road whose contours may not be easily discernible in the short run. The magnitude of success or failure of this mega experiment is likely to have far-reaching repercussions both inside and outside China. Evidence suggests that both success and failure are built into the Dengist model. Despite its current status as a 'developing country', China is fast emerging as one of the powerhouses in the global political economy with the most rapid rise in incomes in living memory. With economic transformation, however, comes social dislocation of unprecedented proportions. Both aspects of the reform provide useful insights into the hitherto uncertain trajectories of development and underdevelopment under conditions of a rapidly evolving global political economy.

The linchpin of Chinese *perestroika* was first reform in the rural areas, still the mainstay of nearly 80 per cent of China's population. A 'contract responsibility system' (*zeren zhi*) was introduced, linking income to output. Under the new system of market socialism, communes were abolished and replaced by individual initiative and local government. Peasants were granted primary responsibility for production decisions. This gave peasants virtual ownership rights on land. After meeting a state-set quota for produce, they could now dispose of the surplus as they deemed fit. The result of this system has been the rise of both a commodity economy in farm products and a market for labour-power with legal rights to hire labour. By the mid-1980s, this system was fully in place. Purchase prices of agricultural products came close to reflecting market prices. In addition, there was a proliferation of rural industries and the rise of commodity economy in the countryside. Both village and township enterprises in nearly all sectors of the economy – agriculture, industry, commerce, construction, services, transportation – mushroomed at a phenomenal pace. Acting mainly as an appendage to the agricultural sector via processing agricultural products and servicing machines, these enterprises have been a key, if ineffective, deterrent against mass exodus to the cities. Village and township enterprises, according to a 1995 survey by *The Economist*, have raised their share of China's industrial output from 10 per cent to 40 per cent in 15 years and employ 120 million workers.

Reforms in the rural areas have changed the face of modern China. The major difference is in the rural social structure, with a large non-agricultural population now co-existing with actual agricultural producers. Women have been particularly affected by these changes, with rural enterprises opening up new employment opportunities, though a UNU study found resistance against trading activity, attributable to negative attitudes among women towards money-making. The study also reported that, despite these reforms, the influence of established ideas remain a major fetter on development. Women are unable to acquire the technical knowledge of their male counterparts, underemployment is still wide spread and male supervision is applied in economic activity. The historical bias against women has been particularly acute in the light of China's one-child population policy, attaching special favour to mothers of sons while diminishing the status of mothers of daughters. 'Little emperors', a term to describe the limitless care, attention and pampering reserved for male children, is symptomatic of a societal context in which women tenuously negotiate their position in the family, while they struggle for equality in other spheres in civil society. A study by anthropologist Ellen Judd thus indicates that the culture of rural China is marked by a pervasive devaluation of women that is constantly denied in the practice of everyday life.

The reforms have also failed to stop the exodus from the countryside to the cities. Official Chinese estimates record over 100 million people (nearly 10 per cent of China's population) as the new migrants. A floating population (*liudong renkou*) of this size portends untold problems for central planners. With China adding an additional 12 to 15 million people to its population each year, the shrinkage of cultivatable land – due to urban construction, industrial and infrastructural development, and the proliferation of recreational sites, including China's new emphasis on golf courses and a rise in agricultural productivity – is expected to spawn another flight of 100 to 200 million peasants in the years ahead. This surplus population is generating additional obstacles to sustainable development in China. Diminishing state capacity to provide services for this marginalized element, rising crime rates associated with this group's plight as well as slum-like conditions in China's biggest cities – already mega-centres by global standards – could make China's economic 'miracle' less sustainable in the long run.

Chinese cities offer the most visible contrast to the spartan days of the past. Resembling one large construction site, urban China is in the throes of a building fever. High-rise buildings, department stores, five-star hotels, new residential and commercial blocks, highways, and airports are to be found in the major urban centres. Guangdong, one of China's poorest provinces in the 1970s, is now the richest, contributing 9 per cent of China's GDP. Fuelled by foreign capital and technology, mainly from Hong Kong, Taiwan and Macau, between 1986 and 1992, Guangdong absorbed over $10 billion of FDI. Up the Pearl River first came Hong Kong's obsolete machinery in search of cheap labour and land in the 1970s. Small-scale enterprises, mostly in light industry, offered a new home for enterprises from Hong Kong. The 1980s saw a wave of investments from Taiwan and south-east Asia, in part to fill the gap in the aftermath of the Beijing Massacre, which sparked a temporary departure of Western capital. Deng Xiaoping's southern sojourn in 1992, in which Shenzhen was slated by the paramount leader as China's model industrial centre, started the most recent wave of investments from the USA and other countries to garner the Chinese market. In 1994 alone, China received nearly $30 billion of FDI.

Despite rampant privatization of the Chinese economy, the state sector remains an ideological relic of the planned economy, but mostly as a prized source for influence and power of the party. Out of the more than 100 000 SOEs, two-thirds report losses, absorbing 70 per cent of state investment funds. Virtually subsidized by the 'private' sector, the SOEs provide employment and other benefits to 100 million workers. In 1992, however, Deng decided to carry out an extensive structural reform to give these enterprises more room to manoeuvre, set prices, hire and fire employees and select areas of possible investment. Hitherto, SOEs have had to rely heavily on bank credit to pay the wage bill and provide for worker benefits. It is estimated that without state subsidies, 20 million workers would be without work. Apprehension of catching the so-called 'Polish disease' – the symbiosis of industrial unrest and dissidence that allowed Solidarity to overthrow the communist system – plagues central authorities. SOEs remain a major barrier against such a movement.

The marriage of private enterprise and socialist planning has not been without turbulence. Income disparity, corruption, social instability and regionalization are some of the more troubling consequences of socialist China's embrace of market rationality. While urban incomes of 4 million inhabitants increased 12-fold by 1993 and 32 times the rural average, as reported by Orville Schell and Todd Lappin, 400 million people experienced a decline. Real income growth has not kept up with the 20 per cent annual rate of inflation caused by failing SOEs, a budget deficit and the massive dosage of foreign capital. The gap between the urban and rural areas as well as between the provinces is growing at a frightening pace. Urban workers earn three times the income of rural workers and enjoy better benefits. In the mid-1990s, the Chinese press reported several hundred incidents of rebellion in the rural areas.

To the extent that industrial growth is concentrated in the southern provinces, regional disparities have intensified. In turn, provinces have sought fiscal autonomy from Beijing, making it difficult to raise sufficient tax revenues. Immediately following the reforms, fiscal revenues represented nearly one-third of the GNP. Within 15 years, they had fallen to 13 per cent. Fiscal chaos is traceable to China's vast potential as a speculative market. Combined with one of the highest saving rates in the world (30 per cent), speculation, especially the emergence of stock markets, has contributed greatly towards economic volatility. Stock markets have proved to be a highly unstable affair, triggering riots in Shenzhen (an EPZ previously described by the Chinese authorities as 'a test tube of capitalism') in 1992.

No aspect of Chinese political economy reveals the effects of market-driven growth better than the environment. Against a historical legacy of abuse and neglect of the natural habitat, in both prerevolutionary and communist China, Deng's market socialism lifted all barriers to the exploitation of China's already endangered environment. The drive to raise agricultural productivity meant the heavy use of chemicals. The decline in arable land has been met by more intensive methods of cultivation, resulting in long-term loss in fertility. Qu Geping and Li Jinchang, two prominent experts on China's environmental problems, for instance, note a drop from 6 per cent to 2 per cent in the organic content of soils in parts of southern China. Population increase, with 16 million newborns a year, has raised the demand for timber and firewood, threatening China's forests, already among the world's poorest, ranking 131st by percentage of forest coverage. Depletion of grasslands, which destroyed them at the rate of 15 per cent per year in the 1970s, reached 30 per cent in the 1980s. Moreover, deforestation and grassland depletion are causing the extinction of species. According to official estimates, reported by Qu and Li, 15 to 20 per cent of vegetation faces extinction.

In addition, air pollution in China has reached dangerous levels. Coal consumption, currently at one ton per capita a year, is the main contributor to poor air quality. Acid rain is a chronic problem. Nearly 45 per cent of the samples of rainfall from 23 provinces, regions, and municipalities found acid rain. Key Chinese cities, including Changzhou, Changsha, Guangzhou, Guilin, Hangzhou and Suzhou, recorded acid rain. Noise pollution, notably from traffic, exceeds set standards in 94 per cent of major Chinese cities.

Drainage from industrial waste in 1990 was nearly three billion tons. Large sections of rivers traversing China's urban centres contain some of the heaviest metals, including lead, mercury, petroleum waste, phenols, and arsenic cyanides. Figures for 1990 show 580 tons of solid industrial waste produced in China. Chinese rivers absorbed 10 million tons of this mostly untreated waste. Large residues of waste, mostly in urban areas, pose another major problem.

Soil erosion, a consequence of deforestation, overgrazing or woodcutting, has reached unprecedented levels at five billion tons per annum, or 17 per cent of the world's total. The Yangtze River is a monument to neglect and industrial excesses. With the decline in soil fertility, 15.5 per cent of China's total land mass has turned into desert.

Undergirding environmental problems, China's race to the market is a corrosion of the social system and the undermining of social norms. Notwithstanding periodic appeals for moral rectitude and campaigns against 'spiritual pollution', corruption in bureaucratic and party circles is growing. Only the scale of China's accumulation rate conceals its real effects. China's highest leaders are struggling to regulate the country's banking and tax systems, electing to strengthen the legal code without initiating political reform as a means to control the pace of China's economy. For the most part, these efforts have slowed the tide. A combination of inflationary pressures and discontent among intellectuals, students and the urban poor contributed in 1989 to a massive pro-democracy movement, which anxious CCP leaders crushed with unmitigated ferocity. Etched in the memory of both leaders and masses, the Tiananmen Massacre betrays the zigzag of China's transition to a market economy, revealing the shortcomings of market-Leninism.

China's re-entry into the global political economy suggests both the opportunities and uncertainties of development in an evolving world order. Autonomous inward-looking policies in the first three decades of the New China guaranteed that it would not be pushed around like many other underdeveloped countries. Resolute leadership, consolidation of the state and a spirit of egalitarianism gave economic strength and confidence. Yet to break out of a demand-restricted economic pattern with meagre consumer industries, and to escape technological stagnation, Chinese planners found no alternative to riding the waves of globalization, especially the currents of the advanced industrial economies. With the legitimacy of the post-Mao leadership tied to economic prosperity as opposed to collectivist experimentation, this engagement acquired a built-in logic of self-reproduction. But with the 'open door' have come ideas and practices that unravel the socialist strategy altogether. The ascendancy of market relations in China, not subordinated to larger societal concerns, is spawning all-too-familiar inequities. In the absence of democratization, political repression is the CCP's main recourse to orchestrate China's embrace of globalization.

8 The Alternative Path, Weaving through Global Capitalism: Mozambique

Shortly after independence in 1975, a Marxist government in Mozambique sought to loosen its ties to South Africa's *apartheid* system. Mozambique approached transnational corporations in the USA and Western Europe to do business. Their reply was: sorry, chum, you must deal with our regional affiliate (which is in Johannesburg). Even today, if a parent company does agree to fill an order, say, for urgently needed spare parts, delivery time from Europe is at least four or five months. It can take weeks to get a technician out to Mozambique from Europe to repair one of the country's few printing presses, but only a couple of days from Johannesburg, an eight-hour drive from Maputo.

In Mozambique, the practicalities of what is required to break out of the web of underdevelopment cannot be understood without reference to the country's past. It is not enough to recount the activities and practices that exist today, because to gain an appreciation of the current situation, one must explain how present patterns took shape in the colonial era, and then examine the independent government's programme for reconstructing the national political economy.

THE COLONIAL LEGACY

Only two aspects of the historical context need concern us here: the peculiarities of Portugal's position in Europe and the all-important shift in colonial policy in the 1960s locking Mozambique into the southern African orbit. Traditionally, not only was Portugal the weakest country in Europe, but also the metropolitan economy itself was subordinate to that of England. Dating from 1373, the Anglo-Portuguese pact is one of the most durable alliances on record. The 1703 Treaty of Methuen assigned to Portugal the role of providing primary products for British manufactured goods. With the deterioration of Lisbon's textile industry and the development of a chronic trade deficit, economic dependence became the pattern. In the twentieth century, under the longest lived fascist regime in history, Portugal neither promoted industrialization nor modernized the agricultural sector, as did other European countries. At the 1884–5 Berlin Conference, at the behest of England, Portugal agreed to take state control in Africa to ward off French and Belgian claims to hegemony. In Mozambique, Portugal skimmed surplus from traditional colonial activities without engaging substantially in the modern sectors, which were largely the province of the non-national concerns. Big business in Lisbon did not invest heavily in the colonies, preferring instead safer markets elsewhere in Europe and Brazil. Seeking to guard against the 'denationalization' of Portuguese interests in the empire, Prime Minister Antonio Salazar introduced protectionism in the 1930s; however, when the colonial wars erupted in 1961, he was forced to reverse this policy, for the government desperately needed funds from foreign sources to fight a military campaign in three territories in Africa: Angola, Guinea Bissau and Mozambique.

With Portugal faltering in its efforts to bear the burden of empire in the 1960s, the hinterland territories of South Africa and Rhodesia took a commanding position in the economy of Mozambique. They oriented it not to the needs of the mother country, but to their own burgeoning economies, and investment concentrated on developing infrastructure. Indeed the basis for transforming Mozambique into a service economy linked to the interior had been established early in this century in a series of agreements between Lisbon and Pretoria. Lisbon was to supply a vast amount of cheap labour to fuel capital accumulation on the Transvaal. More precisely, Portugal would export at least 100 000 African workers per year to the mines provided that South Africa routed at least 47.5 per cent of its Transvaal transit trade via Mozambique's traffic facilities. After the first six months of their 12–18 month contracts, the workers received deferred payments for 60 per cent of their wages. With the introduction of the two-tier gold price in 1968, the mines remitted this premium to Lisbon in gold valued at the official rate of $42 per ounce, which the metropolitan treasury then sold at the free market price of $162 per ounce, retaining a windfall profit of perhaps $150 million per year. Largely as a result of this transaction, South Africa provided, before 1975, between 50 and 60 per cent of Mozambique's foreign exchange earnings. In addition, from 1965 to 1976, Maputo and Beira were the principal sanctions-breaking routes for Rhodesia, handling 85 per cent of Salisbury's imports and exports. From this traffic, Mozambique derived about 13 per cent of its total annual exchange earnings.

Portugal built and improved railways for use by the neighbouring countries without linking up domestic transportation routes. Today the rail line between Maputo and Beira, Mozambique's two major cities and ports, runs through Zimbabwe, and that between Beira and Nacala, the country's third largest harbour, is in Malawi. The railways all stretch east–west, from the coast to the interior; there is no all-weather road from north to south in this long, narrow country. Around this transportation network emerged an elaborate service sector to administer port traffic as well as major tourist centres for South Africans and Rhodesians.

The foremost monument to the combination of Portuguese political will and South African capital is Cabora Bassa, the largest dam in Africa and the fourth in size in the world. Portugal launched the project in 1969 with the intention that it would develop the whole Zambezi Valley, attract a large influx of white settlers and thereby serve as a bulwark against FRELIMO (Front for the Liberation of Mozambique). The massive dam was built by Consórcio Hidroelétrico do Zambeze, a multinational consortium led by the Anglo-American Company of South Africa. South Africa was not only a major sponsor of Cabora Bassa but is also the chief beneficiary of its hydroelectric power; all current on the DC high voltage line from the dam's giant generators, even for Mozambique, must be relayed via the Apollo converting station in the Transvaal.

Colonialism thus implanted a mega-infrastructure without laying the foundations upon which Mozambicans themselves could build a nationally integrated economy. We can now turn our attention to how independent Mozambique has sought to extricate itself from the colonial heritage.

MOZAMBIQUE'S STRATEGY OF ACCUMULATION

Following one decade of armed struggle, Mozambique promptly formulated a postcolonial development strategy. In the initial phase, its principal features were creating new party and state organs, hastening a rural transformation, promoting heavy industry and redefining links with the international economy. After calling attention to Mozambique's professed goals, we will turn to the strengths and weaknesses of this strategy.

The Party State

At the core of the political programme was an effort to form a tightly knit organization between the leadership and the masses. Whereas the front had been a broad coalition of anti-colonial elements, the party was launched at the Third Congress of FRELIMO in February 1977 as a vanguard of workers and peasants. It retained the name FRELIMO, and was open exclusively to those politically engaged citizens who did not collaborate with the colonial government. In order to enlarge the working-class component of the party, preference among applicants was given to the proletariat, which numbered only about 200 000. While embracing the familiar Marxist tenet that the working class is the 'leading force' in society, the Third Congress took issue with the classical Marxist position which views the peasantry as a residue of an antiquated mode of production, and accorded a central role to Mozambican peasants. Not only does the peasantry constitute the largest stratum in Mozambique, but it also 'had already great proof of its engagements in the revolutionary transformation of our society'.

Following the completion of a campaign known as 'structuring the party' in 1978, FRELIMO had primary responsibility for dismantling the colonial state, and was assigned a leading role in relation to the new state. In practice, FRELIMO had proceeded gingerly in winnowing the colonial legacy. Without going into detail, it was clear that remnants of the old state machinery – in particular, complicated administrative departments such as customs – remained intact. However, Mozambique, like other countries which aimed at a socialist transition, promptly introduced measures to place the economy under state control. The government nationalized the main branches of the economy, including private banking in 1978, and invited foreign concerns to submit claims for compensation. The assets and liabilities of the private banks – Casa Bancaria de Mozambique, Banco de Credito Comercial Industrial and Banco de Angola – were transferred to the Bank of Mozambique. A newly created People's Development Bank replaced the Portuguese quasi-state banks – Banco de Fomento and Banco Pinto e Sotto Mayor – which were given one year to conclude their business in Mozambique without incurring new assets and liabilities.

Added to this, the state took over all private property in land, apartment buildings and rental properties. It nationalized funeral parlours and all activities in the fields of medicine, law and education. But apart from such basic necessities in sectors related to social services, the state nationalized relatively few holdings (in most cases abandoned or sabotaged enterprises).

There were numerous other innovations in the state apparatus. Among them, the army was a new entity; the Ministry of Foreign Affairs was created from scratch without the typical crash-training in diplomacy being provided by the departing colonial power; the Ministry of Agriculture established extension services that the metropolitan authorities would not furnish; and the legal system was being remoulded along the lines of the juridical principles established in the liberated zones. (The commission charged with the task of revamping the legal system studied the practices of various other countries, including the socialist ones. While this was an instructive exercise, it was immediately obvious that the law as it evolved in other countries had limited applicability in Mozambique. In capitalist countries courts sanction principles which Mozambicans did not wish to uphold. In socialist countries such as Cuba, courts have no experience settling disputes over, say, polygamous marriages or initiation rites, which are major sources of civil conflict in Mozambique.) In 1978, the Law on Judicial Organization, which established a court hierarchy of tribunals, was passed. At all levels of the court hierarchy, lay judges were popularly elected. As a matter of policy, out of the three to five judges in each tribunal, at least one should be a woman. In the whole system in 1989, 15 per cent of the elected judges were women.

When Mozambicans began to abuse their positions of authority, FRELIMO inaugurated the 'Political and Organizational Offensive'. In 1980, the then President, Samora Machel, made a dramatic round of surprise visits to state enterprises, exposing incompetence and corruption. The president's initiative was symbolic, signalling FRELIMO's intention to revitalize inefficient structures and to call upon the people to take state institutions to task. In the wake of the president's announcements, some leading members of FRELIMO were relieved of their ministerial duties. Their new responsibility was to reinvigorate the party and, in a subsequent move towards decentralization, top officials were assigned to the provinces. As a result, many key figures in FRELIMO were no longer based in Maputo.

Special mention should be made of the social sector, an area where there was nearly a void under Portuguese rule. In health care, the situation was appalling. Of the 440 doctors in Mozambique on the eve of independence, only 87 remained in the country. An expensive private medical system catered to white settlers in the towns. Apart from traditional medicine, health services were practically unknown in the countryside. Thus not only did FRELIMO ban private medicine, but it also organized a rural health service and emphasized preventive rather than curative medicine. Most importantly, FRELIMO introduced free medical treatment, including a massive vaccination campaign that reached 90 per cent of the population by 1979. The number of health clinics more than doubled from 446 to 1039 between 1975 and 1981. Within five years of independence, infant mortality declined by 20 per cent. And against a background of a 5 per cent literacy rate at independence, 27 per cent of the population could read and write eight years later.

To give substance to this programme at the grass-roots level, locally elected mobilizing committees (known as dynamizing groups) organized political education projects, instilling FRELIMO's ideology into the rank and file. The dynamizing groups, envisaged as transitional entities, were gradually supplanted by party cells, which FRELIMO regarded as a more mature form of political institution. To stimulate greater political participation by the workers and peasants, the party drew on the 'mass democratic organizations': the women's movement, the youth movement, and production councils.

Even before independence, FRELIMO emphasized the significance of the participation and liberation of women. Samora Machel, during the opening conference of the Organization of Mozambican Women (OMM) in 1973, declared: 'The liberation of women is a fundamental necessity for the revolution, the guarantee of its continuity and the precondition for its victory.' (Coincidentally, the independence of the country came at exactly the same time as the beginning of the United Nations Decade for Women.) The 1975 Mozambican Constitution proclaimed equal rights for women and men, and stated that 'the emancipation of women is one of the State's essential tasks'. This entailed concrete steps to foster greater participation by women in the transformation of production: that is, an increased role for women not only in politics, but in industry and agriculture. For example, to involve women in the government's state farm programme, two weeks were set aside during which only women applicants were accepted. Other efforts included the OMM's emphasis on literacy for women. They also gained access to technical training through the cooperatives which had been limited to men.

The party's major step was to hold elections throughout the country for people's assemblies. In 1977, for the first time, all adult Mozambicans (except for those who had served the colonial state) were entitled to vote for candidates for political office within the single-party framework. The composition of these assemblies was a telling measure of the state's social base. Tabulations by a Mozambican weekly publication showed that at the district level 20 per cent of the deputies elected were workers and 40 per cent peasants; at the Popular Assembly, the country's national parliament, 32 per cent of those elected were workers and 29 per cent peasants. An indicator of changing social relations and the increasing role of women, too, was the representation of women in Mozambique's legislative bodies. Proportionally there were more women in Mozambique's Popular Assembly than in the US House of Representatives. Of the 219 deputies in the Assembly, 28 were women. Their presence was more pronounced in the local and district assemblies, where 28 and 24 per cent respectively of the deputies were women. In 1991, according to the UNDP *Human Development Report 1993*, 16 per cent of the seats of the Assembly were occupied by women, compared to 12 per cent for all developing countries, and 9 per cent for industrialized countries.

The party attempted to stimulate political consciousness by organizing a weekly meeting in ministries on Saturday mornings to discuss texts, party documents and speeches. At these sessions, which were essentially political science seminars, men and women were encouraged to voice their opinions and criticize the implementation of socialism in Mozambique. Some Saturday morning meetings were lively and constructive, while others were boring and ineffectual.

The decisions taken at the Third Congress marked a new stage in the growth and evolution of FRELIMO's ideology. The guiding principle in FRELIMO's thinking was the notion that the lessons of the liberated zones could be generalized to provide the basis for developing the entire country along socialist lines. For FRELIMO the liberated areas were the key, the embryo of the future Mozambique. Unfortunately there was no easy explanation for understanding what constituted a liberated area. Its essence lay in how problems were solved, how the people were organized and how social relationships had changed. Integral to this process were debate, discussion, criticism and self-criticism. In principle, Mozambicans were to talk out trying issues until mutually satisfactory solutions were reached. This procedure derived from the practices of self-rule established before independence day, when peasants engaged in armed struggle to oppose Portugal's attempt to move them into protected villages. Also known as strategic hamlets, they were modelled on those used by the USA in Vietnam. Given that Mozambicans were scattered throughout the countryside, they had to concentrate their forces and join together, forming new communities to counter the Portuguese offensive. These dramatic changes in the lifestyles of peasants generated the impetus for dispensing with antiquated agricultural practices, adopting improved technologies, and altering work habits.

Lessons from the popular struggle – the need for continual self-criticism and innovation – played an important role in the debates at

Fourth Congress, held in 1983. Jarred by military raids from South Africa, widespread drought and its own management errors, especially overcentralization, FRELIMO ran the risk of losing peasant support. The economy had pushed the peasantry into subsistence, for there was little to buy. Neglect of family farming contributed to a material crisis which mushroomed into political and ideological crises. Planners, meanwhile, believed that there were no fundamental problems because the class base of the state was in order. The Fourth Congress thus developed a sharp critique of the Marxism practised by FRELIMO. It was viewed as too abstract and outside the popular experience. Questions of policy and options, it was said, must be kept open. In the political realm, the primary problem was heavily economic: how to generate a socialist accumulation fund. According to the congress, the solution was to develop new linkages between agriculture and industry, between rural and urban areas, in order to revive the economy.

A Rural Transformation

Central to the deliberation at the Fourth Congress was the plight of the countryside, where FRELIMO had sought to reorganize production units in order to take advantage of Mozambique's fertile soil. (Mozambique is also endowed with sizeable mineral deposits including coal, bauxite, iron ore, copper and precious metals, reserves of natural gas, and a large fisheries potential.) Approximately 12 million Mozambicans, out of a population of 15 million (by 1995, 17 million), were involved in agriculture and, FRELIMO believed, only this sector could raise a surplus to rouse other sectors. Increasing agricultural production was deemed an urgent matter because the exodus of Portuguese settlers in 1975 and 1976 caused a sharp decline in yields on commercial farms, and Mozambique faced critical shortages of food.

At independence, FRELIMO established twin vehicles of rural development: state farms and communal villages. Formed from large plantations abandoned by the Portuguese, the 2000 state farms were meant to be the major source of the country's food supply. They were seen as the key to reducing food imports and to generating surpluses that could be invested in peasant production. While allocating considerable funding to the state farms, the government made a political decision not to transfer appreciable resources to the communal villages. Before 1983, 90 per cent of centrally planned agricultural investment went to the state sector. The purpose of the village scheme, which in 1982 encompassed almost two million people (nearly 15 per cent of the population), was to regroup peasants in order to provide them with social services and to increase production. FRELIMO called on residents to work together to build temporary housing, which was subsequently upgraded through self-help projects and small loans tendered by the state. In theory, the villages will achieve self-sufficiency and serve as the poles of socio-economic development throughout the countryside.

The resettlement strategy was most successful in the Limpopo Basin and the Zambezi Valley, the areas devastated in February 1977 and March 1978 by the worst floods of this century in Mozambique, impelling thousands of peasants to seek a new life. The pace was not as fast elsewhere, and some peasants returned to their former homelands. Let us see why and how FRELIMO responded.

Peasants in Mozambique are in a different position from their counterparts in neighbouring Tanzania or other African countries. Flying over rural Mozambique, one is struck by the diffuse distribution of the population. Peasants are generally grouped in clusters of two or three homesteads. They do not form medium-sized communities as in the adjacent countries, and neither do they live in large villages as do peasants in parts of West Africa. This pattern reflects a combination of historical factors: ancient wars among ethnic groups and the slave trade depopulated certain provinces; the Portuguese dispersed Mozambicans to prevent resistance to colonial rule; and many Mozambicans fled to avoid serving as contract labourers, often preferring to work in South Africa and Rhodesia. Distinct difficulties were encountered in the formation of communal villages, owing partially to the isolation and narrowness of rural existence which was quite pronounced even in comparison to other African countries.

Inspired by its success with the techniques of education and persuasion, FRELIMO encouraged peasants to attend meetings whose task was to examine Portuguese colonialism and the objectives of FRELIMO. Organizers explained that the form of settlement obstructed economic advancement and the provision of social services. Organizers reviewed the fundamental principles of agricultural economics, showing concretely the prospect of improvement. Then when a village was formed, peasants from nearby areas were invited to visit, to see for themselves the material and social benefits of living and working together, including increased productivity, schools, clinics and bore holes for water.

In some cases, peasants were simply tired of authorities and of moving. In the former war zones in Tete Province, for example, the Portuguese army had shifted a large number of peasants into strategic hamlets and given them free food. Not only were these peasants unaccustomed to hard work, but they expected the postcolonial state to feed them too, and otherwise just wanted to be left alone. FRELIMO was not attempting to transfer them, and sought to continue to sponsor discussions until such time as the peasants would take the initiative to move. Whereas FRELIMO had emphasized voluntarism and persuasion, the structural problem of accumulation still had to be solved. With few consumer goods to buy, peasants lacked the incentive to produce. Without consumer goods to stimulate surplus production, increased foreign exchange earnings were not forthcoming. Such features of the world economy as declining terms of trade for primary products and stiffening conditions for loans exacerbated the accumulation problem in independent Mozambique.

Meanwhile performance in the agricultural sector fell short of FRELIMO's expectations. Total production plummeted after 1975. Most villages grew little on a communal basis, for small farmers still preferred family plots. And, since few resources were set aside for the communal villages, the government was unable to provide needed inputs and services. Key cashew and sugar exports declined. At the beginning of the 1980s, Mozambique produced only about one-third of the food it consumed. Not only did food imports rise, but the government also squandered precious foreign exchange. Heavy equipment for state farms consumed the bulk of the funds budgeted for agricultural development.

FRELIMO made a mistake investing in the large state farms without supporting millions of family farmers who were responsible for a major portion of agricultural produce. In 1983, despite the emphasis on state farms, family farms still contributed 51.2 per cent of the marketed agricultural yield. What explained the lack of goods on the market was a blend of historical factors, bad luck and FRELIMO's own errors. More specifically, the crisis was directly related to capital flight, military raids by South Africa and the rebels it sponsored, adverse weather and a misguided policy of high technology in an impoverished country. FRELIMO's vice-president, Marcelino dos Santos candidly described the problem as follows:

> We are not bothering about manufacturing the hoe, because we are awaiting the arrival of the tractor we must import. We are distributing tinned beans, that cost foreign exchange, in a communal village that produces beans and from which no one has bothered to collect surplus production. We overload the peasants with items he does not use, but do not provide him with a lamp, cloth, a file, or a ham-

mer. Nonetheless, we expect him to exchange his production for goods he does not need.

Having acknowledged its mistakes, beginning in the 1983 Fourth Party Congress FRELIMO shifted its priority from state farms and collectives to family agriculture. Small-scale projects were thus emphasized and state farmland redistributed.

Industrialization

Whereas FRELIMO viewed a viable agricultural sector as an essential element in its quest for socialism, it initially regarded heavy industry as the driving force of an advanced economy. In other words, Mozambique was officially committed to a completely different path from that plotted by Tanzania or the other countries in Africa. In the initial years after independence, industrial activities centred on recovery from acts of sabotage perpetrated by vindictive settlers and from the exodus of skilled labour. The goal, defined by the Third Congress of FRELIMO, was to restore 1973 levels of production by 1980. This was achieved in some sectors but not others.

A noteworthy development in industry was the formation of production councils in each enterprise. Their avowed purpose was to bridge the separation between immediate producers and control of the means of production. To this end, workers in the councils were encouraged to set production targets and play an active role in decision making. To take one example of this in practice, Belita Clothes Factory in Beira, nationalized in 1975 when the owners fled, was subsequently run by its workers. A production council comprising 43 elected members determined goals and procedures. Workers were further organized into teams of 10, each of which included an elected leader and party stalwart. Employees grew their own rice and other food staples on the factory's farm, where they laboured one day ($9\frac{1}{2}$ hours) per working week ($5\frac{1}{2}$ days long). They also participated in sports together, and attended literacy classes (which they requested) at Belita. Production levels and wages reportedly doubled within three years after independence. The extent to which the reorganization at this factory met the broader goals of the country's development strategy was evident. Belita was more successful than most production units in Mozambique, and illustrates what FRELIMO sought to achieve.

To improve working conditions in factories and offices, FRELIMO established labour unions in 1983. The first union, the Organisation of

Mozambican Workers (OTM), drew upon the experiences of its fore-runner, the production councils. The objectives of the new structure · were to increase worker participation and to improve the coordination of state power and workers' action both in the rural areas and urban factories. According to labour legislation, unions were responsible for protecting workers against health and safety hazards. Employers had a legal obligation to provide medical care and disability security. The law affirmed that women had rights equal to those of men in the workplace. There was special provision for mothers, including 60 days of paid leave during or after pregnancy. However laudable, the legislation was not fully implemented. As OTM evolved, rather than representing the workers, the union increasingly served its own hierarchy and the party.

One constraint in organizing the urban proletariat was the large wage differentials among industrial workers emanating from the colonial period and hiked in the wake of wildcat strikes in 1974. After independence, FRELIMO imposed wage ceilings in the public sector, but wages in the private sector remained higher and unrestricted. Building heavy industry was problematic, too, because even in comparison to other parts of Africa the level of technology in Mozambique was very low. At the tea estates in Gúrùe, for instance, the Portuguese proprietor did not import machinery directly from the UK, where it was manufactured, but purchased second-hand equipment from Malawi and India. In any event, most operations at Gúrùe were manual, not automated. A tea factory in Mozambique staffed by 70–100 workers produced a yield equivalent to that of a factory in Kenya with a complement of 10.

In the short term, top priority was accorded to strengthening consumer industries and building agricultural-processing activities. The long-term goal was to develop transforming industries in order to reduce dependency on foreign imports and to expand exports. Thus the government constructed textile plants, aluminium smelting facilities, a paper and pulp complex and an iron and steel mill. Planners envisaged that many of the industrial projects would be placed in northern Mozambique, close to most of the country's raw materials and away from the axis in the south designed by colonialism and overshadowed by Johannesburg. But before Mozambique could forge ahead with new industrial units, more detailed information was needed about the country's resource base and about industrialization in neighbouring countries. To this day, duplication must be avoided, and it is crucial for Mozambique to coordinate its industrialization strategy with those of Tanzania and Zambia.

Ties with the International Economy

In international economic relations, FRELIMO charted a middle course between acquiescing to the situation it inherited from colonialism and rejecting established ties. Having professed a desire to expand economic dealings with countries of diverse orientations, Mozambique first had to decide how to deal with Rhodesia and South Africa. Maputo distinguished between them in principle in that the former was a colony and the latter is a sovereign country. Unwilling to tackle both minority regimes simultaneously, for to do so would have been economic suicide, FRELIMO initially challenged the more vulnerable of the two. Thus FRELIMO complied with UN sanctions, closing its border with Rhodesia in March 1976, forfeiting its lucrative transit-trade earnings and causing large-scale unemployment in the transport sector. According to UN figures, the direct financial cost to Mozambique of imposing sanctions was $550 million.

FRELIMO repeatedly expressed its determination to end its dependence on South Africa, but it understood that it would be self-defeating to attempt an overnight divorce. In the short run Maputo and Pretoria still needed each other. The long-run strategy for disengagement from South Africa was to build an independent home economy and to diversify international economic relationships. Thus the number of Mozambican mineworkers in the white redoubt tumbled from a peak of 115 000 in 1975 to less than 40 000 in 1983. FRELIMO wanted to cut back the supply of migrant labourers in the future. However, this decline was directly attributable to the decision of the mining industry to vary the countries of origin of foreign labour and to increase the size of the domestic contingent as well as to the South African government's desire to punish Mozambique. The effective abolition of the gold bonus, resulting from South Africa's revaluation of its gold reserves in 1978 in conjunction with an amendment to the Articles of Agreement of the IMF, deprived Mozambique of its major source of foreign-exchange earnings. To compensate for a portion of this drop in revenue, postcolonial Mozambique raised the price of Cabora Bassa energy above the amount agreed to by Lisbon and Pretoria, and jacked up the harbour dues charged to South African shippers.

FRELIMO viewed international assistance as a stop-gap measure to unshackle itself from the colonial heritage. Burdens arising from the application of sanctions and numerous costly attacks on Mozambique by South Africa and rebel forces compounded Mozambique's need for aid. Special UN and Commonwealth funds, though substantially less than the amount requested, met a portion of the country's stated requirements.

Maputo carefully considered the question of membership in international institutions. After enlisting in the African Development Bank, Mozambique joined the Lomé Convention of the European Economic Community and applied to COMECON, but was rejected. Whether Mozambique would benefit by entering the World Bank group has been more controversial. Mozambique was eager to receive the concessionary terms that the International Development Association, the soft-loan arm of the World Bank, offers to the least developed countries, but initially balked at the idea of joining its Bretton Woods partner, the IMF, as a precondition. Having noted the influential role which the Fund plays in such countries as Portugal and Zaire, FRELIMO was wary of its enormous power. The IMF aroused suspicions in Mozambique when it urged Zambia to reopen its border with Rhodesia, and FRELIMO knew that the Fund typically insisted on conditions – reductions in government spending, especially in the social sector – that were inconsistent with the goals which FRELIMO sought to achieve.

By the end of 1983, the government was out of money and unable to import even essential goods. On 30 January 1984, the country declared bankruptcy and defaulted on its loans. However, creditors refused to renegotiate any of the country's debt unless it joined the IMF. Beset by widespread drought, direct South African military raids, attacks by insurgents, as well as an economy in severe crisis, Mozambique thus joined the IMF in 1984, a move calculated to right the country for access to external capital (a globalizing tendency which we will examine on pp. 208–12).

On balance, Mozambique's strategy for overcoming underdevelopment was bold, yet tentative and perilous; by its very nature it injected profound tensions into the social fabric and engendered a distinctive set of problems.

ACHIEVEMENTS AND DIFFICULTIES

Having emerged from the experience in the liberated areas, there was, if only during the early postcolonial period, a deeply ingrained tradition of collective leadership in FRELIMO (and this was what set Mozambique apart from many other Third World countries). The nucleus of FRELIMO was compact and united. It comprised a highly cautious group with a penchant for protocol and painstaking analysis. A visitor may have been surprised to find revolutionary élan and old-world formality bound up together in Mozambique. FRELIMO's orderly style, too, distinguished it from revolutionary groups whose political gatherings were, by comparison, impassioned and undisciplined.

At first, the strength of FRELIMO was a theoretically sophisticated leadership combined with grass-roots support. Those at the top combined intellectual acumen with practical skills. They took a long view of politics, approaching it historically in the light of broad social forces and movements, not as an arena of personalities and episodes. The main challenges to FRELIMO's rule were an abortive military uprising in December 1975, which did not receive civilian backing, and protracted attacks by the Mozambique National Resistance Movement (RENAMO), a contra movement that operated in every province in Mozambique.

FRELIMO's leaders came to theory through diverse routes. President Machel, an intellectual driving force in his own right, was a former medical orderly and military commander. He explained that his first political education came 'not from the writing in books. Not from reading Marx and Lenin. But seeing my father forced to grow cotton for the Portuguese and going with him to the market where he was forced to sell it at a low price – much lower than the white Portuguese cotton grower.' It was practical experience in Mozambique as a wage earner, Machel added, which impelled him to seek theoretical understanding. Following Machel's death in a plane crash in 1986, FRELIMO's Central Committee elected Mozambique's next president, Joaquim Chissano, the foreign minister since 1975 and prime minister in the nine-month transitional period leading to independence in 1975. In colonial Mozambique, he was one of the first black students enrolled at Maputo's principal secondary school and received a scholarship to study medicine in Lisbon. He later went to Paris, where he met Marcelino dos Santos and helped to unite rival Mozambican liberation movements. Dos Santos, who became FRELIMO's vice- president, is an accomplished poet who spent many years in the circle around Jean-Paul Sartre in France. Dos Santos is widely regarded as a profound thinker and an eloquent speaker.

How deep in FRELIMO has this sophistication run? Historically, a major weakness in Mozambique is an acute shortage of middle cadres. There are simply too few qualified lieutenants to maintain links between top and bottom. This gap developed because Portugal denied Africans access to higher education and because FRELIMO expected the anti-colonial war to last longer than it did. The upshot is that not enough intermediaries were trained. It may be hypothesized – though conjecture cannot change history – that if the war against colonialism had continued for a longer period, the liberated areas would have been extended to other provinces (but at the cost of much greater loss of life) and FRELIMO could have had a stronger foundation for building socialism.

To provide scientific and technical personnel capable of organizing a modern society, Mozambique sought to upgrade its educational system. At the time of independence, fewer than 30 Mozambican Africans were represented in an enrolment of over 2000 at Lourenço Marques University. Subsequently, there were too few secondary school graduates to fill the places for full-time students at Eduardo Mondlane University, as it is now called. Some of the students at the university were products of the old elitist system, and embraced the values transmitted by their former teachers.

Mozambique, like many underdeveloped countries, required foreign technicians to meet its immediate manpower needs. At least half of the 240 000 Portuguese in Mozambique quit the country by independence day, and perhaps 90 per cent of them departed within the next year. The government recruited *cooperantes*, contractees from Eastern and Western countries who were technically skilled and politically committed, to fill the void. In addition, in March 1980 the government invited former residents to return to Mozambique and invest in the private sector. Small businesses, shops, garages and so on, which had come under state control when their owners had gone into exile, were placed in private hands. For some commentators abroad, this policy signified a retreat from socialism. Other observers held that at independence, the state, faced with sabotage, abandonment and the lack of know-how by Mozambicans, had no choice except to fill the vacuum in commerce and transportation; it was not surprising that, in the first five years of independence, the state had failed at these tasks. In the light of this admitted failure, Machel counselled that the state should concentrate on the priority sectors (production and social activities such as education, health and housing), rather than on selling matches, eggs or a dress.

Another question worth considering is whether FRELIMO confined resolution of major issues within too narrow a circle. Practical matters, especially social programmes, were aired in public, but little became known about divergent views among the leaders. Axiomatic to democratic centralism is the tenet that various oppositions engage each other until a decision is reached. The case for competition among different tendencies is predicated on the belief that a broad exchange of perspectives is essential to party life and that a battle between rival positions is the surest way to rectify mistakes.

Surely no party is free of schisms, and FRELIMO is by no means a monolith. It is inconceivable that Mozambique's senior officials would be of one voice: by definition a front is a broad coalition of elements. Further, since a transition to socialism subsumes two or more modes of production and spurs conflict between them, divergent interests necessarily clash and the contention is reflected in a political party.

FRELIMO tempered internal criticism because attempts by external forces – the minority regime in Rhodesia, former Portuguese settlers, ex-PIDE (secret police) agents and RENAMO forces – to discredit and divide independent Mozambique were relentless. It is important to note too that a pitched battle between two factions was fought out at the Second Congress in 1968, when the socialists defeated a moderate nationalist group. Thus a centrist FRELIMO position and collective leadership formed in order to temper sharp differences from the turbulent pre-independence years.

Another problem was the proliferation of state bureaucracies caused by socialist development. This tendency was inherent in the transition period owing to the rapid expansion of the state sector and the simultaneous contraction of the private sector. The question, however, at bottom is one of social relations rather than scale. Bureaucratism is a qualitative condition, in this case the awkward combination of archaic Lusitanian practices and modern revolutionary zeal, in part old ideological habits and the persistence of state structures from the colonial era, and in part a manifest inability to match political cohesion with administrative cohesion. After independence, coordination among ministries was inadequate and liaison between Maputo and the provincial capitals was weak. While top officials in the bureaucracy were competent, the standard dropped perceptibly as one moved down the ladder. At the middle and lower levels youthful exuberance was admirable, but executive experience and pronounced capacity were lacking. Only a small coterie of extremely hard-working officials was willing or able to make decisions, and those people were saddled with countless minor issues. Thus the Council of Ministers handled routine matters which are managed by an intermediate echelon in other countries. Candidly expressing his concern for this problem, President Machel, in a key speech, spoke out against corruption in the State Housing Corporation. He also made a series of unannounced visits to ports, warehouses, factories and clinics, exposing red tape and black marketeering.

The formation of a National Planning Commission in July 1977 was a step in the right direction to the extent that it spotlighted the need to streamline the bureaucracy. In 1979 the commission formulated a detailed ten year economic plan for the 1980s. Implementation was delayed by the combined effect of natural calamities, the dire situation created by the RENAMO insurgency, a shortage of trained personnel and lack of statistical data. Fashioning the planning mechanism remained an urgent matter; investment choices required clear definition; and finely honed techniques and specific timetables needed to be worked out. Converting a market economy into a planned economy proved to be a protracted and complex process, for, to use Antonio Gramsci's felicitous phrase, democratic centralism can degenerate into bureaucratic centralism.

A closely related danger is repression. Remember that in a transitional period, fragments of both capitalism and socialism co-exist. The attempt to achieve socialism is punctuated by a constant struggle between unregulated market forces and the planned state sector of the economy. The capitalist classes typically favour restoration, and seek succour in foreign countries for the *ancien régime* or another form of reaction. They do not stand idly by as their interests are thwarted, but instigate capital flight and perhaps sabotage. Under these conditions it is exceedingly difficult for the fledgeling economy to meet the weight of economic ills. Then coercion may be used again, this time against disgruntled labourers as well as against the bourgeoisie, to ensure the survival of the new order. Coercion is not aberrant but endemic to attempts to exit capitalism. In the long run, there remains the problem of how to disembowel the repressive apparatus so that democratic alternatives can flourish.

The question of repression has been raised by both top government officials in Mozambique and their critics. In a 1981 address to the nation, President Machel reported on official corruption and abuses of power by the police, members of the security forces, the army and the people's militia. The president called for popular control so that the perpetrators could be punished. The director of Machava Prison was dismissed over complaints of mistreatment of prisoners. In the face of alleged police brutality, several police and security officers were similarly discharged. FRELIMO made clear its intention to continue to invite popular redress to stem repression.

This pledge was evidently discounted by the US government, particularly in the Department of State's human rights reports. For example, the 1983 report on Mozambique, required by Congress, concluded that

FRELIMO had made important advances in health care and education. Despite the Marxist regime's differences with the Catholic Church, FRELIMO loosened control of organized religion. However, the State Department did express reservations about restrictions on political participation imposed by a 'small cadre of senior officials' which dominated all political activity in the country. Acknowledging that there were no indications of government-sponsored disappearances, the State Department noted the practice of detention without trial in 'reeducation centers' where political prisoners and other 'antisocial elements' were interned.

FRELIMO's case was that the colonial power had not been blacklisted for violations of human rights; meanwhile, the liberation movement led the campaign to attain the main right to political independence. After the ravages of colonialism, FRELIMO contends, it is no wonder that Mozambique's urban centres – like Saigon (today Ho Chi Minh City) – were replete with prostitutes, drug addicts and smugglers. In the early postcolonial period, the government had in fact closed prisons, not opened them, according to FRELIMO.

By most accounts, the major problems were that the length of time to be spent in a centre was unspecified and that the administrative system for releasing those who had completed the re-education process was faulty, causing some inmates to serve for indeterminate periods. Medical personnel who treated inmates revealed that conditions were grim, but then again peasant life in Mozambique is spartan, and facilities in the centres were no worse than those in rural areas generally. The crux of the matter is that Mozambique's re-education centres had to be considered in the national context as well as in relation to universal standards of human rights. Quite clearly, Western standards are not a historical alternative for Mozambique. A balance must be struck between a cultural-relativist position and a position which would establish global norms. One yardstick is the situation that obtained before independence and the direction in which Mozambique has moved. That Mozambicans readily dissented and were encouraged to voice criticism in the single party, but not in public, was certainly a step forward from what they knew under colonialism. Limits on open and democratic participation have been attributable both to Mozambique's internal dynamics and external pressure on the country.

In terms of human rights, an important step was FRELIMO's recognition that the transformation of society must include changes in the status of women. During the founding conference of the OMM, Machel exhorted the delegates: 'the main objective of the revolution is to destroy the system of exploitation and build a new society which releases the potential of human beings...This is the context within which the question of women's emancipation arises.' Furthermore, 'the decisive factor for the emancipation of woman is her involvement in the principal task – the task of transforming the society'. Concretely, FRELIMO sought to encourage women's participation outside the household in both agriculture and industrial production. For instance, in Moamba State Farm, one of the largest, women were employed for the first time. Five of the 16 tractor drivers for 'block one' were women.

The integration of women into production did, however, exhibit weaknesses. FRELIMO stressed the participation of women as wage labourers in state farms, but ignored their contributions to the agricultural sector on family farms. The state's tendency to focus on state farms only reduced the resources available to women responsible for producing food elsewhere. The eventual shift of emphasis to small farmers still resulted in support for cash crops, which were the domain of men. Subsistence farming failed to receive the state's backing. Unequal gender relations were reinforced so long as men brought in money while women were expected to put food on the table and remained exclusively or primarily responsible for domestic chores. Although women were encouraged to participate in production, gender inequality in the domestic sphere was not adequately addressed. Rhetorical pronouncements about the public realm did not effect equality at home. Nina Berg and Aase Gundersen underscored the crucial point: 'true emancipation for women cannot be brought about by formal equality only, even if it leads to increased opportunities in public life and equal rights on fundamental issues ..The notion of equality must also challenge the relations inside the family.'

THE GLOBAL CONTEXT

The Subcontinent

In foreign affairs, one of Mozambique's avowed goals is to strengthen relations with neighbouring countries and all of southern Africa. As a front-line state, Mozambique sought to coordinate its foreign policy with those of Angola, Botswana, Tanzania, Zambia and Zimbabwe. It is cordial to other African countries whose political systems differ from its own. The adjacent kingdom of Swaziland, for example, is landlocked and relies on port facilities at Maputo.

To build their economies and to reduce dependence on South Africa, Mozambique and eight other states (Angola, Botswana, Lesotho, Malawi, Swaziland, Tanzania, Zambia and Zimbabwe) formed the Southern African Development Coordination Conference (SADCC) in 1979. Each member state was placed in charge of a functional aspect of cooperation. SADCC, renamed the Southern African Development Community (SADC) in 1992, delegated responsibility for transportation and communications, perhaps the most important part of the plan, to Mozambique. Over 40 per cent of this subregional grouping's budget was earmarked for expenditure in Mozambique.

Meanwhile Mozambique sacrificed dearly in giving material and political support to southern African refugees and liberation movements. It hosted training camps for guerrillas belonging to the Zimbabwe African National Union wing of the Patriotic Front but did not permit military preparation within its borders against *apartheid* rule. In all likelihood, repeated bombing raids emanating from Rhodesia were meant to pressure Machel to embrace Cuba and the former Soviet Union and thus draw in the USA against the insurgents. But Mozambique refused to allow the Salisbury regime to internationalize the war in any way. Maputo's policy was to encourage the Patriotic Front to enter into negotiations while keeping up the armed struggle. FRELIMO understood, too, the differences between conditions in Mozambique which led to the demise of colonialism and those in other territories which impeded a transfer of power. It believed that the impetus for change must be internal. The Mozambique Revolution could not be exported.

For Maputo the critical policy issue was its relationship with Pretoria. After the collapse of settler domination in Rhodesia, South Africa targeted two military attacks on African National Congress (ANC) residences in Matola, a suburb of Maputo, and nurtured RENAMO. Created by the white authorities in Rhodesia, RENAMO was initially composed of a medley of former members of the Portuguese colonial army, secret police and defectors from the liberation struggle. The insurgents terrorized the civilian population, destroyed numerous development projects and fundamentally disrupted transportation and communications facilities. RENAMO's favourite targets were health clinics and schools. Of 5886 primary schools opened in 1983, no fewer than 2655 had been closed by the end of 1987. So, too, 42 per cent of the country's rural health clinics had been destroyed or shut down. Throughout its military campaign, RENAMO offered no ideology or governmental alternative to FRELIMO. Its only goal was destruction.

The costs of the destabilization campaign were enormous. In January 1984, the government of Mozambique assessed its losses since 1975 at $556 million ($6 million above the UN estimate) for destruction and sanctions during the Rhodesian war; and since Zimbabwe's independence in 1980, $3463 million for South Africa's reduction in railway-port traffic and mine-worker recruitment, plus $333 million for direct military aggression by South Africa and RENAMO. Against a GNP of $2.05 billion in 1982, a seven-year loss of $4.02 billion is a staggering sum. A 1987 study commissioned by SADCC estimated the direct and indirect costs of destabilization in Mozambique at $6 billion. This sum was nearly twice the country's external debt and 60 times the value of Mozambique's exports in the year in which the study was carried out. The money lost, however, cannot compare with the number of lives sacrificed. The United Nations Economic Commission for Africa estimated the number of war-related deaths from 1980 to 1988 at 900 000. Other accounts place this figure at one million. Of those who died from the war between 1981 and 1986, 320 000 were children. Furthermore, 4 million people were forced to leave their homes, with more than one million from their ranks living in refugee camps in neighbouring countries.

Under heavy military and economic stress, Mozambique had signed the 1984 Nkomati Accord, a non-aggression pact with South Africa. Buffeted by direct military raids from South Africa and attacks by insurgents, FRELIMO committed as much as 46 per cent of the national budget to defence in the mid-1980s. Clearly, resolving the security situation was key to economic revitalization. Pretoria and a beleaguered Maputo agreed to halt insurgents from attacking the other country and to pave the way for improved economic relations. Not only did South Africa want to seal the Mozambican border, but also the *modus vivendi* was an opportunity to split the coalition of front-line states and liberation movements. Military ventures cost South Africa dearly: over $1 billion per year for the occupation of Namibia alone. In the mid-1980s, the overall financial pressure continued to mount appreciably: a sagging gold price, a severe drought, poor export performance and mushrooming government spending in several sectors. Yet another source of pressure was the Reagan administration's needs during an election year. President Reagan's aides advised him to achieve diplomatic victories in order to silence critics who accused the administration of militarizing foreign policy in such Third World areas as Lebanon, Grenada and Central America. Hence the USA urged *apartheid* South Africa – described by Mr. Reagan as 'a friendly country that has stood behind us in every war we've ever fought' – to tone down its response to the furies of guerrilla warfare. Since South Africa could not have a more supportive president in the White House, it was in Pretoria's interest to comply with Washington's overture.

For war-ravaged Mozambique, striking the Nkomati bargain was a matter of survival. Not only had the country been battered by RE-NAMO, but also a prolonged drought had caused widespread starvation. What Maputo hoped to gain by calling off the undeclared war was time. The diplomatic setback suffered by FRELIMO was supposed to be the means to give Mozambique its first chance to implement its development strategy in times of peace. However, Pretoria continued to train and support RENAMO in violation of its pact with Maputo. In the post-Nkomati period, the conflict with rebel forces worsened and drained Mozambique's economy.

The Socialist Countries

Just as it did before independence, postcolonial Mozambique steered clear of the Sino-Soviet dispute and kept its foreign policy options open. That FRELIMO was cultivating relations with a variety of nations could be best understood by examining how its foreign policy evolved.

In the colonial era, external support played a secondary role, and FRELIMO relied on its own resources because it had to do so. For one thing, unlike Algeria or Vietnam, Mozambique could not count on an anti-war movement in the metropole to constitute an effective force, for the fascist government in Lisbon would not permit dissent. To be sure, in the early 1960s some cadres, including Machel, received military training in Algeria. But confidence in its own ability led FRELIMO to reject an offer of Cuban aid in 1967. Mozambique turned down Cuba's overture after Che Guevara, who had been instructing guerrillas and leading them in battle in the Congo from April to December 1965, travelled to Dar es Salaam and met representatives of FRELIMO. Guevara and FRELIMO differed in their theories of guerrilla warfare. Whereas Guevara advocated that a military campaign carried directly to select localities would trigger a spontaneous peasant uprising, FRELIMO believed in the efficacy of long, patient spadework by political activists as a precondition for a mass-based, armed insurrection. In FRELIMO's view, Guevara was trying to impose theories emerging from Latin America without understanding the concrete conditions that obtained in Mozambique. FRELIMO's own theorists repudiated any attempt to generalize lessons from another context.

By independence, Mozambique and Cuba revived their friendship. The two countries share an Afro-Iberian heritage and speak similar languages; both have experienced foreign rule and fought to cast off the yoke of colonialism. In the late 1970s, there were between 650 and 750 Cubans in Mozambique, a presence far smaller than that in Angola and Ethiopia. At the same time, Maputo maintained cordial but strict relations with Moscow. Shortly after independence, in a celebrated incident, Chissano, who was then foreign minister, publicly rebuked the Soviet ambassador by saying that Moscow should not attempt to pressure Maputo. Chissano was referring to an attempt by the Soviets to persuade FRELIMO to grant them military base facilities, which Mozambique steadfastly refused to do. Nonetheless Mozambique, embracing the ideal of socialist cooperation, voted against the UN resolution deploring Soviet intervention in Afghanistan.

Compared to Soviet technical assistance in Mozambique, the level of Chinese activity remained modest. Sino-Mozambican relations were grounded in the amity established before independence, when Beijing provided instructors and engineers for FRELIMO's training camps. The independence of Mozambique came at a time when China was sorting out its own problems, as well as supporting the National Front for the Liberation of Angola (FNLA) and the National Union for the Total Independence of Angola (UNITA). Unlike Mozambique, which backed the Popular Movement for the Liberation of Angola exclusively, China promoted a united front. In fact their differing policies in Angola did not explain relations between the two countries, as is sometimes argued, for China and Tanzania also took opposing stands on Angola but their relations did not suffer. Nor did Mozambique's condemnation of China's invasion of Vietnam lead to a general deterioration of relations between Maputo and Beijing. In recent years, there has been a general congruence in policy changes. Both Mozambique and China have introduced market reforms and have moved towards an accommodation with the USA.

In seeking technical assistance, FRELIMO took the position that the experiences of socialist countries are closer to Mozambique's than are those of the capitalist world. But FRELIMO found that problems arise in negotiations with all countries, the socialist nations included. Technical assistance is a contractual agreement, and skill and expertise are required to set the terms. FRELIMO has lacked that specialized, practical knowledge. Meanwhile, it made mistakes and some aspects of the signed agreements were not favourable to Mozambique. Particular difficulties were encountered in obtaining technical assistance from planned economies, since orders had to be placed well in advance of the date of delivery; the exigencies of Mozambique's needs frequently would not permit proper anticipation and accurate timing.

The West

Friendship with the socialist world did not preclude cooperation with the West. FRELIMO recognized that Western countries themselves have divergent policies, and distinguishes among distinct interests within each country. It has deeply appreciated the generous assistance tendered by the Nordic states and the concessionary terms granted by the Netherlands and Britain. But until 1982, Mozambique spurned West Germany because Bonn insisted that an agreement include reference to West Berlin. FRELIMO wanted to maintain its ties with East Germany. Mozambique subsequently concluded a food aid agreement with West Germany, tacitly acknowledging Bonn's interpretation of the status of Berlin. Maputo also contracted with Lisbon to purchase small arms, an emblem of rapprochement with the former colonizer and member of the North Atlantic Treaty Organization.

In its relations with the USA, FRELIMO has believed that powerful groups – senators who supported the Byrd Amendment, which allowed chrome imports from Rhodesia, and American executives investing in *apartheid* South Africa – were opposed to Mozambique, and that there are also good friends, both in the government and among the public, who are working for ends which are consonant with those of Mozambique.

Strategically Washington has tried to protect and promote US interests, mainly through South African channels. Before 1989, the aim was to avert confrontation with the Soviet Union and Cuba in southern Africa. Politically, Washington sought to enlist FRELIMO's assistance in assuring an orderly transition to majority rule, anchored to moderate leadership in Namibia and South Africa. Economically, the US has tried to secure a hospitable climate for American firms in the subcontinent. US bilateral interests in Mozambique are nonetheless minimal; private investment is nominal. Although trade with the USA is important to Mozambique, this commerce does not figure seriously in the American global pattern.

To woo US capital, Mozambique organized an investors' conference in New York. General Tire of Akron, Ohio, holds a small equity share in a Mozambican tyre factory, Mabor de Moçambique. In 1983, the government negotiated contracts with Exxon and Shell for exploration of petroleum and natural gas. Other US firms, however, hesitated to operate in Mozambique. Potential investors criticized Mozambique's Decree Law 18/77 of April 1977, the legislation governing foreign investment, for its lack of specificity. Equally problematic, they said, is the paucity of detailed information about the economy.

Of greater concern to Washington than the bilateral stakes in Mozambique was keeping the economies of its Western allies buoyant. Although US trade with, and investment in, South Africa have been marginal to the vitality of the American economy, the sturdiness of the South African economy is directly related to the strength or weakness of Britain. It did not pass unnoticed in Washington that events in South Africa could seriously damage the British economy, which in turn would have major repercussions in the USA.

To understand more fully US-Mozambican relations, recall that at independence, in 1975, the policy of President Gerald Ford and Secretary of State Henry Kissinger was to bring an FNLA-UNITA coalition to power in Angola. Mozambique rightly feared activity by the CIA within its own borders. It is not surprising in the light of this history that the USA was not invited to independence-day celebrations. However, some individuals such as Senator Richard Clark and Congressman Charles Diggs, attended in their private capacities and not as representatives of the government. On that day, after the US Consulate had closed down and was no longer accredited in Mozambique, the former US Consul-General flew the American flag. Added to what FRELIMO regarded as a clear affront was the consistently bad press given to Mozambique in 1975 and 1976 by American journalists, who often picked up their information in Johannesburg or Salisbury from embittered Portuguese *émigrés* and conveyed stereotyped images of 'rigid Marxism' in Mozambique.

In Lusaka on 27 April 1976, Kissinger unveiled what he touted as a completely new US policy in southern Africa based upon acceptance of the principle of majority rule for Rhodesia and Namibia and a commitment to end 'institutionalized inequality' in South Africa. A departure from NSSM-39, Option 2 embracing the white minority regimes, the Lusaka speech conceded that the USA had made mistakes in the subcontinent, a reference to American support for Portugal in the colonial war. The Secretary of State offered $12.5 million in assistance to Mozambique. He sought to engage Machel in settling the Rhodesia issue, but FRELIMO doubted Kissinger's sincerity and scotched his bid to visit Maputo.

The Senate balked at Kissinger's promise to give Mozambique a $10 million grant and $4.7 million in food aid – the figure was raised from the original one of $2.5 million – on the grounds that the country was communist, that assistance would contribute to terrorism and that three Americans were imprisoned in Mozambique. In addition to barring development assistance (though not food aid) to Mozambique, the USA lobbied against loans to Maputo by the African Development Bank. The Ford administration sought to fulfil its prior commitment (of April 1976) to Mozambique, but failed to lift the Congressional ban.

After the Nixon-Ford years, FRELIMO was pleased by signs of change in Washington, such as Ambassador Andrew Young's statement that Cubans are a 'stabilizing influence' in Angola and the repeal of the Byrd Amendment in 1977. FRELIMO looked favourably on participation by the United States in the UN Conference in Support of the Peoples of Zimbabwe and Namibia, held in Maputo in 1977, but disapproved of Young's performance there, especially his patronizing refrain about his own experience in the US civil rights movement. Mozambicans did not want an American solution to African problems. They did not regard the legislative techniques used to accomplish integration in the American South in the 1950s and 1960s as a model for ending colonialism and accelerating the struggle in southern Africa in the 1980s and 1990s.

In a sharp reversal of policy, in December 1980 Secretary of State Edmund Muskie certified that aid to Mozambique would be in the foreign policy interests of the USA. While planning was under way for aid to Mozambique, FRELIMO exposed CIA activity and charged that the agency had relayed information which facilitated a South African raid on Maputo. As a result, the United States suspended plans to provide development assistance.

Section 512 of the Foreign Assistance and Related Programs Appropriation Act, 1982, specifically bans development assistance to Mozambique, unless the president favours a waiver of the prohibition and reports to the Congress that furnishing assistance would further the interests of the USA. In 1982–3 there was talk in the Congress of enacting new legislation to supersede Section 512 and to place Mozambique in the category sometimes facetiously referred to as 'the hit list'. Set forth in Section 513 of the Act, the hit list comprised the countries proscribed from development assistance under any conditions: Libya, Iraq, South Yemen, Angola, Cambodia, Cuba, Laos, Vietnam and Syria.

In the spring of 1984, however, President Reagan and Congress waived the ban on development assistance to Mozambique and approved commencement of three bilateral aid programmes. These were a $40 million programme which funded input and equipment to large private farmers, increased food aid, and launched projects by two NGOs, CARE and World Vision (a right-wing, anti-communist organization known for its links with repressive military regimes in Central America). In 1984 the Reagan administration allocated more emergency food aid to Mozambique than to any other African country. Weighing into the decision to reverse US aid policy were the emergency situation in Mozambique, FRELIMO's overtures to US investors, the easing of relations between Maputo and Pretoria and, perhaps, to some small extent the administration's desire to moderate its hard-line image during an election year.

ABOUT-FACE

By the end of 1983, the crisis in Mozambique was severe. Destabilization continued to have a devastating impact on both infrastructure and exports, exacerbating the shortage of foreign exchange. Local production suffered due to a lack of imported materials. The government had run out of money and had no choice but to default on its debts. Destabilization and natural calamities had taken a heavy toll on the country. In January 1984, the government estimated that 1.4 million people needed to be supplied with all their food and another 3.1 million needed some food support. Hence, from 1981 to 1985, foreign aid more than doubled, from $171 million to $359 million. By 1988, Mozambique was the largest recipient of US aid in sub-Saharan Africa.

Foreign aid thus became a major source of external finance, in 1987 constituting 40.9 per cent of GNP. (During the 1981 to 1987 period, Mozambique's GNP had declined from $2.24 billion to $1.24 billion.) Although donors from more than 50 countries and organizations agreed to provide Mozambique with $354 million in emergency aid in 1989, they indicated that they were tired of emergency conferences on Mozambique. At a UN-sponsored meeting in New York in 1989, the third in a series of such annual meetings, donors used phrases like 'aid fatigue' and 'waste of resources'. Most donors said that they were satisfied with the way the FRELIMO government had managed the emergency operation, but cautioned that their capacity to infuse funds is limited, especially because the disintegration of socialist regimes in Eastern Europe had prompted Western donors to reassess their priorities.

In the face of these deteriorating conditions, the government adopted an Economic Action Programme for the 1984 to 1986 period. It included an export retention scheme, which allowed export enterprises to use a portion of their foreign exchange earnings for imports of inputs. The programme also involved a new code to facilitate direct foreign investment. Other measures were enabling legislation for some enterprise managers to lay off workers and reward increased productivity. Agricultural policies focused on augmenting production in the family sector through the provision of farming tools and production incentives. In industry, rehabilitation centred on the manufacture of textiles, shoes and other consumer goods.

The Economic Action Programme provided the basis for debt rescheduling under the aegis of the Paris Club in 1984. The IMF and the World Bank regarded Mozambique's reform programme as an improvement in management but insufficient to engineer an economic turnabout. Doubtless, the fund and the bank conveyed these observations in their discussions with the government of Mozambique in 1985 and 1986, paving the way for agreements with London Club banks and Paris Club creditors in 1987. These agreements afforded debt rescheduling and commitments for new loans, including concessional interest rates.

To create the structural conditions for economic revitalization, the government introduced the Economic Rehabilitation Programme, known by its Portuguese acronym PRE, in 1987. The 1987–88 PRE focused on reversing the cycle of economic decline and restoring output by 1990 to a level approximately equal to that of 1981. The PRE sought to realize this objective while boosting production and correcting financial imbalances. The idea was to shift the terms of urban/rural trade in favour of rural dwellers and to offer material incentives by rejuvenating industries producing inputs and trade goods for the agricultural sector. Meanwhile, the programme aimed to narrow the gap between the official and parallel market exchange rates. To undercut the parallel market, there were devaluations accompanied by measures to enhance efficiency and incentives for profitable management of productive enterprises. Consequently, in 1987, the metical was devalued from MT40 to the US dollar to MT200 in January and MT400 in June. By October 1988, the metical was MT620 to the dollar; by 1991, MT 1050 to the dollar.

Despite continuing destabilization sponsored by South Africa, the implementation of these neo-liberal reforms had an unambiguous impact on the economy. In 1987, the economy experienced a recovery of gross domestic output of about 5 per cent as well as a substantial rise in production. In 1988, GDP again increased by approximately 4 per cent. It is important to keep in mind the context of this 4 per cent hike:

marked social polarization and a substantial infusion of foreign aid. It is noteworthy that the economy showed signs of recovery in 1986 even before the PRE was announced. Government estimates showed a 1.5 per cent increase in real GDP during that year.

Given the vast scope of the economic distortions, the reform programme was phased over several years, the second stage from 1989 to 1991. The overall objectives of the PRE remained the same as in the first stage and targeted the major policy issues. Priority was accorded to the extension of price controls and a wider scope for market forces to guide price formation. Fiscal policy concentrated on instilling financial discipline and restoring profitability to enterprises. Of considerable importance was improved coordination and utilization of external assistance. Monetary policy continued to be restrictive, with controls on bank credit and emphasis on the provision of credit to enterprises. In agriculture, pricing and marketing reforms were aimed at increasing production and boosting the income of rural dwellers.

Along with modest economic growth during late 1980s, there were serious social dislocations caused by the structural adjustment programmes. The devaluations in 1987 sparked massive price hikes. Though wages rose by 70 per cent, average prices jumped 200 per cent. Budget cuts meant a decline in support for health and education programmes. Per capita spending on health fell from $4.70 in 1982 to $1.40 in 1987, then to $0.90 under the PRE in 1989. Education spending in 1988 was only a third of the amount budgeted for the schools in 1982. While deregulation enlarged the amount of food available in the market and in stores, in 1988 the prices of rice, corn and sugar increased 300 to 500 per cent.

The problems accompanying structural adjustment intensified during the 1990s. Mozambique's imports became more expensive relative to the prices of its exports. Exports covered only 15 per cent of the country's imports. The external debt in 1993 reached $5.3 billion, almost four times Mozambique's GNP.

The impact of the IMF framework is evident in the lowering of the quality of education and limiting access to it. There is a marked shortage of certified teachers and no budget for in-service training. Similarly, services in health care continued to spiral downward, with per capita expenditure dwindling to as little as an estimated $.10. The privatization of health care has led to a substantial hike in the price of examinations, hospital fees and medicine. These high costs result in fewer visits to clinics and hospitals. It is women who bear the burden, caring for family members who are ill and children without school fees.

Women thus absorb the tasks shed by public institutions. Structural adjustment makes women work longer and harder. Although women are heads of over 60 per cent of Mozambique's households, they still have no access to the land except through their husbands. Nonetheless, women are the major food producers.

Faced with sudden increases in food prices in the 1990s, the urban poor rioted in Maputo, blocking roads, stoning vehicles, and storming market places. Similarly, served by only a handful of buses, angry urban residents mounted street barricades and marched in protests over the doubling of fares of private minibuses. Also propelled by the dire economic conditions at home, large numbers of Mozambicans seeking employment in South Africa have been the target of hostile attacks in townships and mines around Johannesburg, causing them to return and join the throngs of demobilized soldiers searching for jobs.

Within this framework, civil society in Mozambique has not developed according to the Western model of spontaneous organization of voluntary associations. Rather, in the absence of local funding, Mozambican NGOs, which are mostly located in the capital, not in the rural areas where 70 per cent of the population lives, are closer to the donor agencies than to the social base they are supposed to represent. The partnership being forged is with international donors, not across Mozambican communities or with civil societies throughout southern Africa. The top-down vertical ties are taking precedence over a bottom-up thrust of civil society.

Mindful of these conditions, Reginald Green of Sussex University's Institute of Development Studies noted that 'a third of the urban, half of the peri-urban, and more than two-thirds of the rural population lived in "absolute poverty"'. The World Bank listed Mozambique as the world's poorest country for 1992, with a per capita income of $60. Also in the early 1990s, official development assistance constituted 98 per cent of GNP! This injection of foreign funding was conditional on economic liberalization and accompanied by political reform.

The government transferred power to elect the president from the party's central committee to the People's Assembly (renamed the Assembly of the Republic in 1990), in which non-FRELIMO members have seats. At FRELIMO's Fifth Party Congress in 1989, references to Marxism-Leninism were dropped from party statutes and programmes. The congress decided to redefine the party as a 'vanguard party of the Mozambican people' rather than a vanguard of a worker-peasant alliance. Mozambique's legislature approved a new constitution in 1990, clearing the way for a multi-party system, with provisions for universal suffrage and secret ballot. The 206-article constitution called for the separation of the executive, legislative and judicial branches of government.

In 1990, FRELIMO and RENAMO opened talks which culminated in the General Peace Agreement for Mozambique, signed in Rome by President Chissano and, for the opposition, Alfonso Dhlakama. The UN Security Council deployed 7500 troops, police and civilian observers to oversee the demobilization process and national elections. In 1994, nearly 88 per cent of the 6.1m registered voters went to the polls. In a field of 12 candidates for the presidency, Chissano and FRELIMO scored more than 53 per cent of the ballots, well ahead of second place finisher Dhlakama, with 34 per cent. Among 14 parties, FRELIMO gained a narrow majority (129 seats) in the 250-member Assembly, and RENAMO, at 112 seats, came in close behind. Each of the two top parties carried the vote in five of the country's ten provinces.

Protagonists on both sides of the war cooperated with international forces. Although peace could not have been achieved without the political will of Mozambicans, it came at a cost. The country had to relinquish yet another slice of sovereignty, this time to a multilateral military presence. Also, UN affiliates—donor agencies—deepened their commitment to buoy Mozambique's economy. Partly to open further the spigot of foreign assistance, in 1995 Mozambique joined the Commonwealth as well, the first non-English-speaking country to be admitted.

With its economy coiling in crisis, Mozambique was anything but a free agent. It had little choice but to yield to the demands of more powerful governments and international institutions. A donor-driven strategy of development means that a country is integrated into the global political economy on someone else's terms. In stark contrast to Mozambique's attempt to secure its autonomy in the 1970s, the locus of decision making shifted outward. Today, with an external debt more than 1000 times larger than its exports, Mozambique has lost whatever control it had over the development process. An ever-tightening web of conditionality constricts Mozambique's economic and political options. This vulnerability limits its ability to formulate policies appropriate to national needs. Hence, when IMF and World Bank officials came to Maputo to tell Mozambicans to tighten their belts, local authorities were incredulous. Knowing full well that many of their compatriots are so thread-bare poor that they must substitute potato sacks for clothing, the government's negotiating team matter-of-factly responded that the people did not have belts to tighten.

PROBLEMS AND PROMISES

To sketch out the main points, Mozambique has encountered an awesome combination of natural and social disasters: the departure of most of the country's skilled personnel, a consequent decline in productivity and critical food shortages, the return of thousands of exiles and migrant workers, the loss of the major source of foreign exchange (South African gold paid for black labour), a drop in world prices for the nation's agricultural exports, costly border wars, an insurgency backed by a powerful neighbour and severe floods followed by drought and famine. Even though Mozambique was not converted into a Bantustan (a black ethnic reserve dependent on *apartheid* South Africa), it encountered objective conditions which favoured opposition to an alternative strategy of development. Perhaps the main problem is that in a climate of insecurity, when the survival of the state is at stake, security, not development, necessarily takes precedence. The diversion of resources from development to war drained the economy. Under such conditions accumulation for productive investment could not be a reality. By all accounts the economy has been in a state of acute distress.

Yet several vital factors which foster development may be found in Mozambique. Among them are substantial reserves of arable land, vast mineral wealth, abundant energy and a proven ability to redress grievances. To get out from under, social forces must not only offer a vision, a conception of a better and an achievable future, but also unmistakably demonstrate the capacity to execute a plan in keeping with the priorities of the independent institutions of civil society. Mired in particularly abject conditions of underdevelopment, Mozambique, for a time, more than most countries, produced a clear idea of how to move itself ahead. Mozambique's leaders had freed themselves of the fallacies enshrined in prevalent ideologies of accumulation, and replaced them with a strategy of development which blended theoretical understanding and their own indigenous experience.

To be sure, attempting to implement an egalitarian strategy of accumulation under inauspicious circumstances undermined FRELIMO's legitimacy. Specifically, the state had to intervene massively in the economy, even in sectors where its capacity was notably lacking. When intervention in the accumulation process did not work, the state lost legitimacy. The difficulty is that without other sources of accumulation, the state sought to extract surplus from the peasant sector. At the same time, those who held state power also relied on the peasants as their source of political support. Large numbers of rural dwellers, however, would not wilfully play this dual role. As FRELIMO became less democratic, it was increasingly insensitive to the needs of the peasants and indifferent to the desires of some other groups of Mozambicans. Poverty served as a crucible for mounting corruption and the arbitrary use of power. Even though Mozambique's dilemmas have overwhelmed FRELIMO's emancipatory project, elements of its strategy for escaping underdevelopment cannot be erased from historical memory and could suggest important lessons for the Third World.

Part IV

The Big Question

9 What Works in the Third World?

When an acquaintance in Dar es Salaam invited me (JHM) to visit her family in an *ujamaa* (communal) village, I jumped at the opportunity. Hemmed in by the Indian Ocean on one side and groves of mango trees, coconut palms, jackfruit (which resemble large basketballs) and the infamous durian plant, with its succulent pulp of fine flavour but skunk-like smell, on the other, we careered southwards for 100 miles along a washboard road to the Rufiji River. There we navigated inland over a series of dirt paths until we reached our destination: numerous clumps of neat, thatched huts nestled astride the river bank.

Following a warm welcome, an exchange of gifts and a tour of the village, an elder recounted the origins of the community, whose inhabitants had been moved to this location by the government. Asked whether she preferred to live in this communal setting or her former domicile, this wizened old woman merely shrugged. My question was too iffy for her taste. Perhaps she thought that such hypothetical matters may interest naive Westerners, but given the practicalities of the struggle to scratch a jagged patch of earth for subsistence, why bother?

Later, after establishing some rapport, I asked whether force had been used to transfer rural dwellers to this site. 'No,' she said. 'Was the army present?' 'Yes.' 'Did the soldiers carry guns?' 'Yes,' she nodded knowingly. The implications were obvious, and so the conclusion drawn by various commentators was that, as in other resettlement schemes in Africa, the threat to use force was as effective as actual coercive practices.

The homegrown rice served for lunch was delicious, much better than the American and Chinese varieties in the supermarkets in Dar es Salaam, where Tanzanian rice, an export item, was not available. Malnutrition was quite apparent, for the children's bellies protruded markedly. But how could the sons and daughters of fishermen suffer from protein deficiency? The villagers explained that the government had decreed that the catch was for export only and that violators faced stiff penalties.

We were surrounded by another vital source of protein, an abundance of cashew trees. The villagers said that cashews, too, were an export product. I then inquired about the price paid to the producer of

cashew nuts: 'One shilling and five cents per kilo.' Asked if they knew
the retail price for the same grade of cashews in Dar es Salaam, the villagers replied unhesitatingly, '20 shillings per kilo.' Allowing for transportation costs and processing the crop, is a producer price pegged at
about 5 per cent of retail justified? Or is a relatively large surplus being
siphoned? If the latter is the case, are the peasants truly aware of the
mechanisms of exploitation?

The matter was resolved when I inquired about the extent of communal farming versus family farming. I was told to look yonder at the
communal plot. 'We till those fields only on the days when government
officials make their rounds. Otherwise, we produce for our own families, just as we've always farmed.'

The conflict of interest between the direct producers and the state
was unmistakable. Resistance was passive, not active. Although political consciousness was rudimentary, the peasants shared a notion that
they did not wish to feed the consumption habits of a voracious bureaucratic bourgeoisie. Such is the blockage that often restrains productive
forces in underdeveloped countries.

Whether this blockage can be cleared is controversial. The argument
to be developed in this chapter is basically positive. Some things do, or
can, work in the Third World. After all, there are glimmers of hope in
a number of countries once viewed as sunk in despair. From the standpoint of *national* development, the forecast is neither dismal nor im-
probable. Dramatic changes in the global political economy portend
both barriers and opportunities for development. Though several Third
World areas experience increasing marginalization, initiative, creativity
and innovation promise new avenues of bringing vast populations out
from underdevelopment. A generation ago, East and South Asia offered few silver linings. Thirty years ago who would have thought that
India could learn to feed itself? Bangladesh, until quite recently, was
touted as a basket case. China, shunning both Soviet-style socialism
and Western capitalism, was in the grips of political turmoil and economic dislocation. Malaysia and South Korea presented observers
with little to cheer about. Not that these countries have found the mas-
ter-key to escape underdevelopment, but some guiding principles illu-
minate the way out from under. These principles do not offer an
instantaneous solution. There are no magic remedies. However, the
lack of a simple solution does not lessen the urgency of the problem.
With wide variations within and among regions of the world, there is a
continuing need to adapt these principles to changing realities, learning
from experience as we proceed. This is not to celebrate the triumphs of

the few while the many continue to face colossal difficulties – usually dismissed in neo-liberal accounts of the success stories – but to provide a glimpse of the possible.

WHAT IS THE PROBLEM?

In the final analysis, underdevelopment is a multilayered historical process culminating in the stifling of human creativity, skill and self-confidence. From colonial rule to decolonization to postcolonial social construction, the path of development is *embedded* in historical and cultural contexts. Throughout the initial postcolonial phase, underdevelopment in the Third World was seen as a product of the exterior squeeze of a changing world economy and the inner functioning of an exploitative social system. In the context of dependent capitalism, this process was reproduced and extended by such structures as international agencies, foreign aid, technology, TNCs and banks. This course of affairs appears to have changed, though the effects of underdevelopment show remarkable similarity: hunger and want, malnutrition and marginalization. Structures designed to advance international capital have become more complex, providing contradictory potential for national development. Steered by an alliance with broad popular support, accumulation with redistributive mechanisms is indeed possible. Adjustment to a new global political economy may be exacting, but also opportune if social forces are aligned in novel ways.

To head off any misunderstanding, it must be clear that for both liberals and more critical minds, the principles that elucidate the way out from under cannot be abstracted from human agency. By human agency, we mean a general capacity for moral personality and individuality. Liberals and Marxists agree that the abolition of systematically oppressive conditions – slavery, serfdom and contemporary discriminatory practices – is a prerequisite for the realization of human good, including individuality. The main liberal claim is that a legitimate political regime must facilitate individual agency, and vice versa. Likewise, Marxists defend such broad judgements about human good, but locate the basis of inequality in specific constellations of accumulation and distribution. Just as slavery is at odds with modern individuality, 'wage slavery' conflicts with self-respect. Marxism's moral claims stem from a notion of social agency. The central argument rests on an appreciation of a society which nurtures social individuality. Specifically, it suggests that the social structures within which individuals are embedded limit and define the range of individual choice. The central issue that concerns us here is the relationship between structural determination and human will, which enables (or impedes) intervention in pursuit of social change. More simply, from the standpoint of 'underdevelopment', structural constraints serve also to restrict the scope of collective action. Very concretely, the question of agency is tied to such matters as the relationship between the dictates of global political economy and local inventiveness in the Third World, moral and material incentives as spurs to productivity, and what drives individuals to join movements for collective action.

To take this one step further, the problem of underdevelopment is multifaceted, having both subjective and objective dimensions. As far as the subjective aspect is concerned, fatalism and defeatism on the one hand and a naive romanticism on the other obscure possible solutions to the hard core of underdevelopment. Since achieving political independence, many Third World nations have oscillated between these two extremes. Remnants of both types of thinking cast an enduring shadow on societal consciousness and its mediators in the West.

Fatalist attitudes precipitated by economic frustration can be illustrated briefly in Mauritania, a country whose external debt exceeds its GNP, and home to an ancient desert culture that may already be dead. Today the desert is void of what was one of the world's largest nomadic populations and their tireless caravans. Before the drought hit, Mauritanian farmers were growing enough sorghum, wheat and other grains to feed the country, accounting for but a fraction of total food consumption. Most of what Mauritanians ate represented donations, causing concern about creating dependencies on foreign aid.

In the mid-1980s the drought in Mauritania intensified hunger, but the problem had been several centuries in the making. Desertification goes back at least 2500 years, and humans have increasingly compounded the impact of atmospheric pressure systems. When the Sahara was mostly grass, and parts of North Africa were the breadbasket of the Roman Empire, large caravans began to denude the prairies of trees used for firewood. In the eighteenth and nineteenth centuries, Europeans destroyed the gum forests along Mauritania's coast (now part of the desert). Boundaries drawn by the colonizers made it difficult for nomads to migrate to greener pastures in neighbouring lands, and overgrazing quickened the pace of the spreading sand.

Efforts to stave off the desert, which is expanding at about four miles per year, are not succeeding. The construction of dams is costly for a country whose principal export, iron ore, fetches low prices on the world market. Fishing has potential, but Mauritania lacks a navy to patrol against foreign fleets exploiting its marine resources. Officials have authorized oil exploration, without result.

For Mauritanians, disillusionment is an obstacle to surmounting underdevelopment. Conjoined to uncertainty is a reliance on faith, the expectation that nothing of significance is willed except by God. Asked to foretell his future, a herdsman balked, saying there is only one option: 'In sha Allah' ('Whatever God wills'). Reflecting the attitude with which these wanderers have coped with the drought and desert, he added, 'We are ready for whatever comes from God.'

Many Westerners take that man's gesture as pessimism, failing to wrestle with cultural complexity. Instead, with an ease furnished by compulsions of Western rationality, a coterie of artists and writers smuggle hopelessness into the equation. Prognoses of the African condition only highlight the 'coming anarchy' and Malthusian horrors. The breakdown of state structures, as in Somalia and Rwanda, has perpetuated the sentiment that nothing hopeful can or will come out of Africa. Prominent among those who share the doomsday scenario is V.S. Naipaul, himself a gifted spinner of tales about 'half-made societies', flawed civilizations, places where 'the West is packing its boxes, waiting for the helicopters'. The theme that ignites Naipaul's pages is the area of darkness just outside town; in the trail of colonial empires, always the bush remains. By 'the bush', Naipaul means ignorance and obscurity: contempt for what he left behind in his native Trinidad, dubbed 'a place with no history', where his grandfather, a Brahmin from Uttar Pradesh, India, had arrived as an indentured worker.

Naipaul, the winner of every major literary award in Britain, and often described as quite possibly the greatest author writing in the English language today, claims that he is not the spokesman for anything. He sees little hope for a Third World whose future and past travel along parallel paths in the present. In over 20 books of fiction and non-fiction, a psyche that has internalized colonial values reflects a pervading pessimism, a dark vision.

Naipaul's view of Third World politics is uncomplicated: a quicksand of corruption, decadence and vice. Without liberal democracy, non-Western countries have only barbarism. There is no middle ground, no alternative route. Naipaul's description of Argentina is a prototypical account of all Third World countries: 'Politics reflect a society and a land. Argentina is a land of plunder, a new land, virtually peopled in this century. It remains a land to be plundered, and its politics can be nothing but the politics of plunder.' Something must be wrong with all

Argentines. Evidently the missing element is Western laws, achievements and aspirations. As with Africa, life in this Third World setting,
clearly an unnecessary country, is but a graveyard. 'You were in a place
where the future had come and gone.'

Naipaul's pessimism resonates with many precisely because it lends
authenticity to what for too long has been seen as self-evident in the
West: the link between 'underdevelopment' and Third World cultures.
Since fatalism – the deficiency of purposive will in the face of a reli-
giously mandated destiny – is often inscribed in Third World consciousness, the institutions of state and economy erected by these
societies betray the deficiency of reason and, consequently, progress.

Whereas Naipaul's odysseys made by people who became aliens in
other civilizations point to a basic political conservatism and forlorn
acceptance of the status quo, one variant of Third World romanticism
originates with a one-sided reading of Frantz Fanon, another West
Indian writer. Also an interpreter of the mind of the colonized, Fanon
provided one of the most powerful inspirations to revolutionaries in
the Third World's early quest for building alternatives to Western
capitalism and Soviet-type economies. Born in Martinique in 1925,
Fanon studied medicine in France, fought in the French army during
the Second World War, and served as a psychiatrist in Algeria, where
he experienced revolution as both an observer and participant. He
died young of leukaemia at the age of 36, before the independence of
Algeria. One can only conjecture about the impact of the masterly books
which this prolific author would have composed had he lived longer.

For Fanon, Third World countries, not social classes, are the agents
of change, and psychological factors are the main movers of history.
Racism should be understood not as an independent phenomenon but
rather as 'the most visible element of a given structure'; it is an ideological weapon accompanying domination. The underlying dynamic is
decolonization, an inherently violent phenomenon; the nation is
consecrated in blood, and the creative power of revolution is purified
by the flame of violence. According to Fanon, it is repressive violence
which breeds revolutionary violence. When the electrodes are put to
the genitals, the native becomes a man and can no longer afford random or purely destructive outlets for repressed aggression. Thus violence often occurs as collective behaviour, allowing for the possibility
of social transformation. Far from celebrating violence as an end,
Fanon looks to its transcendence by a new and higher social order.

When nationalist movements in Algeria, Angola and elsewhere were
developing into social revolutions, Fanon, unlike many of his contem-

poraries, warned about emerging forms of dictatorship and about the pitfalls of the one-party state, potentially a shield for private ambition. The bourgeoisie in the Third World, he claimed, is not the inventive, productive, entrepreneurial class of the *Communist Manifesto* but a parasitical stratum profiting from a subordinate economy. Also the proletariat in the Third World is not a suppressed class but a privileged element with much more to lose than its chains. In Fanon's view, the key sources of revolutionary change are the peasantry and the lumpenproletariat, both natural allies of urban intellectuals.

Fanon's writings contain more fresh ideas on the nature of colonialism than any piece of scholarly literature and have had an enormous impact on the thinking of social movements, but his notion of spontaneous peasant revolution represented a romanticized vision of Third World alternatives, a harbinger of the misplaced optimism of some of his followers. Fanon's idea of spontaneous peasant revolution could not account sufficiently for political organization, ideological work and discipline: who is to mobilize the peasantry? And how is political consciousness to be formed? Moreover, Fanon's emphasis on psychology and the individual displaced a careful scrutiny of the lumpenproletariat. Without presenting examples of revolutionary dynamism among the lumpenproletariat and failing to distinguish between the hard-core lumpen and the urban proletariat, Fanon placed his hope in this social stratum for transformation. While many of Fanon's prophecies concerning decolonization and settler rule have come to pass, his programme was fairly imprecise. His more enduring legacy lies in the importance of the psycho-cultural dimensions of development, the decolonization of the imagination.

Both aspects of the subjective barrier to identifying possible solutions to underdevelopment – a cornucopia of defeatism and romanticism – resonate among contemporary Western observers. In the pregnant controversies over whether the developed countries have a moral responsibility to share resources with the Third World, one option sometimes advocated, though under a different banner, is *triage*, a term first used in reference to the treatment of the most severely wounded during the First World War. Given scarce medical resources, those who could not be easily saved were allowed to die. Such hard-nosed politics is epitomized in the 'lifeboat ethics' of the biologist, Garrett Hardin. Those nations which can not make it on their own should not be admitted to the lifeboat of the rich lest we lose our safety factor and threaten our own, as well as our progeny's, survival. The ethics of the lifeboat mean that sharing is impossible; the downtrodden should be permitted to go their own way even if innocent people die, harsh though that may be. As far as Hardin is concerned, there are no solutions for Third World countries. Let them wallow in the mire.

Recent neo-liberal thinking which regards the self-regulating market as the only panacea for development without recognizing its socially disruptive and polarizing aspects may not seem as drastic, but parallels Hardin's prescription. A retreat from statist redistributive policies – welfare capitalism – and stress on individual charity as an answer to inequality and want present the humane side of *triage*. In contrast to Hardin's gloomy interpretation, neo-liberal triumphalism offers a rosy outlook. The most recent expression of this view is celebration of the so-called East Asian 'miracle', regarded as a beacon for the Third World. Sympathetic observers invoke the promise of the NICs without taking a hard look at the severe structural problems endemic to either the makings of the 'miracle' economies or their social and environmental costs.

Leaving aside prevalent attitudes and culturally laden expressions, the objective nature of underdevelopment seems, at first sight, straightforward. Today almost 20 per cent of the global population resides in advanced countries. But as population skyrockets in the rest of the world – while holding steady in the developed countries – the proportion cocooned in the advanced nations is expected to tumble to only 4 per cent by the middle of the twenty-first century. Unless the poor become richer, 24 out of every 25 people will then be living in poverty.

In fact the persistent and mounting problem in the global political economy cannot be solved by economic growth, but only with growth *and* redistribution. A large portion of the world's population is still unable to get a foothold in an expanding economy. In a capitalist market economy where survival (of individuals and countries) hinges on their success in participating in the market, those that fail to do so risk extinction. However, the task is to negotiate the rough waters of the world economy *and* preserve a sense of social connectedness, community and identity. Usually, the currents favour the first part of the equation, not the latter.

In some cases, slow economic growth over past decades has worsened the ravages of underdevelopment, and rapid economic growth itself is not a cure. This is especially acute for those nations whose development capacity has disintegrated from within and who find themselves unable to compete in the global political economy. The problem for others is that on a world scale there is a fundamental disproportion between accumulation, a profitable rate of return, and consumption. Burgeoning economies require increasing capital accumulation, but the current reality is insufficient profit and, more especially, irrational disposal of surplus.

Capitalist accumulation is not only a ceaseless process, but also a necessary, albeit insufficient, condition for augmenting the value of labour. In another historical era in Western Europe, capitalist accumulation became the spearhead of social development. Throughout the 1960s and 1970s, dependent development characterized the bulk of Third World nations. For these nations, internationalization of capital meant redirecting a large share of surplus, the margin between production and consumption, from one sphere to another sphere of the global economy. For a capitalist economy to become self-sustaining, the bulk of the surplus must be invested in domestic production, not transferred to other countries. Yet this transfer from underdeveloped countries to the advanced capitalist world was seen as a hallmark of global economic relations. Although capital flows in both directions, a startling feature of the global economy was a net transfer from the Third World to the advanced countries. With mounting interest payments and amortization of debts exceeding total new loans and investment, uneven flows of finance capital augment global structural inequality.

With post-Fordism and the globalization of both production and finance, national boundaries have acquired a new meaning in global political economy. Dependent development, a feature of the international division of labour and *national* strategies of development, is now subordinated to new constellations of production and power. With its instantaneous mobility, finance has attained even greater significance in the geographical allocation of resources. Electronic transactions tend to outpace the rhythm of industrial progress. The notion of a *niche* economy appears as a more relevant characterization of global production than that of a dependent economy. In the present era, time-space compression marks global production, not simply the relative advantages of spatial organization of production. Emulation of the industrialization strategies of two decades ago is inappropriate for a globalizing phase of capitalism. The quest for development, correspondingly, must adapt to the new realities.

With neo-liberalism, capitalist economies in the underdeveloped world are extroverted organisms. Their outward orientation welcomes international capital, and adjusts domestic policies to the global political economy. If so, the long-term effect is to mould internal social relations to conform to the emerging social structure of accumulation on a world scale.

This process has dovetailed nicely with the use of foreign aid as an instrument of policy. Increasingly the aid policies of Western governments have discouraged state intervention in Third World economies and have favoured the expansion of the private sector. With emphasis upon strengthening dominant socio-economic structures, much aid has been earmarked for the military in the Third World. In times of waning global welfarism, trade has replaced aid as a mainstay of Western policy towards all but the most underdeveloped countries. The structural adjustment policies of international financial institutions help to implement this project: downgrading aid externally and diminishing the scope of the state internally in favour of open markets for capital and technology flows and the regime of private capital.

Initially driven by Cold War pressures, the build-up of arms also lessened the ability of some states to make effective policies. Official development assistance remained only a small fraction of world spending on armaments. In 1980, for instance, total aid came to a mere $20 billion per year, while overall military expenditure was around $450 billion per year. As observers as far apart as the Brandt commissioners and Fidel Castro argued, if only a small share of the money, effort and research devoted to military uses were ploughed into development, the availability of resources would make the prospects of the Third World look much brighter. Each dollar sunk into military procurement may be viewed as an opportunity lost in development expenditure. Military dollars reduced security, for the war economy makes the world poorer. With the end of the Cold War, military build-ups are still operative. The spiral of military spending in the post-Cold War period is disconnected from the global rivalry between two ideological adversaries and linked to competition between regional powers, as in the case of China and India, or perhaps among the three macro-regions: North America, the European Union and Asia-Pacific.

Long before it became fashionable for contemporary conservatives to argue that military spending is beneficial to the economy, conventional Keynesians claimed that the Second World War had remedied the problems of the depression of the 1930s. In 1940, John Maynard Keynes declared that it seemed 'politically impossible for a capitalist democracy to organize expenditure on the scale necessary to make the grand experiments which could prove my case – except in war conditions'. This was to upholster the old Marxist argument that war is a capitalist means to realize surplus value through military production.

In fact, military expenditure yields fewer jobs per dollar than does most American business, according to the US Bureau of Labor Statistics. Military contracts bid up the cost of skilled labour and provide employment for expensive, technical people. Moreover, a large ratio of military to civilian capital formation saps the civilian economy. Extensive research by Seymour Melman showed that, in the USA, capital was increasingly concentrated in a fund that renders no goods useful for consumption or further production. Taking his figures for 1977, out of every $100 of new (producers') fixed capital formation, the USA applied $46 to the military economy. In Japan, the figure was $3.70. Melman observes that the investment of Japan's capital in productive economic growth was no doubt a major feature of that resource-poor country's amazing industrial surge.

In recent years, the advanced countries have helped to pay for the huge cost of developing their new weapons systems through arms sales to the Third World. Export sales have offset the rising cost of weapons research and have enabled Western (and former Eastern Bloc countries) to go on producing sophisticated equipment for their own forces. The spiral of arms sales to the Third World has been astounding: an increase in current dollars from $19.7 billion in 1975 to $45.6 billion in 1980 (US Library of Congress figures). In 1990, the developed countries exported $36 billion in arms to the Third World. Some Third World countries, most notably Brazil, have developed arms industries of their own and compete with the big suppliers – the USA, Russia and France – in the export market.

The key problem for Brazil, like other underdeveloped countries, however, is not guns or bombs or population. By what grotesque priorities could this troubled nation give birth to a billion-dollars-a-year arms industry? Despite new possibilities for development at the end of the Cold War, the peace dividend remains ephemeral. The existence of military industrial complexes in advanced countries and the emergence of new military machines in the Third World have precluded substantial reductions in defence spending. Some states have taken the dismantling of communism in the Soviet Union and Eastern Europe as a signal to covet military might.

Fundamentally, the challenge of underdevelopment is how to both reduce structures of inequality and build an accumulation fund. Some state capitalist countries, such as Brazil, have achieved higher levels of capital formation and have broadened social inequalities. The structural changes made by countries aiming at socialism before its collapse lessened social inequalities but did not fuel the accumulation process. Herein lies the dilemma: how to generate wealth and ensure an equitable distribution?

WHAT HAS BEEN TRIED?

To say that Third World countries are tottering is to overlook the differences. Some strategies have provided the material base to expand the domestic economy.

The 'miracle' of *unfettered capitalist accumulation* was built on a fundamental premise: a transfer of wealth from the needy to the well-to-do would power the engines of capital accumulation. The dominant strata would then take the economy in tow, expanding the stock of machinery and other productive equipment. Putting this strategy to work, with a nod towards regulating the worst abuses by foreign capital, Brazil became a paragon of rapid industrialization. The gains of dependent capitalist development were quite considerable during the 1970s. Pushing for growth at any cost, Brazil erected numerous factories, attained profit rates that were among the world's highest, and offered stable right-wing rule.

Brazil is one of a galaxy of Third World countries, an original NIC, often touted as a viable model for the rest of the Third World. The NICs, as indicated, are defined in the mainstream as a category of countries in which the per capita income exceeds, and the share of the manufacturing sector in the GDP surpasses, a given statistical threshold. It is also the particular position that a country has reached in the international division of labour which denotes its status as an NIC. Usually NIC specializes in the production of intermediate, manufactured goods.

Abstracting from our analysis (Chapter 6), the main features of the NIC model are maximum integration in the world economy, especially through TNCs, direct *state-led* industrialization, low wages and a predisposition for strong rule. What has facilitated industrialization in these countries is a substantial domestic market, or access to one, heavy investment in economic infrastructure and large-scale external aid.

To what extent is the NIC model an exemplar for the rest of the Third World? Since the category itself glosses over the diversity among countries, it can only be employed with great caution. Given the historical embeddedness of the economic performance of the East Asian NICs, it is unlikely that, in an era of globalization, export-oriented strategies will guarantee NICdom.

There are at least two groups of NICs. The so-called modern Japans, or 'Asian Dragons' (Hong Kong, Taiwan, Singapore and South Korea), maintain fairly open economies. They differ in essential respects from the large Latin American NICs, namely Brazil, Mexico and Argentina. One major difference is that extensive land reforms in South Korea and Taiwan contributed importantly to relative income equality. No significant land reforms were undertaken in Brazil and Argentina, countries with a highly skewed pattern of income distribution. Following reforms in Mexico during the 1930s, there was a reconcentration of landholdings and worsening inequality. Additionally, unlike the comparatively open economies of Asia, the Latin American NICs have at times applied extremely high tariffs. To safeguard infant industries, powerful local entrepreneurs have at some critical junctures sought to maintain a high level of protection. Brazil, especially, has drawn on its huge domestic market, large population and vast resources.

Within each group, the divergence is striking. Most especially, as city states and entrepôts without a substantial agricultural sector, Hong Kong and Singapore are unlike the other NICs. Also, the resource endowments and historical trajectories marking the various national experiences are quite dissimilar. For example, Taiwan's success in the export of manufactures was accompanied by such factors as the proximity of the Japanese market, massive aid, the presence of a formidable entrepreneurial class and favourable trade conditions arising from the Vietnam War. In the case of South Korea, it is clear that a broad range of import-substitution industries was developed and that various non-price measures were used to promote export industries.

The chances of the East Asian experience being repeated in most parts of the Third World – in, say, sub-Saharan Africa – are slim. As global capitalism continues to expand, some national economies, much like competing firms, will emerge as winners and others as losers. The rise of a global division of labour has already begun to bring about a reversal of fortune, at least at the margins. What is to prevent Brazil and England from switching places? But in the medium run, the underlying system will remain in place. There is no reason to think that the NIC experience illuminates the way to wipe out underdevelopment. Even for the handful of NICs whose economies grow rapidly, questions can be raised about authoritarian structures as well as the social and environmental costs of export-oriented industrialization. The Latin American NICs suffer severely from the debt burden and have adopted austerity measures that ride on the back of the poor, whereas the other economic parvenus, the modern Japans, are still stalked by some of the pangs of underdevelopment.

The term 'modern Japans', increasingly in currency, is a misnomer. The Japanese pattern of independent capitalism is not an option for contemporary Third World countries. For one thing, Japan was never a colony. In 1638 the Tokugawa Shogunate adopted a policy of strict seclusion, and the imperialist powers became ensnarled in rivalries in more lucrative areas, especially the Middle East, India and China. The heyday of imperialism was punctuated by such explosions as the Crimean War (beginning in 1854) and the US Civil War, tying down the Western powers. Lacking raw materials of its own, Japan sought to keep foreign capital at arm's length until the state could control it. Unequal treaties were imposed, however. Gradually coming out from isolation, Japan proscribed the importation of luxury items and cheap consumer goods, purchasing instead raw materials and capital goods for industry. Subsequently, Japan launched a sustained drive to become the world's third leading economy, engaging in military adventurism and colonial conquest, rapidly expanding its munitions and export industries. Japan itself emerged as an imperialist power: a course that obviously is not the way for Third World countries to surmount underdevelopment.

Is there evidence to commend the policy of seclusion as a prelude to a high rate of capital accumulation? Not in the few instances when *go-it-alone strategies* have been tried in the context of underdevelopment.

A telling case is Burma (today Myanmar) where, following the 1962 *coup d'état*, a technocratic-bureaucratic regime backed by the military proclaimed autonomy as its goal, but ever since it has run into a tangle of political and economic troubles, especially maintaining minimal living standards, with the parallel or subterranean economy posing an intractable problem. The attempt of Pol Pot's Kampuchea to withdraw from the world economy was more extreme. Rusticating the urban population and striving for an agriculturally self-sufficient rural order, the regime relied on repression and provoked the ire of many other countries, as the Vietnamese invasion showed.

As we have seen, China under Mao also inaugurated an inward-looking policy. Faced with US intransigence and Soviet pressure to toe the line, Beijing cut itself off from Moscow, its major source of foreign investment and aid, largely excluding itself from the world economy. The burden of accumulation weighed heavily on the agricultural sector. Peasants were required to hold consumption near subsistence, and the state soaked up the rest of what they produced as surplus for investment. Yet a labyrinthine bureaucracy hindered productive investment, ritualized participation and discouraged peasant initiative. With a new class in the making, China's inward-looking strategy could not attain requisite levels of accumulation for mounting an industrial base. The legitimacy of the socialist order was severely tested in the aftermath of the Cultural Revolution, revealing the basic shortcomings of an inward-looking development strategy. China's enthusiastic embrace of the global political economy presaged the negative effects of its relative isolation. Clearly a country cannot forge an autonomous path to development merely by breaking its external ties and initiating central planning. The way out from under lies not in seclusion, but in the maelstrom of international relations: today – globalization – with its integrating and disintegrating tendencies.

More concretely, if it is agreed that autarchy is not the solution, the task becomes one of participating in the global political economy while simultaneously undercutting a contradictory world order. More purposefully than most countries, Mozambique has tried this route (see Chapter 8). Drawing on substantial support from the popular classes, FRELIMO, in an initial phase, adopted a strategy of *managing the ties of dependency* inherited from colonialism.

Before waging a frontal assault on the colonial state, the liberation movement wrought multidimensional changes in civil society. FRELIMO accorded priority to establishing alternative norms and laying new social foundations in zones wrested from Portuguese colonialism. The goal was to assign socio-economic content to political independence. Rejecting various formulas for decolonization handed down by Lisbon, FRELIMO accelerated the moral-intellectual aspects of revolutionary development and fostered a different cultural-ideological milieu. This entailed a 'war of position', a concept developed by Gramsci to refer to the erosion of the ideological bonds which cement the ruling class and popular classes, a process that paves the way for winning control of, or transforming, the state apparatus. The essential element in challenging the hegemony is the moulding of a new culture and innovative institutions within the old order.

From independence in 1975 to the Third Congress in 1977, FRELIMO opened a debate on how to conquer underdevelopment. FRELIMO envisaged state farms and communal villages, along with heavy industry, as the locomotives which would pull the economy out of the rut that it was left in by almost 500 years of Portuguese colonialism. In the international sphere, Maputo sought to diversify its economic relationships, reducing some forms of dependence on South Africa, developing ties with the socialist world and selectively engaging in trade and securing assistance from the West.

The period between the Third Congress in 1977 and the Fourth Congress in 1983 was one of trial and error. The experimentation entailed both a refinement of the development strategy and serious mistakes. FRELIMO invested substantially in large state enterprises without supporting millions of family farmers. Heavy industry remained but an intention. In foreign economic relations, FRELIMO sought more actively to engage foreign capital, yet until 1984 withstood pressure to conform to the policies of international monetary institutions. FRELIMO paid a heavy price for its blunders during this period: a substantial demobilization of the peasantry. After the Fourth Congress, FRELIMO attempted to correct its errors by ploughing capital into family farms, the source of livelihood for 80 per cent of the population. Top priority was assigned to building agricultural processing industries and to producing more consumer goods. The long-term goal was to develop transforming industries in order to reduce dependence on foreign imports and also to expand selected export sectors. FRELIMO tried to create an independent home economy while encouraging private investors to help meet the country's immediate objectives.

Thus in terms of social relations, though not economic accomplishments, the significance of the Mozambique Revolution is that it is a prototype of building counter-hegemony in the Third World. Vast modifications in society took place under the surface of formal institutions. In the wake of the ideological erosion of the old order, Mozambicans developed an acute understanding of their predicament and conceptualized the requirements for transforming what was an underdeveloped economy in utter shambles at the time of independence. Unlike most countries in the Third World, Mozambique for a time relied primarily on local initiative. But all of this political and theoretical activity failed to produce the economic bonanza FRELIMO had hoped for. The debilitating effects of Mozambique's security situation and the drought in the 1980s, along with ill-advised attempts to implement the development strategy, are a stoppage that FRELIMO has been unable to clear out.

The South African-based insurgency was not primarily the result of FRELIMO's inept policies. It stemmed from Pretoria's fear of a non-racist and democratic socialist alternative on its border. But as long as Mozambique was pummelled by its powerful neighbour, it could offer no definitive evidence that a tightrope approach to the global political economy is the path to success. With hindsight, this strategy is more promise than positive performance. Like other underdeveloped countries, Mozambique is still saddled with the problem of how to gather an investable surplus for productive investment.

WHETHER TO JOIN, LEAVE OR WEAVE?

Having noted the merits and shortcomings of strategies that embrace, repudiate and balance ties with global capitalism, let us underscore the principal trade-offs in terms of who benefits and who loses. Evidently, the way to achieve the highest rate of economic growth is to embrace global capitalism. But maximum integration in world capitalism heightens a national economy's vulnerability to external forces. Moreover, economic gains for the few do not necessarily help to overcome underdevelopment, understood as removal of the blockage that warps a social structure and prevents the interests of the majority from becoming increasingly dominant. Although disengagement from global capitalism (an option pursued by some nations before the advent of economic globalization and the delegitimation of a command economy) does not generate substantial economic growth, it permits the redistribution of wealth and an egalitarian ethic. This is not to overlook the ascendancy of a new bureaucratic class, anchoring another set of rigidities in the social system. The strategy of selectively managing the ties of dependency also has a poor record for economic growth, yet there are historical elements in this programme that deserve notice. The possibility of subordinating external capital to the requirements of the local (or regional) economy and providing channels, both internal and external, for the creation of an accumulation fund, are clearly elements that can be revisited in a new form. The strategy of submerging the blockage in the social structure and repeatedly adopting measures to stop abuses of power are still relevant. Without being laudatory or blind to the costly mistakes of policy makers, it is evident that a strategy of balancing ties to the global political economy offers a clear chance for productive economic growth on terms consistent with the needs and aspirations of ordinary people. With a highly differentiated global political economy, however, no across-the-board solution to underdevelopment is possible: only broad principles to inform practitioners who can adapt them to the unevenness of capitalism and historically specific conditions.

Objections to the principle of managing the ties of dependency have been voiced by critics who believe that, historically, it has invited foreign intervention. It is true that (as with Mozambique) a country adopting a balancing strategy was likely to become a tempting target for foreign intervention, but surely the sceptics' argument was a classic case of blaming the victim. Another challenge, one with much substance, is the call for evidence of successful economic performance. Setting aside debates over the yardsticks for measuring economic performance, we have already shown that in at least one instance where this balancing act was tried, the economy was prostrate. Nonetheless, flawed execution of a strategy does not invalidate its underlying concept. If we were living in the late fifteenth century in Western Europe, how could one 'prove' the potential of capitalism, whose stirrings did not match the achievements of feudal units of production? Evidence would have been altogether lacking.

Looking to the future, some writers flatly assert that independent national development is impossible within global capitalism, thus making development strategies a delusion, at least within that system. Those who advance this position hold that, to be meaningful, anti-systemic change must come at the world level. Others argue that practical development strategies can be enhanced through a Third World partnership based on self-help. It is claimed that in these hazardous times, collective self-reliance is the key to Third World power.

Although politically empowering, the idea of self-reliance must give pause. Implicit in the notion is the assumption that, as an ideal and strategy, self-reliance offers a distinctive road out of underdevelopment. To treat this uncritically, however, leads to a misconception of both the nature of capitalism *per se* and recent changes in the global political economy. As a particular way of ordering the economy, capitalism makes globalization its organizing principle. Just as precapitalist self-reliance gave way to a social division of labour, so too national self-reliance remains an unrealizable ideal in the contemporary global capitalist economy. Second, inasmuch as changing modes of competition in the global economy render global market shares (as opposed to territories or resources) most critical, the strategy of national self-reliance does not hold much promise. What, then, are the results of collective action by the South?

Emblematic of the potential for concerted action by Third World producers was the hike in the price of oil from $1 per barrel in 1970 to over $30 per barrel in 1980. The drama of how Colonel Muammar el-Qaddafi of Libya successfully spearheaded a rebellion against big oil, while too convoluted to rehearse fully here, is instructive in its implications for a collective response to the problems of underdevelopment. Setting the stage for OPEC's price explosion, the international oil companies exercised a near monopoly and disciplined any producer who tried to evade their price controls. The major oil companies, or Seven Sisters (Exxon, Gulf, Texaco, Mobil, Socal, British Petroleum and Shell), derived enormous profit from their power to determine where and how much to prospect, set levels of production, command refinery technology, dominate world markets, and share pipelines and tankers among themselves.

Playing the independent oil companies against the majors, Qaddafi employed a divide-and-rule strategy against those who had practised it so successfully in the past. The Libyan leader singled out Occidental as his first target, abruptly cutting the amount of oil the company could produce. There was no love lost between Occidental and the Seven Sisters. Not only did the other oil companies refuse to defend Occidental, but the US government chose this inopportune moment to abandon its long-standing support for the companies. Relative to Western Europe and Japan, the USA stood to gain from the boost in oil prices because it was only partially dependent on imported oil. Moreover, financial reinforcement for the Shah and the Saudis would strengthen two regional powerhouses allied to the USA. As the syndicated columnist Jack Anderson and his colleague James Boyd point out in their book, *Fiasco*, President Nixon and his National Security Adviser (later Secretary of State), Henry Kissinger, maintained that the oil companies should accede to Qaddafi's demands, Nixon because of his reluctance to expand domestic production and Kissinger because he was wrapped up in his grand strategy of high politics. The Nixon administration's oil expert, Jim Akins, advised that the oil companies had no reason to fear that a leapfrog would take place among the oil-producing countries. With this avenue of opposition to Qaddafi closed, the oil companies acquiesced in the negotiations. The oil companies lost what they had fought for decades to win: control over production. The die was cast for a group of underdeveloped countries, organized since 1960 into OPEC, to initiate the era of high-cost oil and to raise the spectre of producer power.

Indeed, the short period of OPEC power was a genuine challenge to the international order. In the 1980s, however, the price of oil cascaded into a depressed market. Although OPEC succeeded for a time in jacking up oil prices, it never effectively regulated production. The organization set production quotas, but it had no means of enforcing them. Conflicting interests among its 13 members hobbled common action. A territorial dispute between Iraq and Kuwait, culminating in the Gulf War in 1990, and the protracted war between Iraq and Iran (1980–8) are but two of the rivalries that bedevilled the organization. Other measures of OPEC's diversity include geography, population and average per capita income. Algeria is more than 30 times the size of the United Arab Emirates (UAE). Indonesians number about 200 million, over

700 times the population of Qatar. And the average per capita income in the UAE is $26 850, in excess of 60 times that of Indonesia.

OPEC's problem has not only been how to share a dwindling market among its members, but how to organize itself to share demand with non-OPEC exporters. Mexico and the North Sea producers acquired the option of offering cheaper oil. To adjust to a reduced market, some OPEC members moved increasingly from pumping oil to processing and marketing it. Indeed, as control of oil reserves shifted, the companies became service outfits, specializing in high technology activities, buying smaller energy concerns and purchasing big businesses outside the energy field. And as oil prices rose in the period from 1973 to 1980, energy company profits soared. Critics accused American oil companies and OPEC nations of being allies in profiteering, placing the heaviest burden on ordinary people in both the advanced countries and the non-oil-exporting countries in the Third World. Notwithstanding the phenomenal run-up in oil prices, the gains for producer countries were primarily at the state level. Although there were noticeable gains in living standards, the income distribution in the OPEC countries remained grossly skewed. The collapse of OPEC signalled the difficulties of Third World nations, through their producers' associations, to capture the bulk of the surplus from the sale of their resources because they lack a common identity of interests and a monopoly of key minerals. OPEC, with less than half of the world's oil output, is an assembly of producers, not a cartel whose members are bound to act in unison.

A cartel implies massive concentrated power. In the second half of the twentieth century, its activities are tightly coordinated and backed by government and other concerns. Failure to comply with the cartel's policy means that enforcement action will be taken. By this definition, the underdeveloped countries are faced with what amounts to a creditors' cartel.

Not only do private lending institutions command vast resources, but the banks concert their policies and protect each other through cross-default clauses: a declaration of default against one bank in effect trips an automatic pronouncement against others, ensuring joint action by creditors in many countries. Private banks are bolstered by their governments, the IMF and the World Bank. A break with these lending institutions would be likely to cause the cessation of all international credit, thus cutting off trade with foreign countries. The structural power of capital remains entrenched in global institutions that primarily serve the interests of the advanced capitalist sectors of the global political economy.

Can a debtors' cartel exercise reverse leverage over the creditors' cartel? In Cuba, Fidel Castro has long called for a suspension of all debt by Latin American countries. In Peru, President Alan García Peréz unilaterally set a limit – 10 per cent of annual export earnings – on the debt service his nation would pay foreigners.

Threatened by the debt bomb, Western bankers moved swiftly to prevent the superdebtors from ganging up on them. The Westerners sought to separate Mexico and Brazil from the rest of the pack. In the 1980s, these two countries owed over two-thirds of the total Latin debt and more than one-third of the debt of all underdeveloped countries. Hence Jacques de Larosière, managing director of the IMF, reportedly informed Mexico that it would receive easier terms than other debtors for putting its economic house in order. Similarly, Walter B. Wriston, a confidant of President Reagan, told Brazil that it, too, would receive favoured treatment for complying with prescribed policy. Guarding their options, the big banks bought up Brazilian debt notes from the smaller banks, which were more likely to knuckle under.

Additionally, lending countries can always play their trump card – the food weapon – as a means to enforce financial discipline. After all, most countries are borrowing in order to eat. Debt repudiation is unlikely as long as creditors can impose famine as a penalty for violating the rules of the international financial system.

Many borrowing countries are in fact in arrears on their debt payments, but all parties tiptoe around the term 'default', preferring instead euphemisms like 'rescheduled agreements' and 'stretch-outs'. Insolvent borrowers obviously do not have the economic wherewithal to pay, and their governments would find it politically suicidal to try to do so. Therefore, as Celso Furtado has argued, the only way to avoid a showdown between debtors and lenders is for the private international banks to strike a deal with their central banks. If Western governments do alleviate the burden of the debt, they will defuse the worst aspects of the problem. But the system that produced the debt trap in the first place will remain intact, with the majority of the world's population still ravaged by ingrown structures of underdevelopment.

WHAT HAS BEEN LEARNT?

If it is by no means self-evident that tried national strategies of development and tested forms of international action point the way out from under, what general lessons can be derived from a sometimes diffuse and contradictory experience in the Third World? Although there are no ready-made formulas for overcoming underdevelopment, it would be wrong to muddle through with improvised solutions. The task is to identify principles which can be adapted to varied conditions.

The first step is to recognize that *Third World countries cannot break the structures of underdevelopment by relying on the impulses generated in the heartlands of world capitalism.* The stimulus cannot come from the advanced capitalist countries, although elements within those countries may play an important role in the process. Closely related, one impulse that reinforces underdevelopment and strengthens world capitalism is an export-promotion strategy in the Third World, if it spins out of popular control.

The establishment of export platforms for Third World industrialization is but one aspect of a historical process rooted in the economic crisis of the 1930s and accelerated after the Second World War. In that wrenching realignment of the international division of labour, underdeveloped countries began to assemble and manufacture industrial goods. The advanced countries have increasingly focused on the service sector, particularly banking and insurance, and high-technology, specialty products, such as seamless pipe for the oil industry and alloys for the aerospace industry. Meanwhile, underdeveloped countries have continued to supply commodities for the West, and an entire range of low- and medium-technology products that they can make cheaply. In this segmented system of world production, however, large ratios of underdeveloped countries' manufacturing activities are within the province of foreign affiliates of TNCs. Since this contemporary version of an export-oriented industrialization strategy accentuates reliance on external market forces, and thus widens the gulf between domestic production and local consumption, it is not the answer to the problem of underdevelopment.

Export-led industrialization must also be historically contextualized. The NIC option may have been effective at a specific time and place. With the globalization of finance and production and the compression of time and space, however, a development strategy premised primarily on exports may not be economically or socially sustainable in the long term. The task, instead, is to generate and expand domestic demand, as South Korea has begun to do, and find resources to match it.

The second lesson is that *it is possible to set limits to exploitation.* Underdeveloped countries are not suspended in a state of torpor, and by learning from experience along the way, they can embark on a purposeful course to reduce the outflow of surplus and to redirect it for social needs. Although specific policy proposals would take us too far afield, it may be useful to offer some guidelines for practical action.

With the redeployment of industrial activities from the advanced to the underdeveloped countries, the old international division of labour is a dead letter. Underdeveloped countries now compete with the advanced countries in a number of sectors. For example, six producers – Brazil, Argentina, Venezuela, Mexico, Taiwan and South Korea – became exporters of basic steel when their new-found capacity outstripped domestic demand. South Korea's state-of-the-art steel mill, designed and built by Japan, has stirred resentment in Tokyo, where steel makers plead that the world market is already overclogged and that the government should adopt a policy of import protection. Their counterparts in the West have switched to increasingly sophisticated products, conceding basic steel making to cheaper producers. Some analysts thus see a growing symbiosis between enterprises in the advanced and underdeveloped countries.

The emerging global division of labour does not, however, include thoroughgoing redeployment of scientific and technological activities. Most Third World countries are passive users, relay agents and imitators in international production. Creative capacity in the accumulation process continues to be concentrated in the advanced countries. At issue are not only resources but also resourcefulness. Inventions are less important than inventiveness. Indigenous, innovative capacity goes to the heart of releasing human energies, which is the essence of development.

In the drive to develop an innovative capacity, Third World producers can take effective measures to curb TNCs – entities with no inherent interest in advancing indigenous scientific potential in host countries – and to assert greater control over the home economy. Health care is one sector in which such action is essential. The vast majority of the population in the Third World urgently needs drugs for disease control and primary medical care; the lack of these drugs is an important constraint on development. Research carried out by transnational pharmaceuticals is not geared to the development of tropical drugs for diseases predominant in the Third World. Their resources are directed instead to the production of 'me-too drugs', goods similar to existing ones. These goods are produced not primarily to improve health care but to boost a firm's market share and profit margins.

In the face of the drug companies' enormous market power, most Third World countries have appeared helpless; however, before its economic crisis in the 1990s, Cuba's challenge to the pharmaceuticals suggested the type of limits that may be placed on exploitation. Before the revolution, the Cuban drug market was unregulated, with little coordination among government agencies. In 1958, imports represented 80 per cent of Cuba's drug supply. However, by 1980, domestic drug production met 81 per cent of local needs. The government vested responsibility for the procurement and distribution of drugs in one agency, the Ministry of Public Health. The ministry established a national formulary guide, which identified the drugs deemed essential and their active ingredients. Only drugs listed in this guide could enter the country, reducing the inflow from 20 000 medicinal products in 1962 to 689 products in 1979. Next the ministry launched facilities to manufacture, test and carry out research on phamaceuticals. The research and development effort was centred on the health problems of Cuba, and allowed for quality control and inspection of drugs purchased abroad. Special attention was given to the veracity of advertising claims and safety hazards.

The government also created MediCuba, a foreign commerce enterprise that imported and exported all items in the medical-pharmaceutical sector. As the sole link between the international and the local drug market, MediCuba was able to offer TNCs exclusive access. Rather than relying on the public tender system, MediCuba began inviting bids from select companies: those with proven performance as well as some new bidders. In discharging this responsibility, MediCuba gathered systematic data on previous purchases, including volume, delivery time, terms of payment and price fluctuations. MediCuba also collected information on the economic profile of suppliers, their production capacities, the latest technical and scientific advances and so on. The Cuban strategy in the health care sector was not to try to get rid of TNCs but to harness them by changing the environment in which they operate. Now, with globalization, transnational companies have entered the lucrative bio-technology field and seek market consolidation to maximize profits. In the 1990s, Cuba's economic woes have forced a more relaxed attitude towards the transnationals.

By playing on the competition for foreign markets among enterprises which, according to capitalism's own inner logic, require expansion, underdeveloped countries can turn adversity to advantage. The first measure is to empanel a centralized agency to regulate the procurement and distribution of goods. This should not be a bureaucratic jungle where the economically fit thrive; safeguards are required to prevent undemocratic control, a profusion of state organs and corruption. An equally important measure is qualifying access to the internal market.

To perform both of these tasks in a shrewd and enlightened manner, policy makers must be apprised by a market intelligence system equipped to provide information on the latest developments in the advanced countries.

Building an innovative capacity and limiting the excesses of TNCs would, however, be an incomplete programme if the problem of foreign exchange flows were left to fester. The question that arises, therefore, is what are the alternatives for underdeveloped countries trying to cope with the awesome financial challenges confronting them while avoiding the pitfalls of IMF structural adjustments? Since the Fund has few powers of enforcement apart from the withdrawal of its seal (and hence international credit), what is the touchstone of formulating a strategy which forges macrobalance and growth, equity in income distribution and national economic integration?

To answer this question, it is not necessary to start from scratch. A great deal can be learnt from the structural adjustment programme Tanzania negotiated with the IMF and the World Bank, some elements of which have been implemented and others abandoned. According to economist John Loxley, the alternative to the IMF model of accumulation centres on shifting purchasing power to rural areas after the provision of incentive goods up-country. In other words, goods would first be made available in the stores and then producer prices would rise. Subsequently, adjustment policies would be phased in after emergency balance of payments support became available. This would mean a postponement of most investment projects, with concentration instead on rehabilitation and the utilization of existing capacity. Equally important is increased efficiency in state agencies, allowing cooperatives and small traders to fill gaps, as well as a reduction in recurrent budget expenditure in the areas of administration and defence. The monies thereby released would be used to protect minimum wage earners through wage adjustment and basic needs expenditure.

Foreign exchange would be targeted on directly productive activities, especially essential goods, export earnings and recurrent budget revenue. This strategy entails lessening dependence on project aid and heightening state action to ensure coordination among aid donors. The task is to enhance both production and efficiency, while shunning shock treatment, all-out export promotion and an unbearable burden on poor urban workers.

Obviously one should not be utopian about this scheme's chances of success. Its feasibility hinges on the presence of a resolute political will within the state apparatus, the depth of support or opposition among

local classes, the options for outside financing, and the danger of destabilization, whether the political riposte is threatened or real. Equally
important is the interface of domestic social forces and the global political economy that has a bearing on the *nature* of political will constituted within a country.

WHAT SHOULD BE DONE?

Some readers of the first edition of this book have suggested that we
should take another intellectual step and flat-out prescribe 'solutions'
for underdevelopment. But what is meant by a solution? A blueprint?
A manual? How-to-do-it instructions that pertain across the board?
Clearly not, for historical structures, resource endowments and cultures differ greatly. Then a national development plan? Not in the traditional sense, given the lessening of autonomy in the context of
globalization. Rather, what is wanting are sharply defined principles
upon which actual policies can be based. Put differently, knowledge
and practice have always been tied. To dichotomize theory and practice
is to employ a false dualism. Theory is a means of production of action.
As we have seen, different theories portend diverse policies ranging,
for example, on a spectrum from heightened state intervention to measures to unleash market forces. The argument for particular policies
requires sober analysis: policies are applied knowledge. An analysis
rooted in the rigours of political economy offers diagnosis, if not prescriptions. If we have accomplished the former, then it is the task of
those engaged in praxis under markedly distinct conditions and most
directly in touch with the specific contradictions that beset their lives
to derive lessons from the basic knowledge in this book as well as to
carry out the programmatic work.

In a pioneering analysis, *Dependence and Transformation*, Clive
Thomas (an economist from Guyana) broke new ground by showing that
the situation in the Third World is far from hopeless and by outlining
an alternative to orthodox doctrines of development. He argues that
for underdeveloped countries the way out is to design a programme of
'dynamic convergence'. The core idea is to converge resource use, local
demand and basic needs. There follow two 'iron laws' of transformation:
one is realigning resources and demand, and the other is realigning
needs with demand. The overall objective is to harmonize the sectors
of an economy so that indigenous peoples produce what they consume
and consume what they produce. This principle would govern invest-

ment choices, encourage the growth of local technologies, suggest new possibilities for resource-based industries and point the way towards an integrated, self-sustaining economy.

Up to a point, Thomas is right about the need for a basic economic realignment. Yet in the absence of a strong political will among the masses, domestic resources would be used to meet local demand which, in turn, would be luxury goods coveted by the well-to-do. A country that adopted this strategy could wind up in the position of Brazil, with its industries ringed by squalor and poverty. In other words, a strategy of dynamic convergence could lend support to technocratic, nationalist interests.

Thomas assumes that, if this strategy is to be implemented, the popular classes must first control the state. This presupposition wishes away such vexing political questions as how do classes acquire political consciousness, organize themselves, manage the coalition, and grab state power? Clearly it is not sufficient to focus on productive forces and to evade the issue of social relations.

Restructuring is a continuous process both in the physical aspects of production and the social organization of production. In this context, restructuring means that the majority of direct producers comes to dominate the use of resources and state power. Although the forms will vary from country to country, thoroughgoing political participation is essential to continually orient the state to meet mass needs and to correct abuses of state power. The whole population must be involved in politics and the economy more equitably; without sustained mobilization, the development effort is bound to falter.

Countries where the producers are dispersed, poor and unorganized face formidable obstacles to changing their historical trajectories. Since social structures constantly reproduce underdevelopment, a radical realignment means that we must rearrange human relationships. This is true both in our bonds with nature and in relations between the sexes. Official policy making is dominated by men, but most food in the Third World is produced by women, and yet the state allocates the lion's share of agricultural training, development assistance and rural credit to the male population.

Rehabilitation of a feeble agricultural sector is of major importance for development. So long as the advanced countries can wield the food weapon, the underdeveloped countries will be in a disadvantaged position. Within Third World economies, balance between the agricultural and industrial sectors is a prime necessity. Although there is no pat formula for striking an appropriate balance in each and every case, it is clear that pumping capital into economic infrastructure and neglecting productive activities is the wrong way to go.

In principle, building economic infrastructure can contribute enormously to development efforts by involving peasant producers more fully in the national economy. Nonetheless, in the context of a dependent capitalist economy, sinking investment into this sector may only eliminate impediments to the further penetration of foreign capital, facilitate the exploitation of cheap labour, and reduce the time of turnover of capital, which helps to enlarge the profits reaped by the few. If a key to escaping underdevelopment is to create value from nature's bounty, injecting capital into infrastructure is a means to enable men and women to extract more value; however, first the level of productivity must be raised.

Are the penetration of foreign capital and a policy that emphasizes the mobilization of domestic resources inherently contradictory? Inviting in external capital is risky, but a rupture with the global economy is not the way out of underdevelopment. In theory, it can be argued that foreign capital may help to build the state economy in a transitional period. Credit obtained from abroad increases the accumulation fund: it can provide technical equipment for the sectors of the economy governed by the planning principle, thereby augmenting the forces of production, and allows the state to employ workers who previously had no opportunity to take part in social production. This contribution, however, is contingent upon the conditions of capital. The interest paid must be less than the value created for accumulation. It is a question, too, of what obligations are made to international creditors and how credit is allocated within the domestic economy. Frequently, investment choices are compromises; the state's political resolve is typically weakened by the needs to placate or pay off local groups, play for time and even mortgage development projects to capitalist investors.

Furthermore, in the context of globalization, the role of the state has become more circumscribed, leaving large sectors of the 'domestic' economy vulnerable to global forces. Within the confines of global capitalism, the Third World should do more than set limits to exploitation. *Underdeveloped countries must learn to exploit global market forces and hitch them to the domestic economy.* But they cannot freely select those market forces. Incapable of taking the least dangerous pathway, almost all of these countries are in the position of runners on a track who can at best maintain their distance from the front of the pack by accelerating at about the same rate as the leaders. This analogy, we suggest, correctly captures the reality at the state-to-state level but not at the people-to-people level, each of which requires a fundamental realignment.

One key for overcoming underdevelopment is to *grasp the contradictions driving the global political economy*, especially as these contradictions make an impact on domestic social alignments. An analytic capacity is essential to this task, but it is important to avoid being overly abstract or metaphysical about the contradictions in world capitalism. Structural analysis has its contextual limits. There are always elements that resist market forces in the Third World. Recently, the resistance has come from the new social movements, organized around questions of gender, cultural rights, identity and the environment. Situating these movements within the global political economy may reveal their potential and contradictions more clearly as they materialize at the base in local contexts.

Under propitious conditions, contradictions at the commanding heights of the global political economy may offer opportunities to Third World countries. At the risk of a repeating a few points, let us again consider, from another perspective here, the action taken by Libya in the 1970s. Qaddafi cleverly manipulated inter-imperialist rivalries, the contradictions between Western states and TNCs, and the conflicts among the enterprises themselves.

The conditions under which Qaddafi acted are essential to understanding the outcome: the continued closing of the Suez Canal forced oil tankers to take the long route from the Middle East's main energy reserves to Western Europe. Then, too, Syria's decision to shut down the Trans-Arabian pipeline denied half-a-million barrels of oil per day to Europe, previously supplied from Middle Eastern fields, thus heightening the West's reliance on Libyan oil. Western consumers were unable to use nearby oil fields because the legacy of imperialism ensnarled countries such as Nigeria and later Iran in internal turmoil.

The Libyan oil offensive followed a severe winter that had depleted most of Europe's reserve stock and had elevated demand. Compounding the problem of Western vulnerability was the shortage of tankers to carry oil from Saudi Arabia and other exporting countries to Europe and the USA. Despite concern about consumer demand, Western governments were reluctant to rescue the oil companies, which had been widely regarded in the USA as greedy profiteers, culminating in an anti-trust suit filed by the Justice Department and a civil suit during the Eisenhower years. As noted, host governments put pressure on the firms to comply with Libyan demands, and Qaddafi played the contradictions between the state and the TNCs to the hilt.

The oil companies were by no means a united group. Qaddafi adroitly managed the schism between the independent and major oil companies by choosing small fry as his first target. He recognized that the independents were more dependent on Libyan oil than were their heavyweight counterparts, and calculated that their plight would not arouse much sympathy or support from the Seven Sisters. For their part, the Sisters viewed the independents as upstarts who were making foolish mistakes in business negotiations, jeopardizing the control over production and pricing long maintained by the seven majors, and threatening to upset the lucrative, vertically and horizontally integrated oil industry. Noting the ill-will between these concerns, Qaddafi cut the amount of oil Occidental could produce, giving birth to the worldwide oil crisis of the 1970s.

Is this experience singular because of oil's uniqueness as a commodity? Whereas each case has its special features, Libya's action against the oil industry does highlight structural contradictions within global capitalism as well as the latitude for political manoeuvre. Libya's encounter with transnational enterprises illustrates both the possibilities and bounds of what can be accomplished under present historical conditions. Although a large increment of oil revenue flowed into OPEC coffers, these countries were unable to release human creativity and energies because of the rigidities clogging their social systems. From the point of view of democratic values, Qaddafi's authoritarian politics presents little to emulate; Libya's type of social system hinders meaningful international action and, perforce, blocks development. Western capitalists benefited handsomely from OPEC power because inflation reduces real wages, effectively redistributing income to the privileged segments of society. Far-reaching changes were wrought in state-to-state relations without basic transformations in the domestic divisions of labour and power.

A different type of case bears out the opportunities for balancing market forces and hitching them to local resourcefulness, provided there is proper state guidance. India's so-called 'information revolution', based on computers, telephones and software technology, shows that liberalization does not always work to the detriment of domestic industries in the context of globalization. Once stifled by a 'license, permit, quota Raj' (in which private capital acquired the habits of inertia), given India's gargantuan bureaucratic machinery and protectionism against international competition in technology, the country is today witnessing a rapid transformation of its information industry. Despite the existence of durable structures of inequality and poverty, India appears at least relatively successful in riding the crests of globalization, especially in the computer software sector and may well be able to create a niche in the global political economy. Already pegged as one of the most attractive markets for offshore investments, India has recently changed from a mere exporter of human capital to a net exporter of goods in software. Though some attribute this success to recent neo-liberal policies, the direction of state intervention to meet local demand was the main determinant of production gains. Indeed, India's massive military complex and bureaucracy, with an almost insatiable appetite for computers and software, gave Indian software industry its *raison d'être*. Subsequently, public sector and business needs ignited demand for expansion.

The rise of information technology, however, has followed a circuitous route. In the mid-1960s through the first half of the 1980s, the central policy goal for Indian information technology was self-sufficiency. To that end, state production, the dislodging of IBM, and strict regulation of private production were the order of business. Beginning around 1984, with economic liberalization, the first signs of a 'silicon plateau' in Bangalore (in South India) were noticeable. In establishing world-class technical institutes, import protection, tax incentives, export processing zones and 'scientific' parks in cities such as Bangalore, the state's role has been paramount. Formerly a colonial military outpost of the British army and a site for scientific and technical training, Bangalore is today regarded as India's Silicon Valley.

At the root of this transformation was the ready supply of the world's second largest English-speaking technical work-force. State expenditure in education at Bangalore's technical institutes helped to create an entire generation of skilled personnel. While allowing private capital gradual entry into production, the state relaxed import restrictions. A software policy dovetailing the hardware policy spurred export production, with selective alliances with giant transnationals such as Hewlett-Packard and Olivetti under strict rules of equity participation by domestic companies. Hence, private capital and the Indian state formed a partnership to attract foreign capital and technology without compromising either the growth of local industry or local demand. The primary market for Indian computers, for instance, has been domestic. A tangible achievement of the business-state partnership is evident in modernizing Indian railways, the world's second largest.

One advantage of late industrialization was the absence of a mainframe industry, which drove India entrepreneurs to specialize in microcomputers. Paradoxically, this form of leapfrogging has given

India a built-in advantage in the wave of the future or the so-called wave of 'right-sizing,' with companies electing to scale their operations toward microcomputers. A magnet for Indian know-how and products, microcomputers, notably PCs (rather than mainframe), allow India to manufacture software and products domestically instead of subcontracting overseas production. From software production, there is now a growing shift toward services in an expanding market. A major by-product of the 'information revolution' is a check on India's perennial brain-drain problem.

Despite the growth in information technology, the structural problems of underdevelopment inhibit forward and backward linkages. India's anti-monopoly laws, however, blocked small-sized firms that tend to dominate production from achieving economies of scale and lower production costs. With R & D concentrated in the industrialized countries, tensions over intellectual property, notably with the USA, plague India's international position as a software giant. India's relative inexperience in global marketing may be another factor. But the more basic problem is the disjuncture between India's computer hardware and software industries. Indian computers have been only one notch above assembled imported components, underscoring the general pattern of technological dependence of Third World nations on the industrialized countries. Bureaucratic hindrances have also been a fetter on further advancement.

The long-term problem is rooted in social structure. While every district in India has access to computer facilities, preference is given to large businesses and organizations to the exclusion of most common people. With information technology, the income gap between India's 200 million people comprising its upper and middle classes and the 700 million poor is only likely to intensify. Unemployment may be one effect, but the further division of society into technological haves and have-nots may prove to be a more hazardous outcome.

On balance, with strategic support to local industry and gradual reduction in the role of SOEs in place of more competitive private entrepreneurs, the pangs of underdevelopment can be lessened. More basically, not simply building export platforms, but the existence of domestic demand is the bedrock for industrial upgrading. In India, the availability of a technically proficient work-force has also facilitated linking domestic production with export promotion. The Indian case, while not a fundamental transformation, may be regarded as a partial success in setting limits to exploitation and balancing the ties of dependency.

What should Western-based movements do to help bring about basic transformations in the Third World? There are several important measures. One is opposition to military build-ups. Another is lobbying for the conversion of expenditure on armaments to investment in genuine agricultural reform. Similarly, pressure on Western governments to adopt a non-interventionist policy in countries undergoing fundamental structural change is essential. But policy makers do not usually act against the interests of the groups that put them in power. To ask capitalists to refrain from expansionism is to ask them to cease being capitalists. This is not to suggest that tactical decisions are predetermined. Surely the anti-war movement influenced the USA's decision to withdraw from Vietnam. Nonetheless, it is not enough to stop Western states from interfering in the Third World.

Basic change must come about within underdeveloped countries themselves. In this process, Western support for realigning the domestic divisions of labour and power in the Third World should be linked more closely to the internal situations within the advanced countries. Just as production is increasingly global, struggles in various parts of the global political economy must be intertwined. As the ideological struggles intensify, moralizing about the evils of exploitation should not replace sober analysis of changing global structures.

Equally important for Westerners to contemplate is the question of what has not been done adequately or at all. Although state actions must be continually challenged, it is wrong to allow those who hold the reins of power to set the agenda. Unfortunately, many Westerners who oppose their governments' policies in the Third World have been largely reactive, their strategies crisis-oriented. Typically, critics have formed single-issue movements. For example, some US citizens regarded the anti-*apartheid* struggle in South Africa as a 'minority issue', a foreign policy matter for African-Americans to contest; Latin Americanists pursue their causes; and so on. What is required is an interlinking of movements that mobilize constituencies around such diverse issues as militarism, feminism, ecology and underdevelopment in different parts of the world. It is essential to bring home to workers, community groups and intellectuals precisely how individuals are personally involved in Third World struggles. Are bank deposits, pension funds and taxes supporting repressive structures in the Third World? How can these levers be used to gain control and change policy?

Surely there is a long road to travel before underdevelopment is overcome. Setting aside the exaggerated optimism of the early postcolonial period and the profound pessimism about the Third World which ensued, it is a truism to say that massive struggles in earlier historical epochs, such as the passage from feudalism to capitalism (a transition which engulfed the entire globe), have spawned fundamentally new world orders. It is out of the crucible of crises and from hard-fought struggles that new social forces emerge and invent creative solutions to deeply embedded problems. The praxis of struggle cannot be defined in advance. Improvements do not come steadily; there are traps and confusions, followed by sudden breakthroughs. And even then it can be hard to measure progress. Although the escape from underdevelopment calls for a monumental feat, we can devise novel ways to abolish the grim conditions in which the majority of humankind has been condemned to live and chart strategies for the course ahead.

The end of the Cold War and the dismantling of Soviet-style command socialism offer new opportunities for underdeveloped nations. Although short-term benefits from playing one patron against another may have receded, and even if several economies face the rude long-term prospect of undoing their socialist construction, a departure from an overly statist development model allows a mobilization of new social forces. Autarkic strategies are neither imaginable nor possible in an era of globalization, but a release from the fetters of the Cold War opens up major venues of domestic mobilization and participation. Demilitarization may be more viable in periods of more fluid global rivalries and democratic transitions.

Reliance on cultural resources derived from either everyday experience or piety offers many in the Third World at least a part of the way out from the prison-house of underdevelopment. Social movements with a localized expression are often propelled by marginalization accompanying West-centred globalization. Understanding the impetus of these movements from a shared cultural basis, as they relate to changing forms of state and strategies of accumulation, may allow a bridge between the developed countries and the Third World. The chief propellant of new possibilities lies in globalization itself. But it is the interface between globalization and local forces that will establish the way for creativity to find its ultimate release and realization.

Postscript

For a very long time the 'Third World' has appeared to Western observers as a bundle of problems, with violence and suffering being fixed signs of its naturalized state. Images of gun-toting religious fundamentalists in the Middle East, bloody civil wars in Africa, and drug-traffickers in Latin America regularly fill the television screens, as do images of Mother Teresa's orphans in hapless slums, disaster-prone Ethiopians or nameless victims of natural and human disaster in mysterious places, usually with strange names. In this tired and predictable representation, the Third World is a world to be analysed, controlled, managed, even salvaged; a laboratory for endless social engineering. Imbued with what Ashis Nandy calls a 'secular theory of salvation', *development* has offered the splendid prospects of 'modernization': from poverty alleviation to democratization, from building new institutions of capitalism to helping save the environment. The list of solutions is unending, subject to multiplication with the changing times. Underpinning policy prescriptions is the proposition that the Third World cannot cope with its problems. Its own solutions are reckless, its understanding of society defective, and its sensibility irrational.

The obverse, seemingly benign, representation sees the Third World as necessarily esoteric, ruled by self-denial, mystery, asceticism or playfulness. Thus, if it is not the recent corruption of tyrants or the ageless insolence of patriarchy, it is the ascription of the Third World as the natural habitat of spirituality or pre-civil chastity that is on offer. Both forms of representation – the Third World as a problem requiring outside scrutiny and help, or a spiritual panacea and vehicle for the cultural validation of alienated Westerners – prevent access to its complexity.

THE THIRD WORLD AS 'CAREER'

'The East is a career,' noted Benjamin Disraeli, Earl of Beaconsfield, arch-imperialist, and prime minister at the apex of British power. Disraeli's nineteenth century world has changed radically: the 'East' is no more the colonial, but the Third World. Remarkable similarities, however, persist. Like the East, the Third World appears to be an imperfect place with abundant material and cultural riches, a world ready and anxious to be transformed from without.

Having presumed this latent deficiency (congealed in the term 'Third World' itself), on the scales of wealth, power or culture the opportunity for prognosis and policy making is vast. As the object of economic and social analyses, the Third World provides fertile ground for policy makers; as a source of 'cultural capital', an investment that reaps rich dividends. Disraeli's sentiment finds resonance in the Third World's transition to postcoloniality. Often with good intentions, deciphering the ills and pains of otherness can be a lucrative business or simply an adventure to fill the personal and social void an advanced market culture often produces.

Encounters with otherness inform, but rarely have they bridged the gulf separating societies that resist the expanding market and those that affirm it. Seldom do the self-descriptions of those *analysed* in the development discourse enter the analyses. 'Can the subaltern speak?' as Gayatri Spivak, paraphrasing Marx, has put it. On the face of it, the problem lies, we are told, with misperceptions. It is assumed that greater emphasis on widening the information base and a concerted effort to promote factual accuracy would solve the problem: hence study-abroad programmes, consciousness raising social service sojourns in Third World regions, and travel to remote lands are designed to overcome ignorance. The idea that imperfect information is at the root of misperception assures – we cannot be held accountable for what we do not know. However, (mis)representations reveal at bottom a deeper structure of thought, make-believe and fantasy: a structure that has constructed the Third World via a particular mode of inquiry. On this view, there are no *mis*perceptions, simply the perceptions constructed by the categories of representation. It is the *context of representation* that needs explication, not simply a critique of recurrent (mis)perceptions about the Third World. Rarely is access to the Third World negotiated on a neutral or even footing. Structures of meaning, representation and interpretation produce knowledge of societal mores, political and economic processes and culture. Conditions of unequal power relations thus generate mutual understandings.

Specifically, awareness of the Third World resides in power relations and the cultural hierarchy these relations have produced and continue to promote between the West and the Third World. Equipped with specific categories of representation, as Edward Said has brilliantly analysed in *Orientalism*, the West meets the Third World, only to further existing hierarchies.

A decisive effect of power in exchange is the cultural separation between the West and the 'developing' non-Western world. Between the two stand armies of interlocutors, seeking to bridge separate worlds, but seldom succeeding in bringing them together. Often, the categories of representation accentuate, rather than mitigate, the differences. Too frequently, cultural embeddedness becomes a casualty of interlocution. Hence, in Richard Attenborough's simplistic portrayal of nationalist leaders in the all-too-well-known film *Gandhi*, the complexity of India's colonial history is reduced to a celebration of the mesmerizing practice of *Ahimsa* (or non-violence). 'History' becomes yet another site for the reproduction of otherness for its Westernized liberal interpreters. Accessing one-dimensional characters from a different world is infinitely more manageable than deciphering complexity. Attenborough's *Gandhi* makes it exceedingly difficult to undo historical representation. Once the film's narrative becomes a part of popular consciousness, access to India is mediated through Attenborough's version of Indian history. By contrast, the hypothetical world of *The Gods Must Be Crazy* is less pernicious. With its self-orientalized images of half-naked innocence triumphantly out-manoeuvring technical reason, the film does not seize the arteries of historical representation like *Gandhi*. The Third World only provides a brief site for playfulness.

Historically, to many in the Third World, often those who have placed themselves in relation to the developing world have wished to dominate it, some in the name of a civilizing mission, others in search of ethnicity. Not willing to engage marginality in their own society, or fearful of a close encounter with difference, many have elected a safer 'otherness' to realize their self. Ideally, travel for recreation or study in the Third World would produce greater affinity between the two worlds. Instead, it has facilitated greater access to the Third World upper classes in different social spheres (economic, political and social), thus empowering the foreign 'expert'. Imbued with the credentials afforded by a legitimate 'field' experience, 'experts' return home armed with 'authentic', experiential knowledge of the Third World, culturally enriched, ready to capitalize their hard-won cultural assets. Strategically positioned, relative to their less informed and provincial compatriots, the expert can provide testimonials to policy makers and captains of industry alike.

With some exceptions, on the other hand, the inner circles of Western societies and their power structures are difficult to penetrate. Not only is this echelon of the West accessible only to the privileged few but, more significantly, the terms of discourse are set in the West. Third

World intellectuals, as Arturo Escobar shows, share the 'theoretical imaginary of the West'. The dominant structures of knowledge, especially those focused on development, reproduce the characterizations and prescriptions of West-centred imagination. Alternative modes of knowledge and representation, unless backed by political power, remain on the margins of inquiry and understanding. Unequal access to either world, largely the effect of structural power, undergirds discourses of representation.

BEYOND ORIENTALISM AND OCCIDENTALISM

Against this background, Jim Mittelman's invitation to collaborate on a revised edition of *Out from Underdevelopment* was an enormous challenge. Having grown up in Pakistan, one of the Third World's 'emerging areas,' I (MKP) had read the first edition with great interest, and appreciated a political economy analysis of the Third World's condition. But I was quite unsure, until the project gained momentum, how I could contribute. Was this the occasion to bridge the relevant development issues with my own experiential knowledge? Given the irresistible practice of self-referential positioning in these times, could I escape the discrete charms of some inscrutable native sensibility? I saw the collaboration as a daunting task, one fraught with many perils. To start with, there was the danger of objectifying oneself. Such an enterprise may carry either the inducement to advance cultural relativism or simply to accept the established terms of discourse.

Working on the project allowed me to revisit the idea of *development*, but also furnished the opportunity to see the process of how the Third World is constructed in the academy. In addition, it reinforced the claim that many in the economically poor regions see themselves through categories that may not entirely be their own. The collaborative effort was to bridge a journey into the Third World with a journey out of it. The former sought to unravel the enigma of underdevelopment by subverting received frames of development thought. The latter attempted to examine the idea of development from the vantage point of its object: the Third World itself. Both Orientalism (the West's imagined understanding of the East) and Occidentalism (the East's imagined understanding of the West), being mirrored constructions, contort the possibility for mutual cultural recognition. This postscript conjoins the attempt in the book to overcome the lingering presence of Orientalism by challenging the deceptive parsimony of Occidentalism.

POLITICAL ECONOMY

Out from Underdevelopment Revisited adopts a political economy analysis to address enduring questions of development and underdevelopment. A departure from both the mendacious promise of modernization and the time-bound prophecies of the *dependentistas* should capture backwardness in terms of its historical embeddedness, recognizing the burdens of legacy and the creative capacities of human agency. The Third World's past is neither timeless nor static; its future, neither determined nor open-ended. There is possibility, but also the imperatives of structural constraints.

At the time of revisiting *Out from Underdevelopment*, there was an additional problem: the Third World is not the same as imagined only a decade ago. Dramatic changes in the global political economy altered the useful, if misleading, classificatory scheme of the three worlds. The end of the Cold War, the rise of the Asian NICs, the virtual disappearance of the Second World and globalization redrew the map in unanticipated ways. But, perhaps the Third World did not exist in the first place; it was an invention, a convenience. If the Third World had not existed, one may speculate, it had to be invented to materialize a world in the future or to displace the prospect of universalizing human history. It is no coincidence that the idea of *economic* development would become the hegemonic screen to arrange old and 'new' nations on a prefixed totem-pole. Hierarchies of wealth and power are often more palpable than those of culture and civility.

Notwithstanding recent accounts of the coming of a new millennium captured in Francis Fukuyama's 'end-of-history' thesis and Samuel Huntington's foreboding prediction of a coming 'clash of civilizations' between the West and the Rest, there is ample utility in preserving the category 'Third World' as an analytical construct. There exists a growing need to apprehend the great divide between wealth and want, sharpened by global neo-liberalism. Rejecting the liberal promise of the arrival of a global village, a 'Third World' of constraints is patent. Overcoming material want remains a key aspiration of most postcolonial societies. And recognition of cultural integrity, a struggle against West-centred globalization, defines the parameters of politics and identity in this heterodox 'Third World'. Acknowledging its inconsistencies, it was safer to stay with this category. The Third World has not disappeared after all. Perhaps it will cease to be, but not yet. Against the unbearable heaviness of received ideas about the Third World, a political economy analysis offers a correction.

DOMINATING STRUCTURES

Throughout the period following political decolonization, Third World countries embraced the ideology of 'catching up' with the industrialized world. Regardless of its human and ecological cost, whether dependency on First World (rarely Second World) powers, or the subordination of culture, the environment or religion, the pursuit of material riches became the hegemonic design. In different guises, secular-nationalists imitating Western industrial experience inflicted this project upon their own societies with unfettered exuberance. In place of respect for the wisdom of centuries, technical reason was to prevail, supplanting value rationality and spontaneity in human affairs. Irrelevant or costlier medicine displaced preventive medicine, as Vandana Shiva has convincingly shown in *Staying Alive*. Lockean notions of property acquired currency, with little regard for communitarian purpose. Above all, without a corresponding restraint to curb the excesses of a growing market, economic growth and commodity relations would build the adopted social order. Zealous state-builders elected 'nation-building' as the goddess of human progress, wresting sacrifice from their bewildered citizens.

The hazards of social engineering, sanctioned by secular modernization, have become apparent in Iran, Algeria, and even Turkey (a country that has prided itself on being a part of Europe, shunning its Muslim roots). In East and South-east Asia, as the preceding analysis in this book has shown, the costs of modernization provide a sobering picture. In Pakistan, too, the pitfalls of developmentalism have been quite palpable. Nudged by Harvard economists in the late 1950s, Pakistan embarked upon an ambitious 'decade of development', only to produce massive social inequities under the banner of 'functional inequality', the insidious idea of using income disparities to propel growth. Similar results, in some cases more tragic, have been witnessed in other parts of the Third World.

In recent years, the borrowed enterprise of modernization has entered a chronic phase of crisis. In diverse parts of the Third World, people have begun to speak out: in writings on culture and development, in alternative philosophical constructions of modernity and, above all, through practice in new social movements. Though far from discarding the dominant (Western) discourse of development, the idea of 'catching up' is being challenged. In an era of globalization, the forms of resistance are decidedly unfamiliar: the Zapatista uprising in Mexico, resurgent movements in many parts of the Islamic world, and women's self-help organizations in rural India.

Less visible, but perhaps more significant to the creation of an alternative, many aspects of everyday life in the Third World recognize and embody an indigenous consciousness. Notwithstanding MTV and the 'CNNization' of the Third World, cultural and political idioms defy homogenization. A growing indigenous expression (once exclusively the domain of those lacking access to the West, or conversely, those who had savoured 'Western' products – cultural and otherwise – that wealth could buy) is evident. In South Asia, for instance, social expression is increasingly marked by a turn towards non-Western sensibilities. The ascendancy of local cultural forms, exploring religious or historical themes, speak to multilinear trajectories of social development. The indigenization of politics is a visible feature of the rise of political religion in the Third World. Despite the propensity of neo-liberal globalization to homogenize economic policy, the political moment congeals multiple expressions of culture. The resourcefulness of Third World societies reveals itself in the resistance to a globalizing economy. Although an uncritical celebration of all 'native' expression is naive, given that some Third World movements seek to foreclose the possibility of gender equality, religious tolerance and democratic politics, an understanding of these movements must be made on universal, not particularistic (whether Western or non-Western) criteria.

Western representations of Third World politics often fail to capture the milieu of ordinary people. Protest movements frequently pass as societal disequilibria or symptoms of *uncivil* politics. Keenly aware of political forces that dictate the everyday rhythms – whether price hikes decreed by IMF adjustment programmes, local corruption, or political trends in neighbouring countries – people across the Third World know too well the forms of struggle germane to their own societies. The economy is always *conditioned* by politics and, contrary to the perception of some purveyors of neo-liberalism, palpable to those who find themselves on its receiving end. Although it is often said that the Third World is more politicized (comparative studies suggest, as one indicator, that voter turn-outs are persistently higher in 'backward' regions) than the Western countries, this claim lacks appreciation for the deeper implications of the nexus between politics and economics in the context of underdevelopment. Processing politics through categories more appropriate to the political reality of Western societies often misses the logic of politics in the Third World. Often, the purported indicators of political development assume certain patterns that belong to societies with a different historical past. Hence, recognizing the capacity for intense politicization, some observers recommend 'slowing down' the political process, to manage ungovernable populations.

The sharp interface between politics and everyday life may be the most distinctive aspect of the Third World, not squalor or economic want. Development has always appeared as a political process in which power relations are directly implicated. With affluence, perhaps, also comes the comfort of depoliticization. For *economically* underdeveloped countries, however, power appears in more naked forms. Though its actual capacities may be fairly suspect, the state also seems more transparent. An awareness of social hierarchies, *class divisions* between tiny islands of affluence and the very poor, is not an academic exercise, but part of 'normal' existence. In this context, political awareness is not the consequence of a later stage of development, provided consciousness is not equated with a particular brand of ideological commitment.

POST-DEVELOPMENT?

Beyond critique, a recent sentiment seeks to reject the idea of development in its entirety. Against the track-record of developmentalism, and with globalization, this suggestion may not be out of place. However, the project of development has shown remarkable resilience. One alternative, short of total repudiation, is to *humanize* development: to make development conform to more basic principles of societal harmony, ecological balance, and respect for diversity and autonomy.

Recognizing these principles may yield new opportunities to reconstruct development. To that end, an appreciation of alternative constructions of social development, while conceding the constraints that originate in the Third World's participation in the global political economy, may allow possibilities. As many voices in the Third World have observed, *economic* development is only a small part of the total picture. On this view, the quest for dignity in the Third World is neither a sign of timidity nor the struggle for recognition, a 'vestige' of 'traditional society'. To reject (alternative) intentions as legitimate expressions is to deny others unlike us the capacity to structure life along different notions of social development. These issues are central to the development discourse, regardless of its protagonists. In the Third World's continued self-scrutiny and 'decolonization of imagination', they are likely to become more pronounced.

Development thinking must continually address the rudeness of its own prevailing structures of thought that produce and process a certain image of the Third World. Discourses of development generally weigh heavily on wealth creation, without acknowledging the longing for dignity and identity in the Third World. Few frames of analysis have escaped this dominant logic. Material wealth may be a prerequisite for development, but it does not even begin to exhaust the compass of societal aspiration and meaning. In much of the Third World, in fact, the desire for dignity is unconditional, tied neither to a compensatory logic attributed to those in want, nor to the social power that wealth affords. Relating the desire for dignity primarily to structures of poverty, the West ironically denies any basis for it to the Third World. The presumption that material progress affords civility, as for Adam Smith, captures only a part of the whole. The primacy of material production is itself the product of a certain ontology. Underlying this ontology is a cultural outlook that is derived from a particular (Western), not a universal, experience. Only under certain historical conditions does the notion that economic development is the major criterion for distinction between cultures present itself as the hegemonic principle for all humanity. Recognizing the temporal and spatial constrictions of this *materialist* social order constitutes an important step towards social transformation.

1995   MUSTAPHA KAMAL PASHA
Washington, DC

Notes and References

1 Public Platitudes and Unfounded Attitudes

The interview with Fidel Castro by Barbara Walters was aired on 9 June 1977. We have corrected some stylistic errors in the ABC transcript, pp. 8–12, which the television network generously shared with us. Moynihan's statement is noted by Michael Harrington, *The Vast Majority: A Journey to the World's Poor* (New York: Simon & Schuster, 1977) p. 18 (emphasis in original). Brzezinski was interviewed by George Urban. The interview appeared under the title 'The Perils of Foreign Policy: A Conversation in Washington', *Encounter* 56, 5 (May 1981), especially p. 13; and in condensed form, 'A Talk with Brzezinski', *New York Times*, 22 April 1981 (emphasis in original). The discussion on *National Geographic* was from Catherine A. Lutz and Jane L. Collins, *Reading National Geographic* (Chicago: The University of Chicago Press, 1993). Mr Gromyko's quip is taken from 'Russians Come and Russians Go, but Not Gromyko', *New York Times*, 4 October 1982. Material on disease in the Third World draws on 'Media's Portrayal of Ebola Virus Sparks Outbreak of Wild Scenarios', *Washington Post*, 14 May 1995. Xan Smiley's 'Misunderstanding Africa' can be found in *The Atlantic Monthly*, 250, 3 (September 1982), pp. 72, 74. See Ngugi Wa Thiong'o, *Petals of Blood* (New York: Dutton, 1978) p. 326.

The gap between rich and poor countries is discussed by the Independent Commission on International Development Issues, *North-South: A Program for Survival* (Cambridge, Mass.: MIT Press, 1980) p. 32. Indicators of the gap can be found in World Bank, *World Development Report 1993* (New York: Oxford University Press, 1993) pp. 199, 238–9 and 246–7, and the UNDP, *Human Development Report 1993* (New York: Oxford University Press, 1993) pp. 141, 213.

On the meaning of political economy, see W. Ladd Hollist and James A. Caporaso, 'International Political Economy Research: What Is It and Where Do We Turn for Concepts and Theory?', in W. Ladd Hollist and F. LaMond Tullis (eds), *An International Political Economy*, International Political Economy Yearbook (Boulder, Col.: Westview Press, 1985) vol. 1, pp. 27–49, and James A. Caporaso and David P. Levine, *Theories of Political Economy* (Cambridge: Cambridge University Press, 1993). The classical tradition is surveyed by Robert L. Heilbroner, *The Worldly Philosophers: The Lives, Times, and Ideas of the Great Economic Thinkers* (New York: Time Incorporated, 1961). Another valuable study is Ernest Mandel, *Marxist Economic Theory*, trans. Brian Pearce (London: Merlin, 1968). For an overview of various schools of thought, consult Robert W. Cox, 'In Search of Political Economy', *New Political Science*, 5/6, (Winter/Spring 1981), pp. 59–78, and Michael Barratt Brown, *Models in Political Economy: A Guide to the Arguments* (Boulder, Col.: Lynne Rienner, 1985).

Diverse perspectives on the Third World are represented in People's Daily, *The Theory of Three Worlds* (New York: Books New China, 1977); Kwame Nkrumah, 'The Myth of the "Third World"', *Labour Monthly*, 50, 10 (October 1968), p. 465; 'Mrs. Gandhi Welcomes Dawn of Era of Detente', *India News*, 4 Septem-

260

ber 1973, cited by Allen H. Merriam, 'Semantic Implications of the Term "Third World"', *International Studies Notes*, 6, 3 (Fall 1979), p. 14; and Immanuel Wallerstein, *The Capitalist World-Economy* (Cambridge, Mass.: Cambridge University Press, 1979) p. 348. Brief histories of China's theory of three worlds can be found in James C. Hsiung and Samuel S. Kim (eds), *China in the Global Community* (New York: Praeger Publishers, 1980) pp. 28–37, and Samuel S. Kim, *China In and Out of the Changing World Order* (Princeton, NJ: Center for International Studies, 1991) pp. 53–6. The concept of 'new Third World' was suggested by Samir Amin, 'Regionalization in the Third World in Response to the Challenge of Polarizing Globalization', paper presented to the UNU/World Institute of Development Economics Research workshop on 'Globalization and Regionalization', Berlin, 20–3 August 1994.

On the decline of US hegemony, see Robert Gilpin, *The Political Economy of International Relations* (Princeton, NJ: Princeton University Press, 1987) p. 330, and James H. Mittelman, 'The End of a Millennium: Changing Structures of World Order and the Post-Cold War Division of Labour', in Larry A. Swatuk and Timothy M. Shaw (eds), *The South at the End of the Twentieth Century: Rethinking the Political Economy of Foreign Policy in Africa, Asia, the Caribbean and Latin America* (London: Macmillan, 1994) pp. 15–27. Information on the US recovery was from Sylvia Nasar, 'The American Economy, Back on Top', *New York Times*, 27 February 1994. The figures on the debt service of underdeveloped countries were from the UNDP, *Human Development Report 1993*, p. 174.

2 Sources of Received Ideas about the Third World

The quotations from Okot p'Bitek's *Song of Lawino* (Nairobi: East African Publishing House, 1966) are taken from pp. 140, 141, 142, 155, 156, 207 and 208. The backdrop to *Song of Lawino* is the subject of James H. Mittelman, *Ideology and Politics in Uganda: From Obote to Amin* (Ithaca, NY: Cornell University Press, 1975). The comments by Hugh Trevor-Roper, 'The Rise of Christian Europe', *The Listener* (London), 28 November 1963, p. 871, are reported by Ali A. Mazrui, *Cultural Engineering and Nation-Building in East Africa* (Evanston, Ill.: Northwestern University Press, 1972) p. 7. Severeid's remarks were on CBS Evening News, 15 July 1975. The quote from Option 2 can be found in NSSM–39, edited and introduced by Mohamed A. El-Khawas and Barry Cohen, *The Kissinger Study of Southern Africa* (Westport, Conn.: Lawrence Hill, 1976) p. 105. Seymour M. Hersh, *The Price of Power: Kissinger in the Nixon White House* (New York: Summit Books, 1983) p. 263, describes the Nixon-Valdés meeting. Hersh cites material in Armando Urbie's memoir, *The Black Book of American Intervention in Chile* (Boston, Mass.: Beacon Press, 1975) pp. 30–3.

Cecil Rhodes is quoted in *Imperialism, the Highest Stage of Capitalism* (Beijing: Foreign Language Press, 1973) p. 94, by V. I. Lenin. The same theme appears in Sir Sidney James, 'Personal Recollections of Cecil Rhodes; 1, Some Conversations in London', *The Nineteenth Century*, 51 (May 1902), pp. 832, 835.

The five phases on the road to modernization are outlined by W. W. Rostow, *The Stages of Economic Growth: A Non-Communist Manifesto* (London: Cambridge University Press, 1960). The anecdote about peasant farmers is borrowed from Philip Raikes, 'Rural Differentiation and Class Formation in Tanzania',

Journal of Peasant Studies, 5, 3 (April 1978), pp. 315–17. On the failure of modernization theory to come to grips with causality, see Geoffrey Kay, *Development and Underdevelopment: A Marxist Analysis* (New York: St Martin's Press, 1975) pp. x, 2. The legacy of the modernization school is examined by Richard Higgott, 'From Modernization Theory to Public Policy: Continuity and Change in the Political Science of Political Development', *Studies in Comparative International Development*, 15, 4 (Winter 1980), pp. 26–58. The figures on the Sri Lankan economy are drawn from World Bank, *World Development Report 1993* (New York: Oxford University Press, 1993) pp. 244, 276, 278 and 284.

Perhaps the best book in the dependency framework is Fernando Henrique Cardoso and Enzo Faletto, *Dependency and Development in Latin America*, trans. Marjory Mattingly Urquidi (Berkeley: University of California Press, 1975). In responding to criticism levelled by Marxists, Cardoso and Faletto conflate the dependency concept and class analysis. They surrender the distinctive features of this concept – the notion that the mainspring of Third World political economies is the exploitation of the periphery by the centre – and substitute dialectical reasoning rooted in history and identification of contradictions. The thrust of their analysis is therefore dependency in name only. On the origins of underdevelopment, a work which informs our analysis is Walter Rodney, *How Europe Underdeveloped Africa* (London: Bogle-L'Ouverture Publications, 1972). The economic legacy of imperialism and a suggested antidote are presented by Clive Thomas, *Dependence and Transformation: The Economics of the Transition to Socialism* (New York: Monthly Review Press, 1974). This vast literature is reviewed by Ronald H. Chilcote, *Theories of Development and Underdevelopment* (Boulder, Col.: Westview Press, 1984). On the issue of Canada's dependence on the USA see Bruce W. Wilkinson, 'The Canada-U.S. Free Trade Negotiations', in David L. McKee (ed.), *Canadian-American Economic Relations: Conflict and Cooperation on a Continental Scale* (New York: Praeger, 1988) p. 90. The statistics on Canada's economy are drawn from John Robert Colombo (ed.), *1994 The Canadian Global Almanac* (Toronto: Macmillan Canada, 1993) pp. 193, 218–19; and Statistics Canada, *Canada's International Investment Position 1993* (Ottawa: Canada Communications Group, published by the authority of the minister responsible for Statistics Canada, 1994) pp. 72–4.

3 Received Ideas and International Institutions

The quip by an African diplomat is drawn from 'Invasion Debate: U.N. Weakness Displayed', *New York Times*, 5 March 1979. Commentary on the UN by various US delegates can be found in John E. Stoessinger, *The Might of Nations: World Politics in Our Time* (New York: Random House, 1975) p. 301; William F. Buckley, Jr, *United Nations Journal: A Delegate's Odyssey* (Garden City, NY: Anchor Books, 1977) p. 237; and Daniel Patrick Moynihan, A *Dangerous Place* (Boston, Mass.: Little, Brown, 1978) p. 188. In criticizing these views, we are summarizing arguments that have been made elsewhere: James H. Mittelman, 'American Double Standards on African Issues at the UN', *New York Times*, 22 January 1977. The relationship between international organization and capital accumulation is explored by Robert W. Cox, 'Production and Hegemony: Toward a Political Economy of World Order', in Harold K. Jacobson and Dusan

Sidjanski (eds), *The Emerging International Economic Order: Dynamic Processes, Constraints and Opportunities* (Beverly Hills: Sage, 1982) pp. 37–58.

The passage from the Independent Commission on International Development issues (also known as the Brandt Commission) appears in *North-South: A Program for Survival* (Cambridge, Mass.: MIT Press, 1980) p. 264. A sequel to this report is the Brandt Commission, *Common Crisis, North-South: Cooperation for World Recovery* (Cambridge, Mass.: MIT Press, 1983).

For recent data on Tanzania, see George Thomas Kurian, *The New Book of World Rankings*, 3rd edn (New York: Facts on File, 1991). On the pitfalls of foreign aid, see Yashpal Tandon (ed.), *Technical Assistance Administration in East Africa* (Stockholm: Dag Hammarskjöld Foundation, 1973). Apart from the information drawn from personal experience, the sources on Tanzania are 'Third World Saga: Tanzania's Case Shows the Pluses and the Many Minuses of Big Foreign-Aid Programs', *Wall Street Journal*, 27 August 1982, and Andrew Coulson, 'The Automated Bread Factory', in Coulson (ed.), *African Socialism in Practice: The Tanzanian Experience* (Nottingham: Spokesman, 1979) pp. 179–83.

The conventional view on the role of modern technology in a developing economy is exemplified by W. W. Rostow, *The Stages of Economic Growth: A Non-Communist Manifesto* (Cambridge: Cambridge University Press, 1960) pp. 4; 32–3. The need to understand the context for technology transfer is stressed by Harvard professors Robert H. Hayes and Modesto A. Maidique, 'The Technology Gap', *New York Times*, 2 June 1981. Two historical treatises explore this theme in depth: Perry Anderson, *Passages from Antiquity to Feudalism* (London: New Left Books, 1974), especially pp. 203–4, and Maurice Dobb, *Studies in the Development of Capitalism* (New York: International Publishers, 1963) pp. 22–3. On expenditures on research and development, see UNESCO, *Statistical Yearbook* (Paris: UNESCO, 1994). Excellent studies of technology and the changing international division of labour are Folker Fröbel, Jurgen Heinrichs and Otto Kreye, 'The New International Division of Labour', *Social Science Information*, 17, 1 (1978), pp. 123–42; Charles Bergquist (ed.), *Labor in the Capitalist World Economy* (Beverly Hills: Sage, 1984); and Joseph Grunwald and Kenneth Flamm, *The Global Factory: Foreign Assembly in International Trade* (Washington, DC: Brookings Institute, 1985). Transnational-driven research and development efforts in the Third World and India's technology policy are discussed by Helge Hveem, 'Selective Dissociation in the Technology Sector', especially pp. 280, 298–303, in John Gerard Ruggie (ed.), *The Antinomies of Interdependence: National Welfare and the International Division of Labor* (New York: Columbia University Press, 1983). The argument that technology transfer is leakage from TNCs is advanced by Charles-Albert Michalet, 'From Unequal Industrial Development to Unequal Scientific and Technological Development: Toward the New International Economic Order?' (paper presented to the annual meeting of the International Studies Association, St Louis, 1977).

On why TNCs forestall the emergence of centres of innovation and technology in the Third World, see Stephen Hymer, 'The Multinational Corporation and the Law of Uneven Development', in Jagdish N. Bhagwati (ed.), *Economics and World Order: From the 1970s to the 1990s* (New York: Macmillan, 1972). Some of the data cited here on TNCs is derived from John Cavanagh and Frederick F. Clairmonte, 'From Corporation to Conglomerates: A Review of Multinationals over the Last Twenty Years', *Multinational Monitor*, January 1983, pp. 16–19 and 'Fortune's Global 500: The World's Largest Corporations', *Fortune*, 7 August 1994, pp. F1-F4. The quotation by Kissinger appears in Seymour M. Hersh, *The Price of Power: Kissinger in the Nixon White House* (New York: Summit, 1983) p. 265. A compelling account of efforts by the ITT and the CIA to get rid of Allende can be found on pages 258–96 of Hersh's book. Dr Yudkin's report is summarized in 'Western Drugs and Third World Markets', *The Guardian* (London), 21 August 1977. On Balasubramaniam's statement and the example of Pakistan, see 'Health Policy for the Third World,' *Multinational Monitor*, December 1992, pp. 25–9. On the example of pesticide use, see 'U.S. Pesticide Kills Foreign Fruit Pickers' Hopes,' *New York Times*, 6 December 1995. The lessons of the Bhopal tragedy are discussed in 'Disaster in India Sharpens Debate on Doing Business in Third World', *New York Times*, 16 December 1984.

The figures on the ratio of loans to unpaid debt were compiled by Mark Hulbert, 'Will the US Bail Out the Bankers?', *The Nation*, 235, 12 (16 October 1982), p. 365. Data on debt have been derived from *World Economic Outlook* (Washington, DC: IMF, 1994). Dimensions of the debt crisis are examined in Lester B. Thurow, 'America's Banks in Crisis', *New York Times Magazine*, 23 September 1984; 'Records Show Citicorp Acted to Skirt Foreign Bank Rules', *New York Times*, 13 September 1982; Anthony Sampson, *The Money Lenders* (Harmondsworth: Penguin Books, 1981) and *Citicorp Worldwide* (New York: Citicorp, 1989). The emergence of a secondary market which trades international loans at discount is reported in 'The Market for Latin Debt', *New York Times*, 17 July 1985, and Richard S. Weinert, 'Swapping Third World Debt', *Foreign Policy*, 65, Winter 1986–7, pp. 85–97. On debt figures, see *World Debt Tables 1991–1992* Volume 1 (Washington, DC: World Bank, 1991), p. 23. Discussion of Mexico's bail-out is based on 'NAFTA Disaster: The Fall of the Peso and the Mexican "Miracle"', *Multinational Monitor*, April 1995, pp. 8–15. Information on the Brady Plan comes from *The Economist*, especially the issue of 5 January 1991. An appraisal of the IMF's record is provided by John Loxley, *The IMF and the Poorest Countries: The Performance of the Least Developed Countries under IMF Stand-by Arrangements* (Ottawa: North-South Institute, 1984). The increasing frequency of debt rescheduling is documented by the Department of State, Bureau of Public Affairs, 'Foreign Indebtedness to US Government' (October 1983), n.p. The debt rescheduling figures for 1990–1994 are drawn from Jonathon E. Sanford, 'Issue Paper: Debt Relief for African Countries' (Washington, DC: Congressional Research Service, 1995). Analysis of the effects of adjustment in Ecuador is based on *World Development Report 1990* (Washington, DC: Oxford University Press, 1990), p. 104. The quotation by the former Brazilian president appears in Jeff Freiden, 'On Borrowed Time', North American Congress on Latin America, or NACLA, *Report on the Americas* 19, 2 (March-April 1985), p. 2. The political economy of debt is the subject of a special issue of *International Organization*, 39, 3 Summer 1985.

4　Back to the Nineteenth Century for New Ideas

Information on Saudi Arabia is gleaned from recent National Trade Statistical Bank data. The analysis of Saudi economic troubles is based on a special report

entitled 'Saudi Arabia Sorts Itself Out', in *The Middle East*, February 1995, pp. 19–22.
A lucid explanation of why capitalism must expand may be found in Robert L. Heilbroner, *The Nature and Logic of Capitalism* (New York: W. W. Norton, 1985). See especially Chapter 2, 'The Drive to Amass Capital'. Important background readings on the nexus between the state and the market are Charles Lindblom, *Politics and Markets: The World's Political Economic Systems* (New York: Basic Books, 1977); Theda Skocpol, *States and Social Revolutions: A Comparative Analysis of France, Russia, and China* (New York: Cambridge University Press, 1979); and Peter B. Evans, Dietrich Rueschemeyer and Theda Skocpol (eds), *Bringing the State Back In* (New York: Cambridge University Press, 1985).

Walter Wriston's comment appears in 'Wriston: A Summing Up', *New York Times*, 21 June 1984. The parable about the interconnection between production and circulation is taken from Arghiri Emmanuel, *Unequal Exchange: A Study of the Imperialism of Trade* (New York: Monthly Review Press, 1972) p. 152. For the vignette about Zimbabwe, we are indebted to David Martin and Phyllis Johnson, *The Struggle for Zimbabwe: The Chimurenga War* (New York: Monthly Review Press, 1981) pp. 54–5. On land hunger, see also Terence Ranger, *Peasant Consciousness and Guerrilla War in Zimbabwe* (Berkeley: University of California Press, 1985). Marx's comment on his own life is drawn from Martin Nicolaus' Foreword to Karl Marx, *Grundrisse: Foundations of the Critique of Political Economy*, trans. Martin Nicolaus (Harmondsworth: Penguin Books, 1973) p. 11. The illustration about the English manufacturer is provided by Marx, *Capital*, 3rd edn (New York: International Publishers, 1975), vol. 1, p. 766. On Marx's mistaken notion about underdevelopment, see *Capital*, 3rd edn (London: George Allen & Unwin, n.d.), vol. 1, p. xvii, quoted and discussed by Geoffrey Kay, *Development and Underdevelopment: A Marxist Analysis* (New York: St Martin's Press, 1975) p.11. The literary works cited here are Henrik Ibsen, *Arthur Miller's Adaptation of An Enemy of the People* (Harmondsworth: Penguin Books, 1980) and Chinua Achebe, *Man of the People* (Garden City, NY: Anchor Books, 1967).

5 The Conventional Route, Joining Global Capitalism: Track 1 – Brazil

The acquisition of Hills Brothers by Corpersucar is discussed in 'Brazil's Coffee (with Sugar) Billionaire', *Fortune*, 46, 1 (July 1977), pp. 82–8. The scale of Brazil's economy is surveyed by Marsha Miliman, 'Brazil: Let Them Eat Minerals!', *NACLA's Latin America and Empire Report* 3, 4 (April 1973), pp. 5–7. Additional data on the economy can be found in the World Bank's *World Development Report 1993* (New York: Oxford University Press, 1993), and Sandra Steingraber and Judith Hurley, 'Brazil's Debt and Deforestation – A Global Warning' (San Francisco: Institute for Food and Development Policy, 1990) p. 2. The figure for the size of the Brazilian Amazon was from Rachel M. McCleary, 'Development Strategies in Conflict: Brazil and the Future of the Amazon', *Case Study in Ethics and International Affairs* (New York: Carnegie Council on Ethics and International Affairs, 1990) p. 1. Information on the historical backdrop may be found in Alfred Stepan, *The Military in Politics* (Princeton, NJ: Princeton University Press, 1971), and Alfred Stepan (ed.),

Authoritarian Brazil: Origins, Policies, and Future (New Haven, Con.: Yale University Press, 1972). Specifically, we are drawing on Sylvia Ann Hewlett, *The Cruel Dilemmas of Development: Twentieth Century Brazil* (New York: Basic Books, 1980) p. 34, and Peter Evans, *Dependent Development: The Alliance of Multinational, State, and Local Capital in Brazil* (Princeton, NJ: Princeton University Press, 1979) pp. 110–11. The sources for material on Brazil's exploitation of the Amazon are Anthony L. Hall, *Developing Amazonia: Deforestation and Social Conflict in Brazil's Carajás Programme* (Manchester: Manchester University Press, 1989), and Marianne Schmink and Charles H. Wood, *Contested Frontiers in Amazonia* (New York: Columbia University Press, 1992). An excellent discussion of import substitution is provided by José Serra, 'Three Mistaken Theses Regarding the Connection between Industrialization and Authoritarian Regimes', in David Collier (ed.), *The New Authoritarianism in Latin America* (Princeton, NJ: Princeton University Press, 1979) pp. 99–163.

The Johnson administration's view of the Goulart government is quoted by Hewlett, *The Cruel Dilemmas of Development*, p. 72. Data on the resources found in the Amazon were from Shelton J. Davis, *Victims of the Miracle* (Cambridge: Cambridge University Press, 1977) p. 32. On repression and labour organization, see Kenneth S. Mericle, 'Corporatist Control of the Working Class: Authoritarian Brazil Since 1964', in James M. Malloy (ed.), *Authoritarianism and Corporatism in Latin America* (Pittsburgh: University of Pittsburgh Press, 1977) pp. 303–8; Kenneth Paul Erickson and Kevin J. Middlebrook, 'The State and Organized Labor in Brazil and Mexico', in Sylvia Ann Hewlett and Richard S. Weinert (eds), *Brazil and Mexico: Patterns in Late Development* (Philadelphia: Institute for the Study of Human Issues, 1984) pp. 213–63; and Maria Helena Moreira Alves, *State and Opposition in Military Brazil* (Austin: University of Texas Press, 1985). For a discussion of the role of women in Brazilian industry, see John Humphrey, *Gender and Work in the Third World: Sexual Divisions in Brazilian Industry* (London: Tavistock Publications, 1987), especially pp. 13–34. The discussion on workers in the De Millus lingerie factory was drawn from Cecilia Camargo, 'Made with Fear', in Caipora Women's Group, *Women in Brazil* (London: Latin America Bureau, 1993) pp. 37–38. The plight of Brazil's Indians is detailed in Davis, *Victims of the Miracle*. Additional information may be found in Schmink and Wood, *Contested Frontiers in Amazonia*, pp. 74–6. The statement from the World Bank Report was taken from Tad Szulc, 'Brazil's Amazonian Frontier', in Andrew Maguire and Janet W. Brown (eds), *Bordering on Trouble: Resources and Politics in Latin America* (Bethesda: Adler & Adler, 1986) p. 228. The number of Indians affected by the Greater Carajás Programme was from Hall, *Developing Amazonia*, p. 89.

The growth of agricultural exports is discussed in Werner Baer, The *Brazilian Economy: Growth and Development* (New York: Praeger, 1989) p. 346. Delfim's remarks appear in Cheryl Payer, *The Debt Trap: The International Monetary Fund and the Third World* (Harmondsworth: Penguin Books, 1974) p. 161. For information on Brazil's state-run corporations, see Douglas H. Graham, 'Mexican and Brazilian Economic Development: Legacies, Patterns and Performance', in Hewlett and Weinert (eds), *Brazil and Mexico*, especially p. 32; 'Brazil's Economy after the Miracle', *New York Times*, 17 July 1983; and Eul-Soo-Pang, 'Brazil's New Democracy', *Current History*, 82, 481 (February 1983), p. 56. Attitudes on state intervention in the economy are reported by Evans, *Dependent Develop-*

ment, p. 238. On the involvement of multinational corporations in the local economy, see Hewlett, *The Cruel Dilemmas of Development*, p. 135, and 'Brazil', in George Thomas Kurian (ed.), *Encyclopedia of the Third World: Afghanistan to Guinea-Bissau*, rev. edn, (New York: Facts on File, 1982) vol. 1, p. 234. The figures on the repatriation of profit can be found on p. 144 of Hewlett, *The Cruel Dilemmas of Development*. Sources for the discussion on the development of the Amazon are Hall, *Developing Amazonia*; Davis, *Victims of the Miracle*; and Schmink and Wood, *Contested Frontiers in Amazonia*. The quotation from the Amazonian *caboclo* was from Jose Lutzenberger, 'Who is Destroying the Amazon Rainforest', *The Ecologist*, 17 4/5, (1987), p. 156. Data on income distribution are provided by Hewlett, 'Poverty and Inequality in Brazil', in Hewlett and Weinert (eds), *Brazil and Mexico*, pp. 317–38. On the impact on women see John Humphrey, *Gender and Work in the Third World*, and Sonia E. Alvarez, *Engendering Democracy in Brazil: Women's Movements in Transition Politics* (Princeton, NJ: Princeton University Press, 1990). The quotation by Alvarez was taken from p. 260.

The remark by the former cabinet minister appears in Janet Shenk, 'Don't Believe in Miracles', *NACLA Report on the Americas* 12, 3 (May-June 1979), p. 10, citing 'After Fifteen Years, Military Rule Dies Hard in Brazil', *Washington Post*, 31 March 1979. Mr Reagan's gaffe is reported in 'President Promises to Give Brazilians a $1.2 Billion Loan', *New York Times*, 2 December 1982. The declining confidence of international banks in investment in Brazil is noted in 'IMF Plans Pressures on Banks to Help Brazil', *New York Times*, 15 December 1982. The plight of the Pereiras is described in 'Poorer Brazilians are Going Hungry, While the Rich Worry about the Future', *Wall Street Journal*, 6 May 1983. The changing political climate is assessed in 'A Country that is on the Verge of Exploding', *Business Week*, 2 May 1983. President Figueiredo's reaction to the wave of civil unrest is reported in 'Blowup: Jobless Workers on a Rampage', *Time*, 18 April 1983. The European ambassador's statement appears in 'Brazilians Condemn Liberalization Foes', *New York Times*, 11 April 1983; the lawyer's observation is in Penny Lernoux, 'The "Model" Shattered: Brazil, the Banks, the Third World', *The Nation*, 237, 14 (5 November 1983), p. 435.

The figures on Brazil's debt and inflation rate were taken from, 'Brazil's Economy – the Right Stuff', *The Economist*, 9 June 1990, pp. 75–77; Baer, *The Brazilian Economy*, p. 165; World Bank, *World Development Report 1992* (New York: Oxford University Press, 1992); and, Thomas Kamm, 'Brazilian Official Maps Federal Plan Against Inflation', *Wall Street Journal*, 15 June 1993, p. A14. A summary of the different plans designed to counter inflation and attempts to solve the debt problem may be found in James M. Malloy and Eduardo A. Gamarra, *Latin America and Caribbean Contemporary Record, Volume VII, 1987–1988* (New York: Holmes & Meier, 1990) pp. B63–B69. For a detailed discussion of Brazil's relationship with the IMF, see Ernest J. Oliveri, *Latin American Debt and the Politics of International Finance* (Westport, Conn.: Praeger Publishers, 1992), pp. 119–62. On the debtors' cartel and the huge profits reaped by international banks in Brazil, see Pang, 'Brazil's New Democracy', p. 55, and Lernoux, 'The "Model" Shattered', p. 435, respectively. Mr. Delfim's reaction to the pile-up of debt is quoted by Payer, *The Debt Trap*, p. 161.

On dependent state capitalism, see James Petras, *Critical Perspectives on Imperialism and Social Class in the Third World* (New York: Monthly Review Press, 1978) pp. 47, 89, 92. The 1985 economic recovery is reported in 'The Ash Wednesday Awaiting Brazil's Revelling Politicians', *The Economist* (London), 8 February 1986. On the relationship between Brazil's debt and the environment, see Susan George, *The Debt Boomerang: How Third World Debt Harms Us All* (London: Pluto Press, 1992). A statistical profile of trade with Brazil is provided by the US Bureau of the Census, *Statistical Abstract of the United States, 1982–83* (Washington, DC: Government Printing Office, 1983) p. 880. On p. 435 of 'The "Model" Shattered', Lernoux examines the options facing Brazil.

The material on inflation and Cardoso's intended solutions to Brazil's economic difficulties are discussed in Kamm, 'Brazilian Official Maps Federal Plan against Inflation', and 'Brazil Reaches Accord with Large Banks on Cutting its Debt', *New York Times*, 17 April 1994. Sources on indigenous peoples include 'Amazon Indians' Battle for Land Grows Violent', *New York Times*, 11 June 1995, and 'Indians Suffer Arrows of Misfortune in Brazil', *Financial Times* (London), 4 July 1995. The decrease in the external debt is noted in the *Wall Street Journal*, 11 January 1993. The growing problem of debt peonage is reported in 'Slavery on the Rise in Brazil as Debt Chains Workers', *New York Times*, 23 May 1993.

6 The Conventional Route, Joining Global Capitalism: Track 2 – the Asian NICs

Empirical data for this chapter are derived from the *National Trade Data Bank*. Lee Kuan Yew's statement is drawn from 'Determined Trend towards Asian Values', *Financial Times* (London), 24 February 1995. Singapore's GNP per capita ranking is indicated in World Bank, *World Development Report 1995* (New York: Oxford University Press, 1995) p. 163. The analysis on land reform relies heavily upon J. Yager, *Transforming Agriculture in Taiwan* (Ithaca, NY: Cornell University Press, 1988) and Anis Chowdhury and Inyanatul Islam, *The Newly Industrialising Economies of East Asia* (London and New York: Routledge, 1993). The quote from Bruce Cumings regarding the East Asian economies is also drawn from Chowdhury and Islam (p. 28).

Offering varied interpretation, the vast secondary literature on the NICs includes: Alice H. Amsden, *Asia's Next Giant: South Korea and Late Industrialization* (New York: Oxford University Press, 1989); Richard P. Appelbaum and J.W. Henderson, *States and Development in the Asian Pacific Rim* (Newbury Park: Sage, 1992); Giovanni Arrighi, 'The Developmentalist Illusion: A Reconceptualization of the Semiperiphery' in William G. Martin (ed.) *Semiperipheral States in the World Economy* (Westport, Conn.: Greenwood Press, 1990), pp. 11–42; Walden Bello and Stephanie Rosenfeld, *Dragons in Distress: Asia's Miracle Economies in Crisis* (San Francisco: The Institute for Food and Development Policy, 1990); Peter Berger and Hsin-Huang Michael Hsiao, *In Search of an East Asian Development Model* (New Brunswick and London: Transaction, 1990); Manfred Bienefeld, 'The Significance of the Newly Industrializing Countries for the Development Debate', *Studies in Political Economy* 25 (Spring 1988), pp. 7–39; Robin Broad and John Cavanagh, "No More NICs', *Foreign Policy*, 72 (Fall 1989) pp. 81–103.

James A. Caporaso, 'Industrialization in the Periphery: the Evolving Global Division of Labor', *International Studies Quarterly*, 25 (1981), pp. 347–384; Frederic C. Deyo (ed.), *The Political Economy of the New Asian Industrialism* (Ithaca, NY: Cornell University Press, 1987); Folker Fröbel, Jurgen Heinrichs and Otto Kreye (eds), *The New International Division of Labour: Structural Unemployment in Industrialised Countries and Industrialisation in Developing Countries*, trans. Pete Burgess (Cambridge: Cambridge University Press, 1980); Gary Gereffi and Donald L. Wyman (eds), *Manufacturing Miracles: Paths of Industrialization in Latin America and East Asia* (Princeton, NJ: Princeton University Press, 1990); Gary Gereffi and Miguel Korzeniewicz (eds), *Commodity Chains and Global Capitalism* (Westport, CT: Greenwood Press, 1993); Stephen Haggard, *Pathways from the Periphery: The Politics of Growth in the Newly Industrializing Countries* (Ithaca, NY: Cornell University Press, 1990); Gary Hamilton and Cheung-Shu Kao, 'Max Weber and the Analysis of East Asian Industrialization', *International Sociology* 2 (1987), pp. 289–300; Paul W. Kuznets, 'An East Asian Model of Economic Development: Japan, Taiwan, and South Korea', *Economic Development and Cultural Change*, 36 (1988) – Supplement; Robert B. Stauffer, 'Review Essay: Postcolonial Industrialization and NIC-dom – Myths and "Lessons" from East and Southeast Asia', *Bulletin of Concerned Asian Scholars*, 25 (1993), pp. 49–58.

7 The Exit Option, Withdrawing from and Re-entering Global Capitalism: China under and after Mao

The major sources for this chapter are Vivienne Shue, *Peasant China in Transition: The Dynamics of Development toward Socialism, 1949–1956* (Berkeley: University of California Press, 1983) and Andrew Walder's dissertation, 'Work and Authority in Chinese Industry: State Socialism and the Institutional Culture of Dependency' (University of Michigan, 1981). Essential background reading is Lucien Bianco, *Origins of the Chinese Revolution, 1915–1949*, trans. Muriel Bell (Stanford, Cal.: Stanford University Press, 1971) and William Hinton, *Fanshen: A Documentary of Revolution in a Chinese Village* (New York: Random House, 1966).

The land reform is assessed by C. K. Yang, *Chinese Communist Society: The Family and the Village* (Cambridge, Mass.: MIT Press, 1959). Another important work on the rural sector is Nicholas R. Lardy, *Agriculture in China's Modern Development* (Cambridge: Cambridge University Press, 1983). The comparison of economic performance in 1952 and the prerevolutionary period appears in Xue Muqiao, *China's Socialist Economy* (Beijing: Foreign Languages Press, 1981) p. 22. The data on income in the agricultural sector are drawn from Shue, *Peasant China in Transition*, p. 283; her explanations quoted here appear on p. 332. An excellent discussion of relations between the central authorities and local cadres may be found in Ezra Vogel, *Canton under Communism: Programs and Politics in a Provincial Capital, 1949–1968* (Cambridge, Mass.: Harvard University Press, 1969). The incentive system is reviewed in Walder's seminal study, 'Work and Authority in Chinese Industry', *passim*. The tale of Old Guo is told by Liang Heng and Judith Shapiro, *Son of the Revolution* (New York: Alfred A. Knopf, 1983) p. 184. On the shortcomings of the Cultural Revolution, see Victor Lippitt, 'Socialist Development in China', in Mark Selden and Victor Lippitt (eds), *The Transition to Socialism in China* (Armonk, NY: M. E. Sharpe, 1982),

270 *Notes and References*

especially pp. 131–2. A provocative account is provided by Samir Amin, *The Future of Maoism*, trans. Norman Finkelstein (New York: Monthly Review Press, 1983). Debates about the sequel to Maoism appear in Stephan Feuchtwang and Athar Hussain (eds), *The Chinese Economic Reforms* (New York: St Martin's Press, 1983).

Analysis of the women's question is based on Ellen R. Judd, *Gender and Power in Rural North China* (Stanford: Stanford University Press, 1994); All-China Women's Federation, *The Impact of Economic Development on Rural Women in China*, Report of the United Nations University Household, Gender and Age Project (Tokyo: United Nations University, 1993); and Zhang Xianliang, *Half of Man is a Woman* (New York: W. W. Norton, 1988).

Information on economic reforms has been culled from several recent issues of the *National Trade Data Bank* as well as numerous secondary sources and reports, including Nicholas D. Kristof, 'China Sees "Market-Leninism" as a Way to Future', *New York Times*, 6 September 1993 and 'Riddle of China: Repression as Standard of Living Sours', *New York Times*, 7 September 1993; 'China: Birth of a New Economy', *Businessweek*, 31 January 1994; David Shambaugh, 'Losing Control: The Erosion of State Authority in China', *Current History*, September 1993, pp. 253–9; Orville Schell, 'Twilight of a Titan: China—End of an Era', *The Nation*, 17/24 July, 1995; 'A Survey of China', *The Economist*, 18 March 1995; Jonathan Karp, 'Greens for the Reds: China Discovers the Golfing Boom', *Far Eastern Economic Review*, 29 October 1992; Orville Schell and Todd Lappin, 'China Plays the Market', *The Nation*, 14 December 1992; Fuh-Wen Tzeng, 'The Political Economy of China's Coastal Development Strategy: A Preliminary Analysis', *Asian Survey*, 31 (March 1991), pp. 270–84; Benedict Stavis, 'Contradictions in Communist Reform: China Before 4 June 1989', *Political Science Quarterly*, 105 (Spring 1990), pp. 31–52.

Discussion of China's environmental problems relies mainly on He Bochuan, *China on the Edge: The Crisis of Ecology and Development* (San Francisco: China Books and Periodicals, 1991); and Qu Geping and Li Jinchang, *Population and the Environment in China*, trans. Jiang Baozhong and Gu Ran, ed. Robert B. Boardman (Boulder: Lynne Rienner; London: Paul Chapman, 1994).

8 The Alternative Path, Weaving through Global Capitalism: Mozambique

Some of the information in this chapter is drawn from James H. Mittelman, *Underdevelopment and the Transition to Socialism: Mozambique and Tanzania* (New York: Academic Press, 1981) and James H. Mittelman, 'Marginalization and the International Division of Labor: Mozambique's Strategy of Opening the Market', *African Studies Review*, 34, 3 (December 1991), 89–106. The statement on the role of the peasantry appears in Mozambique Information Agency, *Information Bulletin*, 9–10 (1977), p. 6. Changes in the country's legal system, with emphasis on the emancipation of women, are discussed in Nina Berg and Aase Gundersen, 'Legal Reform in Mozambique: Equality and Emancipation for Women Through Popular Justice', in Kristi Anne Stolen and Mariken Vaa (eds), *Gender and Change in Developing Countries* (Oslo: Norwegian University Press, 1991). On the plight of women, we are borrowing from Stephanie Urdang,

And Still They Dance (New York: Monthly Review Press, 1989). The composition of the people's assemblies is described in 'Assembleia Popular', *Tempo* (Maputo), 378, (1 January 1978), pp. 53–4; Allen and Barbara Isaacman, 'A Rare Glimpse of How Mozambique Governs Itself', *Christian Science Monitor*, 27 December 1979; and Stephanie Urdang, 'The Last Transition? Women and Development in Mozambique', *Review of African Political Economy*, 27–8 (February 1984), pp. 13–14. The statistics on the representation of women in national parliaments were drawn from the UNDP, *Human Development Report 1993* (New York: Oxford University Press, 1993) p. 151.

An interpretation of the changing rural economy in Africa that differs from our own is offered by Göran Hyden, *No Shortcuts to Progress: African Development Management in Perspective* (Berkeley: University of California Press, 1983). Hyden hypothesizes that an 'uncaptured peasantry' exits the formal economy. According to him, Africa's precapitalist societies are without states that can be used for economic expansion and development. Undoubtedly, Hyden identifies an important phenomenon – the informal market or parallel economy – but his explanation is open to challenge on the ground that the mode of production in contemporary Africa is predominantly a capitalist, not precapitalist, structure. Moreover, rather than choosing the exit option, peasants are being pushed out of the system. Figures on the state of Mozambique's agriculture were taken from Robert T. Huffman, 'Colonialism, Socialism and Destabilization in Mozambique', *Africa Today*, 39, 1 and 2 (1st and 2nd quarters 1992), pp. 2–27, and Steven Kyle, 'Economic Reform and Armed Conflict in Mozambique', *World Development*, 19, 6 (June 1991), pp. 637–49. The quotation by Marcelino dos Santos was taken from Joseph Hanlon, *Mozambique: The Revolution Under Fire* (London: Zed Press, 1984) p. 110. For a brief discussion of the trade union movement see Adriane Paavo, 'Starting Over: Rebuilding the Worker's Movement in Mozambique', *Southern Africa Report*, 8, 5 (1 May 1993), pp. 12–15.

Samora Machel was interviewed by Herb Shore in Dar es Salaam, Tanzania, in 1970. The interview is quoted by George Houser and Herb Shore, *Mozambique: Dream the Size of Freedom* (New York: The Africa Fund, 1975) p. 11. The US State Department's assessment of Mozambique's human rights performance can be found in *Country Reports on Human Rights Practices* (Report to the Committee on Foreign Affairs, US House of Representatives, and the Committee on Foreign Relations, US Senate, Washington, DC, 1984). Information on the rights of women was drawn from Urdang, *And Still They Dance, passim.*; UNDP, *Human Development Report 1993*, p. 169; and Berg and Gunderson, 'Legal Reform in Mozambique', p. 268.

The costs of South Africa's destabilization campaign have been computed by the Government of Mozambique in its *Economic Report* (Maputo: National Planning Commission, 1984) p. 41. More recent figures were from Mittelman, 'Marginalization and the International Division of Labor', p. 95. Data on the economy are taken from 'Mozambique', *Foreign Economic Trends and Their Implications for the United States* (FET–66) (US Department of Commerce, Washington DC, 1984) pp. 2, 4–5. On the human costs of destabilization see Huffman, 'Colonialism, Socialism and Destabilization in Mozambique', p. 9, and Jane Perlez, 'A Mozambique Formally at Peace is Bled by Hunger and Brutality', *New York Times*, 13 October 1992. The ban on development assistance was contained in *Legislation on Foreign Relations through 1982*, Current Legislation and Related Executive Orders, vol. 1 (Committee on Foreign Relations, US Senate, and Committee on Foreign Affairs, US House of Representatives, Washington, DC, 1983) p. 361.

Much of the information on the impact of structural adjustment was taken from Mittelman, 'Marginalization and the International Division of Labor'; Joseph Hanlon, *Mozambique: Who Calls the Shots?* (London: James Currey, 1991); Huffman, 'Colonialism, Socialism, and Destabilization in Mozambique'; and Robert B. Lloyd, 'Mozambique: The Terror of War, the Tensions of Peace', *Current History*, 94 591 (April 1995), 152–5.

The conclusion derived insights from John S. Saul, 'Mozambique: The "Peace Election"', *Southern Africa Report*, 10, 2 (December 1994), pp. 3–6; Otto Roesch, 'The Politics of the Aftermath: Peasant Options in Mozambique', *Southern Africa Report*, 9, 3, (January 1994), pp. 16–19; Lloyd, 'Mozambique: The Terror of War, the Tensions of Peace', pp. 152–5; and Salim Lone, 'African Debate on Reforms Shifting Focus: Nairobi Conference Urges End to Externally Oriented, Aid-Seeking Approach', *Africa Recovery*, 9, 1 (June 1995), pp. 8–9.

For readers interested in postcolonial Mozambique, the most authoritative studies include Allen and Barbara Isaacman, *Mozambique: From Colonialism to Revolution, 1900–1982* (Boulder, Col.: Westview Press, 1983); Hanlon, *Mozambique: The Revolution under Fire*; Barry Munslow, *Mozambique: The Revolution and its origins* (London: Longman, 1983); and John S. Saul (ed.), *Recolonization and Resistance in Southern Africa in the 1990s* (Trenton: Africa World Press, 1993).

9   What Works in the Third World?

A penetrating essay on human agency, on which we have drawn, is Alan Gilbert, 'Democracy and Individuality', *Social Philosophy and Policy*, 3, 2 (Spring 1986), pp. 19–58. Some of the material on Mauritania is borrowed from 'Drought Turns Nomads' World Upside Down', *New York Times*, 3 March 1985, and 'Poorer Nations Get Poorer as Recession Eases', *Africa News*, 21, 13 (26 September 1983), p. 6. The sentences quoted from V.S. Naipaul can be found in *The Return of Eva Peron* (New York: Alfred A. Knopf, 1980) p. 141, and *A Bend in the River* (New York: Vintage Books, 1979) p. 27. Frantz Fanon's remark on the ideology of racism is taken from 'Racism and Culture', in Fanon, *Toward the African Revolution* (Harmondsworth: Penguin Books, 1964) p. 43. See the commentary by Aristide Zolberg, 'Frantz Fanon – A Gospel for the Damned', *Encounter*, 27, 5 (November 1966), pp. 56–63. Garrett Hardin's views are set forth in his 'Lifeboat Ethics: The Case Against Helping the Poor', *Psychology Today*, 6, 4 (8 September 1974), pp. 38ff.

Seminal work on the 'objective problem' is Celso Furtado, *Accumulation and Development: The Logic of Industrial Civilization*, trans. Suzette Macedo (New York: St Martin's Press, 1983); Celso Furtado, *No to Recession and Unemployment: An Examination of the Brazilian Economic Crisis* (London: Third World Foundation, 1984); and Peter Evans, *Dependent Development: The Alliance of Multinational, State and Local Capital in Brazil* (Princeton, NJ: Princeton University Press, 1979), especially pp. 80–1. Data on arms sales are derived from the Independent Commission on International Development Issues, *North-*

South: A Program for Survival (Cambridge, Mass.: MIT Press, 1980) p. 117; and 'Cost-Effective Job Creation', and 'The Third World Limits Its Arsenals', articles in the *New York Times* on 22 September 1982, and 18 March 1984, respectively. Keynes's comment appears in Donald Moggridge (ed.), *The Collected Writings of John Maynard Keynes: Activities 1939–1945; Internal War Finance* (Cambridge: Cambridge University Press, 1978) vol. 22, p. 149. Seymour Melman summarizes his research findings in 'Looting the Means of Production', *New York Times*, 7 October 1980.

We have borrowed information on the NICs from Stephan Haggard and Chung-in Moon, 'The South Korean State in the International Economy: Liberal, Dependent, or Mercantile?', in John Gerard Ruggie (ed.), *The Antinomies of Interdependence: National Welfare and the International Division of Labor* (New York: Columbia University Press, 1983), especially pp. 132–41 and 185–9. Extensive research on capitalist development in Japan has been carried out by Jon Halliday, *A Political History of Japanese Capitalism* (New York: Monthly Review Press, 1978).

On restructuring ties with the world order, see Furtado, *Accumulation and Development*, pp. 115, 118, and Immanuel Wallerstein, *The Politics of the World-Economy: The States, the Movements, and the Civilizations* (Cambridge: Cambridge University Press, 1984) p. 10. The strategy of managing the ties of dependency is assessed by Robert W. Cox, 'Production and Hegemony: Toward a Political Economy of World Order', in Harold K. Jacobson and Dusan Sidjanski (eds), *The Emerging International Order: Dynamic Processes, Constraints and Opportunities* (Beverly Hills: Sage, 1982) pp. 54–6, and André Tiano, *La dialectique de la dépéndance: Analyse des relations économiques et financières internacionales* (Paris: Presses Universitaires de France, 1977) pp. 402–6. The concept 'war of position' is developed by Antonio Gramsci, *Selections from the Prison Notebooks of Antonio Gramsci*, trans. and ed. Quinin Hoare and Geoffrey Nowell Smith (London: Lawrence & Wishart, 1971), *passim*.

Much of our information on oil is derived from Anthony Sampson, *The Seven Sisters: The Great Oil Companies and the World They Shaped* (New York: Bantam Books, 1976); Jack Anderson, with James Boyd, *Fiasco* (New York: Times Books, 1983); and 'Energy Upheaval: Questions about OPEC, Past and Future', *New York Times*, 3 October 1983. On the leverage of Western banks, see 'Acting to Avert Debtor Cartel', *New York Times*, 20 June 1984, and Joan Robinson, *Aspects of Development and Underdevelopment* (Cambridge: Cambridge University Press, 1979) p. 132. Cuba's policy towards the pharmaceuticals is described by Mike Muller, *The Health of Nations: An Investigation of the Pharmaceutical Industry's Exploitation of the Third World for Profit* (London: Faber & Faber, 1982), especially p. 65, and Luis R. Capo, 'International Drug Procurement and Market Intelligence: Cuba', *World Development*, 11, 3 (November 1983), pp. 217–22. Our discussion of an alternative to the IMF model of accumulation relies very heavily on John Loxley, 'IMF and World Bank Conditionality and Sub-Saharan Africa' (mimeo, n.d.). A compelling critique of Clive Thomas, *Dependence and Transformation: The Economics of the Transition to Socialism* (New York: Monthly Review Press, 1974) has been developed by Andrew Coulson (mimeo, Department of Economics, University of Dar es Salaam, n.d.). The argument about the division of labour in agriculture is presented in Kevin Danaher, *Myths of African Hunger* (San Francisco: Institute for Food and Development Policy, 1985) p. 2. Discussion of India's 'information revolution' is partly based on Peter B. Evans 'Indian Informatics in the 1980s: The Changing Character of State Involvement,' *World Development,* 20 (1992): 1–18.

Postscript

For Ashis Nandy's remark on development as 'a secular theory of salvation', see Tariq Banuri, 'Development and the Politics of Knowledge: A Critical Interpretation of the Social Role of Modernization Theories in the Development of the Third World', in Frederique Apffel Marglin and Stephen A. Marglin (eds), *Dominating Knowledge: Development, Culture, and Resistance* (Oxford: Clarendon Press, 1990) p. 30, n. 4. Disraeli's statement appears on the opening page of Edward Said's *Orientalism* (New York: Vintage Books, 1978). Gayatri Chakravorty Spivak's essay, 'Can the Subaltern Speak?', appears in *Wedge,* 7/8 (Winter/Spring 1985). Marx's statement, 'They cannot represent themselves; they must be represented,' comes from *The Eighteenth Brumaire of Louis Bonaparte* (1852). See Karl Marx and Frederick Engels, *Selected Works,* Volume 1 (Moscow: Progress Publishers, 1973) pp. 394–487.

Arturo Escobar's comment on the 'theoretical imaginary of the West' can be found in 'Imagining a Post-Development Era? Critical Thought, Development and Social Movements', *Social Text,* 10, 2/3 (1992), pp. 20–56. For a detailed formulation of Francis Fukuyama's 'end-of-history' thesis, see *The End of History and the Last Man* (New York: The Free Press, 1992). Samuel P. Huntington, 'The Clash of Civilizations?' article first appeared in *Foreign Affairs,* 71 (Summer 1993), pp. 22–49. Vandana Shiva, *Staying Alive: Women, Ecology and Development* (London: Zed Books, 1989). For an analysis of industrialization during the Ayub era, see Rashid Amjad, *Private Industrial Investment in Pakistan, 1969–1970* (Cambridge: Cambridge University Press, 1982). Prominent Third World voices can be found in Trinh T. Minh-ha, *Woman, Native, Other: Writing Postcoloniality and Feminism* (Bloomington: Indiana University Press, 1989) and Chandra Talpade Mohanty *et al.* (eds), *Third World Women and the Politics of Feminism* (Bloomington: Indiana University Press, 1992). On 'decolonization of imagination' see especially Jan Nederveen Pieterse and Bhiku Parekh (eds), *The Decolonization of Imagination: Culture, Knowledge and Power* (London: Zed Books, 1995). For an analysis of Islamic resurgence in the context of globalization, see Mustapha Kamal Pasha and Ahmed I. Samatar, 'The Resurgence of Islam', in James H. Mittelman (ed.), *Globalization: Critical Reflections,* Vol. 9 of the *International Political Economy Yearbook* (Boulder, Col.: Lynne Rienner, 1996), pp. 187–201.

Index

accumulation 82–7
  dependent development 45, 225
  flexible 55
  international institutions and
    global 78
  modernization theory 41
  Mozambique's strategy 183–94
  primitive 89–91
  profit, consumption and 224–5
  state, class and non-class forces
    91–101
  unfettered capitalist 228
Achebe, C.: *Man of the People* 98–9
achievement, orientation to 41
Acholi 31–3
acid rain 178
adjustment *see* structural adjustment
  programmes
Africa 90–1
  civilizations 47
  history 35
  Mozambique's relations with
    neighbouring countries 200–3
  sub-Saharan 23
  see also under individual countries
African Development Bank 194
agency, human 219–20
Agricultural Producer
  Cooperatives 163
agriculture 14, 243–4, 249
  Brazil 115; agro-export
    economy 107–8
  cash crop production 19, 47
  China 155, 157–9, 169;
    collectivization 160–3; Great
    Leap Forward 165–8; under
    Deng 175–6
  family farms 190–1
  Green Revolution 40, 100
  modernization 38, 39, 138
  Mozambique 188–91, 200
  state farms 188–91
  see also land; land reform

aid, foreign 226, 241–2
  Brazil 110, 111–12
  international institutions 52–9
  Mozambique 193–4, 206–8,
    208, 211
air pollution 178
Akins, J. 235
Allende Gossens, S. 44, 67
Alvarez, S. 119
Amazon, development of 112–15, 118,
  127
Amazonian Indians 115, 118, 128
Amsden, A. 141, 142
Anaconda 67
Anderson, J. 235
Anglo-Portuguese Pact (1373) 181
Angola 204, 206
appropriateness of technology 61–2
Argentina 221–2
Aristotle 24
arms sales 227
  see also military expenditure;
    military production
Asian Development Bank (ADB) 150
Attenborough, R.: *Gandhi* 253
austerity
  Brazil 121, 122
  Mexico 74–5
  see also structural adjustment
    programmes
Australia 88
autarchy *see* self-reliance
authoritarian state 70, 100, 144–7, 153

baking industry 58–9
Balasubramaniam, K. 68
Bangalore 247
Bank of Mexico 74
Bank of Mozambique 184
banking/banks
  Brazil's external debt 124–5
  China 161
  creditors' cartel 236–7

banking *cont.*
　Mozambique 184
　transnational 71–9
Barroso, C.E. 129
Belita Clothes Factory 191
Bello, W. 151
Berg, N. 200
Berlin Conference (1884–5) 182
Bhopal disaster 69–70
Bolivia 73
Boyd, J. 235
Brady Plan 73, 127
Brandt Commission 12, 21, 53, 54
Brazil 62, 105–29, 227, 228, 229
　agro-export economy 107–8
　development of Amazon
　　112–15, 127
　development strategy 106–7
　economic boom 1968–74 115–19
　failed miracle 119–23
　foreign debt 121–2, 123–9, 237
　import substitution 108–9
　military coup (1964) 110–11
　National Privatization
　　Programme 128
　resource endowment 106
Bretton Woods system 26, 37, 75
　see also International Monetary
　　Fund; World Bank
Britain 40, 58
Brzezinski, Z. 7–8
Buckley, W.F. 49
bureaucracy
　China 169–70; campaign
　　against 170–2
　Mozambique 197–8
bureaucratic ruling class 100
Burma (Myanmar) 230

Cabora Bassa 183, 193
Canada 46
capital
　accumulation *see* accumulation
　attracting 70; *see also* foreign direct
　　investment
　concentration 64, 90, 143
　constant and variable 89–90
　industrial and loan 70
　mobility 66

capital goods 60, 120
capitalism
　command 140–3
　dependent statist 126
　global *see* global capitalism
　Japan's independent 229–30
　Marxist theory 83–91
'capitalist roaders' 170–2
Cardoso, F. Henrique 114, 127, 128
CARE 208
'career', Third World as 251–4
cartels 234–7
　creditors' 236–7
　debtors' 237
　see also Organization of Petroleum
　　Exporting Countries
cash crops 19, 47
caste 86, 94, 99, 100
Castro, F. 237
　television interview 3–6
'catching up' ideology 256
cattle-ranching 118
Central Intelligence Agency
　(CIA) 207
centre and periphery 45
chaebol 141, 142–3
Chile 67
China 154–80
　EPZ strategy 70
　First Five Year Plan 160–4
　Great Leap Forward 165–8
　Great Proletarian Cultural
　　Revolution 170–2
　Mao's legacy 173
　'mass production of useless
　　products' 164–8
　migration to Hong Kong 136
　pre-revolution 155–6
　relationship with Hong Kong 148–9
　relationship with Mozambique 204
　Revolution 156–60
　self-reliance 168–70, 230–1
　theory of three worlds 21
　under Deng 173–80
Chinese Communist Party
　(CCP) 136, 173, 174–5
　Great Leap Forward 166–8
　Revolution 156–9
Chissano, J. 195, 204, 212

circulation, facilitators of 85
Citibank 125
Citicorp 72
cities 144–7, 176–7
city-states 34, 144–7
civil society 211
Clark, R. 206
'clash of civilizations' 255
class 18
    accumulation, state, class and non-
        class forces 91–101
    bureaucratic ruling class 100
    China and class consciousness 158
    concept 99–100
    conflict 94–5
    dependency theory 45
    development aid and dominant
        classes 59
    imperialism and class
        formation 47–8
    merchant class 47
    structure in Brazil 107–8; roles in
        exploitation of Amazon 112–15
    working class *see* working class/
        workers
Cold War 136, 143
collective self-reliance 234–7
collectivization 160–4
Collins, J. 8
colonialism 98
    decolonization 36, 222–3
    legacy in Mozambique 181–3
command capitalism 140–3
commerce, international 85, 145–6,
    148–9
communal villages 188–91, 217–18
communes 165, 169, 175
competitiveness, global 22–3
computer industry *see* information
    technology
concentration of capital 64, 90, 143
conditionality 75–6
conflict
    class 94–5
    ethnicity and 10–12
    forms dependent on history and
        culture 19
    social 19, 94–7
Confucian values 133–4

constant capital 89–90
consumption 47, 83–5, 87
    energy 12–15
    mass 38
context of representation 252
contract responsibility system (*zeren
    zhi*) 175–6
control: TNCs and conflict over 66–70
cooperantes (contractees) 196
cooperatives 160–3
copper industry 67
Corpersucar 106
corruption 197, 198
Council for Mutual Economic
    Assistance (COMECON) 159,
    164, 168, 194
crises, capitalism and 90
Cruzado Plan (1986) 123–4
Cuba 203–4, 239–40
cultural hierarchy 252–4
culture
    colonialism and indigenous
        cultures 19
    impact of foreign aid 57
    NICs 133–4
Cumings, B. 135

Daewoo 143
De Gaulle, C. 46
debt
    Brazil: external 121–2, 123–9, 237;
        peonage 125–9
    Mozambique's external 194, 210, 212
    reschedulings 76
    South Korea's external 143
    Third World 55; service 26;
        transnational banking 71–8
        passim
debt-equity swaps 73
debtors' cartel 237
decolonization 36, 222–3
deforestation 118, 127
Delfim Netto, A. 116, 121, 125, 125–6
demand: aligning needs and resources
    to 242–3
demarcation of reservations 128
democracy
    liberal 39
    pro-democracy movement 179

denationalization 42–3
Deng Xiaoping, China under 173–80
dependency
    globalization and 225
    managing ties of 231–2, 233–4
    perspective 43–6, 60
dependent statist capitalism 126
deregulation 42–3
destabilization 201–2, 208
devaluation 42–3, 126
development 25
    Brazil's strategy 106–7
    donor-driven strategy 212
    dynamics 91–2
    and economic growth 81
    ethical aspects 24
    gap 12–15
    Marx's expectations for 91
    models of 34–48
    NIC model 132–5
    post-development 258–9
    transition to 25–6
development assistance *see* aid
development deficit 75
Dhlakama, A. 212
Dibromochloropropane (DBCP) 69
Diggs, C. 206
dignity 258–9
discount purchasing 73
diseases 115
Disraeli, B. 251
distribution 54
    production–consumption cycle
        83–5, 87
    redistribution 224–7
    triage 223–4
distribution/procurement
    agency 240–1
division of labour, global 8–9, 62, 239
domination 86, 94
donor-driven development
    strategy 212
Dos Santos, M. 190–1, 195
Dow Chemical 69
drug companies 68–70, 239–40
dumping, technological 62
Durabolin 69
dynamic convergence 242–3
dynamizing groups 186

Ebola virus 9
Economic Commission for Latin
    America (ECLA) 43
economic growth
    Brazil 115–19, 125–6; failed
        miracle 119–20
    China 162
    and development 81
    'flying geese' pattern 133
    need for redistribution also 224–7
    NICs: 'miracle' economies 130–5;
        underside of growth 149–52
economic nationalism 44
economies of scale 43
education 142, 196
efficiency 241–2
elites, aid and 59
'end of history' 255
energy consumption 12–15
Engels, F. 87
entrepôts 145–6, 147–8
environment theory of human
    diversity 34
environmental degradation
    Brazil 126–7
    China 167–8, 178–9
    NICs 151–2
environmental groups 95
Escobar, A. 254
ethnicity 9–12
evolutionary optimism 39
exchange 83–5, 87
exchange value 88
exoticism 9
exploitation 85–6, 88
    setting limits to 238–42
Export-Import Bank, US 44
export orientation 77
export processing zones (EPZs) 70,
    138
export promotion 54–5, 141–2, 238
exports
    Brazil 120
    colonial economies 47
    devaluation and 126
    exploitation and export
        products 217–18
    and re-exports in NICs 145–6,
        147–9

family farms 190–1
Fanon, F. 222–3
fatalism 220–2
favelados 111, 114–15, 122
Federation of Malaya 135–6
feudalism 40
Figueiredo, J.B. 78, 121, 123
First World 20
fiscal chaos 178
'flying geese' growth pattern 133
food 118
  and export products 217–18
food weapon 237
forces of production 87
Ford, G. 206
foreign aid *see* aid
foreign direct investment (FDI)
  Asian NICs 138; Singapore 144–7
  Brazil 108–9, 117–18; outward 126
  in Canada 46
  China 177
  controlling TNCs 70
  incentives 70, 112, 145, 174
  mode of technology transfer 60
  and mobilization of domestic
    resources 244
  Mozambique 205–6
foreign 'experts' 253
France: TNCs 64–5
FRELIMO (Front for the Liberation
    of Mozambique) 183, 184–214
    passim, 231–2
  elections (1994) 212
  factions 196–7
  guerrilla warfare 203
  ideology 187
  leadership 194–6
  redefinition as 'vanguard party of
    the Mozambican people' 211
Fukuyama, F. 255
Furtado, C. 237

Gandhi, I. 22
Gandhi (film) 253
gap, development 12–15
Geismar, A. 20
gender relations 243
  see also women
Generalized System of Preferences 53

Germany 205
global capitalism 22
  choosing whether to join, leave or
    weave 233–7
  contradictions as
    opportunities 245–50
  exploitation of market forces by
    underdeveloped countries
    244–50
  export promotion and 238
  international organizations 51–2,
    77–9
  joining 105, 228–30; *see also* Brazil;
    newly industrializing countries
  leaving 105, 230–1; *see also* China
  modernization theory 40–1
  weaving 105, 231–2; *see also*
    Mozambique
global cities 144–7
global division of labour 8–9,
    62, 239
globalization 22–3, 55, 225
  China and 179–80
  dynamics 42
  and NICs 152–3
  production and TNCs 63, 65–6
Goulart, J. 110–11
government officials 93
Gramsci, A. 231
Great Leap Forward 165–8
Great Proletarian Cultural
    Revolution 170–2
Greater Carajás iron-ore project 115,
    127
Greek city-states 34
Green, R. 211
Green Revolution 40, 100
Greene Agreement 44
Gromyko, A. 9
gross domestic product (GDP) 14
  growth rates in NICs 131, 140
  per capita by country 13
  see also economic growth
Guangdong 176–7
Guatemala 67, 97
guerrilla warfare, theories of 203
Guevara, Che 203
Gulf War 80, 235
Gundersen, A. 200

Guomindang (National People's
    Party) 156
Gúrùe tea estates 192

Hamilton, A. 10
'hard hats' 99
Hardin, G. 223-4
health care
    Mozambique 185-6
    TNCs and 239-40
Helms, R. 67
Hersh, S.M. 35-6, 67
hierarchy
    cultural 252-4
    of race 8-9
    structured 23
Hills Brothers 106
history
    'end of' 255
    enigmas in Marx's view of 87-91
    legacy and NICs 135-6
    underdevelopment as historical
        process 46-8
Hong Kong 85, 130-53 *passim*, 229
    laissez-faire to market-
        Leninism 147-9
human agency 219-20
human development index 12, 13
Huntington, S. 255
Hyundai 143

Ibsen, H.: *An Enemy of the People* 96
ideology
    'catching up' 256
    class and 99
    FRELIMO 187
    state and 95-7
imperialism 36-7, 44-5, 47-8
import-substitution industrialization
    (ISI) 43
    Brazil 108-9
incentives
    investment 70, 112, 145, 174
    system 170-1
income
    average per capita 12-15
    high-, middle- and low-income
        countries 12
income distribution 128

independence, political 36
Independent Commission on
    International Development
    Issues (Brandt Commission) 12,
    21, 53, 54
India 47, 62
    Bhopal disaster 69-70
    caste 86, 94, 99, 100
    information technology
        industry 246-8
    portrayal of history in *Gandhi* 253
Indians, Amazonian 115, 118, 128
indigenous consciousness 256-8
individuality, social 219-20
industrial capital 70
industrial parks 146
industrial reserve army of labour 90
industrial waste 178-9
    see also environmental
        degradation
industrialization 23
    Brazil 108-9, 112
    import substitution 43, 108-9
    Korea 141-2
    Mozambique 191-2
    NICs 136-40
industry 14
    China 155-6, 159; First State
        Plan 161-2; Great Leap
        Forward 165-8;
        readjustment 169-70; reward
        system 163-4, 166-7; Soviet
        support 164-5
    continuous upgrading in NICs
        139-40, 147, 148-9
    impact of TNCs 63
    strategic industries 138-9, 145
    tradition and modernity 38
infant mortality 119, 131, 186
inflation 122, 123, 150
information technology 146
    India 246-8
infrastructure 82-3, 145, 244
    transportation 58
Institutional Revolutionary Party
    (PRI) 96-7
intellectuals, revolutionary 100
'intelligent island' 146
International Court of Justice 7

international division of labour 8–9, 62, 239
international institutions 22, 26, 49–79
  foreign aid 52–9
  international organization 49–52
  lack of power 7
  modernization theory 37
  Mozambique and 194
  technology 60–3
  TNCs 63–70
  transnational banking 71–9
  see also under individual names
International Monetary Fund (IMF) 37, 132
  Brady Plan 73
  and Brazil 110, 121, 122, 124
  conditionality 75–6
  criticisms of 78
  establishment of 75
  'IMF riots' 76
  and Mozambique 194, 209, 210, 212
  structural adjustment programmes *see* structural adjustment programmes
International Petroleum Company 44
International Telephone and Telegraph Company (ITT) 67
investment
  foreign direct *see* foreign direct investment
  reinvestment and accumulation 83
  state and in Brazil 108–9
  surplus product 81–2
Iran 67
Iran–Iraq war 235
'iron laws' of transformation 242–3
Islamic fundamentalism 9
Islamic movements 95
Islamic societies 92–3

Japan 227
  colonial rule of Taiwan 137, 140
  independent capitalism 229–30
  TNCs based in 64, 65
Jay, J. 10
Judd, E. 176

Kampuchea 230
Kaname, A. 133
Kennecot Copper 67
Keynes, J.M. 18, 226
Khrushchev, N. 164
Kissinger, H.
  attitude towards Third World 35–6
  ITT and Chile 67
  and Mozambique 206
  and oil companies 235
knowledge, sharing 60–1
Korea, South 130–53 *passim*, 229
  command capitalism 140–3
  Mutual Defense Treaty with US 143
Kubitschek, J. 110

labour
  cheap for Transvaal 182
  exchange of labour-power 83–4
  exploitation *see* exploitation
  global division of labour 8–9, 62, 239
  immobility 66
  industrial reserve army of labour 90
  surplus value 88–90
labour law, Brazil 113
laissez-faire 147–9
land
  Brazil: expropriation 111; unequal distribution 128–9
  China 158; private plots 169
  see also agriculture; land reform
land reform 136–8, 140–1, 229
land-to-the-tiller programme 137
Lange, O. 17
Lappin, T. 177
latifundia (landed estates) 94, 118
Latin America
  NICs 132, 229
  transnational banking 71
  US policy towards 35–6, 40
  see also under individual countries
leadership 40–1
  local leaders in China 166
Lee Kuan Yew 130–1, 146
legal system, Mozambique 185

Li Jinchang 178
liberal democracy 39
liberal reformism 34–41
liberalism 219
    see also neo-liberalism
liberation movements 45, 201
Libya 234–5, 245–6
licensing 60
life expectancy 12, 13, 131
'lifeboat ethics' 223–4
literacy 12, 13, 186
    NICs 131, 142, 144–5
loan capital 70
local leaders 166
Lomé Convention 194
Loxley, J. 76, 241
Lutz, C. 8

Machel, S. 185, 186, 195, 197, 198
Madison, J. 10
Malacca 135–6
Malaysia 136
malnutrition 12, 77, 118–19
manufacturing sector 14
    see also industry
Mao Zedong 163, 170
    legacy 173
market
    Brazil's deformed domestic
        market 109
    China's social market
        economy 174–80
    exploitation of global market
        forces 244–50
    international market
        mechanisms 53–4
    neo-liberalism 51–2
    qualifying access to internal
        market 240–1
    secondary loan market 73
    using competition for foreign
        markets 240–1
'market-Leninism' 147–9
marketing practices 68–9
Marshall Plan 55
Marx, K. 16, 99
    enigmas in Marx's view of
        history 87–91

Marxism 18
    agency 219–20
    expansion and capitalism 83
mass consumption 38
'mass production of useless
        products' 164–8
materialism 93, 258–9
Mauritania 220–1
McCone, T. 67
media images of Third World 8–11, 251
MediCuba 240
Mejia Victores, O.H. 97
Melman, S. 227
merchant class 47
Methuen, Treaty of (1703) 181
Mexico 62, 237
    bail-out of peso crisis 74–5
    state and ideology 96–7
middle cadres: shortage in
        Mozambique 195–6
migration 55, 136, 137, 147, 176
military coups 97
    Brazil 110–11
military expenditure 226–7, 249
military production 62, 116
Mill, J.S. 16
'miracle' economies 130–5
misperceptions 252
mobilizing committees (dynamizing
        groups) 186
modernization theory 36–41
    dependency school's critique 45
    IMF 77
    intellectual crisis 41–3, 256
    sharing knowledge 60–1
modes of production 87–8
Montesquieu, C. de 34
Mossadegh, M. 67
Most Favoured Nation (MFN)
        status 154–5
Moynihan, D.P. 6–7, 49
Mozambique 16, 181–214, 231–2
    about-face 208–12
    achievements and difficulties
        194–200
    colonial legacy 181–3
    Decree Law 18/77 (1977) 206
    Economic Action
        Programme 208–9

Economic Rehabilitation
Programme (PRE) 209–10
General Peace Agreement
(1990) 212
global context 200–8; socialist
countries 203–5;
subcontinent 200–3; the
West 205–8
managing ties of dependency 231–2
National Planning
Commission 198
Popular Assembly/Assembly of the
Republic 187, 211–12
problems and promises 213–14
strategy of accumulation 183–94;
industrialization 191–2; party
state 183–8; rural
transformation 188–91; ties with
international economy 193–4
multinational corporations (MNCs)
see transnational corporations
multiple identities 10
Muskie, E. 207
Mutual Aid Teams (MATs) 160

Naipaul, V.S. 221–2
Nasser, G.A. 66
nation-building 256
National Geographic 8–9
national identity 39
National People's Party
(Guomindang) 156
National Security Study
Memorandum-39 (NSSM-39)
Option 2 35
nationalism
economic 44
revolutionary 37
nationalization 111, 184
natural mobility of productive
factors 60
needs: aligning with demand 242–3
Nehru, J. 66
neo-classical economics 16–17, 60
NICs 133
neo-liberalism 224, 225
Brazil 128–9
international institutions'
ideology 51–2, 77

Sri Lanka 42–3
see also liberalism
Netherlands 58
new international economic order
(NIEO) 52–5
newly industrializing countries
(NICs) 19, 130–53, 224,
228–9
city-state to global city 144–7
command capitalism 140–3
historical legacy 135–6
laissez-faire to market-
Leninism 147–9
land reform and
industrialization 136–40
Latin American 132, 229
'miracle' economies 130–5
second-tier 132, 133
underside of growth 149–52
Ngugi Wa Thiong'o: *Petals of
Blood* 11–12
niche economies 225
Nigeria 93
Nixon, R. 35, 67, 172
oil crisis 235
Nkomati Accord (1984) 202–3
Nkrumah, K. 21–2, 66
non-aligned movement 164
non-class forces 91–101
non-governmental organizations
(NGOs) 51, 211
vehicles of development 59
North American Free Trade
Agreement (NAFTA) 74
North-South distinction 21
Nyerere, J. 58

Occidental 235, 246
Occidentalism 254
oil
cartel 234–6, 245–6
Saudi Arabia's revenues 80, 81
open door policy 148, 174
optimism, evolutionary 39
Option 2 (NSSM-39) 35
Organization of Mozambican Women
(OMM) 186
Organization of Mozambican Workers
(OTM) 191–2

Organization of Petroleum Exporting Countries (OPEC) 15, 55
  collapse 235–6
  Libya and 234–5, 245–6
Organon 69
Orientalism 254
orientation to achievement 41
otherness 252, 253
outward orientation 133, 135

Pakistan 256
Paris Club 209
party cadres 158–9
party state 183–8
Pastoral Land Commission 129
Patriotic Front 201
p'Bitek, Okot: *Song of Lawino* 31–3
peasant communes 165, 169, 175
peasant-worker alliance 100
peasants
  China 155; collectivization 160–1;
    contract responsibility
    system 175; incentives 169;
    inequality 162
  Mozambique 213–14; strategic
    hamlets 187, 189–90
  resistance to innovations 39
  spontaneous peasant
    revolution 222–3
Peel, Mr 88
Penang 135–6
People's Action Party (PAP) 146
people's assemblies 186–7
people's banks 161
People's Development Bank 184
Pereira family 122
Peréz, A.G. 237
periphery and centre 45
Peru 44, 237
peso crisis 74–5
pessimism 221–2
pesticides 69, 70
pharmaceutical companies 68–70,
  239–40
Phillip Morris company 64
physis doctrine 24
piece-rate system 163–4
planning, state 43, 160–4, 198
Plato 24

plunder 41
Point Four Program (1949) 36
policy-making: foreign aid experts
  and 58
policy studies 42
polis 24
political change, NICs and 150
political economy 16–18, 255
political independence 36
political participation 243
  dominating structures 256–8
  Mozambique 186–7
political power: accumulation
  and 97–8
political stability 15–16, 146–7
politicians 98–9
politics 19
  indigenization 256–8
  TNCs and local 66–70
  transnational banking and 71
  tribalism and 10–11
Portugal 181–3, 203
position, war of 231
poverty 12
  Mozambique 211
  Third World and 20
power 18
  political 97–8
  'Third World as career' 252–4
  TNCs 64
Prebisch, R. 43
precapitalist societies 25, 47–8
prisons 199
procurement/distribution
  agency 240–1
pro-democracy movement 179
production 241–2
  accumulation and system of 83–6
  China: manipulation of quotas 170;
    'mass production of useless
    products' 164–8;
    organization 163–4
  cycle 83–5, 87
  for exchange 24
  forces of 87
  globalization and TNCs 63, 65–6
  impact of foreign aid 54, 55
  imperialism and 47
  military 62, 116

mobilization of factors of
    production 77
modes of 87–8
Mozambique's accumulation
    problem 190–1
natural mobility of productive
    factors 60
physical organization 85
precapitalist societies 25, 47
social organization 85
structures of 14
Taiwan and adjustment of
    industrial 139–40
production councils 191
productivity, agricultural 162
profits 84–5, 224–5
    reinvestment 83
    tendency of rate of profit to fall 90
    TNCs 67–8; Brazil 117
progress 39
proletariat *see* working class/
    workers
protected villages 187, 189–90
protectionism 141–2, 182
Publius 10
Pye, L. 134

Qaddafi, M. 234–5, 245–6
Quadros, J. 110
quality 167
Qu Geping 178

race, hierarchy of 8–9
race theory of human diversity 34–6
radicalism, Third World 43–6
Reagan, R. 121, 202–3
recession, world 120
rectification campaigns 159
re-education centres 199
regionalism 146, 152–3
regulation
    Singapore 144–5
    TNCs 69–70
RENAMO (Mozambique National
    Resistance Movement) 195, 212
    South Africa and 201–2, 203
rent-seeking 92, 138
representation 252–4

repression 97
    China 179–80
    Mozambique 198–200
research and development 60, 62, 68
reservations, demarcation of 128
resettlement 217
    Mozambique 188–91
resources: aligning with demand
    242–3
revolution, sources of 222–3
revolutionary intellectuals 100
revolutionary nationalism 37
reward system 163–4, 166–7, 170–1
Rhodes, C. 36
Rhodesia (later Zimbabwe) 50, 86,
    182, 193
Ricardo, D. 16
Ríos Montt, E. 97
Rockefeller, D. 71
romanticism 220, 222–3
Rosenfeld, S. 151
Rostow, W.W. 60
rural reforms
    China 175–6
    Mozambique 188–91
    see also agriculture

Said, E. 252
Salazar, A. 182
sanctions 50, 193
Saudi Arabia 80–2
scale economies 43
Scali, J.A. 49
Schell, O. 177
seclusion *see* self-reliance
Second World 20
secondary loan market 73
self-cultivation 140–1
self-interest 161
self-reliance 46
    China 168–70, 230–1
    collective 234–7
services 14
    Hong Kong 149
Sese-Seko, M. 71
Severeid, E. 35
Shanghai Communiqué 172
Shell Oil 69
Shiva, V. 256

Shue, V. 162, 163
Siderbrás steel company 126
Singapore 130–53 *passim*, 229
  city-state to global city 144–7
  Economic Development Board
    (EDB) 145
Skilled Development Fund 147
slavery 41
  upsurge in present day 129
Smiley, X. 11
Smith, A. 16
social conflict 19, 94–7
social contract 52
social engineering 256
social forces 91–101
social individuality 219–20
social market economy 174–80
social movements 94–7, 245
  indigenization of politics
    256–8
  sources of revolution 222–3
  Western support 249–50
social protest
  Brazil 122–3
  China 177–8
  'IMF riots' 76
  Mozambique 211
  NICs 150
social relations
  Mozambique Revolution
    231–2
  of production 87
  technological innovation 61
social sector 185–6
  see also education; health care
social security 78–9
social structures
  as blockage to development 25
  dominating 256–8
  global inequality 54
socialism 170–2
socialist countries: Mozambique
  and 203–5
soil erosion 179
South Africa 181, 182–3, 193, 232
  destabilization of
    Mozambique 201–2
  Nkomati Accord (1984) 202–3
South–North distinction 21

Southern African Development
  Coordination Conference
  (SADCC) (later SADC) 201, 202
Soviet Union 20, 157
  and China 156, 159, 164–5; Sino-
    Soviet split 1960 168
  and Mozambique 204
  Russian Revolution 157
Special Economic Zones 174
spontaneous peasant revolution
  222–3
Sri Lanka 42–3
Stalin, J. 164
state 18
  authoritarian 70, 100, 144–7, 153
  class, accumulation and non-class
    forces 91–101
  developmental 134–5
  intervention in Mozambique
    213–14
  intervention in Saudi Arabia 80
  Korea 141–3
  party state 183–8
  popular classes' control 243
  role in Brazil 108
  Taiwan 138–9
state farms 188–91
state-owned enterprises (SOEs)
  Brazil 116–17
  China 161, 177
  Korea 142
  Taiwan 137, 138–9
state planning 43, 160–4, 198
statism 150
  dependent statist capitalism 126
Stevenson, A. 7
Straits Settlements 135
strategic hamlets 187, 189–90
strategic industries 138–9, 145
structural adjustment
    programmes 26, 226, 241
  impacts 76–7, 78–9
  Mozambique 210–11
structural change 26, 249
structural crisis 77
structural perspective 6
structures, dominating 256–8
sub-Saharan Africa 23
Summer Plan (1989) 124

surplus: generation in China 158
surplus product 81–2
surplus value 88–91

Taiwan 130–53 *passim*, 229
   land reform and
      industrialization 136–40
take-off 38
Tanzania 39, 68, 241
   communal village 217–18
   foreign aid 57–9
taste creation 57
technical assistance 56–9, 204–5
technical experts 56–7, 169–70, 171
technocrats 112–13
technological determinism 61
technology
   appropriateness 61–2
   international institutions 60–3
   modernization and 38
   NIEO 55
   TNCs and monopoly 64
technology transfer 60, 62–3
Terry, F.B. 44
Third World
   as 'career' 251–4
   characterization 19–23
   cultures and
      underdevelopment 222
   debt *see* debt
   images of 8–11, 251
   radicalism 43–6
Thomas, C. 242–3
Tiananmen Massacre 179
torture 113
tourism 57, 149
township and village enterprises
   175
trade 26
   China 154–5, 168–9; embargo
      156–7, 164
   dependency theory 43, 45–6
   forced 41
   Hong Kong 147–9
   Korea 141–2
   Singapore 145–6
   Taiwan 139
   Third World 19
   unequal terms of trade 43

US 26; and China 154–5, 156–7,
   164
see also exports
trade unions 95, 113, 191–2
traditional society 37–8, 40
training 57
Trans-Amazon Highway 115
transformation, 'iron laws' of 242–3
transition from underdevelopment to
   development 25–6
transnational banking 71–9
transnational corporations
   (TNCs) 22, 63–70
   Brazil 109, 113–14, 117–18
   measures to curb 239–41
   oil companies 234–6, 245–6
   pharmaceutical companies 68–70,
      239–40
   technology transfer 62–3
transportation infrastructure 58
Transvaal 182
Trevor-Roper, H. 34–5
triage 223–4
tribalism 9–12
Truman, H. 36
Turkey 256

Uganda 10, 55
underdevelopment 27
   blockage in transformation of social
      structure 25
   defining the problem 219–27
   dynamics 91–2
   as historical process 46–8
   link with Third World cultures 222
   modernization theory's lack of
      explanation of causes 40–1
   transition to development 25–6
unemployment 122–3, 131
Union Carbide 69–70
United Fruit Company 67
United Kingdom 40, 58
United Nations (UN) 7, 37, 61, 212
   General Assembly 49, 50
   Security Council 50
   system 49–51
United Nations Conference on
   Trade and Development
   (UNCTAD) 51

United Nations Development
Programme (UNDP) 12, 51
United Nations Economic
Commission for Africa 202
United Nations Educational,
Scientific and Cultural
Organization (UNESCO) 49–50,
60
United States (US)
Agency for International
Development (AID) 40, 111
banks and Third World debt 72
and Brazil 110, 111–12, 121–2
and China 156; military
containment 156–7; Shanghai
Communiqué 172; trade 154–5;
trade embargo 156–7, 164
criticisms of UN 49–50
dominance of Canada 46
economic problems 26
Foreign Assistance and Related
Programs Appropriation Act
(1982) 207
images of global disorder 7–8
images of Third World 8–11
Mexico peso crisis 74
military expenditure 227
and Mozambique 198–9, 205–8;
pressure on South Africa 202–3
and NICs 136; Hong Kong 148;
Taiwan 138, 139; US–Korea
Mutual Defense Treaty 143
oil crisis 235, 245
and Peru 44
policy towards Latin America
35–6, 40
public opinion regarding Third
World 6–7
Social Science Research Council
Committee on Comparative
Politics 42
TNCs 64, 65; pesticides in Third
World 69
urban settlements 38
use value 88

Valdés, G. 35–6
value, surplus 88–91
value added 84–5, 86

Vargas, G. 110
variable capital 89–90
Velasco, J. 44
vertical integration 63
Vietnam War 143
village and township enterprises
175
villages
communal 188–91, 217–18
protected 187, 189–90
violence 222

wages 89, 151
Brazil 118
China 163–4, 166–7, 170–1, 177
Mozambique 192
Walder, A. 164
Wallerstein, I. 22
Walters, B. 3–6
war of position 231
water, piped 118
Western countries 205–8
*see also under individual
names*
Wilkinson, B. 46
women
Brazil 114, 119
China 155, 176
impact of structural adjustment
76–7
Islamic societies 92–3
Mozambique 186, 187, 199–200
NICs 150–1
women's groups 94–5
work-group system 166–7, 170–1
worker–peasant alliance 100
working class/workers
Brazil 111, 114, 119
China 163–4, 166–7
Mozambique 184
World Bank 37, 128
criticisms of 78
Mozambique and 194, 209, 212
NICs 132
world disorder 7–8
world economy *see* global
capitalism
World Health Organization 9
world recession 120

World Vision 208
Wriston,W. B. 83, 237

Young, A. 207
Yudkin, J. 68

Zaire 9, 71
Zedillo, E. 74
Zhou Enlai 164, 172
Zimbabwe (formerly Rhodesia) 50,
    86, 182, 193